Employee Benefits

Employee Benefits

A Primer for Human Resource Professionals

Sixth Edition

Joseph J. Martocchio
University of Illinois

Mc
Graw
Hill
Education

EMPLOYEE BENEFITS: A PRIMER FOR HUMAN RESOURCE PROFESSIONALS, SIXTH EDITION

Published by McGraw-Hill Education, 2 Penn Plaza, New York, NY 10121. Copyright © 2018 by McGraw-Hill Education. All rights reserved. Printed in the United States of America. Previous editions © 2014, 2011, and 2008. No part of this publication may be reproduced or distributed in any form or by any means, or stored in a database or retrieval system, without the prior written consent of McGraw-Hill Education, including, but not limited to, in any network or other electronic storage or transmission, or broadcast for distance learning.

Some ancillaries, including electronic and print components, may not be available to customers outside the United States.

This book is printed on acid-free paper.

4 5 6 QVS 21 20 19

ISBN 978-1-259-71228-9
MHID 1-259-71228-1

Chief Product Officer, SVP Products & Markets: *G. Scott Virkler*
Vice President, General Manager, Products & Markets: *Michael Ryan*
Vice President, Content Design & Delivery: *Betsy Whalen*
Managing Director: *Susan Gouijnstook*
Director, Product Development: *Meghan Campbell*
Product Developer: *Laura Hurst Spell*
Marketing Manager: *Necco McKinley*
Director, Content Design & Delivery: *Terri Schiesl*
Program Manager: *Mary Conzachi*
Content Project Managers: *Kelly Hart, Karen Jozefowicz*
Buyer: *Jennifer Pickel*
Content Licensing Specialist: *Shannon Manderscheid*
Cover Image: *Ola Dusegard/Getty Images*
Cover Design: Studio Montage, *St. Louis, MO*
Compositor: *Lumina Datamatics*
Printer: *Quad/Graphics Digital*

All credits appearing on page or at the end of the book are considered to be an extension of the copyright page.

Library of Congress Cataloging-in-Publication Data

Names: Martocchio, Joseph J., author.
Title: Employee benefits : a primer for human resource professionals /
   Joseph J. Martocchio, University of Illinois.
Description: Sixth edition. | New York, NY : McGraw-Hill Education, [2018] |
   Includes bibliographical references and index.
Identifiers: LCCN 2016042221 | ISBN 9781259712289 (pbk. : alk. paper)
Subjects: LCSH: Employee fringe benefits—United States. | Compensation
   management—United States.
Classification: LCC HD4928.N62 U637 2018 | DDC 658.3/25—dc23
LC record available at https://lccn.loc.gov/2016042221

The Internet addresses listed in the text were accurate at the time of publication. The inclusion of a website does not indicate an endorsement by the authors or McGraw-Hill Education, and McGraw-Hill Education does not guarantee the accuracy of the information presented at these sites.

mheducation.com/highered

For My Students

—Joseph J. Martocchio

About the Author

Joseph J. Martocchio   *Professor in the School of Labor and Employment Relations, University of Illinois at Urbana-Champaign*

Professor Martocchio earned his Bachelor of Science degree in management and quantitative methods from Babson College, and both his Master's and PhD degrees in human resource management from Michigan State University's School of Labor and Industrial Relations. His research and teaching interests include employee compensation, employee benefits, and employee training and development. Professor Martocchio's research appears in leading scholarly journals including the *Academy of Management Journal, Academy of Management Review, Journal of Applied Psychology, Journal of Management,* and *Personnel Psychology*. He has researched extensively, placing him in the top 5 percent of the most productive researchers published in premier applied-psychology journals in the 1990s, according to a survey conducted by the Society for Industrial and Organizational Psychology (SIOP). Professor Martocchio received the Ernest J. McCormick Award for Distinguished Early Career Contributions from the Society for Industrial and Organizational Psychology (SIOP), and was subsequently elected as a Fellow in both the American Psychological Association and SIOP. Following the attainment of this recognition, he served as the Chair of the HR Division of the Academy of Management as well as in various other leadership roles within that organization. He is the author of the textbook *Strategic Compensation: A Human Resource Management Approach* (Pearson Higher Education) and coauthor of a textbook with Wayne Mondy, *Human Resource Management* (Pearson Higher Education).

Preface

Employee benefits refer to compensation other than hourly wage, salary, or incentive payments. Three fundamental roles characterize benefits programs: protection, paid time off, and accommodation and enhancement. *Protection programs* provide family benefits, promote health, and guard against income loss caused by catastrophic factors such as unemployment, disability, and serious illnesses. *Paid time-off* policies compensate employees when they are not performing their primary work duties, for example, vacation and holidays. *Accommodation and enhancement benefits* promote opportunities for employees and their families, including stress management classes, flexible work arrangements, and educational assistance.

Employee Benefits was written to provide an introduction to the most common employee practices used in U.S. firms. It is an appropriate source of information for those who want to learn the foundation and acquire a breadth of knowledge about these practices. College-level students taking an undergraduate or a graduate course in employee compensation and benefits will build the foundation for understanding the origin of specific benefits practices and fundamental design considerations. Practitioners who work with benefits professionals or are beginning to take on administrative or managerial roles regarding employee-benefits programs will find this book to be an excellent introduction.

This book contains 12 chapters, organized into four parts:

- Part 1: Introduction to Employee Benefits
- Part 2: Retirement, Health Care, and Life Insurance
- Part 3: Services
- Part 4: Extending Employee Benefits: Design and Global Issues

Each chapter contains a chapter outline, learning objectives, key terms, discussion questions, and two brief cases.

NEW TO THE SIXTH EDITION

All the chapters have been thoroughly revised to capture the ever-changing field of employee benefits—and this field changes at a breakneck pace! For instance, the Patient Protection and Affordable Care Act has imposed an employer mandate for offering health-care plans to employees and compliance guidelines. The Dodd-Frank Act requires even greater transparency of executive benefits practices. Although both laws were passed a few years ago, the implementation requirements have rolled out in phases. In addition, for those who will work with benefits practices in other countries, concepts and data have been added to help make cross-country comparisons. Further, substantially more statistics are included to quantify the costs and prevalence of particular benefits as well as trends where available. All statistics were the most current at the writing of this edition. Finally, thanks to feedback from my students, course instructors, and practitioners, substantial rewriting throughout the book better organizes and breaks down the complexity of benefits practices for the book's intended readers.

SUPPLEMENTAL MATERIALS FOR INSTRUCTORS

All supplements are available from the book's Web site at www.mhhe.com/martocchio6e. Given the rapid and substantial changes in the benefits area, the Web site also offers updates to text coverage of important benefits topics and issues.

Instructor Supplements: Instructor's Resource Manual, TestBank, and Power-Point Presentations.

ACKNOWLEDGMENTS

Many people made valuable contributions. I am also indebted to the reviewers who provided thoughtful remarks for the development of the sixth and previous editions: Among them are James C. Coulson from Chapman University; Larry Morgan from St. Mary's University; Lori Olson from Western Technical College; Barbara Rau from the University of Wisconsin, Oshkosh; Joel Rudin from Rowan University; and Carol Spector from the University of North Florida. F. Jack Witt III, Vice President of Human Resources and Administration at Owens Community College, provided meticulous comments that draw not only from his extensive field experience, but also from his expertise teaching an employee-benefits course at Wayne State University.

At McGraw-Hill Higher Education, my gratitude goes to Michael W. Ablassmeir and Laura Hurst Spell for their support and commitment to this project. I thank Kelly Hart for her oversight of this project. At Lumina Datamatics, I thank Srinivasan Sundararajan for his fine work during the final stages of this project.

Joseph J. Martocchio

Brief Contents

Table of Contents

Introduction to Employee Benefits

Chapter One

Introducing Employee Benefits

Chapter Outline

Defining and Exploring Employee Benefits

Defining Employee Benefits
The Fundamental Roles and Sources of Employee Benefits
Employee Benefits in the Total Compensation Scheme

The Field of Employee-Benefits Practice

Legally Required Benefits
Discretionary Benefits
Origins of Employee Benefits

Legal and Regulatory Influences on Discretionary Benefits Practices

Strategic Planning for a Benefits Program

Basic Strategic Planning Concepts
Approaches to Strategic Benefits Planning

Information Used in Strategic Benefit Planning

External Environment
Internal Environment

Key Terms

Discussion Questions

Cases

1. *Understanding Your Employee Benefits: Understanding a Job Offer*
2. *Managing Employee Benefits: Strategic Benefit Planning at Makers Crafts*

Endnotes

Learning Objectives

In this chapter, you will gain an understanding of:

1. The fundamentals of employee benefits and fit in the total compensation scheme.
2. The field of employee-benefits practice.
3. Legal and regulatory influences on discretionary employee-benefits practices.
4. The strategic importance of benefits and approaches to strategically planning a benefits program.
5. Information used to develop strategic benefits plans.

Welcome to *Employee Benefits: A Primer for Human Resource Management Professionals*. Understanding employee-benefits practices is a worthwhile endeavor no matter whether you plan to become a specialist working in an employee-benefits department, a human resource generalist, or a manager in any department. For instance, employee-benefits professionals are experts in paid time-off policy design. These experts work with HR generalists who oversee all HR activities for employee groups and share developments in the employee-benefits offerings. Employee-benefits professionals also work with managers who are ultimately responsible for carrying out HR policies such as approving paid time off or knowing when to encourage a distressed worker to seek help through an employee assistance program. Let's not forget, most people work for a living and either currently have or will likely have access to at least one employee benefit. As a bonus, this book will help you to understand the components of your benefits and the employer's rationale for offering them.

DEFINING AND EXPLORING EMPLOYEE BENEFITS

Let's start off with a brief definition of employee benefits. Next, we put employee benefits in the context of total compensation systems in companies (Exhibit 1.1) and from there expand the definition of employee benefits. Finally, we examine strategic considerations essential for establishing and maintaining effective employee-benefits programs.

EXHIBIT 1.1
Employee
Benefits in the
Total
Compensation
Scheme

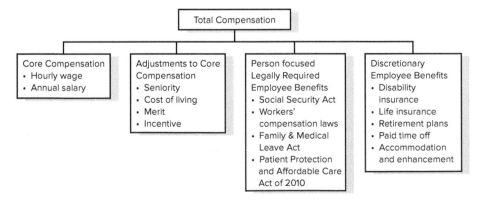

Defining Employee Benefits

Employee benefits refer to compensation other than an hourly wage or salary. Examples of specific employee benefits include paid vacation, health-care coverage, tuition reimbursement, and many more. To organize the vast amount of benefits information efficiently, it is helpful to group benefits based on the role that the benefits serve for recipients and the source of the benefits.

The Fundamental Roles and Sources of Employee Benefits

Three fundamental roles characterize benefits programs: protection, paid time off, and accommodation and enhancement. **Protection programs** provide family benefits, promote health, and guard against income loss caused by catastrophic factors such as unemployment, disability, and serious illnesses. **Paid time-off** policies compensate employees when they are not performing their primary work duties under particular circumstances such as vacation or illness. **Accommodation and enhancement benefits** promote opportunities for employees and their families. Employers may choose to offer one or more of these benefits, including wellness programs, flexible work schedules, and educational assistance.

Employee benefits derive from two broad sources. First, the U.S. federal government requires that most employers, employees, or both make contributions so that certain government-sponsored benefits can be provided to employees. These are referred to as *legally required benefits*. Laws such as the Social Security Act of 1935 mandate a variety of programs designed to provide income to retired workers, disability income, survivor benefits, and health care for older Americans. Legally required benefits can take other forms such as workers' compensation insurance, which the employer purchases and administers. And, it should be noted that some cities and states have legislation that enhance federal government benefits such as paid sick leave. Second, companies may choose to offer additional benefits such as educational benefits and retirement savings plans as just two examples. Choice benefits are referred to as *discretionary benefits*.

Exhibit 1.2 lists typical employee benefits offered in U.S. companies. As this exhibit shows, legally required benefits focus on protection, and companies may choose to offer additional protection programs, which often enhance or supplement legally required benefits. For instance, discretionary disability protection, when added with Social Security disability insurance, could generate a higher income stream than would otherwise be possible.

Prior to the passage of the Patient Protection and Affordable Care Act of 2010, which mandates that most companies provide health-care coverage, companies offered health-care benefits on a discretionary basis. However, some companies still treat health care as a discretionary benefit. In lieu of offering health-care benefits, they are willing to pay a penalty to the federal government based on provisions of the law. More recently, it is possible that employer-sponsored health care will return to discretionary benefit status because President-elect Donald Trump has promised to seek the law's repeal.

Employee Benefits in the Total Compensation Scheme

Employee benefits are a part of a company's total compensation system. **Total compensation** represents both core compensation (wages, salaries, and adjustments), and

EXHIBIT 1.2
Typical
Employee
Benefit
Offerings in
the United
States

Legally Required Benefits	
Old-Age, Survivor, and Disability Insurance (OASDI)	Medicare
	Unemployment insurance
Health-care coverage	Workers' compensation
Prescription drugs	Family and Medical leave
Mental health and substance abuse	
Maternity care	

Discretionary Benefits	
Protection Programs	Nonproduction time
Dental care	Volunteerism
Vision care	
Life insurance	*Accommodation and Enhancement*
Disability insurance (short- and long-term)	*Programs*
	Employees' and family members'
Retirement programs	mental and physical well-being
	Employee assistance programs
Paid Time Off	Wellness programs
Holidays	Family assistance programs
Vacation	Educational benefits for employees
Sick leave	Educational assistance programs
Personal leave	Tuition reimbursement programs
Bereavement or funeral leave	Scholarship programs
Sabbatical leave	Support programs for daily living
Jury duty and witness duty leaves	Transportation services
Military leave	Physical fitness

employee benefits represent compensation other than wages or salaries (see Exhibit 1.1). Compensation professionals establish core compensation programs to reward employees according to their job performance levels or for acquiring job-related knowledge or skills. Monetary compensation lies at the heart of core compensation. After briefly defining specific core and employee-benefits practices, we will subsequently discuss the origins of employee benefits. Understanding the origins enables employee-benefits professionals to better understand the rationale for benefits design.

Core Compensation

Employees receive **base pay**, or money, for performing their jobs. Companies disburse base pay to employees in one of two forms. Employees can earn an hourly pay, or a wage, for each hour worked, or they can earn a salary for performing their jobs, regardless of the number of hours worked. Companies measure salary on an annual basis.

Adjustments to Core Compensation

Over time, employers may choose to adjust employees' base for one or more reasons: increases in the cost of living, differences in employees' job performance, or differences in employees' attainment of job-related knowledge and skills. These elements are defined next.

Cost-of-living adjustments (COLAs) represent periodic base-pay increases often set to periodic changes in the U.S. Bureau of Labor Statistics' Consumer Price Index (CPI). COLAs enable workers to maintain purchasing power by having their base pay adjusted for inflation. Over time, most everything we buy costs more money, such as the price of a gallon of milk. Most companies choose not to apply COLAs to base pay. However, this practice is a common feature in the unionized workforce and in government employment.

How exactly does inflation affect purchasing power? Let's assume, for example, that a local grocery store employs college students, paying them $11 per hour. Let's also assume that a student works 10 hours per week, for a total of $110. Further, let's assume a student typically drives his car, paying $20 per week for gasoline. As gas prices rise, the weekly gasoline cost could increase to $30. As long as the hourly wage rate remains the same, the student will have 10 fewer dollars available for other pursuits. Rising costs erode purchasing power when wages do not increase accordingly.

Seniority-pay systems reward employees with periodic additions to base pay, according to length of service. Over time, employees presumably refine existing skills or acquire new ones that enable them to work more productively. This rationale comes from human capital theory, which states that employees' knowledge and skills generate productive capital, known as human capital. A person employed in a company for a long time knows rules and procedures from which he or she develops the skills (i.e., human capital) necessary to perform a job more quickly than newly hired employees. Today, most unionized private-sector and public-sector organizations continue to base salary on seniority or length of employee service, though the number of unionized workplaces is steadily declining. In 2015, the overall unionization rate was 11.1 percent. During the same period, unionization in the private sector was 6.7 percent and 35.2 percent in the public sector. Members of union-bargaining units whose contracts include seniority provisions, usually rank-and-file as well as clerical workers, receive automatic raises based on the number of years they have been with the company. In the public sector, most administrative, professional, and even managerial employees receive such automatic pay raises.[1]

Merit-pay programs assume that employees' compensation over time should be determined based on differences in job performance. Employees earn permanent increases to base pay according to their performance, which rewards excellent effort or results, motivates future performance, and helps employers retain valued employees. Merit pay increases are expressed as a percentage of current base pay, with higher percentage increases for better performers. For instance, an employee currently earning $25,000 annually receives a 10 percent merit pay increase, making her total annual pay $27,500 after the pay raise takes effect: [$25,000 + (10 percent of $25,000 = $2,500)]. In 2016, employees earned average merit increases of 3.0 percent across all industries, and the projected average increase for 2017 was 3.1 percent.[2] This average increase did not vary significantly, except for nonexempt hourly employees whose average merit increase was 2.9 percent in 2016. In addition, most companies relied on market-based pay increases. Most U.S. companies rely on merit pay to recognize employee performance.

Incentive pay rewards employees for partially or completely attaining a predetermined work objective. Incentive pay is defined as compensation other than base wages or salaries that fluctuates according to the attainment of individual or group goals (for example, $1,000 to a customer sales representative whose customer-service ratings increased each month over a six-month period), or company earnings (for instance, employees share 2 percent of company profits when the company substantially exceeds its performance projections). Commonly used incentive plans include piece rate, gain sharing, and profit sharing.

Person-focused pay rewards employees for acquiring new knowledge and skills through designated curricula sponsored by an employer. This approach recognizes the range, depth, and types of skills or knowledge employees are *capable* of applying productively to their jobs following training. This feature distinguishes pay-for-knowledge plans from merit pay and incentive pay, which reward actual job performance. Some targeted studies and anecdotal information suggest that companies of various sizes use person-focused pay programs. Many of the companies known to be using this kind of pay system employ between approximately 150 and 2,000 employees, the majority operate in the manufacturing industry, and the average age of the companies is approximately 10 years.[3] Overall, the pay method is least commonly used among all U.S. companies, in part because companies fear training employees to join the competition later.

THE FIELD OF EMPLOYEE-BENEFITS PRACTICE

Virtually every company offers at least one benefit to employees, and most companies offer several. This book emphasizes the importance of benefits in achieving legal compliance and competitive advantage and how companies achieve these goals. Meeting these imperatives requires benefits professionals who work in departments within the broader human resource function or as external consultants offering expert advice. Employees in benefits departments span the organizational hierarchy, including clerical staff members, managerial employees, and executives.

One survey revealed that the typical number of employees working in a company's benefits department is 5.3, of whom 3 are professional or managerial staff and 2.3 are support or clerical staff.[4] In addition, the number of staff members varied by company size, ranging from an average of 2.9 employees in smaller companies to 11.3 in larger companies.

So, with which issues do employee-benefits professionals work? According to the *Occupational Outlook Handbook*:

> Benefits managers plan, direct, and coordinate retirement plans, health insurance, and other benefits that an organization offers its employees.[5]

Performance standards are established by members of the profession rather than by outsiders. Most professions also have effective representative organizations that permit members to exchange ideas of mutual concern. Several well-known organizations serve the benefits profession. Among the more prominent are the International Foundation of Employee Benefit Plans and WorldatWork.

Opportunities for employment as compensation and benefits managers are projected to grow at an annual rate of 6 percent through 2024.[6] The median annual compensation for compensation and benefits managers was $108,070, which is more than double the median annual earnings for all jobs.[7] The salary levels vary on a number of factors, including relevant work experience, educational credentials, and industry. For example, the mean annual compensation was lowest in local government ($95,880) settings and highest in the financial securities industry ($158,760).

While the employee-benefits group is on the same team as HR, inevitably tensions arise. Employee-benefits professionals are inclined to develop the benefits program, but competition for limited funds creates challenges. For instance, recruitment professionals may wish to purchase costly selection tests to improve the quality of hires. Training and development professionals vie for greater resources to incorporate expensive technology into curricula. Let's take a closer look at the components of benefits packages to gain an appreciation of the scope of employee benefits.

Legally Required Benefits

Legally required benefits are mandated by several laws, some of which include: the Social Security Act of 1935 (Chapter 7), various state workers' compensation laws (Chapter 6), the Family and Medical Leave Act of 1993 (Chapter 8), and the Patient Protection and Affordable Care Act of 2010 (Chapter 5). All provide protection programs to employees and their dependents. A basic summary of each benefit follows, with detailed treatment deferred to the relevant chapters.

The Social Security Act of 1935

The economic devastation of the Great Depression era prompted the federal government into action because most people had used up their life savings to survive, and opportunities for gainful employment were scarce. **The Social Security Act of 1935** set up two programs: a federal system of income benefits for retired workers, and a system of unemployment insurance administered by the federal and state governments. Amendments to the Social Security Act established the disability insurance and Medicare programs. **Old-Age, Survivor, and Disability Insurance (OASDI)** refers to the programs that provide retirement income, income to the survivors of deceased workers, and income to disabled workers and their family members. **Medicare** serves nearly all U.S. citizens aged at least 65, as well as disabled Social Security beneficiaries, by providing insurance coverage for hospitalization, convalescent care, major doctor bills, and prescription drug coverage.

State Compulsory Disability Laws (Workers' Compensation)

Workers' compensation insurance came into existence during the early decades of the 20th century, when industrial accidents were very common and workers suffered from occupational illnesses at alarming rates.[8] During the early years of industrialization of the U.S. economy, no laws required employers to ensure the health and safety of employees. Seriously injured and ill workers were left with virtually no recourse because social insurance programs to protect such workers were nonexistent. **State compulsory disability laws** created workers' compensation programs. **Workers' compensation** insurance programs are designed to cover employee expenses incurred in work-related accidents or injuries.

The Family and Medical Leave Act of 1993

The **Family and Medical Leave Act (FMLA)** provides job protection to employees in cases of a family or personal medical emergency. FMLA permits eligible employees to take up to 12 workweeks of unpaid leave during any 12-month period. These employees retain the right to return to the position they left when the leave began or to an equivalent position with the same terms of employment, including pay and benefits. The passage of the FMLA reflected growing recognition that the parents of many employees are becoming elderly, rendering them susceptible to serious illnesses or medical conditions as well as the changing role of men regarding child care.

The Patient Protection and Affordable Care Act of 2010

The Patient Protection and Affordable Care Act (PPACA), enacted on March 23, 2010, is a comprehensive law that requires employers to offer health-care benefits to employees. **Health care** covers the costs of a variety of services that promote sound physical and mental health, including physical examinations, diagnostic testing (X-rays), surgery, and hospitalization. Companies can choose to rely on one or more of four broad approaches to providing health care, including **fee-for-service plans, alternative managed-care plans, point-of-service plans**, and **consumer-driven health care**. Companies may offer additional care options: **Dental care** benefits may cover routine preventative procedures and necessary procedures to help restore the health of teeth and gums. **Vision care** plans usually cover eye examinations, prescription lenses, frames, and fitting of glasses. **Prescription drug plans** cover a portion of the costs of legal drugs. **Mental health and substance abuse plans** cover the costs for treating mental health ailments such as clinical depression and alcohol or chemical substance abuse.

Discretionary Benefits

Discretionary benefits fulfill three main roles. The first, *protection programs,* most closely parallels legally required benefits by offering protections to employees and family members due to income loss or ill health. The second, *paid time off,* affords employees time off with pay for many purposes, including illness or to celebrate designated holidays. The third variety, *accommodation and enhancements,* offers improvements to employees and their families in many ways. Wellness programs and educational assistance programs are just two examples.

Protection Programs

Disability Insurance   Disability insurance replaces income for employees who become unable to work on a regular basis because of an illness or injury. Employer-sponsored disability insurance is more encompassing than workers' compensation because these benefits generally apply to both work- and non- work-related illness or injury. Disability insurance programs are reviewed in greater detail in Chapter 6.

Life Insurance   Employer-sponsored **life insurance** protects family members by paying a specified amount upon the employee's death. Most policies pay some multiple of the employee's salary—for instance, benefits paid at twice the employee's annual salary. Employees usually have the option of purchasing additional coverage. Frequently, employer-sponsored life insurance plans also include accidental death and dismember ment claims, which pay additional benefits if death was the result of an accident or if the insured incurs accidental loss of a limb. Life insurance is reviewed in Chapter 6.

Retirement Plans   **Retirement plans**, provide income to individuals and beneficiaries throughout retirement. Individuals may participate in more than one retirement plan. Companies may establish retirement plans as defined contribution plans, defined benefit plans, or hybrid plans that combine features of defined contribution and defined benefit plans. Under a **defined contribution plan**, employees make annual contributions to their accounts, based on chosen percentage of annual pay. At their discretion, companies make matching contributions, which are determined by a formula. The amount each participant receives in retirement depends on the performance of the selected investment choices (for example, company stock or government bonds). A **defined benefit plan** awards a monthly sum equal to a percentage of a participant's preretirement pay multiplied by the number of years worked for the employer. The level of required employer contributions fluctuates from year to year as necessary to ensure that promised benefits will be honored. Retirement plans are discussed in Chapter 4.

Paid Time Off

The second type of discretionary benefits is paid time off. **Paid time-off** policies compensate employees when they are not performing their primary work duties. Companies offer most paid time off as a matter of custom, particularly paid holidays, vacations, and sick leave. In unionized settings, paid time-off provisions are specified within the collective bargaining agreement. Relatively common paid time-off practices are jury duty, funeral leave, military leave, holidays, and vacations.

Accommodation and Enhancement Programs

Accommodation and enhancement benefits promote opportunities for employees and family members. These benefits are discussed in Chapter 9. Following are four objectives, with an example stated in parentheses:

- Mental and physical well-being of employees and family members (e.g., stress management).

- Family assistance programs (e.g., child care).
- Skills and knowledge acquisition through educational programs (e.g., tuition reimbursement).
- Opportunities to manage daily challenges (e.g., transportation services).

Basic Design Considerations for Discretionary Benefits

Employee-benefits professionals possess substantial leeway when designing discretionary benefits. Numerous design considerations are reviewed throughout this book as specific benefits are examined, and general design considerations are discussed in Chapter 10. As noted later in this chapter and in Chapter 2, companies strive to offer cost-effective benefits that will promote the recruitment and retention of highly qualified employees. Chapter 2 addresses these issues from a psychological perspective as well as from an economic perspective. The following is a basic introduction to common features of employee-benefits programs.

- *Eligibility provisions.* Companies must decide whether to limit participation to current employees, their dependent family members, and survivors of deceased current or retired employees. Companies may limit participation to current employees. For instance, many companies exclude part-time employees as a cost-control measure.
- *Kinds of benefits.* Which benefits do companies offer to eligible individuals? Companies may sponsor a variety of broad benefits, including retirement plans, health care, and paid time off. Then they select specific benefits from these broad categories. For instance, defined contribution retirement plans are often preferred because these plans are more cost-effective than defined benefit plans.
- *Level of benefits.* Companies choose benefits based on maximum benefit limits. For example, life insurance policies specify the dollar benefit amount for the death of an employee.
- *Waiting periods.* Waiting periods specify the minimum number of months an employee must remain employed before becoming eligible for one or more benefits. Some waiting periods correspond with the length of probationary periods, while others are limited by law. Companies impose probationary periods to judge a newcomer's job performance, and they explicitly reserve the right to terminate employees who demonstrate low job performance.
- *Financing benefits.* Employers choose from four approaches: noncontributory, contributory, employee-financed programs, or some combination. **Noncontributory financing** means that the company pays the total costs for designated discretionary benefits. Under **contributory financing**, the company and its employees share the costs. Under **employee-financed benefits**, employees bear the entire cost. The majority of benefit plans today are contributory, largely because benefits costs have risen so dramatically.

- *Employee choice.* Traditionally, a company provided the same benefits to most or all employees. Increasingly, companies offer employees varying degrees of choice. **Flexible benefits plans** enable employees to choose from among a set of benefits and different levels of these benefits (Chapter 10). The increasing diversity of the workforce has made standardized benefits offerings less practical because of greater differences in needs and preferences for particular benefits. For instance, workers with preschool-age children find day-care assistance programs most appealing, and workers nearing retirement age find value in company-sponsored retiree health-care benefits. Voluntary benefits provide additional options. **Voluntary benefits are** supplemental benefits that companies offer on an employee-financed basis, whereas flexible benefits provide employees with a choice from a menu of benefits, which follow contributory or noncontributory financing approaches. Examples of voluntary benefits include identity theft protection, home or renter's insurance, college savings plans, or, even pet insurance. Why offer these benefits when employees can purchase them outside the employment setting? Employers negotiate a lower rate than employees could ascertain on an individual basis. Also, the variety of discounted benefits should be appealing to a diverse workforce. For example, younger employees with children may find a college savings plan an attractive benefit compared to employees approaching retirement whose children have already completed their education.

- *Communication.* Oftentimes, employees either are unaware of or undervalue their benefits. Communicating the features and costs of benefits is essential. Effective communication creates an awareness of, and appreciation for, the way current benefits improve the financial security and physical and mental well-being of employees.

Origins of Employee Benefits

Different forces account for legally required and discretionary employee benefits. The U.S. government established programs to protect individuals from catastrophic events such as disability and unemployment. As highlighted earlier, legally required benefits are protection programs that attempt to promote health, maintain family income streams, and assist families in crisis.

Historically, legally required benefits provided a form of social insurance, which were prompted largely by the rapid growth of industrialization in the United States during the late 19th and early 20th centuries as well as the Great Depression of the 1930s. Early social insurance programs were designed to minimize the possibility of destitution for individuals who were unemployed or became severely injured while working. In addition, social insurance programs aimed to stabilize the well-being of dependent family members. Further, early social insurance programs enabled retirees to maintain subsistence income levels. These objectives remain the cornerstones of today's benefits practices.

The first signs of contemporary discretionary employee benefits were evident in the late 1800s, when large companies such as American Express offered retirement plans. For the next few decades, the development in employee-benefits practice resulted from government legislation. Then, discretionary benefits offerings became more prominent in the 1940s and 1950s due in large part to federal government wage freezes. Employee benefits were not subject to those restrictions, allowing expansion of discretionary benefits as an alternative to wage increases or as a motivational tool. During that period, the term *welfare practices* described some of the employee benefits. **Welfare practices** were "anything for the comfort and improvement, intellectual or social, of the employees, over and above wages paid, which is not a necessity of the industry nor required by law."[9]

The opportunities available to employees through welfare practices varied. For instance, some employers offered libraries and recreational areas, while others provided financial assistance for education and home improvements. In addition, employer sponsorship of health care became common. Employee unions also contributed directly to the increase in employee welfare practices. The National Labor Relations Act (NLRA) of 1935 legitimized bargaining for employee benefits. Union workers have access to more benefits, and lucrative ones, than nonunion employees do.[10] Still, unions contributed indirectly to the rise in benefits offerings in nonunion settings. Nonunion companies strive to minimize unionization by offering their employees benefits comparable to those received by employees in union companies.

Employees typically view employer-sponsored benefits as entitlements. Anecdotal evidence suggests that most employees still feel this way: Company membership entitles them to benefits because participation in benefits programs are not tied to job performance. Until recently, companies also treated virtually all elements of benefits as entitlements. However, rising benefits costs, increased foreign competition, and the so-called Great Recession (2007–2009) led companies to question this entitlement ethic. Increasingly, companies are shifting responsibility for the cost of some benefits to employees. For example, in Chapter 5, employer-sponsored high-deductible health care plans are discussed.

LEGAL AND REGULATORY INFLUENCES ON DISCRETIONARY BENEFITS PRACTICES

While employers are free to offer discretionary benefits, specific laws influence the application of these practices. To understand these influences, it is necessary to distinguish between private-sector employers and governmental employers, because different regulations influence discretionary benefits practices in these sectors of the U.S. economy. The private sector refers to nongovernmental employers that strive to maximize profits or offer charitable services to the public in need (nonprofit companies). Apple and PepsiCo are examples of for-profit companies, and the American Red Cross and the United Way are examples of nonprofit companies. In 2016, private-sector companies employed about 122 million persons—all U.S. civilian employees, and most of the companies were for-profit. Profit maximization is the foundation of the U.S. economy. Private-sector employers strive to increase profits, market share, and returns on investment for the owners and shareholders. Employers expect workers to be as productive as possible to promote these goals. At the same time, containing pay and benefits costs contributes to profit maximization.

Conflicting goals between employees and profit-oriented employers necessitate regulations to protect employees from unfair treatment. The following excerpt captures the natural clash between employers and employees, employer profit maximization goals, and employee desires for equitable and fair treatment:

> As competition increased in the textile industry, the original concern of the mill owners for their employees gave way to stricter controls which had nothing to do with the well-being of the workers. Employers reduced wages, lengthened hours, and intensified work. For a workday from 11.5 to 13 hours, making up an average week of 75 hours, the women operatives were generally earning less than $1.50 a week (exclusive of board) by the late 1840s, and they were being compelled to tend four looms whereas in the 1830s they had only taken care of two . . . [The manager] ordered them [the female textile workers] to come before breakfast. "I regard my work-people just as I regard my machinery. So long as they can do my work for what I choose to pay them, I keep them, getting out of them all I can."[11]

Employees strive to attain high wages, comprehensive benefits, safe and healthful work conditions, and job security. Prior to the passage of the National Labor Relations Act, employees were not required to negotiate terms and conditions of employment. As a result, many workers were subjected to unsafe and unhealthful working conditions, inadequate pay and benefits, and excessive work hours. Today, employment legislation and labor unions protect the rights and status of workers, and employer abuses are much less prevalent than before legal protections and labor unions. For example, prior to the Employee Retirement Income Security Act (ERISA) of 1974, employees could easily lose company retirement benefits after decades of service simply because the employer chose to use retirement funds for other purposes that benefited company profits. Also, employees did not possess the right to keep their retirement assets if they left a company before reaching retirement age. Years of congressional testimony and investigations led to the passage of ERISA based on the conclusion that employer-sponsored retirement plans were essential to the country's economic security and as an essential supplement to government-sponsored retirement programs through the Social Security Act of 1935.

Public-sector employers include the U.S. federal government, state governments, and local governments. Approximately 2 million people are employed in the federal government's three branches: executive, judicial, and legislative. Public-sector employers work on behalf of citizens, and none exists to make profits. At the state and local levels, public-sector employers include local police forces, community colleges, state colleges and universities, court systems, social service agencies, and public works departments (such as road maintenance), totaling approximately 20 million workers. Although government employers do not seek profits, they still must operate within a budget to provide pay and benefits to employees and services to citizens.

Also, the government is a buyer and consumer of the products and services that private-sector companies produce. Indeed, the government spends more than $1 trillion each year on these items. The government uses energy to run its buildings, and it engages in contracts with private-sector companies for a multitude of goods and services ranging from building construction to multimillion-dollar defense systems. Various laws require the government to pay contract employees the customary wage in the local area. This is an important fact because many benefits, such as retirement earnings, are tied to pay levels.

STRATEGIC PLANNING FOR A BENEFITS PROGRAM

The development of successful benefits programs matches the priorities of ongoing strategic planning efforts within companies. One survey found that high-performing companies align total compensation programs with business objectives.[12] Many U.S. companies build their success through creating and marketing innovative products and services to customers. Increasingly, companies emphasize the importance of employing diverse workforces to promote the inventive processes necessary for innovation. For instance, Bristol-Myers Squibb pledges to "foster a globally diverse workforce and a companywide culture that encourages excellence, leadership, innovation, and a balance between our personal and professional lives."[13]

Basic Strategic Planning Concepts

Strategic planning entails a series of judgments, made under uncertainty, that companies direct toward making strategic decisions. Companies base their decisions on environmental scanning activities, which are discussed later in this chapter. Business professionals make two kinds of decisions: strategic decisions and, in the context of employee benefits, the design of specific practices such as retirement plans. Briefly, strategic decisions guide the activities of companies in the market. The choice about the design of employee-benefits practices support the fulfillment of strategic decisions, which are discussed shortly. Exhibit 1.3 shows the relationship between strategic decisions as well as the design of employee-benefits practices.

Strategic planning supports business objectives. Company executives communicate business objectives in competitive strategy statements. **Competitive strategy** refers to the planned use of company resources—technology, capital, and human resources (HR)—to promote and sustain competitive advantage. For example, ExxonMobil Corporation, a company in the oil and gas exploration industry, strives to be the world's premier petroleum and petrochemical company by achieving superior financial and operating results while simultaneously adhering to high

EXHIBIT 1.3
Relationship
between
Strategic
Decisions and
Employee-
Benefits
Practices

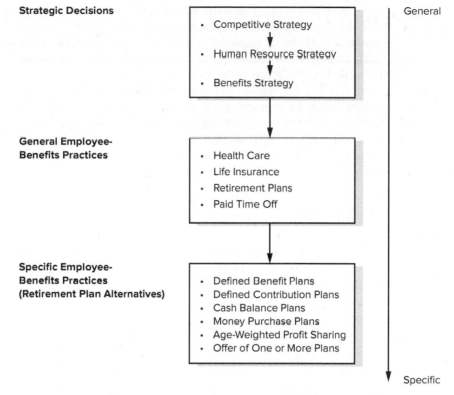

Strategic Decisions

- Competitive Strategy
- Human Resource Strategy
- Benefits Strategy

General

**General Employee-
Benefits Practices**

- Health Care
- Life Insurance
- Retirement Plans
- Paid Time Off

**Specific Employee-
Benefits Practices
(Retirement Plan Alternatives)**

- Defined Benefit Plans
- Defined Contribution Plans
- Cash Balance Plans
- Money Purchase Plans
- Age-Weighted Profit Sharing
- Offer of One or More Plans

Specific

ethical standards.[14] Eli Lilly and Company, a manufacturer of pharmaceutical products, pursues a competitive strategy, which focuses on creating innovative medicines that improve patient health outcomes.[15]

Human resource executives collaborate with other company executives to develop **HR strategies**, which specify the use of multiple HR practices. These statements are consistent with a company's competitive strategy. For example, Eli Lilly is well known for the innovative environment that it creates for employees to make discoveries for pharmaceutical products that will enhance the life of people throughout the world.[16]

Compensation and benefits managers and executives work with the lead HR executive and the company's chief budget officer to prepare total compensation strategies. **Total compensation strategies** describe the use of compensation and benefits practices that support both HR strategies and competitive strategies. Benefits professionals craft **benefits strategies** based on information contained in strategic benefit plans.

Strategic benefit plans detail different scenarios that may reasonably affect the company, and these plans emphasize long-term changes in how a company's benefit plan operates.[17] Companies establish strategic benefit plans based on the interpretation of pertinent information in the external and internal environments, which will be discussed shortly.

At Lilly, it is evident that the use of compensation and benefits practices supports both human resource strategies and competitive strategies. Eli Lilly is well known for offering a balanced compensation and benefits program which recognizes employee contributions and embraces employees through recognition of their needs outside the workplace.

As Exhibit 1.3 shows, managers throughout a company make decisions to specify policy for promoting competitive advantage. Benefits decisions are based on two questions: Does offering particular benefits (e.g., paid vacations) support the company's benefits strategy? and What is the optimal design (of vacation benefits)? Descriptions of five employee benefits practices at ExxonMobil follow.

1. *Education assistance*—After employment, ExxonMobil reimburses 100 percent of college-related expenses for approved courses to maintain or improve your skills.
2. *Matching gifts program*—Three-to-one matching funds for employee and alumni donations to their alma mater.
3. *Volunteer involvement program*—Grant moneys awarded for volunteering at eligible nonprofit organizations.
4. *Flexible work arrangements*—Options for adjustable work hours, telecommuting, part-time extensions for family-care needs, and personal time off.
5. *Life assistance resources*—For child care, elder care, adoption, teen issues, stress, and a variety of other issues.[18]

Approaches to Strategic Benefits Planning

This section begins with a review of two approaches to strategic benefit planning. Afterward, the kinds of information that companies use in this planning process will be touched upon. In most companies, either compensation or benefits-program executives (in some companies, one person is responsible for both) take the lead in strategic benefit planning. Two possible general approaches characterize strategic benefit planning: top-down and backing-in.[19] The **top-down approach** represents a proactive process: Companies regularly review their entire benefits programs or particular parts of the programs. This process may lead to a reformulation of an entire program or specific parts. Exhibit 1.4 illustrates how the top-down approach unfolds and shows the representative time frames for particular stages of this process.

The **backing-in approach** is a reactive process because companies evaluate the benefits program only when unexpected problems arise. Exhibit 1.5 illustrates how the backing-in approach unfolds, along with the representative time frames for particular stages of this process. For instance, Company A, a manufacturing company, built a reputation as a great place to work for many reasons, including competitive pay and benefits. Recently, excessive turnover has occurred among its assembly-line employees, many of whom have taken jobs at another local

EXHIBIT 1.4 A Top-Down Approach to Strategic Benefit Planning: A Conceptual Framework

Source: V. Barocas. *Strategic Benefits Planning* (New York: The Conference Board, 1992), 15.

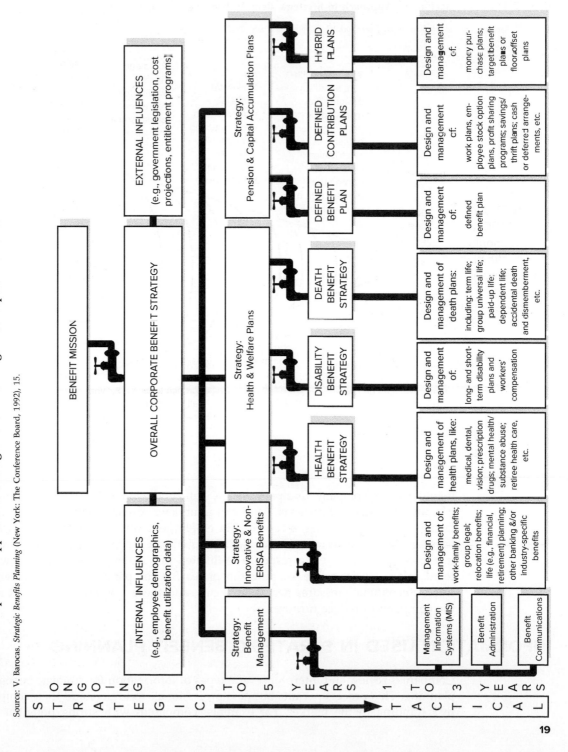

19

EXHIBIT 1.5 A Backing-in Approach to Strategic Benefit Planning

Source: V. Barocas, *Strategic Benefits Planning* (New York: The Conference Board, 1992), 16.

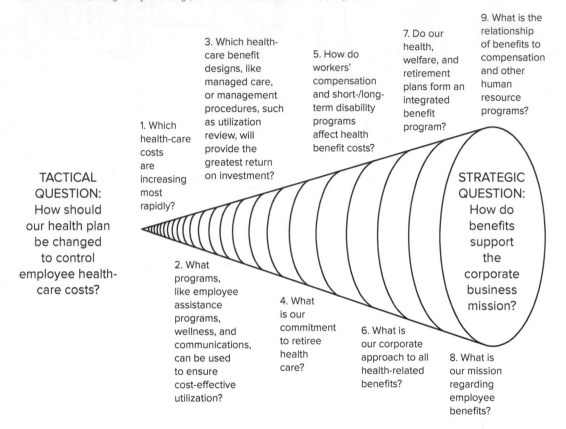

manufacturing company. Company A's HR staff conducted exit interviews to identify possible causes of turnover. Most exit interviews revealed significant dissatisfaction with wage freezes, steep rises in employee contributions for health-care coverage, and the termination of dental benefits. Company management had instituted these changes in response to inflated raw material costs. Its goal was to maintain profits while keeping the prices for company products constant. Intense economic pressures necessitated cuts, and these cuts made it difficult for the company to reduce turnover.

INFORMATION USED IN STRATEGIC BENEFIT PLANNING

Companies review and interpret several types of information for strategic benefits planning. This process permits business professionals to understand their company's standing in the market. For example, companies with strong potential to increase sales levels tend to be in better standing than companies with weak potential to maintain or increase sales. Companies in strong standing should be able to devote more financial resources to fund benefits programs than companies in weak standing. Two information sources include the external market environment and the internal company environment.

External Environment

External environmental factors include:

- Industry prospects, economic conditions, and forecasts
- Employer costs for compensation and benefits
- Government regulation of employee benefits
- Changing demographics of the labor force

Industry Prospects, Economic Conditions, and Forecasts

The first two factors, industry prospects and current and anticipated economic conditions, set the backdrop for establishing strategic benefits plans. Industry prospects and economic forecasts set the backdrop for strategic benefits planning because these factors are indicators of the future of companies. Forecasts indicating growth possibly call for strengthening discretionary benefits offerings and levels to help recruit and retain the most-qualified employees. Pessimistic forecasts emphasize the need to save costs by shifting more of the responsibility on employees. For example, more and more companies require that employees share a greater percentage of the cost of health-care plans. Also, there has been a shift away from employer-sponsored defined benefit retirement plans to employer-sponsored defined contribution plans, which makes it easier for companies to predict their costs. Further, negative outlooks may lead companies to expand outplacement services (i.e., helping unwanted employees find jobs elsewhere) in anticipation of large-scale layoffs. Still, employers will very likely continue to sponsor employee benefits despite economic conditions for two reasons. First, the Internal Revenue Code and the Employee Retirement Income Security Act create tax advantages for companies that offer qualified benefits plans (see Chapter 3). Employers may exclude limited contributions to these plans from taxable annual income, leading to reduced tax payments to the federal government. Second, as we discuss in Chapter 2, generous benefits offerings facilitate a company's attempt to attract and retain the best-qualified employees. Although employer-sponsored benefits costs are significant, well-qualified workforces presumably create lucrative advantages for companies, as evidenced by high-quality customer service, competent business functions such as innovative marketing, and research and development.

Employer Costs for Compensation and Benefits

The U.S. Bureau of Labor Statistics (BLS) regularly publishes current information about employer costs for employee compensation and benefits in the United States (and changes in these costs over time) on its Web site, at www.bls.gov. Benefits professionals may use these data to benchmark current benefits costs against reported averages or as a starting point for budget planning. The following is an excerpt from a BLS news release.

> In the private sector, employer costs for employee compensation averaged $31.53 per hour worked in September 2015, the U.S. Bureau of Labor Statistics reported today. Wages and salaries averaged $21.98 per hour worked and accounted for 69.7 percent of these costs, while benefits averaged $9.55 and accounted for the remaining 30.3 percent.[20]

The BLS presents data for average hourly pay and specific benefits for the entire civilian workforce, private industry, state and local governments, and by particular categories: industry, occupational group, region, establishment size, and worker characteristics, such as bargaining status and full- or part-time status. Employer costs per hour worked are available for five major occupational groups. Employer compensation costs also vary by industry, region, and establishment size. Exhibit 1.6 shows employer costs for employee compensation in the private sector, based on some of those characteristics. Preliminary data for 2016 show minute increases.

Overall, benefits accounted for approximately 30 percent of total compensation costs in the private sector. At first glance, the cost of specific benefits does not appear to be particularly high because employers spent an average of $9.55 per employee per hour to provide discretionary and legally required benefits. However, aggregating these costs for a one-year period (per employee) paints a different picture. Assuming that a typical service employee works 1,850 hours per year, an employer spends $17,667.50 for each employee annually for employee benefits.

Government Regulation of Employee Benefits

Four broad forces contribute to an employer's choice of discretionary benefits and its ability to fund them. The first two, adequacy of legally required benefits and employee expectations, directly influence an employer's choice. The third, the cost of legally required benefits, influences a company's ability to fund discretionary benefits. The fourth entails a variety of economic considerations, which will be discussed in Chapter 2.

First, the workers' plight during the industrialization of the U.S. economy and the Great Depression promoted the rise of many legally required benefits. Examples include workers' compensation and both retirement income and health care under the Social Security Act (Chapters 6 and 7). The U.S. economy is based on free-market principles, not on socialist principles more commonly found in many Eastern European countries and in large segments of the People's Republic of China where government benefits are represent the lion's share of support following injury, disability, or in retirement. In addition, the cost of living has risen more quickly than the dollar amount of government benefits. Finally, legislators during the early part of the 20th century could not anticipate the very high costs of health care due, in large part, to advances in medicine and health-care technology. The entire structure of the health-care industry is fundamentally different

EXHIBIT 1.6 Employer Costs per Hour Worked for Employee Compensation and Costs as a Percent of Total Compensation: Private Industry Workers, by Major Occupational Group and Bargaining Unit Status, September 2015

Source: U.S. Bureau of Labor Statistics, "Employer Costs for Employee Compensation–September 2015," USDL 15–2329.

Compensation Component	All Workers		Occupational Group						Bargaining Unit Status			
			Management, Professional, and Related		Service		Production, Transportation, and Material Moving		Union		Nonunion	
	Cost	Percent	Cost	Percent	Cost	Percent	Cost	Percent	Cost	Percent	Cost	Percent
Total compensation	$31.53	100.0	$55.69	100.0	$14.57	100.0	$27.24	100.0	$46.38	100.0	$30.04	100.0
Wages and salaries	21.98	69.7	38.55	69.2	11.07	76.0	17.94	65.8	27.87	60.1	21.39	71.2
Total benefits	9.55	30.3	17.14	30.8	3.50	24.0	9.30	34.2	18.51	39.9	8.65	28.8
Paid leave	2.17	6.9	4.69	8.4	0.56	3.9	1.65	6.1	3.26	7.0	2.05	6.9
Vacation	1.13	3.6	2.49	4.5	0.29	2.0	0.86	3.1	1.66	3.6	1.03	3.6
Holiday	0.66	2.1	1.37	2.5	0.17	1.2	0.55	2.0	0.95	2.1	0.63	2.1
Sick	0.26	0.8	0.59	1.1	0.07	0.5	0.18	0.7	0.47	1.0	0.24	0.8
Personal	0.12	0.4	0.25	0.4	0.03	0.2	0.06	0.2	0.17	0.4	0.11	0.4
Supplemental pay	1.04	3.3	2.23	4.0	0.24	1.6	0.99	3.6	1.41	3.0	1.00	3.3
Overtime and premium[1]	0.27	0.8	0.19	0.3	0.11	0.7	0.57	2.1	0.89	1.9	0.20	0.7
Shift differentials	0.06	0.2	0.10	0.2	0.04	0.3	0.09	0.3	0.18	0.4	0.05	0.2
Nonproduction bonuses	0.71	2.2	1.95	3.5	0.09	0.6	0.33	1.2	0.34	0.7	0.75	2.5
Insurance	2.59	8.2	3.99	7.2	0.93	6.4	2.95	10.8	6.14	13.2	2.23	7.4
Life	0.04	0.1	0.08	0.2	(2)	(3)	0.04	0.1	0.07	0.2	0.04	0.1
Health	2.44	7.7	3.71	6.7	0.90	6.2	2.78	10.2	5.77	12.4	2.11	7.0
Short-term disability	0.06	0.2	0.11	0.2	(2)	(3)	0.06	0.2	0.18	0.4	0.05	0.2
Long-term disability	0.05	0.1	0.09	0.2	(2)	(3)	0.07	0.3	0.12	0.3	0.04	0.1
Retirement and savings	1.25	4.0	2.54	4.6	0.24	1.7	1.14	4.2	4.05	8.7	0.97	3.2
Defined benefit	0.55	1.7	1.00	1.8	0.10	0.7	0.61	2.2	2.92	6.3	0.31	1.0
Defined contribution	0.70	2.2	1.54	2.8	0.14	1.0	0.53	1.9	1.13	2.4	0.66	2.2
Legally required benefits	2.51	7.9	3.68	6.6	1.52	10.4	2.57	9.4	3.66	7.9	2.35	8.0
Social Security and Medicare	1.82	5.8	3.12	5.6	0.94	6.5	1.53	5.6	2.31	5.0	1.77	5.9
Social Security[4]	1.45	4.6	2.46	4.4	0.76	5.2	1.23	4.5	1.84	4.0	1.42	4.7
Medicare	0.36	1.2	0.65	1.2	0.18	1.2	0.30	1.1	0.47	1.0	0.35	1.2
Federal unemployment insurance	0.04	0.1	0.04	0.1	0.05	0.3	0.04	0.1	0.04	0.1	0.04	0.1
State unemployment insurance	0.20	0.6	0.20	0.4	0.18	1.2	0.21	0.8	0.28	0.6	0.19	0.6
Workers' compensation	0.45	1.4	0.33	0.6	0.36	2.5	0.80	2.9	1.02	2.2	0.39	1.3

[1] Includes premium pay (such as overtime, weekends, and holidays) for work in addition to the regular work schedule.
[2] Cost per hour worked is $0.01 or less.
[3] Less than 0.05 percent.
[4] Social Security refers to the Old-Age, Survivors, and Disability Insurance (OASDI) program.
Note: The sum of individual items may not equal totals due to rounding.

now than it was in the 1930s. Since then, medical research and development have led to the ability to diagnose diseases in the early stages, and thus life expectancy of people born in more-recent years has increased notably. These changes make the funding formulas inadequate to meet today's realities.

Second, the federal government's imposition of wage freezes during World War II gave rise to many present-day discretionary benefits. Employers withdrew costly offerings after the government ended the wage freeze. The withdrawal of these benefits created discontent among employees, because many viewed employer-sponsored benefits as an entitlement. For instance, employees strongly reacted to the withdrawal of health-care benefits. Legal battles followed based on unions' and workers' claims that employer-sponsored health care is a fundamental right. Health-care benefits subsequently became a mandatory subject of collective bargaining in union settings.

Third, the federal government requires companies to support legally required benefits. For example, the **Federal Insurance Contributions Act (FICA)**[21] helps support the Social Security Old-Age, Survivor, and Disability Insurance program (OASDI). Unemployment insurance benefits are financed by federal and, sometimes, state taxes levied on employers. A federal tax is levied on employers under the **Federal Unemployment Tax Act (FUTA).**[22] Both acts are discussed more fully in Chapter 7. Under the **Patient Protection and Affordable Care Act of 2010,** most employers are required to provide health-care coverage to full-time workers; otherwise, they face stiff monetary penalties.

Changing Demographics of the Labor Force

According to the Bureau of Labor Statistics, labor force diversity will continue to increase based on gender, age, race, and ethnicity. An employer-sponsored benefits program is most effective when the workforce is relatively similar in terms of needs and preferences. For example, let's assume that a company's workforce has 60 percent women and 40 percent men. Most of the women are of child-bearing age and most of the men range in age between their 50s and 60s. On the surface, one could say that this workforce is not very similar in terms of needs and preferences for benefits because its composition varies considerably by gender and age. Below the surface, one could reasonably conclude that there will be substantial differences in the needs and preferences for benefits. Chances are that most of the women may place a high value on day-care benefits, while most of the men will not have a need for such benefits because their children are likely to be near or at adulthood.

Employees are more likely to endorse employer-sponsored benefits as long as these benefits fulfill their needs and preferences. Also, employees should believe that contributions to receive benefits are determined fairly. Workforce diversity challenges a company's quest to establish benefits that satisfy the needs and preferences of workers. For example, the younger segment of the workforce may benefit from family assistance programs and educational assistance programs, while the older segments of the workforce rely on generous health-care benefits and defined benefit plans that support progressive retirement-income streams.

Health-care benefits may be redundant for some dual-income families. One spouse or partner will not elect these benefits because he or she already receives coverage as a family member under the other's plan. As employee needs diversify and desires for benefits become apparent to workforce members, some employees will likely protest benefits that they believe disproportionately suit coworkers. Certainly, differences in employee preferences and needs based on life stage and life circumstances call for flexible benefits offerings, which will be discussed shortly.

Internal Environment

Internal environmental factors include workforce demographics and collective bargaining agreements.

Workforce Demographics

The workforce characteristics of companies usually represent the characteristics of the broad labor force. Over time, company workforces have become more demographically diverse as labor force diversity has increased. Not surprisingly, workforce diversity has created challenges for companies in establishing benefits programs. Demographic characteristics to a large extent symbolize employee needs and preferences, which are often associated with life events. Exhibit 1.7 shows typical benefits preferred by employees according to demographic characteristics and probable life events.

Should companies presume the needs and preferences of employees? Probably not. Benefits professionals may use surveys once every year or two to collect information about employee demographics, needs, preferences, recent or

EXHIBIT 1.7
Likely
Preferred
Benefits
According to
Demographics
and Life
Events

Demographics	Life Events Benefits
Unmarried male and female employees (uncoupled employees)	Physical fitness programs Generous vacation allowances
Employees with dependent elderly parents or relatives	Elder care benefits Flexible work schedules
Married male and female employees	Flexible work schedules
Employees with children, male or female, coupled or uncoupled	Day-care assistance Life insurance Health care with dependent coverage Education benefits for children
Older workers (nearing retirement)	Retirement plans with accelerated benefits accumulation Health-care coverage with prescription drug benefits Generous sick-leave allowances Disability insurance Retiree health-care benefits

anticipated life changes, and the extent to which they find particular benefits useful. Statistical analyses will show whether there is an association among these factors. Then, benefits professionals may compare current offerings with survey results. Over time, they can determine whether changes in age, family status, needs, and preferences influence employees' views of benefits.

Collective Bargaining Agreements

Collective bargaining agreements specify terms of employment, including pay, benefits, and working conditions. These agreements arise out of negotiations between management and labor unions that represent some or all employees in a company. In Chapter 3, we discuss the National Labor Relations Act of 1935 established that both labor unions and employers possess a duty to bargain with the other party in good faith over terms of employment. Also, this act sets forth mandatory subjects of bargaining in the benefits area, including retirement plans, health care, and paid time off. Over the years, unions have successfully negotiated generous benefits for employees. As shown in Exhibit 1.6, private-sector employers spend more money on benefits for union workers ($18.51 per hour worked) than nonunion workers ($8.65 per hour worked).

Key Terms

employee benefits, 5
protection programs, 5
paid time off, 5
accommodation and enhancement benefits, 5
total compensation, 5
base pay, 6
cost-of-living adjustments (COLAs), 7
seniority pay, 7
merit pay, 7
incentive pay, 7
person-focused pay, 8
Social Security Act of 1935, 9
Old-Age, Survivor, and Disability Insurance (OASDI), 9
Medicare, 9
state compulsory disability laws (workers' compensation), 10
workers' compensation, 10

Family and Medical Leave Act (FMLA), 10
health care, 10
fee-for-service plans, 10
alternative managed-care plans, 10
point-of-service plans, 10
consumer-driven health care, 10
dental care, 10
vision care, 10
prescription drug plans, 10
mental health and substance abuse plans, 10
life insurance, 11
retirement plans, 11
defined contribution plan, 11
defined benefit plan, 11
paid time-off policies, 11
noncontributory financing, 12
contributory financing, 12
employee-financed benefits, 12

flexible benefits plans, 13
voluntary benefits, 13
welfare practices, 14
strategic planning, 16
competitive strategy, 16
human resource strategies, 17
total compensation strategies, 17
benefits strategies, 17
strategic benefit plans, 17
top-down approach, 18
backing-in approach, 18
Federal Insurance Contributions Act (FICA), 24
Federal Unemployment Tax Act (FUTA), 24
Patient Protection and Affordable Care Act of 2010, 24
collective bargaining agreements, 26

Discussion Questions

1. Describe how employee benefits fit into the total compensation function.

2. Offer some suggestions for how companies might lessen the entitlement mentality among employees toward employee benefits.

3. Companies possess limited budgets to fund employee benefits. From an employee's perspective, which employee-benefits practices should be funded? Which are easily dispensable? Now respond to these questions as a company representative. Explain your answers.

4. Describe the differences between strategic benefits plans and benefits practices. Should strategic benefits plans be developed before setting benefits practices? Explain your answer.

5. Consider the varieties of internal and external information that companies consider when planning a benefits program. Which piece of information do you believe is most important to this planning process? Least important? Explain your answers.

Cases

1. Understanding Your Employee Benefits: Understanding a Job Offer

As a recent college graduate, you are excited to start the search for your first career position. You have already started interviewing for opportunities as a management trainee. You have been fortunate to have two interviews so far, and you identified several other companies to apply to at a recent job fair. From what you have learned, it seems that the starting salary for a job as a management trainee in your area is about the same at all companies. Therefore, you know that salary isn't going to differentiate one job offer from another. It will, of course, be important to understand the work environment and future career opportunities at a given company as you compare offers. As you think back to some of the career-search seminars you've attended, you remember that you should also compare benefit offerings.

As you look through the Web sites of the companies you have applied to, you quickly see that there are lots of different benefits plans offered. In fact, as you look at this information, you start to become concerned that comparing benefits is going to be a challenge. You think that you need to have a better understanding of the value of different benefits when you consider the total compensation you would receive from a company. You decide to start by more closely looking at the benefits offered by your current best prospect, which is a position at a large established corporation where you interviewed last week. You pull up the careers page on the company Web site and find a chart that lists the benefits offered.

Old age, survivor, and disability insurance	Health care	Vacation days
Medicare	Dental insurance	Holidays
Unemployment insurance	Employee assistance program	Sick days
Workers' compensation	Tuition reimbursement	
Family and medical leave	Defined contribution retirement plan	

As you review the chart, you aren't sure what you should pay attention to and what will make a difference in evaluating an offer. You think about lists that you've read on other company's Web sites and think that other companies seem to offer benefits plans very similar to this one. At this point, you think that maybe benefit offerings don't really make a difference. You decide you need to learn more before you go much further in the interview process. If the benefits information provided to you is unclear, you know you should be prepared to ask questions. The future is exciting, but you know that once you receive an offer, it is an important decision that you should make with full information.

1. If two different companies list the same benefits offerings, should you assume that the value of the benefits are the same?
2. What are some benefits offered from this company that you should find more information about in order to fully understand a job offer from the company? Why?
3. Why don't all companies just offer the same benefits?

2. Managing Employee Benefits: Strategic Benefits Planning at Makers Craft

Makers Crafts is facing strong competition in the retail craft chain-store market. Easy Crafts, a new discount craft-store chain, is opening stores in many of Makers Crafts' market areas. Makers Crafts has been a leader in the craft supply marketplace due to the company's superior customer service provided by a well-trained and compensated retail staff that are experts in crafts. Customers have enjoyed the opportunity to gain advice and ideas from the company's talented workers over the years, and customers are loyal to the committed staff. However, the new discount chain is drawing away customers by recruiting the experienced staff from Makers Crafts. Adding experienced staff to the lower prices at Easy Crafts is quickly drawing business away from Makers Crafts, and company executives are concerned.

The sudden employee attrition at Makers Crafts is a top priority for new Director of Human Resources Latonya Thomas. Her initial evaluation of the situation suggests that the company needs to examine its benefit offerings. Makers Crafts has done well at recruiting and training staff; however, little attention has been paid to the company benefits offerings to complement the competitive employee pay. While the company pays its employees above market-average wages, it has slowly changed benefits offerings in response to cost concerns. In the last five years, employee contributions to health-care premiums have increased, and the company has scaled back its contribution to the employee retirement plan. While these changes have helped the company control benefit costs, the changes have led to frustration by the employees.

Easy Crafts has capitalized on employee dissatisfaction at Makers Crafts by offering a generous benefits package to draw away workers. The frustrated employees that have moved to Easy Crafts have accepted minor pay cuts in exchange for benefits that better meet their needs. For example, many of the company workers are older, and their concerns about retirement benefits in particular are more pronounced as they know retirement is not far away. Part of Easy Crafts' strategic planning process to grow its market share included determining the types of benefits that would be attractive to these workers. Thus, Easy Crafts offers a retirement plan that provides more significant contributions by the company than Makers Crafts' plan provides. Given the successful recruitment of so many Makers Crafts workers, it seems that Easy Crafts' planning was effective.

Latonya knows that the company needs to make some changes to its benefits plan. However, she also knows that it is important to not make any hasty decisions in response to this challenge. Latonya needs to begin collecting information in order to start the planning needed to determine appropriate changes to Makers Crafts' benefits plan.

1. What kind of strategic planning approach is Latonya taking for Makers Crafts? Is this an effective approach?
2. What kind of information does Latonya need for the strategic benefits planning process for Makers Crafts?

Endnotes

1. U.S. Department of Labor, "Union Members—2015," USDL 16-0158. Accessed February 19, 2016, www.bls.gov.

2. WorldatWork. "WorldatWork Salary Budget Survey, Top-Level Results." 2016. Accessed October 19, 2016, www.worldatwork.org.

3. A. Mitra, N. Gupta, and J. D. Shaw, "A Comparative Examination of Traditional and Skill-Based Pay Plans," 4 *Journal of Managerial Psychology*, 2011: 278–296.

4. International Foundation of Employee Benefit Plans, "Corporate Benefits Departments: Staffing and Operations: 2015 Survey Results." Accessed March 1, 2016, www.ifebp.org.

5. U.S. Bureau of Labor Statistics, *Occupational Outlook Handbook, 2016–17 Edition, Compensation and Benefits Managers*, 2015. Accessed February 15, 2016, www.bls.gov/ooh/management/compensation-and-benefits-managers.htm.

6. U.S. Bureau of Labor Statistics, *Employment Projections—2014–24* (USDL-15-2327), 2015.

7. U.S. Bureau of Labor Statistics, 2014 wage data. Accessed February 15, 2016, www.bls.gov/oes.

8. F. R. Dulles and M. Dubofsky, *Labor in America: A History*. Arlington Heights, IL: Harlan Davidson, 1993.

9. U.S. Bureau of Labor Statistics, *Welfare Work for Employees in Industrial Establishments in the United States*. Bulletin No. 250 (1919): 119–123.

10. U.S. Department of Labor, *Employee Benefits in the United States, March 2015*. Bulletin No. 15-1432. Washington, DC: Government Printing Office, July 24, 2015.

11. F. R. Dulles and M. Dubofsky, *Labor in America: A History*, 6th ed. Arlington Heights, IL: Harlan Davidson, 1999.

12. J. Kwon and P. Hein, "Employee Benefits in a Total Rewards Framework," *Benefits Quarterly*, first quarter, 2013: 32–38.

13. Bristol-Myers Squibb, Statement on Workforce Diversity. Accessed March 10, 2016, www.bms.com/ourcompany/diversity/Pages/default.aspx.

14. ExxonMobil, "Our Guiding Principles," Accessed March 3, 2016, http://corporate.exxonmobil.com/en/company/about-us/guiding-principles.

15. *Eli Lilly's Annual Report, 2015*. Accessed February 20, 2016, http://investor.lilly.com/annuals.cfm.

16. *Why Lilly?* Accessed March 17, 2016, https://careers.lilly.com/why-lilly.

17. V. S. Barocas, *Strategic Benefit Planning: Managing Benefits in a Changing Business Environment*. Report No. 1012. New York: The Conference Board, 1992.

18. ExxonMobil, description of some ExxonMobil benefits practices offered in the United States. Accessed March 17, 2016, www.exxonmobil.com.

19. Barocas, *Strategic Benefit Planning*.

20. U.S. Department of Labor, "Employer Costs for Employee Compensation—September 2015," USDL 15-2329. Accessed February 15, 2016, www.bls.gov.

21. 26 U.S.C. §§3101–3125.

22. I.R.C. §3121(d); Treas. Reg. §§31.3121(d)-1, 31.3121(d)-2.

Chapter Two

The Psychology and Economics of Employee Benefits*

Learning Objectives

In this chapter you will gain an understanding of:

1. The employment relationship as an exchange relationship and the psychology behind why firms provide employee benefits.

*The material in this chapter pertaining to the psychology of employee benefits was prepared by Professor Niti Pandey, Department of Business Administration, Eastern Connecticut State University, and edited for this edition by Joseph Martocchio. The material in this chapter pertaining to the economics of employee benefits was prepared by Professor Darren Lubotsky, Department of Economics and the Institute for Government and Public Affairs, University of Illinois at Chicago, and edited for this edition by Joseph Martocchio.

2. Employee benefits as part of the psychological contract and how some employee expectations about benefits might be formed.

3. How employee perceptions of justice or fairness are important to understanding how pay and benefits practices influence employee attitudes.

4. The economic rationales for why companies offer employee benefits.

5. Who pays for employee benefits.

The purpose of this chapter is twofold. First, it is important to learn about the *psychological* basis of employee benefits. Employers can use this knowledge to understand how employee benefits influence the attitudes and performance of their employees. Also, employers can then develop and maintain effective benefits programs aimed at promoting worker satisfaction, commitment, and productivity.

Second, it is important to understand the *economic* basis of employee benefits. Employee benefits are a costly proposition. Even though employee benefits are expensive, most employers continue to offer them. Still, it begs the question pertaining to whether companies should have workers pay for life or disability insurance. After considering the psychology of employee benefits, we will take up topics about the economics of employee benefits.

THE PSYCHOLOGY OF EMPLOYEE BENEFITS

This discussion of the psychology of employee benefits is organized into three sections. First, the employment relationship as social exchange is considered. Second, psychological contracts are discussed. Third, we look at the relationship between having a benefits program and employee attitudes.

Employment Relationship as Social Exchange

Most voluntary human behaviors are driven, in part, by some expectation of outcomes. Work behaviors are no exception. In fact, work behaviors are some of the most deliberated and goal-directed behaviors. In the most general terms, the employment relationship consists of clusters of human resource practices offered to a group of employees along with the resulting employee contributions to the employer.[1]

The basis for understanding the employment relationship lies in the concept of **social exchange**—the most basic concept explaining social behavior. All social behavior can be seen as "an exchange of activity (*work effort*), tangible (*visible performance*) or intangible (*motivation and commitment*), and more or less rewarding or costly (*pay and benefits*), between at least two persons (*employee and employer*)."[2] Thus, social exchange in the employer-employee relationship is one in which the employer offers inducements (e.g., wages, employee benefits) in return for employee contributions (e.g., performance, commitment).[3]

How Employee Benefits Constitute Social Exchange

For companies, employee benefits not only offer cost advantages and tax incentives, but also act as a recruitment tool for attracting and retaining desired employees. Employee benefits provide employees with economic and income security, and also with personal and family welfare. People choose to work in exchange for remuneration. While wages or salary act as basic remuneration, employee benefits act as remuneration for the welfare of employees and fulfill such needs as health care, dependent care, retirement planning, vacations, and education. As such, in exchange, they elicit increased motivation and commitment from employees toward the company and its goals.

The employment relationship can be said to constitute both economic exchange and social exchange.[4] **Economic exchange**, as with wages and salary, is one in which the nature of the exchange has been specified at the time of employment. (Of course, economic exchange can also be renegotiated at any time during employment, as with yearly pay raises). Explicit company policies and procedures help to ensure that each party (i.e., the employer and the employee) fulfills the obligations in the exchange relationship. In other words, in exchange for continued employment and wages, employees are obligated to work for the employer. Certain employee benefits can fall under the category of economic exchange. For example, health insurance can be viewed in monetary terms, since it costs employers to pay for employees to have health insurance and is usually a part of the explicit agreement at the time of employment.

Social exchange tends to evolve over the employment period and is not necessarily established at the time of employment. The nature of the social exchange is left to the discretion of the employer and employee. As employees become aware of policies or use various employer practices over the period of their employment, they reciprocate with increased or decreased job effort and commitment. Employee-benefits practices are numerous and versatile, as indicated by the range and variety of practices presented in Chapter 1. Employees' needs change over the duration of their employment with a company. This change may be in terms of personal career needs or self, family health, and welfare needs. Different employee benefits are likely to be relevant to employees at different circumstances and stages of their lives and careers. If an employer can provide an employee with benefits suitable to an employee's evolving needs, the employee is likely to reciprocate with increased work effort and commitment. Hence, employee benefits are an especially relevant component of the social exchange between the employer and employee.

Workforce Changes and the Employment Relationship

To understand the importance of employee benefits for both employees and employers, it is important to understand the dynamic nature of the employment relationship. The nature of the employment relationship, especially in developed economies, has undergone several changes over the past few decades. Jobs are no longer characterized by traditional job security, strong loyalty to the organization, or the patriarchal role of the organization in the life of the employee. Instead, work arrangements and careers have become more flexible. There has been an increase in part-time and contingent workers. Regular layoffs have been taking place, especially in certain industries, such as manufacturing.

From economic and market challenges, the workforce in the United States and other developed economies is becoming increasingly diverse. Diversity in the workforce is stemming from an aging population[5] poised on the brink of retirement,[6] increased labor force participation by those over the age of 60,[7] decreasing age cohorts,[8] an increase in the proportion of racial and ethnic minorities and immigrants,[9] and an increase in single-person households.[10] Some of these trends and projections for the future are presented in Exhibit 2.1.

Traditionally, the design of compensation and benefits packages had assumed a similarity among employees of attitudes, needs, and expectations, particularly on a white, married, male workforce from a single-earner household. Exhibit 2.1 illustrates the expected changes in workforce demographics through 2024. Through the decades, employees developed a strong entitlement mentality. Until recently, employers did little to manage these expectations. Nowadays, companies are shifting some of the costs of benefits to employers, with one example being higher contributions for

EXHIBIT 2.1
Civilian Labor Force by Age, Gender, Race, and Ethnicity for 1994, 2014, and Projected to 2024

Source: Labor Force Projections to 2024: The Labor Force Is Growing, But Slowly Monthly Labor Review, December 2015. Available www.bls.gov.

Group	Percent Change		
	1994–2004	**2004–2014**	**2014–2024**
Total, 16 years and older	12.5	5.8	5.0
Age, years			
16–24	3.0	-4.4	-13.1
25–54	8.8	-1.3	3.9
55 and older	48.0	47.1	19.8
Gender			
Men	11.5	4.9	4.4
Women	13.6	6.7	5.8
Race			
White	9.0	1.9	2.3
Black	14.7	13.4	10.1
Asian	14.6	39.7	23.2
All other groups	–	45.7	22.2
Ethnicity			
Hispanic origin	60.9	31.6	28.0
Other than Hispanic origin	7.6	1.9	0.6
White non-Hispanic	2.7	-2.5	-3.0

health-care coverage. These dynamics can be better understood by becoming familiar with the role of economic challenges facing companies and changing workforce demographics. Both of these will determine the emerging role of employee-benefits practices in the social exchange relationship between employers and employees.

The cost of benefits surely is noteworthy, with companies often spending about 30 percent of the total compensation budget on employee benefits. Companies stand to miss opportunities to promote employee satisfaction, commitment, and productivity unless the set of employee benefits is placed in the context of the psychological contract. We now will learn about some well-established psychological concepts relevant for explaining the importance, role, and impact of employee benefits for employees and employers.

PSYCHOLOGICAL CONTRACTS

Psychological contracts are an articulation of the exchange relationship between the employer and the employee. A *psychological contract* has been defined as an employee's subjective perceptions of the relationship of mutual obligations with the employer and company.[11] Employee benefits can be a part of the psychological contract that employees hold about the employer's obligations to them in exchange for their work efforts. (Similarly, employers can expect employees to work and be committed to the company in exchange for the benefits they provide.)

Psychological contracts *implicitly* establish terms of employment, which stands in contrast to exchange agreements, such as wage and salary levels. As an example, company policies might imply that an employee will be eligible for educational assistance after five years of continuous employment and satisfactory levels of performance. An employee who is interested in making use of this benefit would reciprocate by remaining with the company and working hard. The employee's psychological contract with the company would include the employee's obligations (five years of hard work) and the employer's obligations (educational assistance). Psychological contracts are not an either-or proposition. Expectations of the employer fall on a coninuum, ranging from pay and promotions to career development and family welfare.

Exhibit 2.2 illustrates the continuum of expectations encompassed between **transactional psychological contracts** and **relational psychological contracts.** Toward the transactional end of the continuum, employees' expectations of the employer are more economic and extrinsic in nature, which translate to expectations of high pay and promotions or career advancement in exchange for hard work represent transactional types of expectations in the psychological contract. Toward the relational end, employees' expectations might focus on either economic or noneconomic, and these expectations are emotional, subjective, and intrinsic in nature. Employees' expectations of job security in exchange for loyalty to the employer represent relational types of expectations in the psychological contract.

Transactional psychological contracts can be understood with an example of short-term employment. An independent contractor or consultant hired by a firm is more likely to have transactional expectations of the hiring firm. The

EXHIBIT 2.2
Transactional–
Relational
Continuum of
Employee
Expectations
(Employee
Benefits as
Examples)

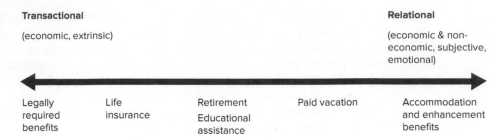

Transactional

(economic, extrinsic)

Relational

(economic & non-
economic, subjective,
emotional)

| Legally required benefits | Life insurance | Retirement Educational assistance | Paid vacation | Accommodation and enhancement benefits |

independent consultant or contractor would expect the firm to provide good pay, as well as the opportunity to build his or her marketability by adding the firm to his or her client portfolio. Once the project or assignment for which the independent contractor was hired is completed, the exchange relationship with the firm might end. Relational expectations can be understood by looking at the employee-employer relationship. Employees hired by a company or firm with the understanding of full-time employment are more likely to hold both transactional and relational expectations of their employer. For instance, not only will such employees expect pay, promotion, and career advancement in exchange for work efforts, but also they will expect job security, recognition, and support in exchange for commitment and loyalty to the employer. The main features of the continuum of expectations in psychological contracts can be summarized in Exhibit 2.3.

Employee-benefits practices could fulfill both transactional and relational expectations. Some employee benefits might fulfill more transactional expectations. For example, as suggested earlier, U.S. employees might expect employers to provide life and disability insurance in addition to competitive wages. Legally required benefits are a part of employees' transactional expectations of the employer. Employee benefits such as the paid time-off and accommodation and enhancement benefits examined might help fulfill employees' relational expectations. An employee might expect longer paid vacation as their tenure increases or educational assistance such as scholarships for their children.

Additionally, some employee benefits might fulfill both transactional and relational expectations of employees, such as retirement plans. For instance, employees might expect the employer to increase matching contributions as organizational

EXHIBIT 2.3
Psychological
Contract
Continuum

Source: D. M. Rousseau, "New Hire Perceptions of Their Own and Their Employer's Obligations: A Study of Psychological Contracts," 11 *Journal of Organizational Behavior,* (1990): 389–400.

	Transactional Contract	**Relational Contract**
Focus	Economic, extrinsic	Economic and noneconomic, Socio-emotional, intrinsic
Time frame	Closed-ended, specific	Open-ended, indefinite
Stability	Static	Dynamic
Scope	Narrow	Pervasive
Tangibility	Public, observable	Subjective, understood

tenure increases. This would increase their sense of security from the employment relationship. Similarly, educational assistance benefits aimed at rewarding continued employment as well as career development would help fulfill both transactional and relational expectations. Exhibit 2.2 presents the transactional–relational continuum of employee expectations in the exchange relationship with some examples of employee benefits.

Psychological contracts usually change over time. If employees have unrealistic expectations of the employer, they are likely to anticipate that the employer will fulfill obligations that may be beyond the employer's scope. For instance, a sense of entitlement might lead employees to expect a company to provide them with certain employee benefits. However, the company might eliminate the matching contribution to retirement plans or substantially raise the employee contribution for health-care coverage. In such instances, companies should keep employees apprised of the changes on a timely basis. If employee benefits are understood to be a part of employees' psychological contracts, then communication and education about the employee-benefits practices of the company is critical in establishing reasonable employee expectations. These approaches to benefits communications will be discussed in Chapter 10.

Psychological Contract Development

Most psychological contracts take shape in the pre-employment phase, when people seek information during recruitment and after receiving a job offer. Employees might seek information about both transactional and relational expectations of their potential employer. For instance, employees might address their transactional expectations by seeking information about a company's health coverage plan and promotion policies before accepting employment. In addition, they might address their relational expectations by seeking more information about the company's employee assistance or family welfare policies. Ultimately, the knowledge gained will help shape expectations along this transactional–relational continuum.

Through direct inquiry, monitoring, and negotiation, employees may gather information from various sources in the company about these issues. It is expected that, over time, the expectations of the employee and employer will match.[12] Employees can form expectations from two sources: interactions with other members of the company, and their perceptions of the company's culture.[13] If either source is inaccurate, employees might form unrealistic expectations.

Psychological contracts are flexible in nature,[14] undergoing constant change based on interactions with the company and other employees. This flexibility allows employees to adapt to changes in the company's practices. If employees hold relatively stable expectations, any changes in the policies and practices will lead to the employees' feeling betrayed unless changes entail offering more rather than less.

Psychological Contract Violation

A violation of the psychological contract occurs when an employee perceives a discrepancy between the promises made by the employer and the actual fulfillment of the promises.[15] If a company withdraws or changes certain benefits, and those practices are an employee's psychological expectation of the company, then that employee will feel that the contract has been violated.

Violations of psychological contracts differ from unmet expectations. The responses to the violation of psychological contracts are likely to be more intense.[16] Violation of employees' expectations can cause feelings of betrayal and the onset of mistrust. There may be two basic causes for violations of psychological contracts: reneging and incongruence.[17] When a company deliberately breaks a promise to employees, either willingly or because of circumstances, reneging is said to occur. Incongruence violations occur when the employee and the employer have different conceptualizations of the employment relationship. In other words, the employee might hold certain expectations of the employer. However, if the employee's actual experiences are different from these expectations, then the employee will feel that the psychological contract has been violated.[18]

Employee Benefits as Constituting Psychological Contracts

If employee benefits are a part of employees' psychological contracts, then it is important for employers to ensure that employee expectations about benefits are clearly articulated and flexible. This will allow employers to avoid any psychological contract violations and the associated costs (lawsuits, lost trust, low morale, turnover, etc.). Sometimes, employees may not be affected by minor contract violations. In the course of adjusting to the work environment, employees might also overlook certain violations. However, any serious violations can be avoided by clear communication and education about the nature and scope of the employee-benefits practices offered by the company. For instance, a company with a large Spanish-speaking workforce might be well served by providing information about its benefits practices in both English and Spanish. Companies also can hold training sessions where explanations of the design and eligibility requirements are explained. This will allow employees to form clear and accurate expectations about employee benefits as part of their psychological contracts.

Just as employees have expectations of the employer, the employer is also likely to have expectations of the employee. Incomplete effort, bad citizenship behavior, voluntary turnover, and low motivation can all be perceived by an organization as breaches of contract by the employee. The actions of the employee might also in some way contribute to the violations by the organization.[19] Thus, if the organization feels that employee performance is not what is expected, it can decide to withhold certain employee benefits, especially discretionary benefits. Once again, effective communication on the part of the organization could ensure that the psychological contract consists of explicit, rather than implicit, promises.[20]

Employee benefits have, over the years, become a growing source of employees' psychological contract violations.[21] Earlier, we stated that employers are shifting some of the costs for employee benefits to employees. As benefits costs increase, especially health-care costs, an increasing number of companies are shifting benefits costs to their employees. As the employee cost burden associated with benefits increases, particularly when wages become stagnant, employee satisfaction decreases.[22] Additionally, how benefits are administered is also important. Employees will likely perceive a benefit as unfair if they are not receiving it according to either their needs or perceptions of entitlement.[23] Thus, expectations about employees' cost burden, needs, and benefits design will all affect employee satisfaction. While some benefits may not be the most cost-effective way to meet employee needs, to avoid perceptions of psychological contract violations, companies will need to find lower-priced alternatives without sacrificing employee satisfaction.[24]

EMPLOYEE ATTITUDES AND EMPLOYEE BENEFITS

As discussed earlier, employment can be implicit, such as psychological contracts, and explicit, such as documented in a job offer letter or employment handbook. Employee benefits can be a part of both, with some benefits likely to be more explicitly offered while others are more implicitly available. Congruence between employees' and the employer's expectations will lead to greater fit between the employee and the employer as well as a sense of fairness. Violations of contracts will lead to perceptions of injustice.

Justice and Perceived Organizational Support

The concept of justice is concerned with the distribution of conditions and goods that affect individual well-being. In a work setting, the distribution of rewards (such as pay and benefits), information, and other resources will all lead to perceptions of justice. Perceptions of justice may be based on the rules by which distributions are made, the way rules are implemented, or the way decisions are made. The basis on which employees are eligible for benefits, the value of those benefits, how the benefits are administered, and employer decisions about which benefits to offer to employees would all influence employees' justice perceptions.

There are four types of justice perceptions. **Distributive justice** is perceived fairness about how rewards are distributed; **procedural justice** is the perceived fairness of processes; **informational justice** is the fairness of the accounts given for certain procedures; and **interpersonal justice** is perceived fairness of the interpersonal treatment people receive from others.[25] Job satisfaction, organizational commitment, evaluation of authority, organizational citizenship behavior, withdrawal, and performance are all affected by employees' perceptions of justice along these dimensions.[26]

Distributive justice is employees' perceptions of fairness of the outcomes they receive.[27] Where employee benefits are concerned, employees will form perceptions of fairness based on the benefits they are eligible for. If employees believe that the employer should provide them with certain benefits in exchange for their work efforts, and the employer fails to do so, then employees will conclude that the employer is being unfair. As a result, they might withhold effort and lower their commitment to the employer.

Procedural justice deals with employees' perceptions of fairness of the process by which decisions are made and includes the extent to which employees can participate in the process as well as the rules followed.[28] For example, by establishing rules for eligibility and contributions to retirement plans, employers can ensure procedural justice perceptions. Additionally, allowing employees to have voice in the use of such benefits as self-development and education can also enhance their perceptions of procedural fairness.

Interpersonal justice is the perception of the degree to which the employer demonstrates concern and social sensitivity toward employees.[29] As an illustration, managers' awareness and concern for employee development and needs and encouraging employees to participate in the benefits program is likely to lead to fairness perceptions about interpersonal justice.

Informational justice deals with perceptions about the quality of information used to explain organizational decision making.[30] If an employer decided to offer certain benefits or change/withhold others, the accuracy and timeliness of information will influence their perceptions of informational justice. For example, a company eliminates transportation benefits (deeply discounted public transportation passes). If the company intentionally or unintentionally fails to inform and educate their employees about elimination of transportation benefits, employees may judge the employer's decision as unfair.

While earlier human resource practices were standardized, today there has been a shift toward nonstandardized, idiosyncratic work arrangements.[31] This is largely driven by the increased competition to attract and retain top talent on the part of companies[32] as well as increased expectations of employee involvement.[33] Employee benefits can be a part of this new individualized employment relationship.

In addition to perceptions of justice and fairness, employees can also form perceptions of organizational support based on their experiences. **Perceived organizational support** is an employee's perception of the degree to which the employer values the employee's contributions and well-being.[34] Organizational support may implicitly incentivize higher job performance, becoming a part of the social exchange relationship.

Certain employee benefits practices can act to signal organizational support. Employee benefits that signal the organization's concern for the well-being of the employee, such as mental health benefits, wellness programs, smoking cessation programs, and stress management, as well as those aimed at recognizing the employees' contributions such as recognitions and rewards, will help in fostering perceptions of perceived organizational support.

Emotionally committed employees have increased performance, reduced absenteeism, and decreased likelihood of turnover. Employers can ensure commitment by showing support to employees in the form of pay and promotion, approval and respect, and other aids needed to be effective in the company.[35] Certain rewards and job conditions are more likely to lead to perceived organization support, such as recognition, pay, promotions, job security, autonomy, and training.[36]

Those human resource practices that indicate investment in human capital and demonstrate recognition of employee contributions will certainly promote perceptions of organizational support.[37] For instance, educational assistance programs are an example of investment in human capital, and pay raises and promotions recognize employee contributions. Thus, these practices will lead to employees feeling supported by the company.

From a social exchange perspective, employees will value the employer's discretionary efforts more highly than those that are beyond the employer's control.[38] Thus, discretionary employee benefits, offered to employees at the employer's own choice, are more likely to generate perceptions of organizational support than legally required benefits. Additionally, those discretionary benefits that address most closely the employee's needs for well-being and development are more likely to elicit perceptions of organizational support. The importance of flexible benefits practices, suited to the diverse necessities of the changing workforce, can hence be understood in terms of critical employee attitudes such as perceptions of fairness and perceived organizational support.

Organizational Citizenship Behavior

Employees' discretionary behavior, not explicitly or directly recognized by the formal reward system of the employer, but in aggregate promoting organizational effectiveness, is termed as **organizational citizenship behavior.**[39] Thus, behaviors such as helping other employees, looking out for the employer's interests, going beyond job requirements to help achieve company goals, are all examples of organizational citizenship behavior. Satisfied employees engage in good citizenship behavior. A company's employee benefits practices can influence employees' satisfaction.

Organizational citizenship behavior is discretionary—it is not enforceable but rather a matter of personal choice. Citizenship behaviors tend to go beyond the formal job requirements. Such behaviors are not easily governed by individual incentive schemes because they are often difficult to discern and measure.[40] For instance, an employee who is helping a coworker to succeed without any motive of recognition or reward from the employer is exhibiting citizenship behavior. Organizational citizenship behavior is a deliberate attempt by the employee to maintain the balance in the social exchange between the employee and the employer and is directly intended to benefit the employer.[41] If employees perceive their employer as generous and fair, they will seek to reciprocate by showing good citizenship behavior (in addition to job performance and commitment).

Employees' perceptions of both distributive and procedural justice are likely to affect citizenship behavior. If employees perceive that the employer is unfair, they will withhold good citizenship behavior.[42] For instance, if an employer decides to stop offering flextime benefits to an employee, and the employee perceives this as unfair, the employee can decide to stop putting in extra hours of work that she was previously doing in order to finish a project faster. Employee-benefits practices that lead to perceptions of injustice or feelings of contract violations might also lead not only to poor performance, reduced commitment, and increased likelihood of turnover, but also reduction in extra-role, prosocial behaviors to help the employer be effective.

As stated earlier, job satisfaction can lead to organizational citizenship behavior that has effects on job performance.[43] There could be two reasons why job satisfaction would lead to organizational citizenship behaviors. It could be because people tend to reciprocate those who benefit them. Hence, if satisfaction comes largely from work, then employees may reciprocate with helping behaviors in the workplace. Also, employees who are satisfied and experience positive mood states tend to engage in good citizenship behaviors.

The concept of organizational citizenship behavior is based on social exchange. As such, employee benefits can be seen as eliciting job satisfaction and citizenship behaviors. In exchange for generous benefits and human resource practices, employees can use good citizenship behaviors to reciprocate and signal commitment and loyalty to the employer. Thus, employee benefits are an important part of the social exchange process that characterizes the employment relationship. They can be an important component of employees' psychological contract with the employer.

How companies design, communicate, and implement employee benefits can lead to varying perceptions of fairness and organizational support. As a result of these attitudes, employees will engage in related organizational outcomes such as job performance, commitment, and citizenship behavior. Thus, the role of employee benefits in eliciting organizational effectiveness is undeniably important.

THE ECONOMICS OF EMPLOYEE BENEFITS: WHY DO EMPLOYERS OFFER BENEFITS?

Most employers compensate employees with some combination of cash and benefits, such as health insurance. This combination of cash and benefits represents the extrinsic component of total compensation, as discussed in Chapter 1. At first glance, it might seem that employees and employers would both prefer a cash-only compensation package rather than a mixture of cash and benefits. After all, employees can use cash to buy life or disability insurance, save for retirement, or buy any other goods or services they want. This freedom would allow employees who want a generous life insurance plan to have it, while employees who prefer a cheaper life insurance plan could spend less on life insurance and have more money available for other goods and services. Additionally, benefits are expensive and time-consuming for employers to administer. Year-to-year changes in the costs of health insurance make benefits planning particularly difficult. It would seem, therefore, that employers also might prefer to pay all employees in cash only. So what advantages are there to employers and employees from having benefits?

Before answering this question, it is important to clarify that the question is not meant to ask whether an employer should pay, for example, a salary of $50,000 per year plus a tuition reimbursement plan and a retirement plan, or whether the company should pay $50,000 per year without the tuition reimbursement and retirement plans. Clearly, if an employer could recruit and retain the same workforce with both pay packages, it would prefer not to offer the costly benefits. Instead, the question is whether an employer would want to reduce the amount of cash compensation and substitute the tuition reimbursement and retirement plans. The relevant choice for the employer might be between paying $50,000 a year plus benefits versus paying $75,000 a year and providing no benefits; or, the choice might be between paying $50,000 a year plus a generous and expensive retirement plan versus paying $60,000 a year plus a less-generous and cheaper retirement plan.

An employer might choose to include benefits in its compensation package for three primary reasons:

- A cost advantage to the employer
- Recruitment of certain types of workers
- Tax incentives

Cost Advantage

The first reason an employer may want to provide a benefit is that the employer may be able to buy the product or service at a lower cost than employees would pay if they tried to buy it on their own. Health insurance is a perfect example: Employers can generally purchase health insurance for a substantially lower premium per enrollee than the amount employees would have to pay for identical coverage if they bought the insurance on their own. A particular insurance plan might cost $1,000 per employee when purchased by an employer that employs 500 workers, but the same insurance plan might cost $2,500 if purchased by a single individual. Employees are therefore better off getting the health plan through their employer and having their cash wages reduced by any amount less than $2,500. The employer is better off by providing the health insurance to its employees and reducing their wages by anything more than $1,000. Together, this means that both the employer and the employees will be better off if the compensation package includes the health plan and salaries are decreased by an amount between $1,000 and $2,500. When the employer can buy a benefit for a lower cost than the employee could buy it, the employer is essentially acting as a buying agent for the worker. Retirement annuities and disability and life insurance are other leading examples of benefits that tend to be cheaper when purchased as part of a large group.

Why does health insurance become less expensive when the size of the insurance group increases? Many products are sold with quantity discounts. Is health insurance just another example? Actually, it isn't that simple. Three primary reasons explain why insurance costs tend to fall as the insured group—also known as the insurance pool—gets larger. First, as the group gets larger, insurance becomes less risky to provide. Second, insurance companies need to worry less about the phenomenon of high-risk individuals driving out low-risk individuals in large insurance groups in which all members are required to buy insurance. Third, as the group gets larger, fixed administrative costs can be spread out among more people. These factors will be discussed in turn.

As the size of the insured group gets larger, it becomes much easier for the insurance company to predict the total medical expenses for the group. That means it is less risky to provide health insurance to a larger group than to a smaller group. For example, in 2013, average total medical expenditures were $4,855 per person and by age:

- $1,980 for children aged 5 to 17
- $3,665 for adults aged 18 to 44
- $6,737 for adults aged 45 to 64
- $10,125 for adults aged 65 and older

Medical expenses also tend to be higher for women than for men, and higher for whites than for minority groups.[44] Medical expenses are also naturally higher for people who have experienced medical problems in the past. Insurance companies can use these and other data, in combination with information on the characteristics of the group to be insured, to come up with an estimate of the expected medical expenses that the group will generate over the upcoming year. In very large groups, total medical expenses are likely to be close to those predicted by the age, gender, and past medical history of the group. The number of people who have particularly bad luck and have larger-than-expected medical expenses is likely to be offset by a roughly equal number of people who have smaller-than-expected medical expenses. In a small group, by contrast, there is much less certainty that the number of people with bad luck will roughly offset the number of people with good luck. That is, it is much more difficult to predict the medical expenses a small group will experience in the future.

A different way to think about this is to note that if you flipped a coin four times, you would expect to get two heads and two tails, but you would not be terribly surprised if you got three heads and one tail. By contrast, if you had the energy to flip the coin 1,000 times, you should be very suspicious about the authenticity of the coin if you ended up with 750 heads and 250 tails. The more times you flip a coin, the more likely it is that you'll receive roughly the same number of heads as tails. In the case of health insurance, the more people in the group, the more likely that total medical expenses will be close to those predicted by the characteristics of people in the group.

The fact that total medical expenses—and hence the amount that insurance companies have to pay out to medical care providers—are more predictable for larger groups of people means that insurance companies bear less risk when they insure these larger groups. They are therefore willing to provide the insurance at a lower cost to larger groups than to smaller groups. Smaller groups, by contrast, tend to face higher insurance costs to compensate insurance companies for the added risk they bear. Similarly, an insurance policy that covers a single individual or family will tend to be more expensive than a similar policy that covers a small group of people. Because of the riskier nature of individual and small group policies, they are more likely to be subject to what is called **medical underwriting,** a process by which employees provide information on their past medical history in a questionnaire or physical examination. Insurers use this health information to exclude coverage or to tie premiums more closely to past medical history.

The bottom line is that employers can purchase group health insurance at a better rate than individuals could purchase the same policies on their own. This gives employers and employees an incentive to have a compensation package that includes group health insurance in lieu of some cash wages or salary. It also means that this incentive is relatively larger for big employers than for small employers, which explains in part why small employers are less likely to offer health insurance to employees.

A second motivation for employer-provided insurance is to avoid an inherent problem in insurance markets that is referred to as **adverse selection**. This is the tendency of an insurance pool to disproportionately attract "bad risks" and discourage the participation of "good risks." Suppose a health insurance company operating in a particular city does market research and concludes that the average resident has medical expenses of $5,000 per year. On this basis, the insurance company offers residents a comprehensive health insurance policy with a premium of $5,500 per year. Which residents would choose to buy this plan?

Clearly, people who think that they are relatively healthy and therefore unlikely to have anywhere close to $5,000 in expenses are not going to buy this health insurance plan. On the other hand, people who think that they are more likely to have high expenses are likely to buy the plan. Thus, the average medical expenses of people who buy the plan will be greater than $5,000, since only people with relatively high medical expenses will purchase the plan. The insurance company has a risk pool composed mostly of "bad risks." The result is that the insurance company can no longer afford to offer this plan for $5,500 and will have to raise its premium. This will lead the insurance pool to become even more unbalanced as some of the healthier policyholders decide that the policy is too expensive given their own expected medical costs.

Adverse selection in insurance markets stems from the fact that individuals know more about their own health status than does the insurance company. One solution to this problem is for the company to gather as much information as possible about each participant's risk profile and then offer the insurance at a lower price to healthier people and at a higher price to less-healthy people. This is referred to as **experience rating** and is how most automobile insurance policies work. It is also how most individual, single-family, and small-group health insurance policies work.

A different solution to the adverse selection problem is for a large group of people who come together for some other purpose to buy group insurance together, with the requirement that all group members must buy into the insurance pool. A group of people who come together to build and sell television sets, provide investment advice, or teach college students, for example, are unlikely to be composed of disproportionately good or bad risks. In any event, as long as everyone in the group is required to participate in the insurance pool, the insurance company can set the premium accordingly without fear that relatively good risks will drop out.

Avoiding the adverse selection problem is one reason why employment-based insurance is so popular, especially among large and medium-sized employers.

It also helps to explain why employers provide a whole range of insurance products as part of a benefits package, including disability insurance and life insurance. Indeed, avoiding the adverse selection problem is one justification for various government-provided insurance programs, such as Social Security, Medicare, and workers' compensation programs.

Finally, administering an insurance policy involves a good deal of paperwork, claims processing, and other administrative functions. Many of these functions are not much more time-consuming and expensive to perform for a large group than for a smaller group, a process referred to as **economies of scale.** Because of this, as the group gets larger, the fixed costs of these administrative tasks can be shared among a larger number of people, thereby reducing the average cost per insured person.

Recruiting Certain Types of Workers

A second reason that employers may want to offer a compensation package that includes both cash and benefits is to aid in recruiting and retaining certain types of employees, particularly when the employer's managers have a difficult time observing all relevant characteristics of potential employees. In management's perfect world, job applications would contain all relevant information about a potential worker, such as his or her future productivity, work habits, career plans, commitment to the employer, and commitment to undergoing future training. Unfortunately, many important characteristics are not observed, and managers may have a difficult time eliciting such information. By offering a compensation plan that includes both cash and benefits that are more highly valued by some applicants than by others, an employer may be able to get applicants to reveal some of these characteristics themselves.

For example, suppose the ideal candidate for a particular employer is a highly motivated recent college graduate who would like to work for a few years and then go to graduate school to earn an MBA. Looking at the job applications received by the employer, however, it is difficult to tell which potential employees actually fit this description. How should the employer go about selecting a candidate?

One strategy is that the employer could simply ask each applicant whether he or she is highly motivated and would like to earn an MBA. However, talk is cheap, which makes this strategy problematic. All of the applicants would likely say that they fit this description if they think it will increase their chances of getting the job. Also, potential employees may not know for sure whether they will want to go on to earn an MBA or may not know what the employer defines as being "highly motivated." The employer needs a way to separate those applicants who are truly motivated and interested in getting the advanced degree from those who are not.

A second strategy is that the employer could offer a pay package that includes a slightly reduced salary and also the promise to pay tuition in an MBA program. (In Chapter 9, **tuition reimbursement benefits,** which fully or partially reimburse an employee for expenses incurred for education or training, will be discussed.) This package would be valued relatively more by the exact employees whom the employer wants to recruit. Potential employees who feel that there is little chance they would seek an MBA would prefer to take a job with a higher salary without the promise of tuition assistance. Offering the tuition assistance in the compensation package would induce highly motivated potential employees to reveal valuable information about themselves to the employer.

Offering particular benefits in a compensation package could also have unintended consequences for the types of employees most attracted to the employer. For example, an employer that touts its generous benefits for mental health services or substance abuse treatments may feel that it is offering a progressive benefit package. However, it may also find that the types of employees who are most likely to accept a position with the employer, or who are most likely to stay with the employer, are those suffering from conditions that require such services or treatments. In some cases, this may not be the outcome that the employer intended.

Tax Incentives

A third reason that employers may want to offer benefits is that the U.S. federal tax code—the Internal Revenue Code (IRC)—provides financial incentives to do so. The most important tax provision is that many benefits are not taxed as income to employees. Suppose an employee has a 25 percent marginal tax rate. If the employer increases her pay by $1,000 in cash, she must pay $250 of that to the government, leaving her with $750 in after-tax income. By contrast, if the employer gives her a benefit that costs $1,000, she receives the full benefit and does not incur any tax burden. A different way to see the effect of taxes on benefits provisions is to suppose an employee wants to buy a life insurance policy that costs $1,000. If she were to buy the policy on her own, she would have to earn $1,333.33. Of this, she would pay 25 percent, or $333.33, in taxes to the government, which would leave her with $1,000 in after-tax income needed to purchase the insurance. She would be better off receiving the plan as part of her compensation package and having her salary reduced by any amount less than $1,333.33. If her employer could buy the same policy for $1,000, the employer would also be better off by including the insurance in the compensation package and reducing the employee's wage by any amount over $1,000. Within these stated limits, the employer and employee are both better off if the insurance plan is part of the compensation package and the salary is reduced by any amount between $1,000 and $1,333.33. Retirement plans are a second example of a benefit that is partly driven by generous tax treatment. More details about tax treatment of benefits are provided in Chapter 3 and in other chapters, as relevant.

All three of the preceding motivations presuppose that employees value a particular benefit and are willing to give up something to receive it. There are two important consequences of this. First, employers need to figure out the cash value that employees place on a particular benefit and which types of employees value the benefit more than others. Second, if employees are willing to give up something to receive a particular benefit, then the cash component of wages and the types and amounts of benefits an employer offers will be inexorably linked. This link is the subject of the next part of this chapter.

Students usually give two other answers when asked why they think employers offer benefits. The first answer is that employers are just trying to match what every other employer is doing. This probably has a lot of truth to it: A lot of businesses do a lot of things simply because everyone else is doing it. Managers may not have the time, inclination, or expertise to investigate every alternative business practice, so why not cut some corners and follow the pack on compensation practices? This argument, though, doesn't really answer the question—it just leads us to ask, Why does every other employer offer benefits? If all employers continued to follow unprofitable compensation practices, then presumably, new employers would enter the market to take advantage of unrealized profit opportunities. Existing employers would either follow the lead of new, more-profitable employers or eventually find themselves out of business.

The second answer is that employer managers want their employees to be well, so they provide wellness plans, or they want their employees to be well prepared for retirement, so they offer retirement plans. It is clear that most employers' managers do, in fact, want their employees to be well, but it is not obvious that this is why employers offer wellness benefits. First, is directly providing wellness benefits or a retirement plan the most effective way for an employer to promote these goals? Second, why would employers choose to promote these goals in their compensation policies rather than promote other worthy goals?

WHO PAYS FOR BENEFITS?

One of the biggest misconceptions about employee benefits is that employers give them as "free add-ons" in compensation packages and that employees do not give up anything to receive these benefits. The truth is that, in large part, employees pay for all of their benefits in the form of lower cash wages or salaries than they would have otherwise received. An important consequence of this is that when the cost of providing a benefit increases, it is employees who pay for the increase; employers' profits are generally not affected.[45]

The degree to which an increase in benefits costs is passed along to employees in the form of lower cash wages generally depends on four factors:

- The cash value employees place on the benefit.
- The degree to which employers will increase or decrease their hiring when the market compensation level decreases or increases, and the degree to which employees will change their desire to work when the market compensation package changes.
- Whether the benefits cost increases for all employers in a market or only for a particular employer.
- Whether the hiring decisions of a particular employer affect the market compensation level.

Let's begin by more precisely defining the concept of the "value that employees place on the benefit." Suppose you've just accepted a new job and your employer offers you the choice of a $75,000 annual salary plus a comprehensive educational assistance plan, or a $90,000 salary and no educational assistance. Which compensation package would you choose? Both options probably would have some takers. Those who want to earn a graduate-level degree will tend to place a relatively higher value on the educational assistance benefits, and they are therefore more likely to forgo the extra $15,000 in salary. On the other hand, people with graduate degrees are more likely to choose the extra salary in lieu of the educational assistance benefits.

Some people may be uncomfortable with the concept of placing a dollar value on educational assistance benefits or on any product. Although we aren't always conscious of it, every time we buy a product or service, we are implicitly deciding that we value the product more than (or equal to) what the merchant is charging for it. Workers make choices about which job to accept, how many days or hours to work each week, and even whether to work at all, based in part on a comparison of the value of compensation packages and the value they place on their leisure time or time spent doing unpaid work at home.

The first lesson is that the greater the value employees place on a benefit, the larger the reduction in cash wages that they will accept if the benefit is introduced into a compensation package. Suppose an employer currently offers a compensation package that only includes a cash salary of $100,000 per year, but she is thinking about introducing new benefits that cost her $10,000 per year. If she simply added the benefits to the $100,000 salary, her total profits would decrease by $10,000 times the number of employees. For the employer to consider offering the new benefits and also maintain her profit level, she would have to reduce the salary she offers by at least $10,000.

Would the employer be able to recruit and retain the same workforce if she reduced the salary from $100,000 to $90,000 per year? This depends on the value that potential employees place on having additional benefits. An employee who values the plan at exactly $10,000 would be indifferent to a change from the current compensation package of $100,000 plus no new benefits to a new package that includes a salary of $90,000 plus the new benefits. In general, though, there are bound to be some employees who value the plan at less than $10,000 per year and some who value it at more. Any employee who values the plan at less than $10,000 per year would view this move as a cut in compensation and would likely seek employment elsewhere.

By contrast, employees who value the new benefits at more than $20,000 per year would view this as an increase in compensation. The employer could cut the salary from $100,000 to $85,000 per year and these employees would still be better off (because they gave up $15,000 per year in salary and received additional benefits they valued at $20,000 per year). What's more, the employer's profits would rise, because labor costs would go down by $5,000 per employee per year. In effect, the employer would be buying additional benefits and providing these benefits to employees at a lower cost than the amount that employees value the benefit.

Let's think through what would happen if the employer introduced the $10,000 benefits but kept cash wages at their initial level of $100,000 per year. At the same time, other employers would either continue to pay a salary of $100,000 per year with no additional benefits or would offer a lower salary and include the additional benefits. One consequence is that profits would fall by $10,000 times the number of employees. The employer may try to raise the price that she charges her customers, but competition from other employers with lower labor costs would certainly make it difficult to sustain this strategy. Thus, faced with reduced profits, the likelihood that this employer will go out of business is increased. In extreme situations, such as in the commercial airline industry, employees will be willing to accept significant cuts in pay and benefits to help the company remain in business.

If the employer remains in business, workers at other companies and people out of the labor force would realize that the employer was offering a significantly more-generous compensation package than those offered by other employers. The employer's human resource manager would soon realize there are many more applications than there are positions. The employer would find herself in a position in which she can be choosier about which employees to hire and also find that she can fill her staffing needs at a lower salary. Thus, it's unlikely that the employer would continue to offer an above-market compensation package.

What would happen if the employer decided to cut wages by more than the amount that employees value the additional benefits package? Let's assume that the employer cut salaries from $100,000 per year to $80,000 per year, but employees only value the new benefits at $10,000 per year. In this case, employees would view their total compensation package as being worth $90,000, or $10,000 less than what it was previously. Some employees would decide that they would prefer to work for another employer, or not work at all, rather than take a pay cut. To fill her staffing needs, the employer would have to raise her cash wage to maintain the value of the total compensation package.

A related but more common scenario is that an employer already offers a compensation package that includes both salary and benefits, and the cost of providing some benefit increases. The leading example is the steady rise in health insurance costs experienced by most U.S. employers. Suppose you are a human resource manager and your CEO tells you that your health insurance company is going to raise the rate it charges your employer for health insurance by 10 percent for the coming year. Since this rise stands to cost the company a lot of money, one option that the CEO proposes is to scale back a planned salary increase for the coming year from 5 percent to 3 percent. This 2 percent savings will offset the 10 percent increase in health insurance costs. What is your reaction to this proposal?

Do you think a decline in the growth of wages will lead some employees to leave the employer? What factors are important in answering the question?

One thing to consider in this situation is the underlying reason for the rise in health insurance costs. The following are some examples:

1. The rise reflects a general improvement in medical technology and health-care quality, but also more-expensive technology.
2. Legal changes allow doctors to unionize and thereby charge higher prices for the existing services they provide.

3. Health insurance costs rose by 10 percent only for this employer because the company workforce is a year older and is at an increased likelihood of contracting additional medical conditions and hence generating additional medical costs.

4. Health insurance costs rose by 10 percent only for this employer because the employer decided to lay off a significant portion of employees, thereby reducing the size of the insured group.

These scenarios are distinguished by whether the rise in medical costs reflects something that adds to employees' valuation of the insurance (Examples 1 and 3) or does not add value (Examples 2 and 4), and by whether health insurance costs rise for all employers (Examples 1 and 2) or for just this particular employer (Examples 3 and 4). Take some time to think about whether your reaction to the CEO's proposal depends on which of the four preceding explanations is the cause of the increased health insurance rate.

The conclusion reached earlier that employees' cash wages will tend to fall whenever benefits are fully valued also holds when benefit costs rise. That is, wages will tend to fall when health insurance cost increases derive from improved quality of care (Example 1) or an increased use of care among employees (Example 3). From this viewpoint, gloomy assessments of the recent increases in health-care costs may have missed the point entirely. If rising health insurance premiums signal that health care is more valuable, then recent rises in health-care costs are good news for employees—at least for those who use medical care.

On the other hand, if increased health insurance costs are not accompanied by an increase in employees' valuation of the insurance, as in Examples 2 and 4 above, cash wages may not be able to adjust downward. Whether or not cash wages will, in fact, fall depends on two additional factors: (1) whether health insurance costs rise for this particular employer only or for all employers in the market, and (2) the degree to which workers and employers will change their labor demand and supply when compensation costs change.

When health benefits costs rise for a single employer in a market, the employer will likely not be able to pass along the benefits costs to workers if the workers' valuation hasn't changed (or has increased, but by less than the increased benefit cost). Let's work through an example. Suppose that to hire an average-quality lawyer with 10 years of litigation experience, a law firm in New York City must offer a total compensation package worth about $100,000. An offer of less than that will likely only attract the lowest-quality lawyers, if any at all. Let's suppose the firm of Lawyers Inc. currently meets the market by offering a compensation package of $80,000 in salary and a health insurance package valued at $20,000 by the current employees. Now suppose that the employer lays off a quarter of its staff, thereby reducing the size of the insurance pool. Thus, the same policy now costs the employer an extra $5,000 per employee per year. Could the law firm reduce the salary level from $80,000 to $75,000?

Probably not. The increase in health insurance costs were not accompanied by any increase in employees' valuation of the insurance, so employees still value their insurance at $20,000 per year. If the market compensation level remains at $100,000, the law firm must maintain the $80,000 salary in conjunction with the insurance to meet the market and retain its current workforce.

The salient factors in the last scenario are that the employer must meet the market compensation level and that health insurance costs rose only at this law firm. Thus, the employer must pay the increase in costs.[46] Many commentators and business leaders mistakenly apply that conclusion to the more general scenario of when health insurance costs rise for all employers. The same logic does not carry over, however. To investigate the response of wages to an economy-wide increase in benefit costs, let's pick up with Example 2 above, in which health insurance costs rise because doctors' fees increase. Clearly, the employees' valuation of their health insurance plan has not changed. There is a still a possibility for wages to offset the health insurance cost increase, however. The degree to which wages will fall—that is, the degree to which employees pay for the cost increase—depends on the degree to which workers will drop out of the labor market when their compensation level falls and on the degree to which employers will reduce their workforce when employment costs rise. To understand this, let's consider two relatively polar opposite cases.

In the first case, employers are relatively insensitive to changes in compensation costs, but workers are sensitive. That is, employers would go about hiring approximately the same number of people if compensation costs rose or fell by 10 percent. By contrast, if total compensation fell by 10 percent, many workers would decide that they have better uses for their time (such as raising children at home, staying in school a little longer, or retiring a little earlier) and choose not to work anymore. If total compensation rose by 10 percent, some people who are not working might choose to do so.

In this situation, employers that would not generally be able to pass along higher benefits costs to their employees instead will end up paying for the benefits out of their profits. What would happen if an employer did try to pass along the benefits costs to employees? Since employees' valuation of their benefits did not change, the decrease in salary would certainly be viewed as a decrease in total compensation. Thus, some employees would likely begin looking for employment elsewhere. Workers in general would gravitate toward employers that maintained their salary base in the face of higher benefits costs. However, we've assumed in this scenario that employers' hiring needs are relatively insensitive to compensation costs. That is, employers still need about as many workers now as they did prior to the benefits cost increase. Thus, employers that cut wages and lost employees would need to hire additional workers to replace them, which would necessitate raising their compensation level—the result being that the employer would pay the increase in benefits costs.

What if all employers could somehow agree to pass along the higher benefits cost to employees, perhaps through contributory financing or employee-financed methods, so that workers didn't have the option of moving to higher-wage employers? Workers in this scenario have the option of leaving the workforce altogether. Thus, if all employers decided to cut wages, some workers would leave the labor market, leaving some employers understaffed. The smaller workforce would force employers to raise their wage offers to fill their staffing needs. The bottom line is that if workers are willing to leave the labor market when compensation falls and employers have relatively inflexible staffing needs, employers will tend to pay for some or all of the benefits cost increases. (In practice, more companies would lower their costs for providing health-care benefits by selecting options with higher deductibles or copayments [Chapter 5] instead of reducing wages or salaries.)

In the second scenario, employees are totally insensitive to market-wide changes in compensation levels. That is, if total compensation fell by 10 percent with all employers, no workers would reduce their hours or weeks of work or drop out of the labor market in response. This is what is meant by "insensitive." Although this view of workers' behavior may sound rather extreme, there's actually quite a bit of evidence that most prime-age workers (those aged 30 to 54) behave this way, especially men. By contrast, the groups most likely to adjust their labor supply—and thus fit the previous scenario—are women with young children, the elderly, part-time workers, and young workers.

In the situation in which employees are totally insensitive to changes in market-wide compensation levels, all the increase in benefits costs will be passed along to employees in the form of lower salary levels, even if employees' valuation of the benefit has not changed. An employee whose salary was reduced by the cost of the benefit might at first perceive a cut in his pay relative to what he could receive at other employers, and thus he would try to seek employment elsewhere. However, all employers have experienced the same increase in benefits costs, and thus all employers will be seeking to cut salaries. Thus, the employee would soon find that, although his salary has been cut, so have the wages at other employers. The employee's only options are to drop out of the labor market altogether or accept the lower pay, and we've ruled out the former. Exhibit 2.4 summarizes whether employers or employees will tend to pay for a benefits cost increase in various scenarios.

EXHIBIT 2.4
Summary of the Incidence of Employee Benefits Cost Increases

Does employees' valuation of the benefits increase?	Employees' valuation increases at least as much as the benefits cost increases.	Employees' valuation of benefits does not increase.	
Do costs increase for all employers in the market?	Costs increase for single employer.		Costs increase for all employers.
Who pays for benefits cost increases?	Employees pay for all benefits cost increases.	Employer pays for all benefits cost increases.	Employers and employees split the cost increase. The party that is least likely to adjust tends to pay more.

Most workers with employer-sponsored health insurance pay a token monthly contribution toward their health insurance premium, which is typically deducted from each monthly paycheck. According to data from the 2015 National Compensation Survey, most employees were required to make a contribution to their health insurance costs. The typical monthly contribution ranged between approximately $28 and $300 for single coverage and between $86 and $1,279 for family coverage.[47] The monthly premium is usually paid from pretax dollars and usually represents only a small fraction of the actual cost of the health insurance. Importantly, this monthly payment should not be interpreted as employees' only contribution to their health insurance. Rather, the view advanced in this chapter is that the full cost of health insurance is paid for by employees. Part is paid for through this monthly contribution, and the remainder is paid for through lower cash wages.

It may seem peculiar that employers charge employees these monthly contributions since they come from after-tax dollars. One advantage of these fees, however, is that they easily allow employers to charge different health insurance prices to people with different family sizes, or to people who choose health plans of different quality. A second advantage is that employers can more easily raise these contributions when benefits costs increase, making it more evident to the workers that health costs have increased.

Business managers and human resource practitioners sometimes question whether economists' view of the relationship between cash wages and benefits is correct, because, they contend, employers are rarely observed cutting wages when a new benefit is introduced or the cost of providing an existing benefit increases. In fact, such wage cuts happen much more frequently than some might think. An employer may scale back a scheduled bonus or reduce the year-to-year rate of growth of cash wages. An employer may also hire new workers at a lower wage rate than that which existing workers are paid. If there is relatively fast turnover, the wage decrease will quickly filter through the employer. Finally, an employer may increase employees' "contribution" to their health insurance premiums. An increase in the contribution is in effect taking compensation out of the hands of employees, which has the same effect as a reduction in cash wages. A difference is that increasing the benefits contribution helps employees realize that their wage cut results from an increase in their benefits costs, not from, for example, a decrease in the employer's profitability. For an employer with both employees who receive health insurance and employees who don't, increasing the contribution may be a particularly effective way to target a wage decrease on those employees whose benefits costs were actually affected.

Summary

This chapter discusses the psychological basis of employee-benefits practices from the point of view of employees, as well as the economics of employee benefits from the perspective of employers. Taken together, these topics illuminate the importance of offering employee benefits. Psychologically, employee-benefits practices can fulfill employees' transactional and relational expectations of the employer and the employment exchange relationship. If employees view their employer's benefits program as fair and meeting their expectations, then those employees will be satisfied and productive. When employees are satisfied and happy with the way the employer is treating them, they will be committed to the employer and even engage in good citizenship behaviors. Hence, it is important for employers to understand employee perceptions and attitudes about employee benefits. This will allow employers to design and communicate benefits programs that can attract and retain productive and committed employees. The economics of employee benefits explore why employers offer a mixture of cash and benefits and whether workers tend to pay for benefits cost increases in the form of lower cash wages. The primary reasons why employers offer benefits are that they can purchase the benefits at a lower cost than could employees on their own, employers use benefits to attract particular types of employees, and the government gives employers a tax incentive to provide some benefits. Whether workers or employers pay for benefits cost increases depends crucially on why costs increase, whether costs increase for all employers in the market, and how willing employees and employers are able to adjust their labor supply and demand when compensation costs change.

Key Terms

social exchange, *32*
economic exchange, *33*
psychological contracts, *35*
transactional psychological contracts, *35*
relational psychological contracts, *35*

distributive justice, *39*
procedural justice, *39*
informational justice, *39*
interpersonal justice, *39*
organizational support, *41*
organizational citizenship behavior, *39*

medical underwriting, *44*
adverse selection, *45*
experience rating, *45*
economies of scale, *46*
tuition reimbursement benefits, *46*

Discussion Questions

1. Discuss the concept of social exchange as it relates to the employment relationship. How does this concept apply to employee-benefits practices?

2. What are psychological contracts? Discuss the main features of psychological contracts and how they develop. Discuss how employees' psychological contracts might be violated and the consequences of these violations for employers.

3. How do perceptions of employee-benefits plans influence organizational justice and organizational citizenship behavior?

4. One reason employers offer benefits is that the benefits may be cheaper for the employers to provide than it would be for the employees to purchase on their own. Even if a particular benefit is cheaper for an employer to provide, would that employer always want to provide it? Why or why not?

5. A major theme of this chapter is that employers need to know the dollar value that employees place on benefits. Explain concisely why this type of information is important for employers to have. What methods do employers actually use to gauge their employees' valuation of benefit packages?

Cases

1. Understanding Your Employee Benefits: Forgoing a Benefits Package

As you consider how to move ahead in your career, it seems like a good time to explore other job opportunities. You generally like your current job but feel that your future opportunities are limited within your company. You are fortunate that your skill set is in demand and you have already received a couple of offers, but you are surprised by the variation of the compensation in the offers. You know that, as you consider an offer, you should consider both the salary and the value of the benefits. As you compare the offers, you start to consider what you really value in compensation.

The most recent offer you received is a surprising, yet tempting, offer. The job is a step up for you from a career-growth perspective, and while most of the jobs you have interviewed for have offered a 5 to 10 percent increase over your current pay, this job is offering you a 30 percent increase over your current pay. However, the job offers no benefits beyond a basic paid time-off allowance. Therefore, if you want life insurance coverage or retirement savings set aside, you will have to pay for both on your own.

The extra cash appeals to you as you think about your needs. For example, you are confident in your ability to invest savings for your retirement. You already have an Independent Retirement Account (IRA) set up and contribute some of your current earnings to the account. You consider yourself disciplined and think that you could easily set aside some of your monthly pay for your retirement savings.

You've discussed the offer with some friends and family and have been cautioned that it might be better to pursue an offer that includes insurance and retirement benefits. They have suggested that it is difficult to find affordable insurance on your own, and that it is easy to be distracted by other needs and fail to save for your retirement. However, you know that employer-sponsored life insurance in particular is not always guaranteed. You know of many friends who have faced cuts in their health insurance benefit that are explained by higher premium rates that are passed along to employees. You think that if you could end up paying more for insurance from an employer anyway, maybe you should just pay for it yourself. On the other hand, you know that the increase in the availability of cash may tempt you to spend the money on things other than your retirement savings. As you consider the offer, you are getting excited about the position, but you just aren't sure about the compensation.

1. Why would a company offer salary with no benefits?
2. Do you think the offer without benefits is worth pursuing?

2. Managing Employee Benefits: Cutting Benefits at Generals Construction

As Generals Construction moves into its 10th year, the company's future is promising. The company has continued to grow and profit, but the CEO has asked company leaders to examine expenses to ensure that the company is financially stable going forward. As the Director of Human Resources, Jane Smith is examining opportunities to cut employee-related expenses while maintaining employee satisfaction and morale. However, Director of Finance Ann Lane is pushing some cost-cutting measures that Jane thinks may have a negative effect.

Generals Construction employs over 100 full-time construction workers and about 40 other workers that include construction supervisors, office staff, and management. Right now, all employees receive the same basic employee-benefits package, which includes a health insurance plan fully paid by the company and a generous vacation allowance. After 30 days of employment, all employees can enroll in the health plan and receive coverage for themselves and their families, and the company pays the full premium. New hires receive 5 vacation days, employees with one year of service receive 10 vacation days, and employees with three years of service receive 15 days. Finally, the company also provides a modest retirement plan benefit. The benefit offerings were determined when the company was started, before Jane joined the company. At the time, the CEO needed to hire nearly 50 workers in a short period of time to fulfill a new contract, and the attractiveness of the health insurance and vacation benefits in particular were instrumental in meeting the company's recruitment goals.

Ann suggests that the company make some significant changes to the benefits offerings in order to stabilize company finances for the future. While Jane agrees that the benefits that the company offers are fairly generous compared to those of competitors, she does not think the cuts Ann is suggesting are a good idea for the company. First, Ann wants some dramatic changes to the health insurance plan. Ann thinks the employees should bear more of the cost of the health insurance plan, including asking the employees to pay at least half of the cost of the premiums for individual coverage and the full premiums for family coverage. This shift would result in an increase of several hundred dollars in deductions from the biweekly pay of many employees.

Ann also suggests a cut in the number of vacation days, but only for the construction workers. She thinks construction workers should receive 5 vacation days after one year and 10 vacation days after three years of service. However, she states that these cuts are not necessary for other workers, including the supervisors, office workers, and management. She argues that the vacation time for the construction workers is costing the company too much money because they must pay overtime and hire temporary workers to cover the absences. She notes that when others are absent, the same coverage is not required, and thus, it won't cost the company anything to keep the same vacation allowance.

While Jane understands that some reduction in employee-benefits expenses is needed, she is concerned that the cuts Ann is recommending are too drastic and may be perceived as unfair. While she knows the employees will understand that they may have to contribute to their health insurance premium eventually, she thinks that the changes Ann is proposing are too much of a change at one time. Further, Jane has serious concerns with offering different vacation allowances for the front-line construction workers and the other employees. As she prepares to meet with the CEO to discuss reducing expenses, she needs to consider her response to Ann's recommendations.

1. Does Jane have a valid concern?
2. What kind of changes could the company make to benefits to address Jane's concerns?

Endnotes

1. A. S. Tsui, J. L. Pearce, L. W. Porter, and J. P. Hite, "Choice of Employee-Organization Relationship: Influence of External and Internal Organizational Factors." In G. R. Ferris (ed.), 13 *Research in Personnel and Human Resource Management.* Greenwich, CT: JAI Press, 1995: 117–151.

2. G. C. Homans, *Social Behavior: Its Elementary Forms.* New York: Harcourt, Brace, & World, Inc., 1961.

3. J. G. March and H. A. Simon, *Organizations,* 2nd ed. Cambridge, MA: Blackwell, 1993.

4. P. Blau, *Exchange and Power in Social Life.* New York: Wiley, 1964.

5. C. E. Weller, "Retirement Benefits: The Increasingly Diverse Labor Force," 29 *Employee Benefits Journal,* 2004: 16–21.

6. E. E. Gordon, "The 2010 Meltdown: Where Will We Find Workers?" 19 *Employee Benefit News,* 2005: 9.

7. M. Gendell, "Older Workers: Increasing Their Labor Force Participation and Hours of Work," *Monthly Labor Review,* Jan. 2008: 41–54.

8. M. F. Riche, "The Demographics of Tomorrow's Workplace." In O. S. Mitchell et al. (eds.), *Benefits for the Workplace of the Future.* Philadelphia: University of Pennsylvania Press, 2003.

9. *Ibid.*

10. *Ibid.*

11. D. M. Rousseau, "New Hire Perceptions of Their Own and Their Employer's Obligations: A Study of Psychological Contracts," 11 *Journal of Organizational Behavior,* 1990: 389–400.

12. *Ibid.*

13. W. H. Turnley and D. C. Feldman, "The Impact of Psychological Contract Violations on Exit, Voice, Loyalty, and Neglect," 52 *Human Relations,* 1999: 895–922.

14. N. Anderson and R. Schalk, "The Psychological Contract in Retrospect and Prospect," 19 *Journal of Organizational Behavior,* 1998: 637–647.

15. Anderson and Schalk, "The Psychological Contract in Retrospect and Prospect."

16. S. L. Robinson and D. M. Rousseau, "Violating the Psychological Contract: Not the Exception but the Norm," 15 *Journal of Organizational Behavior,* 1994: 245–259.

17. Turnley and Feldman, "The Impact of Psychological Contract Violations on Exit, Voice, Loyalty, and Neglect."

18. J. S. Bunderson, "How Work Ideologies Shape Psychological Contracts of Professional Employees: Doctors' Responses to Perceived Breach," 22 *Journal of Organizational Behavior,* 2001: 717–741.

19. L. McFarlane Shore and L. E. Tetrick, "The Psychological Contract as an Explanatory Framework in the Employment Relationship." In C. L. Cooper and D. M. Rousseau (eds.), *Trends in Organizational Behavior,* vol. 1, New York: John Wiley and Sons, 1994.

20. D. E. Guest and N. Conway, "Communicating the Psychological Contract: An Employer Perspective," 12 *Human Resource Management Journal,* 2002: 22–38.

21. M. A. Lucero and R. E. Allen, "Employee Benefits: A Growing Source of Psychological Contract Violations," 33 *Human Resource Management,* 1994: 425–446.

22. G. F. Dreher, R. A. Ash, and R. D. Bretz, "Benefit Coverage and Employee Cost: Critical Factors in Explaining Compensation Satisfaction," 41 *Personnel Psychology,* 1988: 237–254.

23. E. Kossek and V. Nichol, "The Effects of On-Site Child Care on Employee Attitudes and Performance," 45 *Personnel Psychology,* 1992: 485–509.

24. Lucero and Allen, "Employee Benefits."

25. R. Cropanzano, Z. S. Byrne, D. R. Bobocel, and D. R. Rupp, "Moral Virtues, Fairness Heuristics, Social Entities, and Other Denizens of Organizational Justice," 58 *Journal of Vocational Behavior,* 2001: 164–209.

26. J. A. Colquitt, D. E. Conlon, M. J. Wesson, C. O. Porter, and K. Y. Ng, "Justice at the Millennium: A Meta-Analytic Review of 25 Years of Organizational Justice Research," 86 *Journal of Applied Psychology,* 2001: 425–445.

27. J. Greenberg, M. Roberge, V. T. Ho, and D. M. Rousseau, "Fairness in Idiosyncratic Work Arrangements: Justice as an I-Deal." In J. J. Martocchio (ed.), *Research in Personnel and Human Resource Management,* vol. 23, 2004: 1–34.

28. *Ibid.*

29. *Ibid.*

30. *Ibid.*

31. *Ibid.*

32. M. D. Lee, S. M. MacDermid, and M. L. Buck, "Organizational Paradigms of Reduced-Load Work: Accommodation, Elaboration, and Transformation," 43 *Academy of Management Journal,* 2000: 1211–1226.

33. J. W. Budd, *Employment with a Human Face: Balancing Equity, Efficiency, and Voice.* Ithaca, NY: ILR Press, 2004.

34. R. Eisenberger, R. Huntington, S. Hutchinson, and D. Sowa, "Perceived Organizational Support," 71 *Journal of Applied Psychology*, 1986: 500–507.

35. L. Rhoades and R. Eisenberger, "Perceived Organizational Support: A Review of Literature," 87 *Journal of Applied Psychology*, 2002: 698–714.

36. *Ibid.*

37. D. G. Allen, L. M. Shore, and R. W. Griffeth, "The Role of Perceived Organizational Support and Supportive Human Resources Practices in the Turnover Process," 29 *Journal of Management*, 2003: 99–118.

38. Rhoades and Eisenberger, "Perceived Organizational Support: A Review of Literature."

39. D. W. Organ, *Organizational Citizenship Behavior: The Good Soldier Syndrome.* Massachusetts: Lexington Books, 1998.

40. C. A. Smith, D. W. Organ, and J. P. Near, "Organizational Citizenship Behavior: Its Nature and Antecedents," 68 *Journal of Applied Psychology*, 1983: 653–663.

41. K. Lee and N. J. Allen, "Organizational Citizenship Behavior and Workplace Deviance: The Role of Affect and Cognitions," 87 *Journal of Applied Psychology*, 2002: 131–142.

42. B. P. Niehoff and R. H. Moorman, "Justice as a Mediator of the Relationship between Methods of Monitoring and Organizational Citizenship Behavior," 36 *Academy of Management Journal*, 1993: 527–556.

43. M. Schnake, "Organizational Citizenship: A Review, Proposed Model, and Research Agenda," 44 *Human Relations*, 1991: 735–759.

44. U.S. Agency for Healthcare Research and Quality. *2013 Medical Panel Expenditure Survey.* Table 1: Total Health Services—Median and Mean Expenses per Person with Expense: United States. Accessed March 16, 2016, www.meps.ahrq.gov.

45. The effect of benefits costs on cash wages, employer profits, and employment is complex. A more in-depth discussion of the economic issues surrounding employment-based health insurance can be found in Mark V. Pauly, *Health Benefits at Work: An Economic and Political Analysis of Employment-Based Health Insurance,* Ann Arbor: University of Michigan Press, 1999.

46. An alternative is that when faced with a large increase in health insurance costs, an employer may be more likely to drop health insurance altogether and instead raise employees' salaries.

47. U.S. Bureau of Labor Statistics, *National Compensation Survey: Employee Benefits in the United States, March 2015* (Bulletin 2782). Accessed February 12, 2016, www.bls.gov.

Chapter **Three**

Regulating Employee Benefits

Learning Objectives

In this chapter, you will gain an understanding of:

1. The need for government regulation in the employment setting.

2. The National Labor Relations Act of 1935.

3. The Internal Revenue Code.

4. The Fair Labor Standards Act of 1938.

5. The Employee Retirement Income Security Act of 1974 (ERISA) and key amendments such as the Pension Protection Act, COBRA, and HIPAA.

6. The Patient Protection and Affordable Care Act of 2010.

7. Equal-opportunity employment laws.

This chapter is an introduction to some of the complex federal regulations that shape benefits practice. A sound working knowledge is essential for effectively managing employee-benefits programs. Exhibit 3.1 lists the laws that we review in this chapter.

THE NEED FOR GOVERNMENT REGULATION

To understand why we spend time reviewing the regulation of employee benefits, it is important to answer the following question:

How much can Congress or the courts tell an employer how to run its business, who it should hire or fire, and how it should treat its employees? Legal experts Bennett-Alexander and Hartman shed light on this question:

The freedom to contract is crucial to freedom of the market; an employee may choose to work or not to work for a given employer, and an employer may choose to hire or not to hire a given applicant. As a result, the employment relationship is regulated in some important ways. Congress tries to avoid telling employers how to manage their employees. . . . However, Congress has passed employment-related laws when it believes that the employee is not on equal footing with the employer. For example, Congress has passed laws that require employers to pay minimum wages and to refrain from using certain criteria, such as race or gender, in arriving at specific employment decisions. These laws reflect the reality that employers stand in a position of power in the employment relationship. Legal protections granted to employees seek to make the power relationship between employer and employee one that is fair and equitable.[1]

The main focus of this chapter is on the regulation of employee benefits in the private sector—for-profit companies such as Walmart and not-for-profit agencies such as the American Cancer Society—rather than the on the public sector—municipal, county, state, and federal governments. A complex set of public laws across the levels of government determine the regulation of benefits in the public sector, and these topics are largely outside the scope of this book. For instance, most features of public-sector benefits are not subject to every provision of the Employee Retirement Income Security Act (ERISA). Nevertheless, it is imperative to note that many states and municipalities have adopted laws that seemingly overlap with federal regulation. For example, many states have minimum wage laws that set the minimum wage higher than the federal minimum wage.

EXHIBIT 3.1
Legal
Influences on
Discretionary
Benefits
Practices

- The National Labor Relations Act of 1935
- The Internal Revenue Code
- The Fair Labor Standards Act of 1938
- The Employee Retirement Income Security Act of 1974 (ERISA) and noteworthy amendments:
  - The Consolidated Omnibus Budget Reconciliation Act of 1985 (COBRA)
  - The Health Insurance Portability and Accountability Act of 1996 (HIPAA)
  - The Pension Protection Act of 2006 (PPA)
  - The Patient Protection Affordable Care Act 2010 (PPACA or ACA)
- Equal Employment Opportunity laws:
  - The Equal Pay Act of 1963
  - Title VII of the Civil Rights Act of 1964
  - The Age Discrimination in Employment Act of 1967
  - The Pregnancy Discrimination Act of 1978
  - The Americans with Disabilities Act of 1990
  - The Civil Rights Act of 1991
  - The Genetic Information Nondiscrimination Act of 2008 (GINA)

LABOR UNIONS AND EMPLOYEE BENEFITS

The National Labor Relations Act of 1935

Congress enacted the **National Labor Relations Act of 1935 (NLRA)** to restore equality of bargaining power between employees and employers. As discussed in Chapter 1, the industrialization of the U.S. economy and the economic devastation during the Great Depression placed workers at a disadvantage; they were subject to poor pay, unsafe working conditions, and virtually no job security. Workers banded together to negotiate better terms of employment, but employers were not willing to negotiate because collective action could jeopardize their control over the terms of employment. Consequently, employees continued to experience poor working conditions, substandard wage rates, and excessive work hours.

For example, a tragedy occurred at the Triangle Shirtwaist factory located in New York City in 1911. Approximately 150 teenage girls perished when a fire broke out on the eighth floor of the building. Most were burned alive in their work areas, and others jumped out of the windows to their deaths on the sidewalks about 80 feet below. The company routinely kept the exits locked during work shifts, and a single fire escape could not support the weight of the people attempting to escape.

A strong public reaction across the country led politicians to embrace the idea that one of the responsibilities of government is to protect the welfare of workers. Ultimately, the New York Factory Investigating Commission, established to investigate the circumstances of the fire, led to the passage of New York State's Industrial Code, providing the impetus for national laws such as the NLRA to help protect the interests of workers.

Coverage

The NLRA applies to private-sector companies, except for companies whose main business is passenger or freight rail, or air carrier. The act does not extend protection to agricultural workers; domestic service workers; independent contractors; or employees of the federal, state, or municipal governments. The **National Labor Relations Board (NLRB)** oversees the enforcement of the NLRA.

Relevance to Employee Benefits

Section 1 of the NLRA declares the policy of the United States to protect commerce "by encouraging the practice and procedure of collective bargaining and by protecting the exercise by workers of full freedom of association, self-organization, and designation of representatives of their own choosing for the purpose of negotiating the terms and conditions of their employment."

Collective bargaining refers to the process in which representatives of employees (e.g., General Motors employees are represented by the United Auto Workers union) and representatives of company management negotiate the terms of employment. Under the NLRA, the possible subjects for bargaining fall into one of three categories: mandatory, permissive, or illegal. **Mandatory bargaining subjects** are those that employers and unions must bargain over if either constituent makes proposals about them. The following employee-benefits items are mandatory subjects:

- Disability pay—supplemental to what is mandated by Social Security and the various state workers' compensation laws (Chapter 6).
- Health (Chapter 5).
- Paid time off (Chapter 8).
- Retirement plans (Chapter 4).

Permissive bargaining subjects are those subjects on which neither the employer nor the union is obligated to bargain. The following employee-benefits items fall in the permissive subjects category:

- Administration of funds for employee-benefits programs.
- Retiree benefits (e.g., medical insurance).
- Workers' compensation, within the scope of state workers' compensation laws.

Illegal bargaining subjects include proposals for contract revisions that are either illegal under the NLRA or violate federal or state laws. For example, employers and labor unions may not bargain over particular standards for employee-benefits plans set forth by the Employee Retirement Income Security Act of 1974 (ERISA), including minimum funding standards; minimum participation standards; minimum vesting standards; benefit accrual standards; and joint, survivor, and preretirement survivor benefit requirements.

The role of labor unions goes well beyond the collective bargaining process. Increases in layoffs and plant shutdowns promote immediate cost savings for companies, but these activities threaten the bargaining power of unions. Unions are sometimes willing to accept lower pay and benefits in exchange for job security. Unions also were instrumental in securing the **Worker Adjustment and Retraining Notification (WARN) Act**, which generally requires that management give at least a 60-day advance notice of a plant closing or mass layoff. An employer's failure to comply with the requirement of the WARN Act entitles employees to recover pay and benefits for the period for which notice was not given, typically up to a maximum of 60 days.

THE INTERNAL REVENUE CODE

The **Internal Revenue Code (IRC)** is the set of regulations pertaining to taxation in the United States (e.g., sales taxes; company or employer income taxes; individual or employee income taxes; and property taxes). Taxes represent the main source of revenue to fund federal, state, and local government programs. The Internal Revenue Service (IRS) is the government agency that develops and implements the IRC, and it levies penalties against companies and individuals who violate these regulations. Since the early 20th century, the federal government has encouraged employers to provide retirement benefits to employees with tax breaks or deductions. In other words, the government has allowed employers to exclude retirement plan payments from their income subject to taxation. This "break" has reduced the amount of a company's required tax payments. In general, the larger the contributions to retirement plans, the greater the reduction in the amount of taxes owed to the government.

The IRC contains multiple regulations for legally required and discretionary benefits. As noted in Chapter 1, the Federal Insurance Contributions Act (FICA)[2] taxes employees and employers to finance the Social Security Old-Age, Survivor, and Disability Insurance (OASDI) program. Unemployment insurance benefits are financed by federal and, sometimes, state taxes levied on employers. Federal tax is levied on employers under the Federal Unemployment Tax Act (FUTA).

The IRC provides incentives for employers that offer discretionary benefits and for employees as recipients of these benefits. In general, an employee may deduct the cost of some benefits from his or her annual income, thereby reducing tax liability. Employers may also deduct the cost of benefits from their annual incomes when the costs are ordinary and necessary expenses of companies' trade or business. For example, the costs of electricity for a factory and the purchase of raw materials to manufacture products are ordinary and necessary expenses. Payroll costs and benefits costs also qualify as ordinary and necessary business expenses.

The tax deductibility of the costs of some benefits also requires that employers meet the provisions of the Employee Retirement Income Security Act of 1974. Benefits qualify for tax deductibility when nondiscrimination rules are followed. In the case of retirement plans, **nondiscrimination rules** prohibit employers from giving preferential treatment to key employees and highly compensated employees—for example, by contributing a larger percentage of annual salaries to executives' retirement accounts and a smaller percentage to other employees' retirement accounts; and, health-care benefit offerings are the same for all employees. We take up the definitions of key employees and highly compensated employees in Chapter 11 on executive employee benefits.

THE FAIR LABOR STANDARDS ACT OF 1938

The **Fair Labor Standards Act (FLSA)** contains provisions for minimum wage, overtime pay, and child labor.

Coverage

The FLSA provisions apply to private-sector employers and federal, state, or local government agencies. The U.S. Department of Labor enforces this act.

Of particular importance is the act's overtime pay provision. The overtime pay provision applies to employees whose jobs are classified as nonexempt by the act and excludes jobs that are classified as exempt by this act. Generally, executive, administrative, learned professional, creative professional, computer, and outside sales employees are exempt from the FLSA overtime provision. Most other jobs are nonexempt. Nonexempt jobs are subject to the FLSA overtime pay provision.

Determining whether jobs are exempt from the FLSA overtime pay provision has become even more complex since the U.S. Department of Labor introduced revised guidelines, known as the **FairPay Rules**, in August 2004. Previously, an employee was considered exempt under the FLSA overtime pay provisions if he or she earned more than the minimum wage and exercised independent judgment when working. Under the new FairPay Rules, workers earning less than $47,476 per year—or $913 per week—are guaranteed overtime protection.

Relevance to Employee-Benefits Practices

Under the overtime pay provision, nonexempt employees are entitled to pay at an amount equal to one and one-half times their normal hourly rate for hours worked in excess of 40 hours during a workweek. A workweek, which can begin on any day of the week, is seven consecutive 24-hour periods, or 168 consecutive hours. Employee benefits linked to pay, as in the case of unemployment insurance and contributions to a retirement plan, increase correspondingly during those overtime hours. For example, let's assume that a nonexempt employee contributes 5 percent of annual pay to a retirement account. Let's also assume that this employee's hourly pay equals $14.42 without overtime pay. Her annual contribution equals $1,500 ($14.42 per hour × 40 hours per week × 52 weeks per year × 5 percent). If this employee works 300 hours on an overtime basis, a

5 percent contribution would be greater. Her additional hourly pay would equal one-half of her normal hourly pay rate—$7.21 ($14.42/ 2). This employee's *additional* contribution to retirement equals $108.15 ($7.21 × 300 overtime work hours × 5 percent).

THE EMPLOYEE RETIREMENT INCOME SECURITY ACT OF 1974

The **Employee Retirement Income Security Act of 1974 (ERISA)** regulates the establishment and implementation of several employee-benefits practices. These include medical care (Chapter 5), life and disability insurance programs (Chapter 6), and retirement programs (Chapter 4). Deficiencies in the private-sector pension system, which undermined workers' retirement security, prompted this law's passage. For example, prior to ERISA, employers could arbitrarily determine when employees could begin participation in the company's retirement plan. It was in employers' interests to set a high minimum age or years of service to qualify for participation because older workers would have fewer years of employment than younger workers. As we will see later, the years of service criterion is oftentimes important in determining retirement benefits amounts.

ERISA is a far-reaching and complex law. Some law schools devote one or more courses to ERISA regulations. As is the case with other laws, various stakeholders, including employees, employers, and even the government, have comprehended its language differently, which has led to a multitude of court rulings to help guide interpretation. Moreover, ERISA has been amended several times to further balance the interests of employees and employers. For example, COBRA mandates that former employees have the opportunity to continue health-care coverage for a period of time by paying the premium. The Pension Protection Act of 2006 permits an employer to automatically enroll employees in its defined contribution retirement plan and to deduct a small amount of pay for deposit into an employee's account. Prior to this law, permitting automatic enrollment, many employees who had the choice to participate did not do so. Ultimately, the federal government stepped in to promote savings for retirement because of concerns that a significant number of people would not have sufficient funds to retire.

Coverage

ERISA generally covers private-sector employee-benefits plans. The following employee-benefits plans are not subject to ERISA requirements: federal, state, and local government plans; church plans; workers' compensation plans; plans maintained outside the United States for nonresident aliens; and top hat plans, which we discuss in Chapter 11, and which refer to deferred compensation plans for a select group of managers or highly compensated employees. Finally, ERISA excludes plans covering only business partnerships or sole proprietors. The U.S. Department of Labor enforces ERISA.

EXHIBIT 3.2
Summary of
ERISA Titles

Title I: Protection of Employee Rights

1. Reporting and disclosure
2. Participation and vesting
3. Funding
4. Fiduciary responsibilities
5. Administration/enforcement
6. Continuation coverage and additional standards for group health plans
7. Group health plan requirements

Title II: Amendments to the Internal Revenue Code Relating to Retirement Plans

Title III: Jurisdiction, Administration, Enforcement, Joint Pension Task Force

Title IV: Plan Termination Insurance

Relevance to Employee-Benefits Practices

Until the passage of ERISA in 1974, employer-sponsored retirement plans were largely unregulated. The IRC, the Taft–Hartley Act of 1947, and the Federal Welfare and Pension Plans Disclosure Act of 1958 applied limited restrictions to the operation of employer-sponsored plans.

ERISA has several major objectives:[3]

- To ensure that workers and beneficiaries receive adequate information about their benefits plans.
- To set standards of conduct for those managing employee-benefits plans and plan funds.
- To determine that adequate funds are being set aside to pay promised pension benefits.
- To ensure that workers receive pension benefits after they have satisfied certain minimum requirements.
- To safeguard pension benefits for workers whose pension plans are terminated.

ERISA has four broad titles and general sections contained within each title. Exhibit 3.2 displays a listing of the titles and sections. Title I specifies a variety of protections for participants and beneficiaries. Title II includes the IRC provisions pertaining to the taxation of employee-benefits and pension plans. Title III addresses the administration and enforcement of ERISA, including the jurisdiction of relevant federal agencies. Title IV contains terms for pension insurance programs, including the establishment of the Pension Benefit Guarantee Corporation (PBGC).

Titles I and II contribute several minimum standards necessary to "qualify" retirement plans for favorable tax treatment. Additional regulations (e.g., U.S. Treasury rules) also contribute minimum standards for the same purpose. Failure to meet any of the minimum standards "disqualifies" pension plans for favorable tax treatment. Pension plans that meet all of these minimum standards are known as **qualified plans**. **Nonqualified plans** fail to meet at least one minimum standards. We take up a review of the ERISA minimum standards in this chapter and in subsequent chapters where there is relevance to a particular benefits practice.

Defining Pension Plans and Welfare Plans

ERISA applies to **pension plans** and **welfare plans**. Pension plans are any plan, fund, or program that:

> (i) [P]rovides retirement income to employees, or (ii) results in a deferral of income by employees for periods extending to the termination of covered employment or beyond, regardless of the method of calculating the contributions made in the plan, the method of calculating benefits under the plan, or the method of distributing benefits from the plan.[4]

ERISA defines a welfare plan as:

> any plan, fund, or program which was heretofore or is hereafter established or maintained by an employer or by an employee organization, or by both, to the extent that such plan, fund, or program was established or is maintained for the purpose of providing for its participants or their beneficiaries through the purchase of insurance or otherwise, (A) medical, surgical, or hospital care or benefits, or benefits in the event of sickness, accident, disability, death, or unemployment, or vacation benefits, apprenticeship, or other training programs, or day care centers, scholarship funds, or prepaid legal services, or (B) any benefit described in section 302(c) of the Labor Management Relations Act, 1947 (other than pensions on retirement or death; and insurance to provide such pensions).[5]

The two most commonly used pension plans in companies are defined benefit plans and defined contribution plans, which are discussed in great detail in Chapter 4. For the purposes of introducing ERISA, a brief definition of each is warranted, because some of the ERISA provisions refer to one type versus another. A **defined benefit plan**, also referenced as a pension plan in the law, guarantees the retirement benefits. This benefit usually is expressed in terms of a monthly or an annual sum equal to a percentage of a participant's preretirement pay multiplied by the number of years he or she has worked for the employer. Although the benefit in such a plan is fixed by a formula, the level of required employer contributions fluctuates from year to year. The contribution depends on the amount necessary to ensure that benefits are paid as promised. Under a **defined contribution plan**, employers and employees make annual contributions to separate accounts established for each participating employee, based on a formula contained in the plan document. The amount each participant receives in retirement depends on the performance of the selected investment vehicle (e.g., company stock, government bonds). Typically, formulas call for employers to contribute a given percentage of a participant's annual pay each year. Employers invest these funds on behalf of the employee in any of a number of ways, such as company stock, diversified stock market funds, or federal government bond funds.

EXHIBIT 3.3
Permissible
Benefits in
Taft-Hartley
Plans

- Health-care benefits
- Pension benefits
- Life insurance
- Unemployment benefits
- Accident insurance
- Occupational illness/injury benefits
- Training and education (including apprenticeships and educational scholarships)
- Pooled vacation, holiday, and severance benefits
- Financial assistance for housing
- Child-care centers
- Disability/sickness insurance
- Legal services

Another important term is **multiemployer plans** (also known as **Taft-Hartley plans**). The Labor Management Relations Act of 1947, also known as the Taft-Hartley Act, spurred the growth of multiemployer plans in the private sector. Multiemployer plans may include pension or welfare benefits for workers generally in industries where it is common to move from employer to employer when work becomes available, such as in the skilled trades (e.g., carpentry), the trucking industry, mining, public utilities, and the entertainment industry (theater and film companies). The participating companies are generally small. As the name indicates, multiemployer pension plans cover workers with more than one employer, compared to most pension and welfare plans, which are sponsored by a single employer.

Particular characteristics of Taft-Hartley plans include the following:

- A limited set of employee benefits, which are listed in Exhibit 3.3.
- Employers' contributions must be held in trust for the purpose of paying benefits to employees and their dependents.
- Labor and management must be equally represented in the administration of the joint trust fund, with an established procedure to resolve stalemates.
- The trust fund must be audited annually by a neutral organization.
- A separate trust fund must be established to hold contributions for pensions. Pension fund money cannot be mixed with a welfare fund (e.g., health care and disability).

Scope of Coverage for Pension Plans and Welfare Plans

Although ERISA covers both pension plans and welfare plans, most of its provisions pertain to pension (retirement) plans. The protection of employee rights (Title I) addresses seven issues, which are described next. Only two issues (1 and 4) apply to welfare plans; two additional issues (6 and 7) address group health plans exclusively.

Title I: Protection of Employee Rights

Title I contains provisions that provide employees protections for benefits rights:

1. Reporting and disclosure.
2. Minimum standards for participation and vesting.
3. Funding.
4. Fiduciary responsibilities.
5. Administration and enforcement.
6. Continuation coverage and additional standards for group health plans.
7. Group health plan portability, access, and renewability requirements.

Congress endorsed the need for Title I based on four major considerations. First, Congress observed that many companies terminated pension plans after employees completed several years of service. Second, many companies were forced to terminate pension plans due to insufficient funding. Third, many companies did not provide employees information about their pension plans (e.g., the rate at which benefits accumulate over time). Fourth, the absence of federal regulations setting minimum standards for funding pension programs resulted in the financial failure of many pension plans, leaving beneficiaries without any retirement benefits. Altogether, these problems threatened employee security and self-sufficiency in retirement. As noted earlier, most employees do receive Social Security retirement benefits, but oftentimes the amounts are insufficient to fully fund individuals through retirement.

Part 1: Reporting and Disclosure

These provisions impose three requirements on employers regarding pension plans and other employee-benefits plans. First, employers must provide employees with understandable and comprehensive summaries of their pension and welfare benefits plans, information about changes to these plans, and advance notification of planned termination of these plans. Second, employees are entitled to receive reports on their status in the plans, including service credits and accumulated benefits. Third, employers are required to report detailed financial and actuarial data about the plans to the U.S. Treasury Department. Companies may satisfy this reporting requirement by completing **Form 5500.** This form can be obtained from the IRS Web site at www.irs.gov.

Part 2: Participation and Vesting

Strict participation requirements apply to pension plans. Specifically, employees must be allowed to participate in pension plans after they have reached age 21[6] and have completed one year of service (based on 1,000 work hours).[7] These hours include all paid time for performing work and paid time off (e.g., vacation, sick leave, holidays). The one-year requirement may be extended to two years if the company grants full vesting after two years of participation in the pension plan. In addition, companies may not exclude employees from participating in pension plans because they are too old. (Too old is not defined in the law. It references an employer's choice of age for limiting participation.) **Vesting** refers to an employee's nonforfeitable rights to pension benefits.[8]

Part 3: Funding

ERISA imposes several funding requirements. Essentially, employers must contribute sufficient annual funding for all pension benefits earned by employees. In the event of underfunding, companies must notify plan participants. Failure to comply with this funding requirement leads to monetary penalties, which are expressed as a percentage of the amount in question. The percentage may vary based on the length of time an employer remains in violation. In the event of underfunding, employers must make the necessary adjustments to meet future liabilities. Failure to correct underfunding entitles the federal government to place liens against the employer's assets; that is, the government takes charge of assets until the underfunding situation is resolved.

Part 4: Fiduciary Responsibilities

Fiduciaries are individuals who manage employee-benefits plans. A variety of individuals or organizations may serve as fiduciaries. Common ones include:

- Employers.
- Insurance companies.
- Attorneys.
- Corporate directors, officers, or principal stockholders.

ERISA requires fiduciaries to use care in the exercise of their duties while charging reasonable fees and costs to fulfill their responsibilities.[9] Three additional **fiduciary responsibilities** include:[10]

- Using the care, skill, and diligence that a prudent person would use under similar circumstances.
- Diversifying plan investments to minimize the risk of large losses.
- Acting according to the plan document, as long as it is consistent with ERISA.

Part 5: Administration and Enforcement

Three federal government agencies share responsibility for the administration and enforcement of ERISA provisions: the U.S. Department of Labor, the Internal Revenue Service (IRS), and the Pension Benefit Guarantee Corporation (PBGC). Title III of ERISA empowers the U.S. Department of Labor and the IRS to administer and enforce specific sections of this act. Title IV established the PBGC.

Part 6: Continuation Coverage and Additional Standards for Group Health Plans

The **Consolidated Omnibus Budget Reconciliation Act of 1985 (COBRA)** amended ERISA by providing employees and beneficiaries the right to elect continuation coverage under group health plans if they would lose coverage due to a qualifying event. COBRA and such concepts as qualifying events are reviewed later in this chapter.

Part 7: Group Health Plan Portability, Access, and Renewability Requirements

The **Health Insurance Portability and Accountability Act of 1996 (HIPAA)** is another amendment. HIPAA imposes requirements on group health and health insurance issuers relating to portability, increased access by limiting preexisting limitation rules, renewability, and health-care privacy. HIPAA is reviewed later in this chapter.

Title II: Amendments to the Internal Revenue Code Relating to Retirement Plans

Title II amends the IRC relating to the tax treatment of pension and welfare benefits plans. Benefits professionals often describe the interplay between ERISA and the IRC as the "carrot and the stick." The IRC provides the carrot, or incentive, for employers to establish employee-benefits plans by granting favorable tax treatment. ERISA serves as the stick, or deterrent to possible illegal employer treatment, by providing legal remedies to employees and beneficiaries.

Some of these amendments mirror the following Title I provisions: participation, vesting, and minimum funding standards. Additional amendments pertain to nondiscrimination of coverage requirements (Chapter 4, for the treatment of employer-sponsored retirement plans), contribution and benefits limits to company-sponsored retirement plans (Chapter 4), and Individual Retirement Accounts and Keogh Plans for self-employed persons.

The first two amendments are reviewed later in the relevant chapters. The third amendment falls outside the scope of employer sponsored plans.

Title III: Jurisdiction, Administration, Enforcement, Joint Pension Task Force, and Other Issues

Title III of ERISA grants power to the U.S. Department of Labor for administering and enforcing Title I of ERISA: reporting and disclosure requirements and fiduciary responsibility. The U.S. Department of Labor's **Employee Benefits Security Administration**, an agency of the department, possesses responsibility for enforcing Title I. The Employee Benefits Security Administration enforces ERISA by conducting investigations through its 10 regional offices and five district offices located in major cities throughout the country. These field offices conduct investigations to gather information and evaluate compliance with ERISA's civil law requirements as well as criminal law provisions relating to employee-benefits plans.

Title IV: Plan Termination Insurance

Title IV established the Pension Benefit Guarantee Corporation (PBGC), which is a tax-exempt, self-financed corporation created to insure defined benefit pension plans. Its operations are financed by insurance premiums set by Congress and paid for by sponsors of defined benefit plans, investment income, assets from pension plans trusteed by the PBGC, and recovery of at least some money from the companies formerly responsible for the plans. The PBGC pays monthly retirement benefits, up to a guaranteed maximum. It is also responsible for providing the current and future pensions for those who have not yet retired. Since 1974, the PBGC has provided payments to about 1.5 million workers in 4,800 failed plans and, in 2015 alone, paid total benefits of approximately $5.7 billion.

The PBGC currently insures about 27,500 private defined benefit pension plans covering more than 44 million American workers and retirees. Under the PBGC's pension insurance programs, the administrators and plan sponsors have a number of reporting and administrative responsibilities.

THE CONSOLIDATED OMNIBUS BUDGET RECONCILIATION ACT OF 1985

COBRA is a substantial amendment to ERISA, Title I (Part 6: Continuation Coverage and Additional Standards for Group Health Plans).

Coverage

COBRA applies to private-sector companies with at least 20 employees. However, ERISA does not apply to state or federal government employment.[11] The U.S. Department of Labor enforces COBRA.

Relevance to Group Health Plans

Companies are required to permit *qualified beneficiaries*[12] to elect *continuation coverage* under group health plans if they would lose coverage due to a *qualifying event*. A **qualified beneficiary** generally is an individual covered by a group health plan on the day before a qualifying event who is an employee, an employee's spouse, or an employee's dependent child. **Qualifying events** are certain events that would cause an individual to lose health coverage. In other words, an employee or his or her dependents may continue to receive employer-sponsored health insurance for a designated period of time. To fully understand COBRA, it is necessary to know the meanings of qualifying events, qualified beneficiaries, and continuation coverage.

Qualifying events include the following:

- Death of the covered employee.
- Termination or reduction in hours of employment (other than by reason of misconduct).
- Divorce or legal separation.
- Dependent child ceasing to meet the health plan's definition of a dependent child.
- Covered employee becoming eligible for Medicare benefits under the Social Security Act.[13]

Qualified beneficiaries may be the covered employees themselves when the qualifying event is termination of employment (other than by reason of misconduct) or a reduction in work hours.

The **election period** generally refers to the period that begins on or before the occurrence of the qualifying event, and it extends for at least 60 days.

Beneficiaries are responsible for paying the insurance premium. Companies are permitted to charge COBRA beneficiaries a premium for **continuation coverage** of up to 102 percent of the cost of the coverage to the plan. The 2 percent markup reflects a charge for administering COBRA. Continuation coverage must be identical to coverage offered to active employees in terms of deductibles, coinsurance, plan options, and benefit limitations. For instance, an employer pays $250 per month per employee to provide health insurance protection. A qualified beneficiary would generally pay the monthly premium plus an additional 2 percent. In this case, that amount would be $255 =[$250 + (2% × $250)].

THE HEALTH INSURANCE PORTABILITY AND ACCOUNTABILITY ACT OF 1996

The Health Insurance Portability and Accountability Act of 1996 (HIPAA) is a substantial amendment to ERISA, Title I (Part 7: Group Health Plan Portability, Access, and Renewability Requirements). This act contains three main provisions. The first provision ensures that employees (and their dependents) who leave their employer's group health plan will have ready access to coverage under a subsequent employer's health plan, regardless of their health or claims experience. The second provision limits the length of time that health plans and health plan issuers may impose preexisting conditions and identifies conditions to which no preexisting condition may apply. As we discuss in Chapter 5, preexisting health condition generally refers to a medical condition for which a diagnosis was made or treatment given prior to enrolling in a health-care plan. The third provision protects the transfer, disclosure, and use of health-care information.

Coverage
HIPAA applies to all employers offering group health plans. The U.S. Department of Health and Human Services enforces HIPAA.

Availability and Portability
HIPAA prohibits discrimination against individuals and beneficiaries based on health status and related factors. Specifically, health plans may not create rules that would limit eligibility for initial enrollment, terminate continued eligibility for currently covered employees and beneficiaries, or require higher premiums based on any of the reasons listed in Exhibit 3.4.

Health-Care Privacy
Effective February 2003, covered health-care entities must receive a patient's consent for use and disclosure of health records.[14] Covered care entities include health

EXHIBIT 3.4
Prohibited Reasons for Limiting Participation in Group Health Plans under HIPAA

Source: 29 C.F.R. §2590.702.

- Health status.
- Medical condition, including physical and mental illness.
- Claims experience.
- Receipt of health care.
- Medical history.
- Genetic information.
- Evidence of insurability (including conditions arising out of acts of domestic violence).
- Disability.

plans, health-care clearinghouses, and those health-care providers who conduct certain financial and administrative transactions (e.g., electronic billing). Also, employers may not make employment decisions based on health status unless they receive written employee consent. Before employers obtain written consent, they must fully disclose how and for what purpose the health information will be used.

THE PENSION PROTECTION ACT OF 2006

The **Pension Protection Act (PPA)** was designed to strengthen employee rights and is an amendment to ERISA. The PPA focuses on bettering employee rights in at least two ways. The first consideration applies to defined benefit plans, and the second applies to defined contribution plans. First, this law should strengthen the financial condition of the PBGC, which is a self-financed corporation established by ERISA to insure private-sector defined benefit plans. Companies that offer defined benefit plans are required to pay an insurance premium to protect retirement income promised by these retirement plans. Companies that underfund these plans pay substantially higher costs for insurance protection because they are at greater risk for not having the funds to pay promised retirement benefits. The PPA aims to strengthen the PBGC financial condition by making it more difficult for companies to skip making premium payments. Finally, the PPA raises the amount that employers can contribute to pension funding with tax advantages, creating an additional incentive to adequately fund pension plans.

Second, the PPA makes it easier for employees to participate in defined contribution plans. Millions of workers who are eligible to participate in their employers' defined contribution plans do not contribute to them. There are a variety of reasons why employees choose not to participate; however, a prominent reason is that most individuals feel they do not have sufficient knowledge about how to choose investment options that will help them earn sufficient money for retirement. In addition, once employees make the decision to participate in these plans and have been making regular contributions, they are not likely to stop. With these issues in mind, the PPA enables companies to enroll their employees automatically in defined contribution plans and provides greater access to professional advice about investing for retirement. Finally, this act requires companies to offer multiple investment options to allow employees to select how much risk they are willing to bear.

THE PATIENT PROTECTION AND AFFORDABLE CARE ACT OF 2010

The Patient Protection and Affordable Care Act of 2010 (PPACA or ACA) mandates health-care coverage and sets minimum standards for health-care plans. The goal of so-called health-care reform was to reduce the number of uninsured U.S. residents by 32 million by 2016.[15] The U.S. Congressional Budget Office estimates that the cost of health-care reform over the next 10 years will cost approximately $971 billion through the year 2019,[16] which will be paid by individual taxpayers and companies. Individuals who can afford to purchase health coverage must do so either by participating in an employer-sponsored plan or by purchasing health coverage independently. Companies with at least 50 employees are required to offer affordable health insurance under the law to full-time employees. These requirements are known as the individual mandate and employer mandate, respectively. We discuss the PPACA in detail within Chapter 5 (employer-sponsored health care) because many of the law's provisions are closely intertwined with design elements of health-care plans.

EQUAL EMPLOYMENT OPPORTUNITY LAWS

Several federal **equal employment opportunity** laws prohibit illegal discrimination against protected classes of individuals regarding all employment practices, including employee benefits. The Equal Employment Opportunity Commission (EEOC), a federal government agency, oversees the enforcement of these laws. Job applicants and employees file claims with the EEOC if they have reason to believe that they were discriminated against on the basis of race, color, sex, religion, national origin, age, or disability, or believe that they have been discriminated against because of opposition to a prohibited practice or participation in an equal employment opportunity matter. The EEOC provides a number of services to employers, including training sessions and policy manuals, that help them comply with the following laws:

- The Equal Pay Act of 1963.
- Title VII of the Civil Rights Act of 1964.
- The Age Discrimination in Employment Act of 1967.
- The Pregnancy Discrimination Act of 1978.
- The Americans with Disabilities Act of 1990.
- The Civil Rights Act of 1991.
- The Genetic Information Nondiscrimination Act of 2008.

The scope of coverage varies somewhat for each law. Specific coverage requirements are stated below for each law.

The Equal Pay Act of 1963

Congress enacted the **Equal Pay Act of 1963** to remedy a serious problem of employment discrimination in private industry: "Many segments of American industry have been based on an ancient but outmoded belief that a man, because of his role in society, should be paid more than a woman even though his duties are the same."[17]

Coverage

The Equal Pay Act applies to the same organizations as does the FLSA. The U.S. Department of Labor enforces the FLSA.

Relevance to Employee-Benefits Practices

The Equal Pay Act of 1963 is based on a simple principle. Men and women should receive equal pay for performing equal work. Specifically:

> No employer . . . shall discriminate within any establishment in which such employees are employed, between employees on the basis of sex by paying wages to employees in such establishment at a rate less than the rate at which he pays wages to employees of the opposite sex . . . for equal work on jobs the performance of which requires equal skill, effort, and responsibility, and which are performed under similar working conditions, except where such payment is made pursuant to (i) a seniority system; (ii) a merit system; (iii) a system which measures earnings by quantity or quality of production; or (iv) a differential based on any other factor other than sex.[18]

The definition of *wages* in the Equal Pay Act encompasses employee benefits. The EEOC defined *wages* to include all payments made to, or on behalf of, an employee as compensation for employment. Thus, employers must provide equal employee benefits to male and female employees who perform equal work, along with their beneficiaries, regardless of cost differences.

The Equal Pay Act of 1963 pertains explicitly to jobs of *equal* worth. Companies assign pay rates to jobs according to the levels of skill, effort, responsibility, and working conditions. *Skill, effort, responsibility,* and *working conditions* represent **compensable factors**. Exhibit 3.5 lists the U.S. Department of Labor's definitions of these compensable factors.

EXHIBIT 3.5 U.S. Department of Labor's Definitions of Skill, Effort, Responsibility, and Working Conditions

Source: U.S. Department of Labor, *Equal Pay for Equal Work under the Fair Labor Standards Act.* Dec. 31, 1971.

Skill	Experience, training, education, and ability as measured by the performance requirements of a job.
Effort	Mental or physical. The amount of effort expended in the performance of the job.
Responsibility	The degree of accountability required in the performance of a job.
Working Conditions	The physical surroundings and hazards of a job, including dimensions such as inside versus outside work, heat, cold, and poor ventilation.

Title VII of the Civil Rights Act of 1964

Title VII of the Civil Rights Act of 1964 prohibits illegal discrimination against protected-class individuals in employment. The Civil Rights Act grew out of broader social unrest among underrepresented minorities who spoke out against their unfair treatment throughout society. For example, prior to Title VII, employers could legally refuse to hire highly qualified individuals simply on the basis of race, color, religion, sex, or national origin.

Coverage

Title VII protects employees who work for all private-sector employers; local, state, and federal governments; and educational institutions that employ 15 or more individuals. Title VII also applies to private and public employment agencies, labor organizations, and joint labor management committees controlling apprenticeship and training. The EEOC enforces Title VII.

Relevance to Employee-Benefits Practices

Title VII provides for the following:

> It shall be an unlawful employment practice for an employer—(1) to fail or refuse to hire or to discharge any individual, or otherwise to discriminate against any individual with respect to his compensation *including employee benefits* [emphasis added], terms, conditions, or privileges of employment, because of such individual's race, color, religion, sex, or national origin; or (2) to limit, segregate, or classify his employees or applicants for employment in any way which would deprive or tend to deprive any individual of employment opportunities or otherwise adversely affect his status as an employee, because of such individual's race, color, religion, sex, or national origin.[19]

The Age Discrimination in Employment Act of 1967

The **Age Discrimination in Employment Act of 1967 (ADEA)** prohibits illegal discrimination in employment on the basis of age. The ADEA specifies that it is unlawful for an employer:

> (1) to fail or refuse to hire or to discharge any individual or otherwise discriminate against any individual with respect to his compensation, terms, conditions, or privileges of employment, because of such individual's age; (2) to limit, segregate or classify his employees in any way which would deprive or tend to deprive any individual of employment opportunities or otherwise adversely affect his status as an employee, because of such individual's age; or (3) to reduce the wage rate of any employee in order to comply with this Act.[20]

Coverage

The ADEA applies to all private-sector employers with 20 or more employees; state and local governments, with some exceptions; employment agencies serving covered employers; and labor unions with 25 or more members. The EEOC enforces the ADEA.

Relevance to Employee-Benefits Practices

The ADEA makes specific reference to employee benefits. It also sets limits on the development and implementation of employer "early retirement" practices, which many companies use to reduce the size of the workforce. Most early retirement programs are offered to employees who are at least 55 years of age. These early retirement programs are permissible when companies offer them to employees on a voluntary basis. Forcing early retirement upon older workers represents age discrimination.[21]

The **Older Workers Benefit Protection Act (OWBPA)**[22]—the 1990 amendment to the ADEA—placed additional restrictions on employer-benefits practices. When employers require that all employees contribute toward coverage of benefits, under particular circumstances, they can also require older employees to pay more for health-care, disability, or life insurance than younger employees. This is the case because these benefits generally become more costly with age (e.g., older workers may be more likely to incur serious illnesses, thus insurance companies may charge employers higher rates to provide coverage for older workers than younger ones). However, an older employee may not be required to pay more for the benefit *as a condition of employment*. Where the premium has increased for an older employee, the employer must provide three options to older workers. First, the employee has the option of withdrawing from the benefit plan altogether. Second, the employee has the option of reducing his or her benefit coverage in order to keep his or her premium cost the same. Third, an older employee may be offered the option of paying more for the benefit in order to avoid otherwise justified reductions in coverage. Employers can legally reduce the coverage of older workers for benefits that typically become more costly as employees further age *only if* the costs for providing those benefits are significantly greater than the cost for younger workers. When costs differ significantly, the employer may reduce the benefit for older workers only to the point where it is paying just as much per older worker (with lower coverage) as it is for younger workers (with higher coverage). This practice is referred to as the **equal benefit or equal cost principle**.

The Pregnancy Discrimination Act of 1978

The **Pregnancy Discrimination Act of 1978 (PDA)** is an amendment to Title VII of the Civil Rights Act of 1964. The PDA prohibits discrimination against pregnant women in all employment practices. Congress enacted the Pregnancy Discrimination Act because various court rulings revealed that adverse treatment of pregnant women did not violate the "sex" provision of Title VII. In *Nashville Gas Co. v. Satty*,[23] the court held that excluding benefits for pregnant women from the company's disability plan did not violate Title VII. Its decision was based on the following rationale: Both men and women who were not pregnant benefited from the company's disability plan, and there was no reason to believe that men received more benefits than women.

Coverage

The Pregnancy Discrimination Act applies to the same organizations as does Title VII of the Civil Rights Act. The EEOC enforces this act.

Relevance to Employee-Benefits Practices

Employers must not treat pregnancy less favorably than other conditions covered under employee-benefits plans, including health insurance and disability insurance. For example, an employer that allows temporarily disabled employees to take disability leave or leave without pay must allow an employee who is temporarily disabled due to pregnancy to do the same. The PDA protects the rights of women who take leave for pregnancy-related reasons. Protected rights include credit for previous service, accrued retirement benefits, and accumulated seniority.

The Americans with Disabilities Act of 1990

The EEOC ruled that employers must offer benefits to workers with disabilities on the same basis as those offered for nondisabled employees. To rectify abuses to the disabled, Congress passed the **Americans with Disabilities Act (ADA)** in 1990. In particular, employers are required to provide the same health-care coverage to employees regardless of disability status. Also, an employer may not fire or refuse to hire a person with a disability or any qualified person with a family member who is disabled or dependent with a disability either because the health insurance policy does not cover the disability or because the costs of insurance coverage would increase. Finally, retirement plans cannot impose different requirements on employees with disabilities, such as longer vesting periods.

On September 25, 2008, President George W. Bush signed the **Americans with Disabilities Act Amendments Act of 2008 (ADAAA)**, making important changes to the definition of the term *disability*. These changes make it easier for an individual seeking protection under the ADA to establish that he or she has a disability.

According to the EEOC, Congress found that persons with many types of impairments—including epilepsy, diabetes, multiple sclerosis, major depression, and bipolar disorder—had been unable to bring ADA claims because they were found not to meet the ADA's definition of *disability*. Yet Congress thought that individuals with these and other impairments should be covered. The ADAAA explicitly rejected certain Supreme Court interpretations of the term *disability* and a portion of the EEOC regulations that it found had inappropriately narrowed the definition of disability.

Coverage

The ADA applies to the same organizations as does Title VII of the Civil Rights Act. The EEOC enforces the ADA.

Relevance to Employee Benefits

Lawsuits alleging ADA violations have been extremely complex, particularly regarding benefits. For example, an employee could claim under the ADA that he or she is a qualified individual with a disability and simultaneously apply for disability benefits. These claims appear to be contradictory. On one hand, the employee is capable of working with reasonable accommodation. On the other hand, the same employee's application for disability benefits indicates otherwise.

For example, Giles injured his back while performing his job as a machinist at General Electric (GE). Eventually, he required surgery. Following surgery and a convalescent period, Giles's surgeon gave medical clearance for him to return to work, subject to a permanent lifting restriction of 50 pounds and a "medium physical demand level." These restrictions prohibited Giles from performing his work as a machinist, which led GE to terminate his employment. Giles received company-sponsored long-term disability benefits.

After exhausting these disability benefits, Giles wanted to return to work at GE. He asked GE to make reasonable accommodation for his disability; such accommodation would make him a qualified individual with a disability. At the same time, Giles applied for disability benefits under the Social Security program. GE refused to make reasonable accommodation to support his application for Social Security benefits. Giles pursued a lawsuit claiming that GE violated the ADA, and he won the suit. GE appealed the decision to the U.S. Court of Appeals for the Fifth District. In *Giles v. General Electric Co.*, the appellate court upheld the lower court's decision to award Giles $590,000 for damages, front pay, and attorneys' fees.[24] The Court of Appeals reasoned that the application for Social Security benefits did not contradict Giles's claim that he could work with reasonable accommodation. These benefits would have been denied if GE had reinstated Giles.

The Civil Rights Act of 1991

Congress enacted the **Civil Rights Act of 1991** to overturn several Supreme Court rulings that limited employee rights. Perhaps most noteworthy is the reversal of *Atonio v. Wards Cove Packing Company.*[25] The Supreme Court ruled that the plaintiffs (employees) must indicate which employment practices were discriminatory and demonstrate how so. Since the passage of the Civil Rights Act of 1991, employers must show that the challenged employment practice is a business necessity. **Business necessity** is a legally acceptable defense against charges of alleged discriminatory employment practices under Title VII and the Civil Rights Act of 1991. Under the business necessity defense, an employer must prove that the suspect practice prevented irreparable financial damage to the company.

Coverage

The Civil Rights Act of 1991 provides coverage to the same groups protected under the Civil Rights Act of 1964. The 1991 act also extends coverage to Senate employees and political appointees of the federal government's executive branch. The EEOC enforces this act.

Relevance to Employee-Benefits Practices

Waiting periods based on seniority influence who is eligible to receive benefits. Also, as discussed throughout this book, employers increase the level of benefits based on seniority. For example, employees earn more annual vacation days as their length of service increases. The Civil Rights Act of 1991 overturned the Supreme Court's decision in *Lorance v. AT&T Technologies*,[26] which allowed employees to challenge the use of seniority systems only within 180 days from the system's implementation date. Now, employees may file suits claiming discrimination either when the system is implemented or whenever the system negatively affects them.

The Genetic Information Nondiscrimination Act of 2008

The **Genetic Information Nondiscrimination Act of 2008 (GINA)** protects job applicants, current and former employees, labor union members, and apprentices and trainees from discrimination by making unlawful the misuse of genetic information to discriminate in health care and employment. GINA contains two titles, which went into effect on November 21, 2009.

Title I of GINA applies to employer-sponsored group health plans. This title generally prohibits discrimination in group premiums based on genetic information and the use of genetic information as a basis for determining eligibility or setting health-care premiums.

Title II of GINA prohibits the use of genetic information in the employment setting, restricts the deliberate acquisition of genetic information by employers and others covered by Title II, and strictly limits them from disclosing genetic information. The law incorporates many of the definitions, remedies, and procedures from Title VII and other statutes protecting federal, state, and congressional employees from discrimination.

Coverage

Title II applies to private and state and local government employers with 15 or more employees, employment agencies, labor unions, and joint labor–management training programs. It also covers Congress and federal executive branch agencies such as the U.S. Department of Labor.

Relevance to Employee Benefits

GINA was enacted because of developments in the field of genetics, the decoding of the human genome, and advances in the field of genomic medicine. Genetic tests now exist that can inform individuals whether they may be at risk for developing a specific disease or disorder. As a result, people have concerns about whether they may be at risk of losing access to health coverage or employment if insurers or employers have their genetic information. The EEOC enforces GINA.

Summary   This chapter provides a discussion of important federal regulation of many employee-benefits practices. The regulation of discretionary benefits practices is quite complex, as a variety of laws and regulations play a role, including the tax code and federal equal employment opportunity laws. Familiarity with these laws and regulations is an important foundation for effective employee-benefits practice.

Key Terms

National Labor Relations Act of 1935 (NLRA), *63*
National Labor Relations Board (NLRB), *64*
mandatory bargaining subjects, *64*
permissive bargaining subjects, *64*
illegal bargaining subjects, *64*
Worker Adjustment and Retraining Notification (WARN) Act, *65*
Internal Revenue Code (IRC), *65*
nondiscrimination rules, *65*
Fair Labor Standards Act (FLSA), *66*
FairPay Rules, *66*
Employment Retirement Income Security Act of 1974 (ERISA), *67*
qualified plans, *69*
nonqualified plans, *69*
pension plans, *69*
welfare plans, *69*
defined benefit plan, *69*

defined contribution plan, *69*
multiemployer plans, *70*
Taft-Hartley Plans, Form 5500, *71*
vesting, *72*
fiduciaries, *72*
fiduciary responsibilities, *72*
Consolidated Omnibus Budget Reconciliation Act of 1985 (COBRA), *72*
Health Insurance Portability and Accountability Act of 1996 (HIPAA), *73*
Employee Benefits Security Administration, *73*
termination insurance, *73*
qualifying beneficiary, *74*
qualified events, *74*
election period, *75*
continuation coverage, *75*
Pension Protection Act, *76*
Patient Protection and Affordable Care Act of 2010, *77*

equal employment opportunity, *77*
Equal Pay Act of 1963, *77*
compensable factors, *78*
Title VII of the Civil Rights Act of 1964, *79*
Age Discrimination in Employment Act of 1967 (ADEA), *79*
Older Workers Benefit Protection Act (OWBPA), *80*
equal benefit or equal cost principle, *80*
Pregnancy Discrimination Act of 1978 (PDA), *80*
Americans with Disabilities Act (ADA), Americans with Disabilities Act Amendments Act of 2008 (ADAAA), *81*
Civil Rights Act of 1991, *82*
business necessity, *82*
Genetic Information Nondiscrimination Act of 2008 (GINA), *83*

Discussion Questions

1. Some people argue that there is too much government regulation of employment, while others say there is not enough. Do you think there is too little or too much government regulation? Explain your answer.
2. Describe the differences between pension plans and welfare plans.
3. Explain the differences between COBRA and HIPAA.
4. What is the main purpose of the Pension Protection Act of 2006, and why has it been necessary?
5. Describe three equal employment opportunity laws.

Cases

1. Understanding Your Employee Benefits: Continuing Health-Care Insurance

You've just given notice that you plan to leave your job. You have another job, which begins in a month, but you plan to take some time off before you start. Your final day at your current job is at the end of next week. You are meeting with the human resource manager to discuss terminating your employment with the company. You want to make sure you understand your final paycheck and the termination of your benefits with the company. In particular, you want to learn what happens with your health insurance after you leave.

You participate in your current company's health insurance plan and have coverage for you and your family. The company pays most of the premium, but you contribute $200 per month for the coverage. You've examined the benefits information from your new employer and know that you will be able to enroll in its health insurance plan after 90 days of service. You are concerned because you know that your coverage with your current company will end as of the day you leave the company, leaving nearly four months before you are covered under your new plan. Further, as the parent of young children, you know that you are likely to face a need for health care during that period.

You are told by the human resource manager that you will receive a letter regarding your rights under the Consolidated Omnibus Budget Reconciliation Act (COBRA). This letter will explain your option to continue your health insurance at your own expense after you leave the company. You will be required to pay the full premium for the insurance, which includes what your company previously paid plus your normal monthly contribution. You also must pay a 2 percent administrative fee each month.

The human resource manager lets you know that the total monthly premium for your coverage is $1,200.00, so you know that with the administrative fee, your monthly payment for the coverage will be $1,224.00. This amount alarms you, as you will be without a paycheck for a few months. The human resource manager reminds you that you are not required to elect the COBRA coverage, but there is some risk in not taking it. If you or one of your family members has an accident or some other urgent health-care need, the expenses may be significant. The human resource manager advises you to make sure that you carefully review the COBRA letter before making your decision.

1. Should you plan to elect the COBRA coverage?
2. If you do elect COBRA coverage, what are some important considerations to make sure your health insurance coverage is not interrupted?

2. Managing Employee Benefits: A Discriminatory Time-Off Policy

As Karen Jarrod looked over her notes from the human resources (HR) compliance audit that she conducted at her new company, she decided she needed to take a closer look at the company's time-off policies. Karen joined Staffon Consulting three months ago as the Director of Human Resources for the 1,500-employee company. Her first project in her new role was to review all of the company's HR practices and policies to identify any legal compliance concerns. A report on the gender mix in the company's workforce suggests she should take a closer look at some of the company's policies.

Karen's report suggests some gender imbalance in positions throughout the company. The company essentially has three broad groups of employees: managers, consultants, and clerical staff. As the table below summarizes, overall, women represent nearly half of the company's employees. However, women are poorly represented in both the manager and consultant categories. This is a concern to Karen because the manager and consultant categories are the higher-paying positions in the company and represent greater career opportunities. Only 20 percent of the managers are women, and only 32 percent of the consultants are women. However, women comprise 75 percent of the clerical staff. Karen notes that she needs to examine the company's hiring, performance management, and promotion practices to make sure that those processes are free of bias or barriers that prevent more women from becoming managers or consultants.

Gender Diversity at Staffon Consulting

Position	Men	Women	Total
Manager	160 (80%)	40 (20%)	200
Consultant	476 (68%)	224 (32%)	700
Clerical Staff	150 (25%)	480 (75%)	600
Total	786 (51%)	744 (49%)	1,500

As Karen notes the lack of gender diversity in these positions, she considers the impact beyond the potential problem of the disparate pay of women in the company. In starting to look at the impact, she notes that there may be a concern with the company's time-off policies. The company has two policies for time off, one for employees who are classified as exempt workers under the Fair Labor Standards Act and another for employees that are nonexempt. The time-off allocation for exempt workers is fairly generous. Exempt employees are eligible for two weeks of vacation each year upon hiring and three weeks of vacation after five years of service. Exempt employees also receive five personal days each year and may take sick days on an as-needed basis. Nonexempt employees receive one week of vacation each year after one year of service and two weeks of vacation after five years of service. Nonexempt employees receive two personal days each year and are limited to three sick days each year. Karen's concern is that because the managers and consultants are exempt and the clerical staff is nonexempt, the company's time-off policy may have an adverse impact against women.

1. Do you think that women are underrepresented in Staffon's workforce?
2. Do you think that Staffon's time-off policy is discriminatory?

Endnotes

1. D. D. Bennett-Alexander and L. P. Hartman, *Employment Law for Business,* 5th ed. Burr Ridge, IL: McGraw-Hill/Irwin, 2007: 3.
2. 26 U.S.C. §§3101–3125.
3. B. J. Coleman, *Primer on Employee Retirement Income Security Act,* 4th ed. Washington, DC: Bureau of National Affairs, 1993.
4. ERISA §3(2)(A), 29 U.S.C. §§1002(2)(A).
5. ERISA §3(1), 29 U.S.C. §1002(1).
6. I.R.C. §§410(a)(1), 410(a)(4); Treas. Reg. §1.410(a)-3T(b); ERISA §202(a).
7. I.R.C. §410(a)(3), Treas. Reg. §1.410(a)-5, 29 C.F.R. §2530.200b-2(a), ERISA §202(a)(3).
8. I.R.C. §§411(a)(2), 411(a)(5); Treas. Reg. §1.411(a)-3T; ERISA §203(a).
9. ERISA §404(a)(1)(A).
10. ERISA §404(a)(1)(B)–(D).
11. I.R.C. §4980B(d); Treas. Regs. §54.4980B-2.
12. I.R.C. §4980B(g)(1); Treas. Regs. §54.4980B-3.
12. I.R.C. §4980B(f).
14. 45 C.F.R. Parts 160, 164.

15. U.S. Congressional Budget Office, *Estimate of the Effects of the Insurance Coverage Provisions Contained in the Patient Protection and Affordable Care Act (Public Law 111-148) and the Health Care and Education Reconciliation Act of 2010 (P.L. 111-152)* (March 2011). Accessed April. 4, 2011, www.cbo.gov.

16. U.S. Congressional Budget Office, *CBO's Analysis of the Major Health Care Legislation Enacted in March 2010* (March 2011). Accessed April 4, 2011, www.cbo.gov.

17. S. Rep. No. 176, 88th Congress, 1st Session, 1 (1963).

18. 29 U.S.C. §206.

19. 42 U.S.C. §2000.

20. 29 U.S.C. §623.

21. *EEOC v. Chrysler Corp.*, 625 F. Supp. 1523, 45 FEP Cases 513 (N.D. Ohio 1987) 83.

22. Older Workers Benefit Protection Act of 1990, Pub. L. No. pl. 101-433.

23. *Nashville Gas Co. v. Satty*, 434 U.S. 136 (1977).

24. *Giles v. General Electric Co.*, 5th Cir., No. 99-11059 (Feb. 26, 2001).

25. *Atonio v. Wards Cove Packing Co.*, 490 U.S. 642, 49 FEP Cases 1519 (1989).

26. *Lorance v. AT&T Technologies*, 49 FEP Cases 1656 (1989).

Retirement, Health Care, and Life Insurance

Part Two

Employer-Sponsored Retirement Plans

2. *Managing Employee Benefits: A New Retirement Plan at Grinders Manufacturing*

Endnotes

Learning Objectives

In this chapter, you will gain an understanding of:

1. How employer-sponsored retirement plans are defined.

2. Differences between qualified plans and nonqualified plans.

3. Features of defined benefit plans and defined contribution plans.

4. Specific types of defined contribution plans.

5. Features of various hybrid plans.

Of course, most people work to fund basic needs (food) and wants (vacations). While needs and wants may change over time, we will always have them, even in retirement. Therefore, it is necessary to build financial resources throughout our employment to fund retirement. The U.S. federal government refers to savings for retirement as a three-legged stool, supported by personal savings, government benefits, and employer-sponsored retirement plans. We study two of the three legs in this book: Social Security retirement benefits (Chapter 7) and employer-sponsored retirement plans in this chapter. Benefits professionals play an important role in designing and administering retirement plans and working with other HR professionals and line managers who help employees understand their options.

DEFINING AND EXPLORING RETIREMENT PLANS

We learned in Chapter 3 that retirement plans function by providing:

retirement income to employees, or [result] in a deferral of income by employees for periods extending to the termination of covered employment or beyond, regardless of the method of calculating the contributions made in the plan, the method of calculating benefits under the plan, or the method of distributing benefits from the plan.[1]

We elaborate on this definition throughout the chapter by reviewing three main categories of employer-sponsored retirement plans and specific practices within each category. Before embarking on that discussion, let's explore the origins and prevalence of employer-sponsored retirement benefits followed by understanding the essential distinction between qualified and nonqualified retirement plans. For putting those discussions into context, let's give brief definitions of defined benefit plans and defined contribution plans. A defined benefit plan guarantees the retirement benefits. This benefit usually is expressed in terms of an annual sum equal to a percentage of a participant's preretirement pay multiplied by the number of years he or she has worked for the employer. Defined benefit plans are sometimes referred to as pension plans. Under a defined contribution plan, employees make annual contributions to their individual investment accounts, based on a formula contained in the plan document. Employers may choose to make matching contributions to employees' accounts. The amount each participant receives in retirement depends on the performance of the selected financial investment.

Origins of Employer-Sponsored Retirement Benefits

According to the Employee Benefit Research Institute,[2] the first plan in the United States was established in 1759 to benefit widows and children of Presbyterian ministers. Then, in the private sector, the American Express Company established a formal pension in 1875. Plans were adopted primarily in the railroad, banking, and public utility industries and eventually became increasingly popular in the private sector. It is believed that more and more companies adopted retirement plans to attract and retain employees. But, there were limits to which companies chose to retain employees. Approximately 30 years of service were needed to qualify for retirement benefits, and the mandatory retirement age was 65 in most states during the early 20th century. According to economics professor Joanna Short, "Because of the lengthy service requirement and mandatory retirement provision, firms viewed pensions as a way to reduce labor turnover and as a more humane way to remove older, less productive employees."[3] The most significant growth occurred after favorable tax treatment was established through the passage of the Revenue Act of 1921 and the Revenue Act of 1928. During World War II, government-imposed wage controls led companies to adopt discretionary employee benefits plans, which were excluded from those wage increase restrictions. Finally, as discussed in Chapter 3, the National Labor Relations Act of 1935 instituted retirement plans as a mandatory subject of bargaining between unions and management. This requirement further contributed substantially to the growth of retirement plans in the unionized private sector.

Trends in Retirement Plan Coverage and Costs

According to the U.S. Bureau of Labor Statistics, nearly 55 percent of workers employed in the private sector participated in at least one company-sponsored retirement plan in 1992–1993.[4] Since then, the participation rate has declined slightly, to approximately 49 percent in 2016.[5] However, there has been a noticeable decrease in participation rates for defined benefit plans, over the last 20 years. In 1992–1993, 32 percent of private-sector employees participated in defined benefit plans, and slightly more (35 percent) participated in defined contribution plans.[6] In 2016, only 15 percent participated in defined benefit plans, but there was an increase to 44 percent participation in defined contribution plans.[7]

These trends can be explained by a variety of factors. We focus on two important ones here: industry characteristics and union status. Exhibit 4.1 displays these statistics for all retirement plans, defined benefit plans, and defined contribution plans.

Industry Characteristics

We can observe differences in retirement plan participation between goods-producing industries and service-providing industries where most goods-producing industries offer higher pay and retirement plans. Automobile manufacturing and home building are examples of specific goods-producing industries. Food service and retail are examples of service-producing industries. Many goods-producing companies operate in product markets where there is relatively little competition from other companies, enabling them to offer generous retirement plans. Competition on product costs are lower, such as is the case for coal mining. This phenomenon can be attributed to factors such as higher barriers to enter into the product market. Government regulation and extremely expensive heavy or robotic equipment represent entry barriers. The U.S. defense industry and the public utilities industry have high entry barriers and virtually no threats from foreign competitors.

In addition, goods-producing businesses are typically capital intensive. Capital refers to buildings (e.g., factories, warehouses) and heavy equipment (e.g., hoists used to raise steel in the shipbuilding process). Capital-intensive businesses require highly capable employees who have the aptitude to learn how to use complex physical equipment such as casting machines and robotics. Workers usually receive on-the-job training, sometimes including employer-sponsored technical instruction. In addition, some employers may require specialized training or an advanced degree to qualify for those jobs.

Service industries such as retail and food service are not capital intensive, and most have the reputation of paying low wages and offering less generous benefits, including retirement plans. For example, there are a substantial number of fast-food companies that compete for market share and need to manage costs in order to protect profit margins. Also, the operation of service industries depends almost exclusively on employees who need only relatively common skills. Most retail sales workers receive on-the-job training, which usually lasts a few days to a few months.

Union Status

Union and management negotiations usually center on pay raises and employee benefits. There is greater power to negotiate terms of employment as a collective rather than individually, particularly for low-skilled jobs. We can observe higher pay and more generous retirement and health-care benefits. Union leaders also fought hard for these improvements to maintain the memberships' loyalty and support. Unions generally secured high wages for their members through the early 1980s, when competition from foreign companies offered quality products at similar or lower prices. Even still, unions have managed to maintain lucrative benefits, though more attention to costs has pressured some companies to freeze or terminate pension plans.

QUALIFIED VS. NONQUALIFIED PLANS

The Internal Revenue Code (IRC) and ERISA's Title I and Title II provisions set 13 minimum standards to determine whether retirement plans are qualified or

EXHIBIT 4.1
Characteristics
of Qualified
Retirement
Plans

- Participation requirements.
- Coverage requirements.
- Vesting rules.
- Accrual rules.
- Nondiscrimination rules: Testing.
- Top-heavy provisions.
- Minimum funding standards.
- Social Security integration.
- Contribution and benefit limits.
- Plan distribution rules.
- Qualified survivor annuities.
- Qualified domestic relations orders.
- Plan termination rules and procedures.

nonqualified. Exhibit 4.1 lists ERISA's minimum standards. Employers establish qualified plans when all of the ERISA minimum standards are met. Failure to meet at least one minimum standard results in a plan becoming disqualified. What is the main advantage of offering qualified plans? Qualified plans provide both employees and employers with immediate tax benefits. In most cases, monetary contributions to qualified plans reduce the amount of an employee's or company's annual earnings that are subject to taxation.

Companies establish qualified plans for nonexecutive employees. What about executives? Because most executives earn substantially more than other employees and relative to IRC contribution limits, for example, companies base executive retirement benefits on nonqualified deferred compensation plans (NQDC). We discuss NQDCs in Chapter 11 and the criteria that distinguish between executive and nonexecutive employees. In this chapter, reference is made from time to time to two employee groups, defined in the IRC, who we consider as meeting executive status: *key employees* and *highly compensated employees*.

Participation Requirements

As reviewed in Chapter 3, employees must be allowed to participate in employer-sponsored plans after they have reached age 21 and have completed one year of service (based on 1,000 work hours).[8]

Coverage Requirements

Coverage requirements limit the freedom of employers to exclude employees. Qualified plans do not disproportionately favor *highly compensated* employees.[9] Another important group is *key employees*. Again, as we discuss in Chapter 11 on executive benefits, these groups help distinguish between nonexecutive employees and executive employees. Also in Chapter 11, we provide a full definition of each group and the criteria for determining membership in each one.

Companies demonstrate whether plans meet the coverage requirement by maintaining a nondiscriminatory ratio of nonhighly compensated employees to highly compensated employees based on one of the following two tests:

- **Ratio percentage test.** Qualified plans cover a percentage of nonhighly compensated employees that is at least 70 percent of the percentage of highly compensated employees covered by the plan.

- **Average benefit test.** Qualified plans benefit a "nondiscriminatory classification" of employees and possess an "average benefit percentage" for nonhighly compensated employees that is, at a minimum, 70 percent of the average benefit percentage for highly compensated employees.[10]

U.S. Department of Treasury regulations impose an additional participation standard for defined benefit plans. These plans require coverage of at least 50 employees, or 40 percent of the workforce must benefit from the plan.[11]

Vesting Rules

Vesting refers to an employee's nonforfeitable rights to retirement benefits.[12] In defined benefit employees vest in a specific annual amount, as defined under the terms of the plan, each year after retirement. In defined contribution plans, employees vest in *net* employer contributions. Net employer contributions equal gross employer contributions plus investment gains or minus investment losses. Title I of ERISA requires that companies follow an allowed schedule for vesting rights: cliff vesting or six-year graduated vesting.

Cliff vesting schedules must grant employees 100 percent vesting after no more than three years from beginning participation in the retirement plan. This schedule is known as cliff vesting because leaving one's job prior to becoming vested is tantamount to falling off a cliff—an employee loses all the accrued employer contributions. Alternatively, companies may use a gradualted vesting schedule. The **six-year graduated schedule** allows workers to become 20 percent vested after two years and to vest at a rate of 20 percent each year thereafter until they are 100 percent vested after six years from beginning participation in the retirement plan. Exhibit 4.2 shows an example of the six-year graduated schedule. For example, let's assume that an employer has adopted the six-year graduated vesting schedule. Also assume that this employer has contributed $15,000 to an employee's retirement account since he began his employment two years ago. According to the gradualted vesting schedule, this employee has earned a 20 percent nonforfeitable right to the employer's contribution—that is, $3,000 = (20 percent × $15,000). Plans may have faster vesting

	Years of Vesting Service	Nonforfeitable Percentage
EXHIBIT 4.2 Sample of a Six-Year Graduated Vesting Schedule under ERISA	2	20%
	3	40%
	4	60%
	5	80%
	6	100%

schedules, which reach 100 percent vesting in fewer than six years. The graduated schedule is preferable to employees who anticipate changing jobs frequently because they will earn the rights to keep part of the employer's contribution sooner. Moreover, employees recognize that layoffs are more common in today's volatile business environment, and they stand to benefit by earning partial vesting rights sooner than earning full vesting rights at a later date. On the other hand, employers prefer the cliff vesting schedule. The use of this schedule allows employers to reclaim non-vested contributions for employees who leave before becoming vested.

Accrual Rules

Qualified plans are subject to minimum accrual rules based on the Internal Revenue Code (IRC) and ERISA.[13] **Accrual rules** specify the rate at which participants accumulate (or earn) benefits. Defined benefit and defined contribution plans use different accrual rules, which are discussed in subsequent sections of this chapter.

Nondiscrimination Rules: Testing

Nondiscrimination rules prohibit employers from favoring highly compensated employees in making contributions or benefits, availability of benefits, rights, or plan features.[14] Also, employers may not amend retirement plans so that highly compensated employees are favored.

The nondiscrimination requirement may be fulfilled in one of two ways: safe harbors or a facts-and-circumstances testing. *Safe harbors* refer to compliance guidelines in a law or regulation. Retirement plans that meet safe harbor conditions automatically fulfill the nondiscrimination requirement based on particular design features. Failure to reach safe harbors requires passing at least one of two facts-and-circumstances tests (not discussed in this book). It is important to note that the safe harbors and facts-and-circumstances tests differ between defined benefit and defined contribution plans. Safe harbors are reviewed in this chapter.

Top-Heavy Provisions

A **top-heavy** plan[15] provides non-key employees with a minimum benefit if it is a defined benefit plan or a minimum contribution if it is a defined contribution plan:

- A defined benefit plan is top-heavy if the present value of the accrued benefits (PVAB)* under the plan for the key employees exceeds 60 percent of the PVAB under the plan for all employees.
- A defined contribution plan is top-heavy if the total of the accounts of the key employees under the plan exceeds 60 percent of the total of the accounts of all employees under the plan.
- A top-heavy plan must also provide a special vesting schedule:
  - 3-year 100% vesting schedule, or
  - 6-year graduated vesting schedule.

*Present value is the value today of an amount of money in the future. The accrued benefit is the amount that a participant has earned under the plan's terms at a specified time.

Minimum Funding Standards

Minimum funding standards ensure that employers contribute the minimum amount of money necessary to provide promised benefits. As we will see, the standards differ between defined benefit and defined contribution plans.

Social Security Integration

Social Security integration, also known as **permitted disparity rules**, allows employers to explicitly take into account Social Security retirement benefits when determining company-sponsored benefits under a defined benefit plan.[16] Subject to established limits, qualified plans may reduce company-sponsored benefits based on benefits amounts owed under the Social Security program.

Contribution and Benefit Limits

Benefit limits refer to the maximum annual amount an employee may receive from a qualified defined benefit plan during retirement. Contribution limits apply to defined contribution plans. The Economic Growth and Tax Relief Reconciliation Act of 2001 specified annual contribution limits, which are increased from time to time based on inflation rates. The goal is to keep retirement savings from falling behind increases in the cost of goods and services, thereby making retirees less dependent on Social Security retirement benefits (Chapter 7). This act also set limits on annual earnings on which annual retirement pay from defined benefit plans may be calculated, and it specified the maximum annual amount paid from a defined benefit plan. These limits are reviewed in our discussion of defined benefit and defined contribution plans.

Plan Distribution Rules

Distribution refers to the payment of vested benefits to participants or beneficiaries. One of three events triggers a distribution:[17]

- Participant's termination of service with the employer.
- The 10th anniversary of the year the participant commenced participation in the plan.
- The participant's attainment of the earlier of age 65 or the normal retirement age.*

There are three allowable distribution methods. First, **lump sum distributions** are single payments of benefits. In defined contribution plans, lump sum distributions equal the vested amount (the sum of all employee and vested employer contributions, and investment growth, if any, of such sums). In some defined benefit plans, lump sum distributions equal the equivalent of the vested accrued benefit.

Second, **annuities** represent a series of payments for the life of the participant and beneficiary. Annuity contracts are usually purchased from insurance companies, which make payments following the contract terms. Because participants bear the risk of possible investment loss, many purchase annuities to hedge against those losses.

*The *normal retirement age* is the lowest age specified in an employer-sponsored plan. Upon attaining this age, an employee is eligible to take retirement benefits without monetary penalty.

The third form is based on a series of payments paid from a trust fund. In a defined contribution plan, the payments are made over a specified period, not to exceed the life expectancy of the participant or beneficiary.

Qualified Survivor Annuities

Qualified plans provide spouses with a **qualified joint and survivor annuity (QJSA)** or a **qualified preretirement survivor annuity (QPSA).**[18]

A QJSA is a lifetime annuity for the participant and an annuity for the surviving spouse. A qualified preretirement survivor annuity (QPSA) provides a lifetime annuity for the surviving spouse if the participant dies before receiving any retirement benefits. QPSA amounts must be no less than the QJSA amounts. Participants may waive those benefits only after receiving spousal consent.

Qualified Domestic Relations Orders

Qualified plans recognize **qualified domestic relations orders (QDROs).** Domestic courts may issue QDROs that permit a retirement plan to divide a participant's benefits in the event of divorce. Dividing a participant's benefits without a QDRO is a violation of ERISA and the IRC.[19] Without a QDRO, divorced spouses would be ineligible to receive retirement benefits.[20]

Plan Termination Rules and Procedures

Plan termination rules protect employees who participated in either a defined benefit or defined contribution plan that was terminated. According to the U.S. Department of Labor, when a plan is terminated, employees must become 100 percent vested in all benefits amounts. That means that employees would immediately become vested in all amounts regardless of whether vesting requirements were met. Relatively speaking, the procedures for terminating a defined contribution plan are more straightforward than is the case for defined benefit plans. ERISA specifies three permissible types of defined benefit plan termination. We discuss these in the next section.

Having reviewed ERISA qualification criteria, we now move to discuss three types of employer-sponsored plans: defined benefit plans, defined contribution plans, and hybrid plans. Reference to ERISA minimum qualification standards are made as appropriate.

DEFINED BENEFIT PLANS

Defined benefit plans guarantee retirement benefits specified in the plan document. This benefit is defined as an annual sum equal to a percentage of preretirement pay multiplied by years of service. The annual amount is disbursed in equal monthly payments or annuity, usually until the retiree's death. While the benefit in these plans is fixed by a formula, the level of required employer contributions fluctuates from year to year based on two considerations: investment performance and life expectancy. Lower-than-expected investment performance often requires higher future contributions to compensate for the difference. As life expectancy increases, it is not surprising that larger contributions are necessary.

Benefit Formulas

Companies usually choose between two types of formulas for defining benefits: flat benefit formulas and unit benefit formulas. The key factor distinguishing these formulas is whether employees' years of service are considered. Years of service are a factor in unit benefit formulas, but not in flat benefit formulas. The IRC recognizes both formulas as appropriate calculation methods in employer-sponsored plans.

Flat Benefit Formulas

Flat benefit formulas designate a flat dollar amount per employee (*flat amount formula*) or a dollar amount based on an employee's compensation (*flat percentage formula*). Annual benefits are usually expressed as a percentage of final average wage or salary based on the last three or four years of service. Let's assume that in 2017, when Robert plans to retire, his final average salary in the three-year period preceding retirement was $100,000 (based on $99,000, $100,000, and $101,000). Also assume that the plan's designated percentage is 60 percent. Robert's annual retirement income equals $60,000; that is, $100,000 average annual income × 60 percent.

Flat benefit formulas often lead to resentment among employees because length of service is not a consideration. Longer-service employees expect to receive a higher percentage of final average salary during retirement than do employees who retire with substantially less service. There are two possible explanations for these expectations. First, longer-service employees believe they have earned the right to receive a higher percentage, arguing that more years enabled higher productivity than did employees with substantially fewer years. Second, longer-service employees feel that the company owes them a larger percentage in recognition of loyalty and commitment to the company over a longer period.

Unit Benefit Formulas

Unlike flat benefit formulas, **unit benefit formulas** recognize length of service. Typically, employers decide to contribute a specified dollar amount or percentage for each service year worked. Annual benefits are usually based on age, years of service, and final average wages or salary. Retirement plans based on unit benefit formulas specify annual retirement benefits as a percentage of final average salary. Exhibit 4.3 illustrates these percentages for one retirement plan based on age and years of service. Looking at this exhibit, let's assume that Mary retires at age 59, with 25 years of service and a final average salary of $52,500. Mary multiplies $52,500 by the annual percentage of 43.43 percent. Her annual benefit is thus $22,800.75, that is, ($52,500 × 43.43%).

Nondiscrimination Rules: Testing

Defined benefit plans must meet several uniformity criteria, as well as one additional safe harbor criterion, based on the particular characteristics of the plan. *Uniformity* refers to consistent treatment based on factors such as a benefits formula. Exhibit 4.4 describes the uniformity requirements issued by the U.S. Treasury Department. Failure to satisfy safe harbor criteria requires facts-and-circumstances testing for nondiscrimination.

EXHIBIT 4.3
Annual
Retirement
Benefits Based
on a Unit
Benefit
Formula

Years of Service	Age						
	62	**60+**	**59**	**58**	**57**	**56**	**55**
5	8.35						
6	10.02						
7	11.69						
8	—	13.36	12.56	11.76	10.96	10.15	9.35
9	—	15.03	14.13	13.23	12.32	11.42	10.52
10	—	16.70	15.70	14.70	13.69	12.69	11.69
11	—	18.60	17.48	16.37	15.25	14.14	13.02
12	—	20.50	19.27	18.04	16.81	15.58	14.35
13	—	22.40	21.06	19.71	18.37	17.02	15.68
14	—	24.30	22.84	21.38	19.93	18.47	17.01
15	—	26.20	24.63	23.06	21.48	19.91	18.34
16	—	28.10	26.41	24.73	23.04	21.36	19.67
17	—	30.00	28.20	26.40	24.60	22.80	21.00
18	—	31.90	29.99	28.07	26.16	24.24	22.33
19	—	33.80	31.77	29.74	27.72	25.69	23.66
20	—	35.70	33.56	31.42	29.27	27.13	24.99
21	—	37.80	35.53	33.26	31.00	28.73	26.46
22	—	39.90	37.51	35.11	32.72	30.32	27.93
23	—	42.00	39.48	36.96	34.44	31.93	29.40
24	—	44.10	41.45	38.81	36.16	33.52	30.87
25	—	46.20	43.43	40.66	37.88	35.11	32.34
26	—	48.30	45.40	42.50	39.61	36.71	33.81
27	—	50.40	47.38	44.35	41.33	38.30	35.28
28	—	52.50	49.35	46.20	43.05	39.90	36.75
29	—	54.60	51.32	48.05	44.77	41.50	38.22
30	—	56.70	53.30	49.90	46.49	43.09	39.69
31	—	59.00	55.46	51.92	48.38	44.84	41.30
32	—	61.30	57.62	53.94	50.27	46.59	42.91
33	—	63.60	59.78	55.97	52.15	48.34	44.52
34	—	65.90	61.95	57.99	54.04	40.08	46.13
35	—	68.20	68.20	68.20	68.20	68.20	68.20
36	—	70.50	70.50	70.50	70.50	70.50	70.50
37	—	72.80	72.80	72.80	72.80	72.80	72.80
38	—	75.10	75.00	75.00	75.00	75.00	75.00
39	—	77.40	75.00	75.00	75.00	75.00	75.00
40	—	79.70	75.00	75.00	75.00	75.00	75.00
41+	—	80.00	75.00	75.00	75.00	75.00	75.00

EXHIBIT 4.4 **Uniformity Requirements for Defined Benefit Plans**

Source: Treas. Regs. §1.401(a)(4)-3(b)(2).

A defined benefit plan must be "uniform" to meet the safe harbor requirements:

Uniform Normal Retirement Benefit

The same benefit formula must apply to all employees in the plan. The formula must provide all employees with an annual benefit payable in the same form, commencing at the same uniform normal retirement age. The annual benefit must be the same percentage of average annual compensation or the same dollar amount for all employees in the plan who will have the same number of years of service at normal retirement age. The annual benefit must equal the employee's accrued benefit at normal retirement age and must be the normal retirement benefit under the plan.

Uniform Postnormal Retirement Benefits

With respect to an employee with a given number of years of service at any age after normal retirement age, the annual benefit commencing at the employee's age must be the same percentage of average annual compensation or the same dollar amount that would be payable commencing at normal retirement age to an employee who had that same number of years of service at normal retirement age.

Uniform Subsidies

Each subsidized optional form of benefit under the plan must be available to essentially all employees in the plan. In determining whether a subsidized optional form of benefit is available, the same criteria apply that are used for determining whether an optional form of benefit is currently available to a group of employees in the plan. An optional form of benefit is considered subsidized if the normalized optional form of benefit is larger than the normalized normal retirement benefit under the plan.

Uniform Vesting and Service Crediting

All employees in the plan must be subject to the same vesting schedule and the same definition of years of service for all purposes under the plan. For the purposes of crediting service, only service with the employer (or a predecessor employer) may be taken into account.

No Employee Contributions

The plan is not a contributory defined benefit plan. Special rules apply to contributory defined benefit plans.

Period of Accrual

Each employee's benefit must be accrued over the same years of service that are taken into account in applying the benefit formula under the plan to that employee. Any year in which the employee benefits under the plan is included as a year of service in which a benefit accrues.

Accrual Rules

Accumulated benefit obligation refers to the present value of benefits based on a designated date. Actuaries determine a defined benefit plan's accumulated benefit obligation by making assumptions about the return on investment of assets and characteristics of the participants and their beneficiaries, including expected length of service and life expectancies.

The IRS specifies criteria to judge whether an employer's defined benefit plan meets its accumulated benefit obligation. These criteria discourage employers from engaging in a practice known as backloading. **Backloading** occurs whenever benefits accrue at a substantially higher rate closer to an employee's eligibility to earn retirement benefits. Fulfillment of at least one of these criteria ensures that benefits accrue regularly throughout participation in a defined benefit plan: the three percent rule, the 133⅓ percent rule, or the fractional rule.

The Three Percent Rule

Under the **three percent rule**, a participant's accrued benefit cannot be less than 3 percent of the normal retirement benefit, assuming the participant began participation at the earliest possible age and remained employed without interruption until age 65 or until the plan's designated normal retirement age. For instance, Margaret recently retired at age 62 from Company A. She joined the company 41 years earlier at age 21 and immediately began participation in the defined benefit plan. Company A's defined benefit plan awards an annual benefit equal to 70 percent of the four-year average highest salary. Margaret's four-year average annual salary was $50,000, yielding an annual retirement benefit of $35,000; that is, ($50,000 × 70 percent). Under the three percent rule, Margaret's accrued benefit must be no less than $1,050 ($35,000 × 3%).

The 133⅓ Percent Rule

Under the **133⅓ percent rule**, the annual accrual rate cannot exceed 133⅓ percent of the accrual rate for any prior year. For example, a company's retirement plan specifies the following annual accrual rates: 1.5 percent of compensation for each year of service up to 20, and 1.75 percent of compensation for each year of service in excess of 20. This plan satisfies the 133⅓ percent rule because the 1.75 percent annual accrual rate is less than 133⅓ percent of the prior annual 1.5 percent accrual rate: 116 percent; that is, [(1.75% / 1.5%) x 100%].

The Fractional Rule

The **fractional rule** applies to participants who terminate their employment prior to reaching normal retirement age. This rule stipulates that benefit accrual upon termination be proportional to the normal retirement benefits. Said another way, this method compares an employee's plan participation to the total years of participation upon reaching the normal retirement age. For example, let's assume that the annual annuity at the normal retirement age is $20,000. Let's also assume that service years at the normal retirement age would have been 30 years, but terminated her employment at 20 service years. Based on the fractional rule, the annual annuity is $13,333; that is, [$20,000 × (20 years/30 years)]. Paying an annual benefit equaling less than $13,333 would violate the fractional rule.

Top-Heavy Provisions

Each non-key employee must receive an accrued benefit of a designated percentage multiplied by the employee's average compensation. The percentage is the lesser of 2 percent times the participant's number of years of service with the employer, or 20 percent. For instance, an employee with four years of service and an average annual compensation of $75,000 would be entitled to a minimum benefit of $6,000; (that is, 4 years × 0.02% × $75,000).

Minimum Funding Standards

ERISA imposes strict funding requirements on qualified plans. Under defined benefit plans, employers make an annual contribution that is sufficiently large to ensure that promised benefits will be available to retirees. Actuaries periodically review several kinds of information to determine a sufficient funding level: life expectancies of employees and their designated beneficiaries, projected compensation levels, and the likelihood of employees terminating their employment before they have earned benefits. ERISA imposes reporting of actuarial information to the Internal Revenue Service (IRS), which, in turn, submits these data to the U.S. Department of Labor. The Department of Labor reviews the data to ensure compliance with ERISA regulations.

Benefit Limits

The IRC sets a maximum annual benefit for defined benefit plans that is equal to the lesser of $215,000 in 2017, or 100 percent of the highest average compensation for three consecutive years.[21] The annual earnings limit on which the annual retirement benefit may be calculated was $265,000 in 2016. These limits are indexed for inflation in $5,000 increments.[22]

Plan Termination Rules and Procedures

The PBGC's program recognizes three types of plan terminations: distress terminations, involuntary terminations, and standard terminations. Exhibit 4.5 contains a description of these termination types and the PBGC-mandated procedures for conducting them.

EXHIBIT 4.5   Types of Pension Plan Termination

Source: Pension Benefit Guarantee Corporation, Termination Fact Sheet. Accessed April 12, 2016, http://pbgc.gov/about/factsheets/page/termination.html.

The (PBGC) recognizes three types of plan termination, with specific requirements for the termination process.

Distress Termination

A company in financial distress may voluntarily terminate a pension plan if:

- The plan administrator has issued a Notice of Intent to Terminate to affected parties, including the PBGC, at least 60 days, and no more than 90 days, in advance of the proposed termination date.
- The plan administrator has issued a subsequent termination notice to PBGC, which includes data concerning the number of participants and the plan's assets and liabilities.
- The PBGC has determined that the plan sponsor and each of its corporate affiliates have satisfied at least one of the following financial distress tests—though not necessarily the same test:
  - A petition has been filed seeking liquidation in bankruptcy;
  - A petition has been filed seeking reorganization in bankruptcy, and the bankruptcy court (or an appropriate state court) has determined that the company will not be able to reorganize with the plan intact and approves the plan termination;
  - It has been demonstrated that the sponsor or affiliate cannot continue in business unless the plan is terminated; or
  - It has been demonstrated that the costs of providing pension coverage have become unreasonably burdensome solely as a result of a decline in the number of employees covered by the plan.

EXHIBIT 4.5 *(Continued)*

Involuntary Termination

The law provides that the PBGC may terminate a pension plan, even if a company has not filed to terminate a plan on its own initiative, if:
- The plan has not met the minimum funding requirements.
- The plan cannot pay current benefits when due.
- A lump-sum payment has been made to a participant who is a substantial owner of the sponsoring company.
- The loss to the PBGC is expected to increase unreasonably if the plan is not terminated.

The PBGC must terminate a plan if assets are unavailable to pay benefits currently due.

Standard Termination

A plan may terminate only if plan assets are sufficient to satisfy all plan benefits and if the plan administrator has taken the following steps:
- Issued a Notice of Intent to Terminate to affected parties other than the PBGC at least 60 days, and no more than 90 days, before the proposed termination date; it also must inform plan participants that the PBGC's guarantee of their benefits will cease upon distribution of plan assets.
- Informed plan participants of the identity of the private insurer from whom an annuity is being purchased or the names of insurers from whom bids will be sought no later than 45 days before the distribution of plan assets.
- Sent each plan participant a notice that includes the benefits that the participant has earned and data the plan used to calculate the value of the benefits.
- Submitted a termination notice to the PBGC that includes certified data on the plan's assets and liabilities as of the proposed date of distribution.
- Distributed plan assets to cover all benefit liabilities under the plan.

Plans must provide the PBGC with the names of any missing participants and either money to pay their benefits or the names of the insurers holding their annuities. Before sending money to the PBGC, the plan administrator must conduct a diligent search that includes using a commercial locator service.

If assets cannot cover all benefit liabilities, the plan administrator must notify the PBGC and stop the termination process. If the plan administrator does not follow proper procedures, the PBGC may issue a Notice of Noncompliance that nullifies the proposed termination.

Annuity insurer selections are fiduciary decisions and must comply with fiduciary provisions of Title I of ERISA, which is enforced by the Department of Labor.

Termination insurance protects against the loss of vested pension benefits when plans fail. Employers are assessed charges by the PBGC to cover possible plan terminations. Insurance premiums are set by Congress for employers according to the number of covered employees and to whether a pension plan covers employees of just one company (single-employer plans) or a collective bargaining agreement maintains a pension plan to which more than one employer contributes (multiemployer plans).

In addition, the PBGC ensures a basic level of annual benefits to participants in the event that a plan terminates with insufficient assets to pay its obligations. The maximum PBGC-guaranteed annual benefit is adjusted every year.[23] For plans ended in 2016, the maximum annual benefit was approximately $60,000 for those who retire at age 65. The amount is higher for those who retire later and lower for those who retire earlier or elect survivor benefits. The maximum benefit amount is lower for benefits commencing at ages below 65, because younger retirees receive more monthly pension checks over a longer remaining lifespan. Following this logic, the maximum amount is higher for benefits commencing at ages above 65.

Similarly, pension benefit amounts are lower with survivor benefits because the payout will probably extend for a longer period than if benefits terminated upon the participant's death.

DEFINED CONTRIBUTION PLANS

Under **defined contribution plans**, companies set up an account for each employee who chooses to participate. Employees enter into a salary reduction agreement. **Salary reduction agreements** permit an employer to defer a specified amount of pay, often expressed as a percentage of pay, into the employee's account each pay period. The employer may have a matching contribution policy. Employers invest these funds on behalf of the employee, choosing from a variety of investment options such as company stock, diversified stock market funds, or federal government bond funds. Employees may be given a choice of investment options. What is the main difference between defined benefit plans and defined contribution plans?

Defined contribution plans specify rules for the amount of annual contributions, while defined benefit plans specify the annual retirement benefit. Unlike defined benefit plans, these plans do not guarantee particular benefit amounts. Participants bear the risk of possible investment gain or loss. Benefit amounts depend upon several factors, including the contribution amounts, the performance of investments, and forfeitures transferred to participant accounts. **Forfeitures** come from the accounts of employees who terminated their employment prior to earning vesting rights. Companies may choose to offer one or more specific types of defined contribution plans, which we review later in the chapter.

Individual Accounts

Defined contribution plans contain accounts for each employee into which contributions are made, investment losses are debited, and gains are credited. There are three possible contribution sources. First, employee contributions are usually expressed as a percentage of the employee's wage or salary. The second source is employer contributions. In most cases, employers may make contributions to individual accounts contingent on the employee making contributions first. Under these circumstances, employer contributions are referred to as **matching contributions**. Matching contributions are most often expressed as a percentage of the employee's annual compensation, and they may choose to make a full or partial match. Let's look at two examples based on an employee who plans to contribute $6,000, which equals 6 percent of her $100,000 annual salary:

Full match: The company makes a $6,000 matching contribution; the total amount contributed to this employee's individual account is $12,000.

Partial match: The company's policy is to match 50 percent of the employee's contribution. In this case, the company contributes $3,000; the total amount contributed to the individual account is $9,000.

Third, forfeitures come from the unvested employer contribution amounts (and investment gains, if any) of former employees' accounts.

Investment of Contributions

ERISA requires that a **fiduciary** be named. According to the U.S. Department of Labor, fiduciaries have important responsibilities and are subject to standards of conduct because they act on behalf of participants in a retirement plan and their beneficiaries. These responsibilities include:

- Acting solely in the interest of plan participants and their beneficiaries and with the exclusive purpose of providing benefits to them.
- Carrying out their duties prudently.
- Following the plan documents (unless inconsistent with ERISA).
- Diversifying plan investments.
- Paying only reasonable plan expenses.

The duty to act prudently is one of a fiduciary's central responsibilities under ERISA. It requires expertise in a variety of areas, such as investments. Lacking that expertise, a fiduciary will want to hire someone with professional knowledge to carry out the investment and other functions. Prudence focuses on the *process* for making fiduciary decisions. Therefore, it is wise to document decisions and the basis for those decisions.[24]

Employee Participation in Investments

Some companies may allow plan participants to make choices about the investment of funds in their individual accounts. Subject to certain conditions described in Exhibit 4.6, employee participation does not constitute fiduciary responsibility. It is important to note that fiduciaries cannot be held liable for the investment choices of employees.

EXHIBIT 4.6 Conditions Relieving Fiduciary of Responsibility with Employee Participation in Investments

Source: I.R.C. §404(c).

- Participants have the opportunity to choose from at least three diversified investment alternatives. Each investment has different degrees of risk.
- Participants have the opportunity to change their investment allocations at least once each three months. If market volatility is high, this opportunity must be made available more frequently.
- Participants must be given sufficient information to make informed investment decisions.

Nondiscrimination Rules: Testing

Defined contribution plans must meet one of two safe harbor conditions: a uniform allocation formula, or a uniform points allocation formula in the case of profit-sharing plans.[25] Defined contribution plans satisfy the nondiscrimination rules when they offer a uniform allocation formula to each employee based on a percentage of compensation, the dollar amount of allocation, or the same dollar amount for each uniform unit of service. Failure to satisfy safe harbor criteria requires facts-and-circumstances testing for nondiscrimination.

Accrual Rules

The accrued benefit equals the balance in an individual's account.[26] Companies may not reduce contribution amounts based on age. Also, they may not set maximum age limits for discontinuing contributions.

Top-Heavy Provisions

Companies must make minimum contributions to non-key–employee accounts equal to the lesser of 3 percent of annual compensation or the highest contribution credited to key-employee accounts.

Minimum Funding Standard

The minimum funding standard for defined contribution plans is less complex than for defined benefit plans. This standard is met when contributions to the individual accounts reach the minimum amounts as specified by the plan.[27]

Contribution Limits

An **annual addition** refers to the annual maximum allowable contribution to a participant's account in a defined contribution plan. The annual addition includes employer contributions, employee contributions, and forfeitures allocated to the participant's account.[28] In 2017, annual additions were limited to the lesser of $54,000 or 100 percent of the participant's compensation.[29]

The amount of an employer's annual deductible contribution to a participant's account depends on the type of defined contribution plan.[30] The Economic Growth and Tax Reconciliation Act of 2001 raised the allowable contribution amounts in effect before January 1, 2002. In 2017, the maximum contribution to a profit-sharing plan was the lesser of 25% of compensation or $54,000. Section 401(k), 403(b), and 457 plans had contribution limits of $18,000 in 2017. The limit is indexed for inflation in $500 increments.

TYPES OF DEFINED CONTRIBUTION PLANS

Defined contribution refers to a broad classification of different retirement plans that specify who is eligible to make contributions and the formula for making contributions. Beyond that are particular defined contribution practices, the choice of which depends partly on the type of organization. We review the following defined contribution plans:

- 401(k) plans
- Roth 401(k) plans
- profit-sharing plans
- stock bonus plans
- employee stock ownership plans
- savings incentive match plans for employees (SIMPLEs)
- 403(b) tax-deferred annuities
- 457 plans

401(k) Plans

401(k) plans are named after the section of the Internal Revenue Code that created them. These plans, also known as cash or deferred arrangements (CODAs), permit employees to defer part of their compensation to an individual account set up in the qualified defined contribution plan. Only private-sector or tax-exempt employers are eligible to sponsor 401(k) plans.

Section 401(k) plans offer three noteworthy tax benefits. First, employees do not pay income taxes on their contributions to the plan until they withdraw funds. Second, employers deduct their contributions to the plan from taxable income. Third, any investment gains are not taxed until participants receive payments.

Roth 401(k) Plans

The IRC established Roth 401(k) plans in 2006. These plans differ from 401(k) plans in two ways. First, an employee pays income tax on their contributions. Second, upon retirement, employee withdrawals are not taxed. Roth 401(k) plans are becoming an increasingly popular offering to help employees manage the uncertainty of possible changes in future income tax rates. For example, it is not possible to know years in advance what income tax rates will be when an individual retires. The rates could be equal to, lower than, or greater than current income tax rates. Higher future income tax rates would require non-Roth 401(k) participants to withdraw larger amounts to meet retirees' needs. Higher withdrawal rates would lower the value of a 401(k) plan more quickly, as well as reduce the number of years in which it will provide income.

Profit-Sharing Plans

Companies set up **profit-sharing plans** to distribute a portion of profits to employees. Companies start by establishing a **profit-sharing pool**—that is, the money earmarked for distribution. Maximum annual contributions are limited to the lesser of 25 percent of employee compensation or the annual addition limit, $54,000 in 2017.[31]

Employer Contributions

Companies determine the pool of profit-sharing money by application of a formula every year or based on the discretion of their boards of directors. One of three common formulas establishes employer contributions. A **fixed first-dollar-of-profits formula** uses a specific percentage of either pretax or after-tax annual profits (alternatively, gross sales or some other basis), contingent upon the successful attainment of a company goal. For instance, a company might establish that the profit-sharing fund will equal 1 percent of corporate profits. Second, a **graduated first-dollar-of-profits formula** uses a different percentage based on level of attained profits. For example, a company may choose to share 2 percent of the first $10 million of profits and 3 percent of the profits in excess of that level. Third, **profitability threshold formulas** fund profit-sharing pools only if profits exceed a predetermined minimum level but have a maximum payout level. Companies establish minimums to guarantee a return to shareholders before they distribute profits to employees and maximums because they attribute any profits beyond this level to factors other than employee productivity or creativity, such as technological innovation. For instance, a company may choose to share the increment of profits between 2 and 4 percent. There would be no payout below 2 percent or above 4 percent of profits.

Allocation Formulas

After company management selects a funding formula, it must consider how to distribute pool money among employees. Under a qualified defined contribution plan, the chosen allocation formula must not discriminate in favor of highly compensated employees. Usually, companies make distributions in one of three ways: equal payments to all employees, proportional payments to employees based on annual salary, or proportional payments to employees based on their contribution to profits. **Equal payments** to all employees reflects a belief that all employees should share equally in the company's gains to promote cooperation among employees. However, employee contributions to profits probably vary. Accordingly, most employers divide the profit-sharing pool among employees on a differential basis. Companies may disburse profits based on **proportional payments to employees based on their annual salary**. Presumably, higher-paying jobs indicate the greatest potential to influence a company's competitive position. Still another approach is to disburse profits as **proportional payments to employees based on their contribution to profits**. Some companies measure employee contributions to profits based on job performance. However, this approach is often not feasible because it is difficult to directly isolate each employee's contributions to profits.

Stock Bonus Plans

A **stock bonus plan** is a kind of profit-sharing plan paid in employer stock instead of cash. Participants of stock bonus plans possess the right to vote as shareholders. Voting rights differ based on whether company stock is traded in public stock exchanges.[32] In the case of publicly traded stock, plan participants may vote on all issues.

Employee Stock Option Plans (ESOPs)

Employee stock option plans (ESOPs) provide shares of company stock to employees. These plans may be thought of as essentially stock bonus plans that use borrowed funds to purchase stock. ESOPs are either nonleveraged or leveraged plans.[33] In the case of **nonleveraged ESOPs**, the company contributes stock or cash to buy stock. The stock is then allocated to the accounts of participants. Nonleveraged plans are stock bonus plans. In the case of **leveraged ESOPs**, the plan administrator borrows money from a financial institution to purchase company stock. Over time, the company makes principal and interest payments to the ESOP to repay the loan.

Savings Incentive Match Plans for Employees (SIMPLEs)

Congress enacted a law in 1996 that established **savings incentive match plans for employees (SIMPLEs)** working in small companies.[34]

Small companies that meet the following criteria are eligible to establish a SIMPLE plan:

- The company employs 100 or fewer people.
- Each employee's previous year earnings was at least $5,000.
- The company does not maintain another retirement plan.

Companies may establish SIMPLEs as either individual retirement accounts (IRAs) or as 401(k) plans. We briefly consider the SIMPLE 401(k) plan. Employees, employers, or both may make contributions. The employee contribution limit is lower than in regular 401(k) plans. In 2017, employees may contribute up the lesser of 100 percent of compensation or $12,500. Employers may choose to make a regular contribution of 2 percent of annual compensation or a matching contribution. Matching contributions cannot exceed more than 3 percent of annual compensation.

403(b) Tax-Deferred Annuity Plans

Section 403(b) of the IRC established **tax-deferred annuity (TDA)** plans. A TDA is available to a broad range of nonprofit organizations such as churches, private and public schools and colleges, hospitals, and charitable organizations (e.g., the American Red Cross). As with 401(k) plans, contributions come mainly from employers or employees. Employees make contributions through salary reduction agreements with their employers. TDAs, or 403(b) plans, are subject to the same contribution limits as 401(k) plans. TDAs may supplement other employer-sponsored retirement programs, usually defined benefit plans. Private tax-exempt organizations may offer both 401(k) and 403(b) plans, but public organizations are prohibited from offering 401(k) plans.

Not every 403(b) plan is subject to the ERISA minimum standards. Recall that ERISA applies to private-sector organizations; 403(b) plans sponsored by private-sector tax-exempt companies are subject to ERISA requirements. Others are exempt: these include governmental plans (e.g., public university or a state or municipal employer) and church plans. (It is worth noting that private tax-exempt organizations may be exempted from ERISA minimum standards if a variety of U.S. Department of Labor exemptions are met.)

457 Plans

Section 457 plans are nonqualified retirement plans typically for local or state government employees. Until 2002, Section 457 plans were less generous than either 401(k) or 403(b) plans, because maximum annual contributions were substantially lower. Since then, Section 457 plans have the same limits as 401(k) or 403(b) plans. However, unlike 401(k) and 403(b) plans, only employees may contribute to Section 457 plans.

We reviewed both defined benefit and defined contribution plans and the many features of both. We also reviewed several types of defined contribution plans. Exhibit 4.7 summarizes selected differences between defined benefit and defined contribution plans.

HYBRID PLANS

Hybrid plans combine features of traditional defined benefit and defined contribution plans. The following four common hybrid plans will be discussed in turn: (1) cash balance plans and pension equity plans, (2) target benefit plans, (3) money purchase plans, and (4) age-weighted profit-sharing plans.

Many employers have set aside traditional defined benefit plans for hybrid plans. Numerous accounts describe defined benefit plans as **"golden handcuffs"** because they provide generous (golden) retirement income to workers who remain with the same employer (the handcuffs) throughout their work lives. The different career plans of the younger generations have led many employers to conclude that their retirement plans were not beneficial to these younger, more mobile workers. This traditional approach was not conducive to attracting potentially valuable employees that could help increase efficiency.[35]

Cash Balance Plans and Pension Equity Plans

IRS guidelines define **cash balance plans** as "defined benefit plans that define benefits for each employee by reference to the amount of the employee's hypothetical account balance."[36] **Pension equity plans** are similar to cash balance plans, except, as described below, for how benefits are calculated. Both types of plans are relatively new phenomena compared to traditional defined benefit and defined contribution plans. Exhibit 4.8 contrasts cash balance plans and pension equity plans.

Many companies have chosen to convert their traditional defined benefit plans to cash balance or pension equity plans because these plans usually cost less.

EXHIBIT 4.7 **Characteristics of Defined Benefit and Defined Contribution Plans**

Source: U.S. Department of Labor. *What You Should Know About Your Retirement Plan.* 2006. Accessed April 10, 2016, www.dol.gov/ebsa.

	Defined Benefit Plan	Defined Contribution Plan
Employer Contributions and/or Matching Contributions	Employer funded. Federal rules set amounts that employers must contribute to plans in an effort to ensure that plans have enough money to pay benefits when due. There are penalties for failing to meet these requirements.	There is no requirement that the employer contribute, except in the SIMPLE 401(k) and Safe Harbor 401(k), money purchase plans, and SIMPLE IRA and SEP plans. The employer may choose to match a portion of the employee's contributions or to contribute without employee contributions. In some plans, employer contributions may be in the form of employer stock.
Employee Contributions	Generally, employees do not contribute to these plans.	Many plans require the employee to contribute for an account to be established.
Managing the Investment	Plan officials manage the investment, and the employer is responsible for ensuring that the amount it has put in the plan plus investment earnings will be enough to pay the promised benefit.	The employee often is responsible for managing the investment of his or her account, choosing from investment options offered by the plan. In some plans, plan officials are responsible for investing all the plan's assets.
Amount of Benefits Paid upon Retirement	A promised benefit is based on a formula in the plan, often using a combination of the employee's age, years worked for the employer, and/or salary.	The benefit depends on contributions made by the employee and/or the employer, performance of the account's investments, and fees charged to the account.
Type of Retirement Benefit Payments	Traditionally, these plans pay the retiree monthly annuity payments that continue for life. Plans may offer other payment options.	The retiree may transfer the account balance into an individual retirement account (IRA) from which the retiree withdraws money, or may receive it as a lump sum payment. Some plans also offer monthly payments through an annuity.
Guarantee of Benefits	The federal government, through the Pension Benefit Guaranty Corporation (PBGC), guarantees some amount of benefits.	No federal guarantee of benefits.
Leaving the Company before Retirement Age	If an employee leaves after vesting in a benefit but before the plan's retirement age, the benefit generally stays with the plan until the employee files a claim for it at retirement. Some defined benefit plans offer early retirement options.	The employee may transfer the account balance to an individual retirement account (IRA) or, in some cases, another employer plan, where it can continue to grow based on investment earnings. The employee also may take the balance out of the plan, but will owe taxes and possibly penalties, thus reducing retirement income. Plans may cash out small accounts.

EXHIBIT 4.8 Comparison of Features of Pension Equity Plans and Cash Balance Plans

Source: Green, B. L, "What Is a Pension Equity Plan?" *Compensation and Working Conditions*, October 29, 2003. Accessed April 29, 2012, www.dol .gov/ebsa (U.S. Department of Labor).

Feature	Pension Equity Plan	Cash Balance Plan
Benefit formula	Percent of earnings, may vary by age, service, or earnings.	Percent of earnings, may vary by age, service, or earnings.
How benefits are accumulated	Percent of earnings, as determined by the benefit formula, are accumulated each year, but the final benefit is not determined until employee leaves the plan.	Dollar amount (benefit formula times earnings) placed in hypothetical account each year; interest on account balance also credited each year.
Definition of earnings	Total accumulated benefit applied to final earnings, as defined by the plan; final earnings typically those in last 3–5 years before retirement.	Percent applied to each year's earnings.
How to determine value of benefits for current employees	Employees can multiply their accumulated percent of earnings times their final earnings as defined by the plan to determine their current benefit.	Account balance is the current benefit.
Distribution	Specified as a lump sum, but can be converted to an annuity.	Specified as a lump sum, but can be converted to an annuity.

How do hybrid plans work? Let's consider a cash balance plan. First, employers' contributions to cash balance plans are defined, as is the case with traditional defined contribution plans. These plans calculate benefits as a periodic payment, which is similar to defined benefit plans. In cash balance plans, however, the amount of the periodic payment is determined in reference to a "hypothetical balance." As discussed earlier, traditional defined benefit plans typically determine periodic payments based on years of service as well as age and final average pay at retirement. Upon retirement, employees under cash balance plans may elect to take the lump sum or convert the lump sum to annuity payments, based on age at retirement, marital status, and estimated life expectancy. In traditional defined benefit plans, most payouts are in the form of periodic payments for life. In either case, calculating benefits as a lump sum increases the portability of retirement benefits from company to company, thereby benefitting employees who change employers during their working lives. That is, employees may roll over the vested lump sum accumulated in a cash balance plan to another employer's qualified retirement plan. Portability should help place companies in a better position to recruit more mobile workers.

Benefit Formulas

Cash balance plans include individual accounts as is the case for defined contribution plans. Companies calculate benefits by using two types of credits: pay

EXHIBIT 4.9   Account Value Calculations for a Cash Balance Plan

This illustration shows how a cash balance account grows over five years:

Annual Pay Credit: An employee earns an annual pay credit of $1,500, calculated as (3% × $50,000). That is, the pay credit rate multiplied by annual salary.

Annual Interest Credit: The annual interest credit equals $75, calculated as (5% × $1,500). That is, the interest credit rate multiplied by the pay credit amount.

First Year Account Value: The account value equals $1,605.00 based on the following calculation: $1,500 + 75. That is, the sum of the current year pay credit amount and interest credit amount.

Subsequent Year Account Values: At the end of the second year, the account value equals $3,228.75: [($1,575.00 × 5%) + $75.00] + $1,575 + $1,500. That is, the interest credit for year 2 is added to the account value at the beginning of the year and the annual pay credit amount.

The interest credit amount for year 2; that is, [($1,575.00 × 5%) + 75] equals the account value at the beginning of the year multiplied by the interest credit rate, and this value is added to the previous year interest credit amount.

The account for each subsequent year follows the approach used for year 2.

Year	Account Value (beginning of the year)	Annual Pay	Pay Credit (3 percent)	Interest Credit (5 percent)	Account Value (end of the year)
1	$0.00	$50,000	$1,500	$75.00	$1,575.00
2	1,575.00	50,000	1,500	153.75	3,228.75
3	3,228.75	50,000	1,500	315.18	5,043.93
4	5,043.93	50,000	1,500	567.37	7,111.30
5	7,111.30	50,000	1,500	922.93	9,534.23

credits and interest credits. Participants receive a *pay credit* expressed as a percentage of annual pay, and an *interest credit* set at a rate determined by the employer. The interest credit amount is guaranteed, instead of fluctuating based on changes in the interest rate. Employee accounts are often referred to as "hypothetical accounts" because they do not reflect actual contributions to the accounts or actual gains and losses allocable to the accounts. For example, an employer may choose a pay credit of 3 percent of each employee's annual earnings, and these credited amounts grow based on a pre-established interest rate, most often linked to an index such as the one-year U.S. treasury bill rate. Let's assume that the rate is 5 percent. Exhibit 4.9 shows how a cash balance account grows over five years.

Pension equity plans credit employees' accounts with a pay credit points based on years of service. When an employee terminates employment or retires, the benefit is calculated as the product of the employee's average pay (average of one's pay over a career) and the earned credit. Similar to cash balance plans, pension equity benefits are expressed as an account balance.

Years of Service	Pay Credit
Less than 5	2%
5 to 9	4%
10 to 14	6%
15 to 19	8%
20 and above	10%

An alternative formula considers employee age plus years of service. Under this approach, the percentage of pay is based on the sum of the age plus service.

Age Plus Years of Service	Pay Credit
Less than 30	5%
30 to 39	6%
40 to 44	7%
45 to 49	8%
50 to 54	9%
55 to 59	10%
60 to 64	11%
65 to 69	12%
70 to 74	13%
75 to 79	14%
80 or more	15%

Comparing Hybrid Plan Features with Defined Benefit Plan and Defined Contribution Plan Features

As noted previously, hybrid plans contain features of both traditional defined benefit and defined contribution plans. While both traditional defined benefit plans and cash balance plans are required to offer a series of payments for life, these plans differ in an important way. Traditional defined benefit plans define an employee's benefit as a series of monthly payments. Cash balance plans, on the other hand, define the benefit in terms of a designated hypothetical account balance, which can be converted into an annuity.

As we've studied, cash balance plans are defined benefit plans, while plans such as the 401(k) are a type of defined contribution plan. There are four major differences between typical cash balance plans and 401(k) plans:[37]

1. **Participation.** Participation in typical cash balance plans generally does not depend on workers' contributing part of their compensation to the plan; however, participation in a 401(k) plan does depend, in whole or in part, on an employee's choosing to make a contribution to the plan.

2. **Investment Risks.** The investments of cash balance plans are managed by the employer or an investment manager appointed by the employer who bears the

risk of possible investment loss. Neither increases nor decreases in account value affect the benefit amounts promised to participants. By contrast, 401(k) plans often permit participants to direct their own investments within certain categories. Under 401(k) plans, participants bear the risks and rewards of investment choices.

3. **Life Annuities.** Unlike 401(k) plans, cash balance plans are required to offer employees the ability to receive benefits in the form of lifetime annuities.

4. **Federal Guarantee.** If a defined benefit plan is terminated with insufficient funds to pay all promised benefits, the PBGC has authority to assume trusteeship of the plan and to begin to pay pension benefits up to the limits set by law. This is similarly the case for cash balance plans. In contrast, defined contribution plans are not insured by the PBGC.

Concerns about Cash Balance Plans

Two concerns have emerged. The first issue centers on the possible favorable treatment of younger workers and unfavorable treatment of older employees. The second issue is based on the practice of converting traditional defined benefit plans to cash balance plans. Each of these is reviewed in turn.

Age-Related Treatment   At first glance, cash balance plans are said to be age neutral because they do not define benefits as a percentage of final or career average pay or as a flat dollar amount per year of service. Rather, cash balance plans award annual pay-related credits, much as defined contribution plans do, with the contributions appreciating each year based on a specified interest rate. Defined benefit plans are not age neutral because the value of the benefit grows substantially with age and participation, thus favoring older participants. This benefit accrual pattern is often referred to as *backloading*.

Still, some concerns about age-related treatment have been raised. For instance, the U.S. General Accounting Office (GAO) compared the rates of retirement benefit accrual in defined benefit plans and cash balance plans under a variety of assumptions. It concluded that cash balance plan accrual favors younger employees.[38] For example, a 25-year-old employee who is assumed to participate in a cash balance plan until retirement at age 65 accrues an incremental annuity benefit of about $1,660 at age 26 but earns a smaller incremental benefit of about $630 at age 65. Under a defined benefit plan, this same individual earns an incremental annuity benefit of $310 at age 26 but earns a higher incremental annuity benefit of about $2,440 at age 65. The difference in accrual patterns between these plan types has led some people to question whether cash balance plans illegally discriminate on the basis of age. In fact, there are some well publicized court cases about this very issue. We review them shortly.

Converting Defined Benefit Plans to Cash Balance Plans   Converting from defined benefit plans to cash balance plans can be detrimental to older workers unless the amount already earned under the traditional defined benefit plan is fully taken into account when calculating the converted benefit. A potential problem with conversion is known as wearaway. According to the U.S. Department of Labor, **wearaway** is said to occur when the formula in a defined benefits plan is changed to a cash balance formula. Oftentimes, the benefit earned under the defined benefit plan formula may exceed the amount determined under the cash balance plan formula. When this situation arises, an employee may not earn additional benefits until the benefit under the cash balance plan formula exceeds the benefit amount under the defined benefit plan formula.

Not all employees experience wearaway following the conversion of their defined benefit plans to cash balance plans. The GAO study indicated that the wearaway period at conversion is longer for older employees and, in addition, found that the wearaway period is increasingly longer the older the workers are at conversion. Wearaway has two causes. First, a company may create wearaway by setting a participant's hypothetical balance under a cash balance plan lower than the present value of accrued benefits under a traditional defined benefit plan. Currently, no regulations exist for setting opening hypothetical balances. Second, wearaway may occur because of changes in the federally mandated discount rate for determining lump sum distributions from defined benefit plans. The value of lump sum distributions increases when the discount rate falls, while the value of distributions decreases when the discount rate increases. To illustrate this relationship, let's consider the impact of two different discount rates (5 percent versus 10 percent) on the current value of a $10,000 retirement account balance one year from now. Assuming a discount rate of 5 percent, $10,000 today would be worth $9,523.80 one year from now ($10,000/[1 + 0.05]) × 100 percent. At the higher discount rate (10 percent), $10,000 today would be worth $9,090.90 one year from now ($10,000/[1 + 0.10]) × 100 percent.

Several court rulings have been mixed on the issue about whether cash balance plans discriminate on the basis of age. Some courts have concluded that these plans do not violate the Age Discrimination in Employment Act. In *Easton v. Onan Corp.*, a federal district judge ruled that age discrimination prohibitions do not apply to employees younger than normal retirement age;[39] the provisions were set to ensure that employees who chose to work past the normal retirement age continue to accrue retirement benefits. In *Dan C. Tootle v. ARINC Inc.*, the judge ruled that a "sensible approach" to determine whether cash balance plans are discriminatory is to use a test from ERISA for defined contribution plans;[40] specifically, plans are not discriminatory as long as employer contributions are not reduced by age.

However, in *Cooper v. The IBM Personal Pension Plan*,[41] a U.S. District Court judge in southern Illinois ruled in 2003 that IBM Corporation's cash balance plan discriminated against IBM's older employees because the benefit credit provided to older employees purchased a much smaller benefit than the same benefit provided to a younger employee. The judge in the IBM case relied on ERISA-based discrimination tests for defined benefit plans.

Since then, language in the Pension Protection Act of 2006 has tried to resolve the misunderstanding over wearaway provisions. This act makes it illegal for employers to use wearaway provisions when converting a defined benefit plan to a cash balance plan. As a result, cash balance plan provisions must credit a participant with his or her accrued benefit under the old formula, plus full credit for years of service after the adoption of the cash balance formula. The Pension Protection Act also allows employers to create new cash balance plans—or to convert existing defined benefit plans to a cash balance design—with much less fear of litigation.

Shortly after the Pension Protection Act was signed into law, judges from the U.S. Seventh Circuit Court revisited the 2003 ruling in *Cooper v. The IBM Personal Pension Plan*. They reversed the 2003 ruling, concluding that the IBM Personal Pension Plan did not discriminate against employees on the basis of age. Older workers at IBM maintained that "someone who leaves IBM at age 50, after 20 years of service, will have a larger annual benefit at 65 than someone whose 20 years of service conclude with retirement at age 65. The former receives 15 years' more interest than the latter." The Seventh Circuit Court indicated that nothing in the ERISA language legislates against "the fact that younger workers have (statistically) more time left before retirement, and thus a greater opportunity to earn interest on each year's retirement savings. Treating the time value of money as a form of discrimination is not sensible."[42] After that ruling, Cooper made a request to the U.S. Supreme Court to hear this case in the hopes of overturning the Seventh Circuit Court's ruling. The U.S. Supreme Court declined to review the 2006 court decision in *Cooper v. The IBM Personal Pension Plan*. In 2007, Cooper appealed the Seventh Circuit Court's decision. This court refused to rehear the case.

In 2011, a case was decided in which some employees of El Paso Corporation charged that El Paso violated ERISA and the Age Discrimination in Employment Act when it converted to a cash balance plan. The trial court found that El Paso's transition favored, rather than discriminated against, older employees. Accordingly, the Tenth Circuit Court ruled in *Tomlinson et al. vs. El Paso Corporation*[43] that ERISA did not require the employer to provide notification of wearaway periods so long as employees were informed and forewarned of plan changes. In addition, the court held that even if a disproportionate number of older employees are subject to frozen benefits because of conversion, this effect does not violate the Age Discrimination in Employment Act.

Target Benefit Plans

As hybrid plans, **target benefit plans** combine features of defined benefit and defined contribution plans. Target benefit plans calculate benefits in a fashion similar to defined benefit plans based on formulas that use income and years of service. However, target benefit plans are fundamentally defined contribution plans because the benefit amount at retirement may be more or less than the targeted benefit amount based on the investment performance of the plan assets. "Targeted" benefit is based on the assumption that the actual return on plan assets equals the expected return.

Consistent with defined contribution plans, target benefit plan participants have individual accounts. Employers use actuarial calculations of the annual contribution amount that would be necessary to fully fund the retirement benefit at a participant's normal retirement age. These contributions are invested on behalf of the participant. In a defined benefit plan, employers would modify the annual contribution amount according to the performance of the investments to ensure benefit amounts at the time of the participant's retirement. In a target benefit plan, employers do not adjust their contributions. As a result, retirement benefits may be more or less than projected.

Target benefit plans at first glance appear to violate ERISA's nondiscrimination rules because employers contribute greater amounts on behalf of more highly paid employees (usually older employees) than lower-paid employees (usually younger employees). For the moment, let's assume that older workers are more highly paid than younger workers. The *IRS cross-testing rules*[44] permit age-based contributions in target benefit plans and age-weighted profit-sharing plans under the following condition: Lower contributions are permissible for lower-paid (younger) employees because the contributions are projected over a longer period than for higher-paid (older) employees. In the end, plans with age-based contributions are not discriminatory if projected benefits are comparable regardless of age.

Target benefit plans tend to be less expensive than either defined benefit or defined contribution plans. Under defined benefit plans, employers are required to increase contribution amounts to compensate for shortfalls caused by poor investment performance. Employers do not make adjustments to their annual contributions in target benefit plans. As discussed earlier, under a defined contribution plan, the annual contributions of employers are usually based on a fixed percentage of each employee's income regardless of age. Actuarially determined contributions in target benefit plans mean that larger contributions are made for older workers, whose possible lengths of service are shorter than those of younger employees. The costs of target benefit plans in companies with predominantly younger workforces may be less than the costs of defined contribution plans.

Money Purchase Plans

Money purchase plans are defined contribution plans because the benefit is based on the account balance—that is, the employer contributions plus the returns on investment of employer contributions—at the time of retirement. However, these plans possess the funding requirements of defined benefit plans. Employers must make annual contributions according to the designated formula for the plan. These contributions are not tied to company performance indicators, such as profits or stock price.

Age-Weighted Profit-Sharing Plans

As hybrid plans, **age-weighted profit-sharing plans** combine features of defined benefit and defined contribution plans. Fundamentally, these plans are defined contribution plans because benefit amounts fluctuate according to the performance of investments of plan assets. In this regard, age-weighted profit-sharing plans are like profit-sharing plans, which we discussed earlier. Consideration of age makes these plans similar to defined benefit plans. Employers contribute disproportionately more to the accounts of older employees based on a projected hypothetical benefit at normal retirement age. The idea is to fund all employee accounts sufficiently well so that each employee would likely achieve a similar hypothetical retirement benefit.

Summary

This chapter reviews the fundamental concepts of company-sponsored retirement plans. Companies must follow a set of strict guidelines in designing and implementing retirement plans to qualify for favorable tax treatment. Also reviewed were the main features of defined benefit, defined contribution, and hybrid plans.

Key Terms

coverage requirements, *95*
ratio percentage test, *96*
average benefit test, *96*
vesting, *96*
cliff vesting, *96*
six-year graduated schedule, *96*
accrual rules, *97*
nondiscrimination rules, *97*
top-heavy, *97*
minimum funding standards, *98*
Social Security integration, *98*
permitted disparity rules, *98*
distribution, *98*
lump sum distributions, *98*
annuities, *98*
qualified joint and survivor annuity (QJSA), *99*
qualified preretirement survivor annuity (QPSA), *99*
qualified domestic relations orders (QDROs), *99*
plan termination rules, *99*
defined benefit plans, *99*

flat benefit formulas, *100*
unit benefit formulas, *100*
accumulated benefit obligation, *102*
backloading, *103*
three percent rule, *103*
133⅓ percent rule, *103*
fractional rule, *103*
termination insurance, *105*
defined contribution plans, *104*
salary reduction agreements, 104
forfeitures, *104*
matching contributions, *105*
fiduciary, *105*
annual addition, *106*
401(k) plans, *109*
profit-sharing plans, *109*
profit-sharing pool, *109*
fixed first-dollar-of-profits formula, *110*
graduated first-dollar-of-profits formula, *110*
profitability threshold formulas, *110*
equal payments, *110*

proportional payments to employees based on their annual salary, *110*
proportional payments to employees based on their contribution to profits, *110*
stock bonus plan, *110*
employee stock option plans (ESOPs), *110*
nonleveraged ESOPs, *111*
leveraged ESOPs, *111*
savings incentive match plans for employees (SIMPLEs), *111*
tax-deferred annuity (TDA), *111*
Section 457 plans, *112*
hybrid plans, *112*
golden handcuffs, *112*
cash balance plans, *112*
pension equity plans, *112*
wearaway, *117*
target benefit plans, *119*
money purchase plans, *120*
age-weighted profit-sharing plans, *120*

Discussion Questions

1. Describe three criteria of the 13 minimum standards on which plan status is determined to qualify retirement plans for preferential tax treatment.
2. Are employees more likely to favor defined contribution plans over defined benefit plans? What about employers? Explain your answer.
3. Summarize two concerns regarding cash balance plans.
4. Explain why mobile employees might prefer cash balance plans over defined benefit plans.

Cases

1. Understanding Your Employee Benefits: Investing in Your Retirement

After nearly three months at your new job, you believe that you have a good understanding of your responsibilities, as well as the benefits of working at your company. However, you just received a letter from HR informing you of the opportunity to participate in the company's retirement plan. Under company policy, you can begin participating in the retirement plan after 90 days of service. As you review the informational letter, you realize that you are faced with some important decisions about saving for retirement. The company offers employees the opportunity to participate in a Section 401(k) plan. The company will contribute to the savings plan on your behalf, but you must first elect to defer some of your annual income into the plan.

The informational letter outlines the details of the Section 401(k) plan. You can defer up to 10 percent of your annual pay to invest in the plan. The salary deduction agreement allows you to defer your pay through a pretax payroll deduction from your pay each pay period. The company contribution to your retirement savings is a match of what you contribute; thus, you must first decide to defer some of your income into the plan. The company policy is to match 100 percent of what you set aside, up to the first 5 percent of your annual pay. Thus, for example, if you set aside 2 percent of your pay, the company will invest the equivalent of 2 percent of your pay. If you invest 5 percent of your pay or more, the company will invest the maximum match of 5 percent of your pay.

You know that retirement savings is important, so your initial reaction is that you should participate in the plan and set aside the maximum deferral of 10 percent of your pay. However, as you look at the numbers, you have some concerns. Your current pay is $1,500 per pay period, with 24 pay periods each year. If you invest the maximum of 10 percent of your pay, you will have $150 deducted from each pay, leaving you with $1,350. After tax and health-care insurance deductions, your take-home pay will be around $800 each pay period. As you consider your expenses, you worry that your take-home pay won't be enough. With a pile of bills, including rent, utilities, a car payment, and other expenses such as food and entertainment, you see that you will need to stretch your paycheck quite a bit. This concern over paying your bills makes you question deferring the full 10 percent of your pay. While you know that you should start your retirement savings now, you have at least 40 years until you retire.

As you review the letter, you learn that you have a week to make your decision. You must first decide whether or not to participate in the plan, and if you do, you need to decide how much of your pay to defer each pay period. Further, you will also need to decide how to allocate your contributions to the plan. The letter discusses several investment options that include high-risk mutual funds as well as lower-risk federal government bond funds. You decide to take advantage of an upcoming informational meeting mentioned in the letter to learn more, and you start to think about your options.

1. Do you think that you should defer part of your pay to invest in the Section 401(k) plan?
2. If you choose to invest, what percentage of your pay would you defer to the Section 401(k)? Why?

2. Managing Employee Benefits: A New Retirement Plan at Grinders Manufacturing

Grinders Manufacturing faces some tough questions as the organization moves to expand operations. The 75-year old company, with more than 400 employees, produces machine parts, and a new market opportunity will allow the company to expand operations and build a new facility. While Grinders is a business that has endured the test of time, the company has faced many challenges over the past several decades. At one point in the mid-1960s, the company had more than 800 employees. A strong employee union at that time established competitive market pay rates and a generous benefits package that included a traditional defined benefit retirement plan. However, through the 1980s and 1990s, Grinders faced declining sales along with increasing expenses. The company laid off nearly half of its workforce, and while it maintained operations, the company continued to struggle. A frustrated workforce eventually voted to decertify the union, and the plant now remains union-free. However, things seem to be turning around as the new market opportunity for Grinders holds the promise to build back its workforce.

As the company moves forward with its growth plans, Shane Meadow, Director of Human Resources, is examining all of the company's HR management policies and practices to ensure that the company is prepared to meet the future challenges. Employee benefits are also under review, with the retirement plan under particular scrutiny as it is one of the most significant expenses for the company. Shane decides to begin his review by examining the company's retirement plan to determine if the current plan is the most financially responsible plan for the company.

The defined benefit retirement plan set in place through union negotiations years ago is available for all full-time employees. However, the company's declining sales and unstable financial situation have made maintaining the plan challenging. The current plan uses a unit benefit formula that calculates each employee's retirement benefit based on years of service and pay. With many long-term employees, the company makes significant contributions to the plan each year to ensure that the promised benefits will be available. In addition to the financial impact of the plan, Shane has noted that as he hires new staff, they find the plan complex to understand.

Shane is considering transitioning to a defined contribution retirement plan, such as a Section 401(k) plan. His initial thoughts on this change are that the company would be better able to manage the plan financially, as the company contribution to the plan could be a profit-sharing plan that would base the company's contribution to the plan on company profits. He feels this would lower the company's financial risk in supporting the retirement benefit. If it provided a profit-sharing plan as part of a Section 401(k) plan, it would ask employees to contribute to the plan as well. Shane believes that asking employees to invest in their own retirement will help employees understand the value of their retirement benefits.

While the transition process of terminating the defined benefit plan and establishing a defined contribution plan would be complex, Shane believes at this point that it may be a good decision for the company in the long run. Further, the upcoming expansion plans provide a good opportunity to make such a change.

1. Based on the circumstances that Grinders Manufacturing is facing, do you think that Shane's intention to move to a defined contribution plan is a good idea?
2. Who will the change benefit more, the company or the employees?

Endnotes

1. ERISA §3(2)(A), 29 U.S.C. §1002(2)(A).
2. Employee Benefits Research Institute, "Pension Plans" (Chapter 4) in *Fundamentals of Employee Benefits Programs*. Washington, DC, 1997.
3. J. Short, "Economic History of Retirement in the United States." In R. Whaples (ed.), *EH.Net Encyclopedia*, October 1, 2002. Accessed April 13, 2016, https://eh.net/encyclopedia/economic-history-of-retirement-in-the-united-states/.

4. S. L. Costo, "Trends in Retirement Plan Coverage over the Last Decade," *Monthly Labor Review,* Feb. 2006: 58–64.

5. *Ibid.*; U.S. Department of Labor, *Employee Benefits in the United States, March 2016* (USDL 16-1493) July 22, 2016. Accessed October 21, 2016, www.bls.gov.

6. Costo, "Trends in Retirement Plan Coverage over the Last Decade."

7. U.S. Department of Labor, *Employee Benefits in the United States, March 2016.*

8. Internal Revenue Code (hereafter I.R.C.) §§410(a)(1), 410(a)(4); Treas. Reg. §1.410(a)-3T(b); ERISA §202(a) I.R.C. §410(a)(3), Treas. Reg. § 1.410(a)-5, 29 C.F.R. §2530.200b-2(a), ERISA §202(a)(3).

9. I.R.C. §414(q).

10. I.R.C. §410(b); Treas. Regs. §§1.410(b)-2, 1.410(b)-4, 1.410(a)(4)–11(g)(2).

11. I.R.C. §401(a)(26), Treas. Reg. §1.401(a)(26)–2(a).

12. I.R.C. §§411(a)(2), 411(a)(5); Treas. Reg. §1.411(a)-3T; ERISA §203(a).

13. I.R.C. §§411(a)(7), 411(b); ERISA §§204, 3(23); Treas. Reg. §1.411(b)-1.

14. I.R.C. §401(a)(4).

15. I.R.C. §416(g)(1).

16. I.R.C. §§401(a)(5)(C), 401(l).

17. "ABA Section of Labor and Employment Law," *Employee Benefits Law,* 2nd ed. Washington, DC: Bureau of National Affairs, 2000: 252–253.

18. I.R.C. §§401(a), 417(b), 417(c); ERISA §205; Treas. Regs. §§1.401(a)-11, 1.401(a)-20.

19. ERISA §206(d)(1), I.R.C. §401(a)(13).

20. I.R.C. §§401(a)(13), 414(p); ERISA §206(d).

21. I.R.C. §415(b).

22. I.R.C. §404(a)(1)(A)(i)–(iii).

23. I.R.C. §§414(b), 414(c); ERISA §§4011, 4044, 4062(b), 4068; 29 C.F.R. §4011.10; PBGC, Technical Update 00-7.

24. U.S. Department of Labor, "Frequently Asked Questions about Retirement Plans and ERISA." Accessed April 10, 2016, www.dol.gov.

25. Treas. Regs. §1.401(a)(4)-2(b).

26. I.R.C. §411(a)(7)(A)(ii); ERISA §204(b)(2).

27. Prop. Treas. Reg. §§1.412(b)-1(a).

28. I.R.C. §415(c)(2); Treas. Reg. §1.415-6(b)(1).

29. I.R.C. §415(c).

30. I.R.C. §§404(a)(3), 402(g).

31. I.R.C. §404(a)(3).

32. I.R.C. §404(a)(3).

33. I.R.C. §§401(a), 4975(e)(7)–(8).

34. I.R.C. §408.

35. L. B. Green, "What Is a Pension Equity Plan?" *Compensation and Working Conditions,* October 29, 2003. Accessed April 29, 2012, www.dol.gov/ebsa (U.S. Department of Labor).

36. 26 C.F.R. §§1.401(a)(4)-8(c)(3)(I).

37. U.S. Department of Labor, "FAQs about Cash Balance Pension Plans." Accessed April 14, 2016, www.dol.gov/ebsa/faqs/faq_consumer_cashbalanceplans.html.

38. U.S. Department of Labor, Bureau of Labor Statistics, "Questions and Answers on Cash Balance Plans," *Compensation and Working Conditions*, September 23, 2003. Accessed April 29, 2012, www.bls.gov/opub/cwc/print/cm20030917ar01p.htm.

39. *Eaton v. Onan Corp.*, 2000 WL 1459801 (S.D. Ind. 2000).

40. *Dan C. Tootle v. ARINC Inc.*, U.S. Dist. Ct. for .Dist. Maryland, No. CCB-03-1086.

41. *Cooper v. The IBM Personal Pension Plan*, Civil No. 99-829-GPM (S.D. Ill. July 31, 2003).

42. *Cooper v. The IBM Personal Pension Plan*, Civil No. 05-3588, U.S. Dist. Ct. App. 7th Cir., Aug. 7, 2006.

43. *Tomlinson et al. vs. El Paso Corporation*, Civil No.10-1385 (U.S. Dist. Colo. Aug. 11, 2011).

44. ERISA §401(a)(4); I.R.C. §1.401(a)(4)–(8).

Employer-Sponsored Health-Care Plans

Learning Objectives

In this chapter, you will gain an understanding of:

1. Health-care plan concepts.

2. Federal and state laws influencing employer-sponsored health-care plan practices.

3. Health-care plan design alternatives, including fee-for-service, managed care, and consumer-driven approaches.

4. Other health-related benefits.

5. Retiree health-care benefits.

The purpose of this chapter is to review the fundamentals of employer-sponsored health-care plans. We begin with basic definitions, followed by a review of the origins and costs of employer-sponsored plans. Then, key regulations pertaining to health-care plans are considered. Finally, the specific types of employer-sponsored plans are reviewed, for example, fee-for-service plans, managed care plans, consumer-driven health care, and retiree health-care benefits.

DEFINING AND EXPLORING HEALTH-CARE PLANS

Health-care plans cover the costs of services that promote sound physical and mental health, including physical examinations, diagnostic testing, surgery, hospitalization, psychotherapy, dental treatments, and corrective prescription lenses for vision deficiencies. Employers can offer these benefits using *fully insured* or *self-funded* plans. **Fully insured plans** are based on a contractual relationship with one or more insurance companies to provide health-related services for employees and their qualified dependents. Under fully insured arrangements, insurance companies assume the risk for paying medical claims, and insurers take responsibility for administering the plan. When discussing fully insured plans, it is important to understand the difference between *individual coverage* and *group coverage*. Under **individual coverage**, a person chooses to purchase health-care coverage outside the employment setting for herself and qualified dependents. Extending coverage to most or all employees is considered **group coverage**, which is the basis for employer-sponsored health-care plans. Exhibit 5.1 describes the categories of

EXHIBIT 5.1
Types of
Group Plans

- *Single-employer arrangement.* An employer arranges for group coverage of all employees under one policy.
- *Pooled coverage.* An employer pools money with other employers to provide coverage for its employees under one policy. Oftentimes, employers in the same industry with similar workforces use pooled arrangements. Employer contributions are based on a percent of payroll, cents per hour, or dollar amount per worker, per week or per month.
- *Multiple employer trust.* This arrangement is made for employers with relatively small workforces. A single master trust holds each employer's contributions, and premiums are paid from the trust.
- *Voluntary employee beneficiary association.* This arrangement permits tax-deductible contributions to a trust to fund health-care benefits or other types of employee benefits. The return on investment of contributions is also tax-free.
- *Multiemployer (Taft-Hartley) Plans.* Multiple employers sponsor pension and welfare plans (health care); these plans are usually cosponsored by small companies within certain industries such as construction.

group coverage based on the type of plan holder. The contractual relationship, or **insurance policy**, specifies the amount the insurer pays for medical claims. Employers pay insurers a negotiated amount, or **premium**, to establish and maintain health-care plans. How do insurers determine premiums?

Plan providers use mortality tables and morbidity tables as well as experience ratings to determine the terms and premium amount. This decision-making process is known as **underwriting**. **Mortality tables**, created by actuaries (or, statisticians who meet specified certification standards), indicate yearly probabilities of death based on such factors as age and sex. **Morbidity tables,** also created by actuaries, express annual probabilities of the occurrence of health problems. Group plans generally do not exclude any group member based on health status. Instead, these plans focus mainly on establishing the premium for the employer's contract or policy with the health-plan provider. These providers use experience ratings issued by actuaries to set premiums. **Experience ratings** specify the incidence, type, and financial cost of claims for groups (i.e., everyone as a whole covered under a group plan). Experience ratings hold employers financially accountable for past claims, thus establishing the basis for charging different premiums. In other words, premiums will increase for employers whose employees experience greater incidences of hospitalization and surgical procedures than for employers whose employees experience far less of such incidences.

Under **self-funded plans**, the employer determines what benefits to offer, pays medical claims for employees and their families, and assumes all of the risk. Employers pay claims directly from their assets, either current cash flow or funds set aside in advance for potential future claims. The decision to self-fund is based on financial considerations. Self-funding makes sense when a company's financial burden of covering employee medical expenses is less than the cost to subscribe to an insurance company for coverage. By not paying premiums in advance to an independent insurer, an employer retains these funds for current cash flow. There is another important distinction between *single coverage* and *family coverage* that applies to both fully insured and self-insured plans. **Single coverage** extends benefits only to the covered employee. **Family coverage** offers benefits to the covered employee and qualified dependents.

Companies can choose from the following ways to provide health-care coverage, which can be fully insured or self-funded by the employer:

- Fee-for-service plans
- Alternative managed care plans
- Any health-care plan associated with consumer-driven health care

It is also important to mention that health care in the United States is classified as a **multiple-payer system**. In a multiple-payer system, more than one party is responsible for covering the cost of health care, including the government, employers, employees, or individuals not currently employed (e.g., retirees, the unemployed, coverage part-time employees, and independent contractors). As will be discussed shortly, a variety of forces have contributed to the existence of a multiple-payer health-care system in the United States. In contrast, a **single-payer system**, in which the government regulates the health-care system and uses taxpayer dollars to fund health care, as in Canada and some other countries, is discussed in Chapter 12. Single-payer systems are often referred to as **universal health-care systems**, because the government ensures that all of its citizens have access to quality health care regardless of their ability to pay.

Origins of Health-Care Benefits

The predecessor to company-sponsored care benefits appeared in the late 1800s for mining and railroad workers. Those companies hired doctors to provide medical services to employees. The hazardous work of railroad workers, miners, and employees in other industrial businesses led to frequent illnesses and injuries, employee absences from work, and costly disruptions to these businesses. In those days, working-class employees could not readily afford to pay for medical services, so employers quickly recognized that bearing such costs would help maintain a more productive workforce.

The Great Depression of the 1930s gave rise to employer-sponsored health-care plans. Widespread unemployment made it impossible for most individuals to afford health care. During this period, Congress proposed the Social Security Act of 1935 to address many of the social maladies caused by the adverse economic conditions. The act incorporated health-care plans. However, President Franklin D. Roosevelt opposed the inclusion of health coverage under the Social Security Act. Health care did not become part of the Social Security Act until an amendment to the act in 1965 established the Medicare plan, which is mainly limited to individuals age 65 or older.

The government's choice not to offer health-care benefits created opportunities for private-sector companies to meet the public's need. In the 1930s, hospitals controlled nonprofit companies that inspired today's Blue Cross and Blue Shield plans. At the time, Blue Cross plans allowed individuals to make monthly payments to cover the expense of possible future hospitalization. For-profit companies also formed to provide health-care coverage, creating fee-for-service plans.

In the 1940s, local medical associations created nonprofit Blue Shield plans, which were prepayment plans for physician services. Also, the federal government imposed wage freezes during World War II, which did not extend to employee benefit plans. Many employers began offering health-care benefits to help compete for and retain the best employees, particularly during the labor shortage, when U.S. troops were overseas fighting in the war. Also, employers recognized that they could promote productivity with healthier workforces. Without the assistance of employer-sponsored health care, employees could not afford to pay for medical services on their own. Many companies sought ways to promote productivity and morale through the implementation of welfare practices. In Chapter 1, welfare practices were defined as "anything for the comfort and improvement, intellectual or social, of the employees, over and above wages paid, which is not a necessity of the industry nor required by law."[1] Health-care plans were among these practices.

Many companies discontinued health-care benefits soon after the government lifted the wage freeze. The withdrawal of these and other benefits created discontent among employees, who viewed benefits as an entitlement. Legal battles ensued based on the claim that health protection was a fundamental right. In unionized companies, health benefits became a mandatory subject of collective bargaining.

The 1950s were relatively uneventful years regarding employee benefits. In the 1960s, the federal government amended the Social Security Act. Titles XVIII and XIX of the act established the Medicare and Medicaid plans, respectively (see Chapter 6). These public programs provided access to health-care services for a wide segment of the U.S. population in a relatively short period. The demand for health-care services rose quickly relative to the supply of health-care providers, prompting inflation in the price of health-care services.

Congress enacted the Employee Retirement Income Security Act of 1974 to protect employee interests (see Chapter 3). By providing financial incentives to companies, subject to becoming federally qualified, the **Health Maintenance Organization Act of 1973 (HMO Act)** promoted the use of health maintenance organizations. The HMO Act is discussed later in the chapter. Since the beginning of the 1970s, substantial emphasis has been placed on managing costs and the passage of laws put in place to establish employee rights. We discussed a variety of these laws in Chapter 3, and we consider additional laws in this chapter that focus mainly on employer-sponsored health care.

Until recently, employers offered health-care plans on a discretionary basis. President Barack Obama maintained that every American should have health insurance. The Patient Protection and Affordable Care Act (PPACA), enacted on March 23, 2010, is a comprehensive law that requires employers to offer health insurance to employees (the employer mandate). As an aside, if individuals do not have insurance through employment, they are required to purchase their own insurance (the individual mandate). In either case, monetary penalties are assessed for failure to meet the law's insurance mandates. Since the act's passage, the employer requirements have been implemented in phases. The full implementation of all provisions were set to be implemented in 2018; however, the implementation of some (e.g., Cadillac Tax) are extended to 2020. The federal government documents the features and implementations of the PPACA on a dedicated Web site (www.healthcare.org). We take up PPACA later in this chapter.

Health-Care Coverage and Costs

Both employees and employers place a great deal of significance on company-sponsored health-care benefits largely because employer-sponsored plans provide the means to afford expensive health-care services. Companies stand to gain from sponsoring these benefits in at least two ways, as noted above. First, a healthier workforce should experience a lower incidence of absenteeism resulting from sickness. By keeping absenteeism in check, a company's overall productivity and product or service quality should be higher. Second, health-care plan offerings should help the recruitment and retention of employees. Not surprisingly, a large percentage of companies include health-care plans as a feature of employee-benefits programs, extending coverage to substantial numbers of employees and their dependents. At the same time, the rampant rise in health-care prices is putting substantial pressure on cost-conscious companies.

In 2015, 70 percent of all private-sector employees had access to at least one employer-sponsored health-care plan.[2] Employees' access varies by worker characteristics and establishment (company) characteristics. Worker characteristics include occupation, full- versus part-time status, union status, and relative pay level. Establishment characteristics include industry and company size. In general, access to health-care benefits is greater for management employees, full-time employees, unionized workers, more highly paid employees, and workers employed in goods-producing industries. Exhibit 5.2 illustrates these statistics in greater detail.

Health-care premiums are quite high, often amounting to as much as one-half of annual benefits costs. In March 2015, the average monthly health insurance premium was $390.79 per employee for single coverage.[3] Family coverage is substantially higher, averaging $961.22 per employee. Additional statistics are presented in Exhibit 5.2 based on worker characteristics and establishment (company) characteristics. The highest average premium amounts are for union members ($496.96 for single coverage and $1,263.16 for family coverage). Since the 1980s, many plans have extended family coverage to unmarried opposite-sex or same-sex domestic partnerships. A domestic partnership is established by providing evidence of living together, financial interdependence, and joint responsibility for each other's welfare. In 2015, 32 percent of private-sector workers in opposite-sex partnerships had access to health-care benefits. Among private-sector workers, 37 percent of same-sex partnerships had access to health-care benefits.[4]

Many private-sector companies require employees to contribute a portion of health-care premiums because of their considerable cost. Employee contributions varied considerably based on worker and establishment characteristics. Overall, employees contributed 22 percent of the cost for single coverage and 32 percent for family coverage. Union workers paid the lowest share at 13 and 16 percent for single and family coverage, respectively. The highest share of contributions came from the lowest paid workers at 27 and 41 percent for single and family coverage, respectively.[5]

The premiums for fully insured plans are likely to increase, based on the trend in rising prices for medical services. For example, the prices for medical care services overall have increased more than 450 percent since 1984 (compared to a 237 percent increase for all goods and services purchased by consumers during the same period).[6]

The substantially higher rate increases for medical services may be explained by several factors, all of which translate into higher utilization of health benefits:

- Longer life expectancies.
- Aging baby-boom-era individuals, who place higher demands on health care.
- Advances in medical research that include additional diagnostic tests and treatments, such as substantially more effective (and expensive) treatments to save low-birth-weight babies.

- A general tendency for the health profession and family members to treat death as unnatural rather than as a natural ending to life, leading to higher expenditures to prolong the lives of the terminally ill.

There is no reason to expect that health-care costs will decrease in the foreseeable future. Continuing medical research, advanced diagnostic tools, and higher demand due to the aging population, PPACA providing access to more people, and the desire for better treatment will contribute to higher costs.

Types of Medical Expense Benefits

Health-care plans provide three types of medical benefits: hospital expense benefits, surgical expense benefits, and physician expense benefits.

Hospitalization Benefits

Hospitalization benefits defray expenses associated with treatment in hospitals. Plans distinguish between inpatient benefits and outpatient benefits. **Inpatient benefits** cover expenses associated with overnight hospital stays, while **outpatient benefits** cover expenses for treatments in hospitals not requiring overnight stays. Plans also describe the extent of coverage based on a schedule of benefits, usually expressed as the daily amount of the hospital stay.

Inpatient benefits fall into two categories: room and board, and other related benefits. Room and board benefits defray the costs of overnight hospital stays, including the room fee and related expenses. Typical related expenses are nursing care and meals. The second category, other related benefits, defrays a variety of costs associated with hospital stays. These costs include physician-ordered services (e.g., consultation with a physical therapist), pharmaceutical products, laboratory services (e.g., analysis of blood samples), X-rays, and the use of operating rooms.

Outpatient benefits apply to treatments and related expenses not associated with overnight hospital stays. Three types of outpatient benefits include emergency room treatment, preadmission testing, and surgery. Emergency room treatment applies to the sudden onset of serious illnesses or the occurrence of accidents. As the name implies, preadmission testing takes place within a few days prior to hospital admission for surgical procedures. The goal is to determine whether a patient has a medical condition that could place him or her at risk for complications or death from surgery (e.g., an abnormal heart rhythm). Outpatient benefits also cover surgical procedures not requiring overnight stays. Increasingly, medical advancements enable treatment of serious health conditions that avoids close monitoring by doctors and nurses for a period of days following surgery.

Surgical Benefits

Surgical expense benefits pay for medically necessary surgical procedures, but usually not for elective surgeries such as cosmetic surgery. Generally, health plans pay expenses according to a schedule of **usual, customary, and reasonable charges**. A *usual, customary, and reasonable charge* is defined as not more than the physician's usual charge, within the customary range of fees charged in the locality,

EXHIBIT 5.2 Medical care benefits, single and family coverage: Employer and employee premiums by employee contribution requirement, private industry workers, National Compensation Survey, March 2015

Source: U.S. Bureau of Labor Statistics, *Employee Benefits in the United States, March 2015 (Bulletin 2782)*.

(All workers with single coverage medical care benefits = 100 percent)

Characteristics	Single Coverage						
	Total		Employee contribution not required		Employee contribution required		
	Percent of participating employees	Average flat monthly employer premium	Percent of participating employees	Average flat monthly employer premium	Percent of participating employees	Average flat monthly employer premium	Average flat monthly employee contribution
All workers	100	$390.79	15	$516.25	85	$371.05	$121.92
Worker characteristics							
Management, professional, and related	100	410.09	13	498.34	87	396.95	119.03
Management, business, and financial	100	401.61	10	514.86	90	388.42	118.89
Professional and related	100	415.32	15	491.03	85	402.46	119.12
Service	100	374.94	14	510.99	86	354.81	131.17
Protective service	100	386.94	–	–	–	–	–
Sales and office	100	368.45	12	500.35	88	351.62	120.80
Sales and related	100	330.63	9	446.22	91	319.84	128.78
Office and administrative support	100	386.67	13	517.95	87	367.65	116.78
Natural resources, construction, and maintenance	100	404.61	28	583.46	72	351.77	139.90
Construction, extraction, farming, fishing, and forestry	100	417.66	40	582.08	60	346.91	142.81
Installation, maintenance, and repair	100	396.01	19	584.98	81	354.50	138.27
Production, transportation, and material moving	100	389.22	14	514.42	86	368.92	115.66
Production	100	387.76	11	497.05	89	374.04	115.98
Transportation and material moving	100	391.02	18	528.13	82	362.15	115.22
Full time	100	393.15	15	517.34	85	373.19	120.55
Part time	100	354.65	12	492.52	88	339.67	141.91
Union	100	496.96	38	597.07	62	446.51	115.02
Nonunion	100	375.09	11	478.66	89	362.74	122.68
Average wage within the following categories:[1]							
Lowest 25 percent	100	335.61	10	460.94	90	323.61	128.60
Lowest 10 percent	100	317.07	9	512.75	91	302.99	131.50
Second 25 percent	100	376.34	13	488.65	87	360.41	125.51
Third 25 percent	100	396.54	16	520.97	84	373.54	120.30
Highest 25 percent	100	416.40	16	542.25	84	395.18	117.95
Highest 10 percent	100	410.83	13	512.65	87	396.63	116.90
Establishment characteristics							
Goods-producing industries	100	392.82	17	526.20	83	369.91	112.75
Construction	100	409.69	40	560.35	60	342.44	135.55
Manufacturing	100	390.06	10	509.37	90	377.10	107.54
Service-providing industries	100	390.21	14	513.09	86	371.37	124.52
Trade, transportation, and utilities	100	360.19	12	492.57	88	342.76	127.84
Information	100	424.26	23	605.41	77	369.81	114.56
Financial activities	100	394.43	12	575.81	88	369.30	111.53
Professional and business services	100	381.32	13	463.50	87	368.74	134.98
Education and health services	100	429.64	11	520.61	89	418.01	118.15
Leisure and hospitality	100	351.00	21	505.53	79	320.12	124.42
Other services	100	408.77	29	523.00	71	362.09	142.40
1 to 99 workers	100	388.57	19	501.92	81	363.00	132.24
1 to 49 workers	100	390.66	21	495.51	79	365.36	132.64
50 to 99 workers	100	383.52	17	520.82	83	357.53	131.32
100 workers or more	100	392.50	11	536.63	89	376.63	114.76
100 to 499 workers	100	384.25	11	542.59	89	366.60	118.66
500 workers or more	100	402.81	10	528.96	90	389.15	109.89

[1]Surveyed occupations are classified into wage categories based on the average wage for the occupation, which may include workers with earnings both above and below the threshold. The categories were formed using percentile estimates generated using wage data for March 2015.

Note: Because of rounding, sums of individual items may not equal totals. Dash indicates no workers in this category or data did not meet publication criteria.

EXHIBIT 5.2 *(Continued)*

Family Coverage						
Total		Employee contribution not required		Employee contribution required		
Percent of participating employees	Average flat monthly employer premium	Percent of participating employees	Average flat monthly employer premium	Percent of participating employees	Average flat monthly employer premium	Average flat monthly employee contribution
100	$961.22	8	$1,358.53	92	$931.47	$475.84
100	1,032.40	6	1,318.35	94	1,014.68	467.83
100	1,026.08	5	1,422.32	95	1,004.91	470.29
100	1,036.29	7	1,266.77	93	1,020.79	466.29
100	850.51	8	1,416.11	92	818.58	532.68
100	971.16	–	–	–	–	–
100	880.58	5	1,284.14	95	862.36	487.40
100	792.86	4	1,357.58	96	770.95	488.12
100	922.57	5	1,255.57	95	906.52	487.05
100	948.58	21	1,490.87	79	855.74	536.79
100	977.13	32	1,492.61	68	846.75	576.90
100	929.58	12	1,488.74	88	861.09	512.88
100	1,009.78	10	1,332.91	90	975.51	411.59
100	1,016.67	7	1,328.30	93	992.59	399.33
100	1,001.26	13	1,336.16	87	953.06	427.69
100	969.93	8	1,356.63	92	940.04	473.01
100	828.74	6	1,414.13	94	806.04	517.27
100	1,263.16	32	1,484.63	68	1,181.75	375.03
100	916.99	4	1,235.86	96	903.54	487.09
100	765.25	4	1,324.96	96	752.41	524.71
100	717.21	5	1,452.16	95	700.71	530.14
100	894.26	6	1,289.20	94	870.78	501.04
100	978.26	9	1,269.29	91	953.06	466.74
100	1,066.44	10	1,469.03	90	1,027.76	445.45
100	1,066.51	7	1,452.19	93	1,039.07	439.47
100	1,024.89	13	1,379.88	87	984.97	410.54
100	942.96	7	1,348.33	93	916.80	493.75
100	904.56	7	1,375.05	93	871.58	464.05
100	1,085.25	15	1,653.46	85	988.54	399.08
100	980.84	5	1,525.85	95	953.87	445.53
100	918.66	5	1,195.39	95	904.49	530.10
100	1,004.66	5	1,234.49	95	993.18	515.43
100	781.88	12	1,437.28	88	733.52	537.10
100	901.80	14	1,136.70	86	868.03	561.06
100	873.69	9	1,290.30	91	836.61	559.57
100	870.74	10	1,278.55	90	831.80	559.53
100	880.83	8	1,326.45	92	848.01	559.65
100	1,026.64	7	1,427.34	93	1,000.80	414.66
100	967.22	6	1,431.46	94	942.44	449.84
100	1,100.62	8	1,423.78	92	1,075.19	369.80

and reasonable based on the medical circumstances. Whenever actual surgical expenses exceed the usual, customary, and reasonable level, the patient must pay the difference. Finally, health plans cover a physician's charges for services rendered in the hospital on an inpatient or outpatient basis, as well as office visits.

Physician Benefits

Physician benefits defray the costs of physician fees associated with hospital stays or office visits. In extenuating circumstances, health plans provide coverage for home visits. Extenuating circumstances usually refer to instances when travel to a medical facility would jeopardize a patient's life.

REGULATION OF HEALTH-CARE PLANS

A variety of federal and state laws affect employer and insurer practices, respectively. Every state has regulations pertaining to health-care plans.

Federal Regulations

The main federal laws influencing employer-sponsored health plans include the Health Maintenance Organization Act of 1973, the Employee Retirement Income Security Act of 1974, the Americans with Disabilities Act of 1990, and the Patient Protection and Affordable Care Act of 2010. Tax regulations issued by the Internal Revenue Service may influence employer-sponsored health-care practices.

The Health Maintenance Organization Act of 1973

Health maintenance organizations (HMOs), a particular type of managed care, are regulated at both the federal and state levels. At the federal level, HMOs are governed by the Health Maintenance Organization Act of 1973 (HMO Act),[7] amended in 1988, to encourage employers to include HMOs as a choice in their benefits programs. Congress enacted the HMO Act based on the idea that HMOs are a viable option of financing and delivering health care. The act spurred the growth of HMOs by making development funds available to qualifying HMOs and imposing a dual choice requirement on employers that sponsored health benefits. Qualified HMOs provide basic and supplemental health services that follow the U.S. Department of Health and Human Services guidelines and demonstrate sound finances to minimize the likelihood of insolvency. Under the *dual choice* requirement, employers with at least 25 employees had to offer at least one HMO as an alternative to a fee-for-service plan when an HMO formally offered its services to an employer's workforce.

The dual choice requirement was eliminated in 1995 to allow HMOs and other types of health-care plans to compete on a more equal footing in two ways. First, employers now can negotiate rates based on the expected experience of their employee population. That is, the premium amount varies by the likelihood that employees will use HMO services. Oftentimes, HMOs and employers review recent usage of HMO services to predict future usage. Employers whose employees tend to use HMO services more extensively pay higher premiums than employers whose employees tend to use HMO services less extensively.

Second, the HMO Act promotes more equal competition because employers may not financially discriminate against employees who choose an HMO option. In other words, companies must make the same percentage contribution toward an HMO's premium as they do to provide other health-care plans. Suppose, for example, that an employer has paid 75 percent of the premiums for traditional fee-for-service plans. Previously, this employer paid only 40 percent of the premiums to provide HMO coverage. Contributing less is no longer acceptable. This employer now must pay at least 75 percent of the HMO premium to remain in compliance with the HMO Act.

The Employee Retirement Income Security Act of 1974 (ERISA)

In Chapter 3, we discussed that ERISA heavily governs the operation of pension plans and welfare plans. The definition of *welfare plans* encompasses medical, surgical, and hospital care and benefits, and benefits in the event of sickness.[8] Four parts of Title I (protection of employee rights) apply to welfare plans:

- Reporting and disclosure.
- Fiduciary responsibilities.
- Continuation coverage.
- Additional standards for group health plans, and group health-plan portability, access, and renewability requirements.

The latter two provisions are amendments to ERISA since its passage in 1974. The Consolidated Omnibus Budget Reconciliation Act of 1985 established continuation coverage and additional standards for group health plans. The Health Insurance Portability and Accountability Act of 1996 created standards for group health-plan portability, access, and renewability requirements.

An additional amendment to ERISA, the **Women's Health and Cancer Rights Act of 1998**,[9] requires group health plans to provide medical and surgical benefits for mastectomies. Medical and surgical benefits must cover surgical reconstruction of either breast for a symmetrical appearance.

As discussed, ERISA protects the rights of employees regarding retirement and welfare benefit plans. However, a recent Supreme Court decision imposes limits on patients' rights to sue HMOs for malpractice or negligence in particular circumstances. The court reasoned that states with patient protection laws exceeded their authority by interfering with ERISA's exclusive remedy in private sector employee benefit matters.

The Americans with Disabilities Act of 1990

The Americans with Disabilities Act of 1990 (ADA)[10] prohibits illegal discrimination in employment practices on the basis of disability. The U.S. Equal Employment Opportunity Commission (EEOC), the government entity that oversees the administration and enforcement of the ADA, ruled that employers are required to provide the same health-care coverage to employees regardless of disability status. Meanwhile:

> Congress recognized . . . that some types of benefit plans rest on an assessment
> of the risks and costs associated with various health conditions in accordance with

accepted principles of risk assessment. As a result, the ADA permits employers to make disability-based distinctions in employee benefit plans where the distinctions are based on sound actuarial principles or are related to actual or reasonably anticipated experience.[11]

Patient Protection and Affordable Care Act of 2010

The **Patient Protection and Affordable Care Act of 2010 (PPACA)** is a comprehensive law that mandates health insurance coverage and sets minimum standards for insurance. (We discuss health insurance design alternatives later in this chapter.) Specifically, PPACA contains two mandates: *individual mandate* and *employer mandate*. The **individual mandate** requires that individuals who can afford to purchase health insurance must do so either by participating in an employer-sponsored plan or by purchasing health insurance coverage independently. Starting in 2016, the **employer mandate** requires that companies with at least 50 employees are required to offer affordable health insurance to its full-time employees. For the purposes of this law, full-time employees work on average at least 30 hours per week or 130 hours per month. How does the PPACA define affordable health care?

Under employer shared responsibility, large group employers can avoid potential penalties by offering minimal essential coverage to full-time employees and their child dependents under age 26 that:

- Covers at least 60 percent of expected costs for an average person or family.
- Limits an employee's share of the premium contribution to 9.5 percent of the employee's income.
- Is available to at least 95 percent of its full-time employees or five of its full-time employees if that's greater than 95 percent (and also offers that coverage to the employee's child dependents).

Employers and individuals are subject to monetary penalties for failure to provide or carry insurance coverage. Individuals who do not receive coverage through employment or are unemployed pay a penalty; oftentimes, some refer to this as a tax rather than as a penalty. Without this mandate, many individuals would likely put off purchasing health insurance until they need it—that is, at the onset of a serious medical condition, when premium rates are highest (as compared to purchasing health insurance when healthy). This practice would also cause insurance premiums to rise for those who maintain coverage, including the cost of health-care plan premiums to employers: In the case of fully insured plans, rate increases may be levied on all policyholders to protect profits.

Many provisions of the law have a broad impact on employment-sponsored health insurance plans that do not have grandfathered status. PPACA distinguishes between health plans that existed prior to the March 23, 2010, enactment date and those that come into existence afterward. Individual and group health plans already in existence prior to enactment are referred to as **grandfathered plans**. New health plans (or preexisting plans that have been substantially modified after March 23, 2010) are referred to as **non-grandfathered plans**. Grandfathered plans could lose this status if at least one of the following modifications is made:

- Changing insurance carriers for individuals. For example, the employer no longer offers insurance coverage through Blue Cross and Blue Shield, which it had offered prior to the effective date of PPACA, and now offers coverage through Humana Health Care.

- Raising coinsurance by any amount. **Coinsurance** refers to the percentage of covered expenses paid by the insured.

- Increasing copayments. **Copayments** represent fixed payments an individual makes as a condition of receiving services. Grandfathered status will be lost if copayments increase more than $5 plus the rate of medical inflation (e.g., 20 percent), or 15 percent higher than medical inflation (whichever is greater). For instance, raising a copay from $5 to $20 triggers a loss in grandfathered status because the increase exceeds medical inflation plus 15 percent. *Medical inflation* is defined as the medical care component of the Consumer Price Index for All Urban Consumers.

- Increasing deductibles. The **deductible** refers to the amount an individual pays for health-care services before benefits become active. Grandfathered status will be lost if the increase exceeds the rate of medical inflation by 15 percent.

- Increasing out-of-pocket maximums based on the aforementioned criterion. **Out-of-pocket maximum** refers to the maximum amount a policyholder must pay per year.

- Decreasing the amount of an employer's share to provide health coverage by more than 5 percent.

- Eliminating or reducing benefits specific to certain health conditions. For example, a plan would lose its grandfathered status if it terminated benefits for the diagnosis or treatment of diabetes.

Reducing or eliminating coverage for one or more "essential benefits" will cause a grandfathered plan to lose this status. **Essential benefits** include items and services within the following 10 categories:

- Ambulatory patient services
- Emergency services
- Hospitalization
- Maternity and newborn care
- Mental health and substance use disorder services, including behavioral health treatment
- Prescription drugs
- Rehabilitative services and devices
- Laboratory services
- Preventive and wellness services and chronic disease management
- Pediatric services, including oral and vision care

Companies that fail to offer health-care plans are subject to a penalty. These dollar amounts are adjustable for inflation. For 2016, the amounts are $2,160 ($180 per month) for failing to offer coverage, and $3,240 ($280 per month) for failing to offer affordable, minimum-value coverage. These penalties are assessed per full-time employee not appropriately covered (excluding the first 30 employees) on a monthly basis. The penalty is larger ($260 per month) if the company fails to offer affordable, minimum-value coverage. The formula is complex and is subject to modification based on possible legislative rule changes and experience. Oftentimes, a company's decision whether to offer health-care plans is called "pay or play." Companies that do not offer health-care plans or ones that follow the minimum standards specified in the PPACA must pay. Those that offer health-care plans that meet or exceed minimum standards are said to play.

The PPACA instituted requirements that health plans remove annual dollar limits on most health benefits as well as eliminated preexisting condition clauses altogether. (We review both features later in this chapter.) Also, in 2018, a *Cadillac tax* provision was scheduled to take effect, but, its implementation has been delayed until 2020. The **Cadillac tax** will apply to high-cost employer-sponsored health plans. That is, plans that cost more than $10,200 annually for single coverage and $27,500 for family coverage are subject to the Cadillac tax, and these limits are subject to change from year to year. The tax equals 40 percent of the amount that exceeds those limits. For example, if plan for single coverage costs $14,000, the employer would pay 40 percent of $3,800 ($14,000 minus $10,200), or $1,520 for each covered individual (excluding the first 30 employees). The tax was intended to be a disincentive for employers to provide overly rich health benefits, and the cost of the health plan is one way to assess the level of benefits.

It is worth noting that there has been much controversy over this law. For instance, several states, interest groups, and citizens oppose the PPACA, arguing against its legality. The arguments focused on two issues centered on the individual mandate. First, these groups claimed that the PPACA represents an infringement on people's constitutional rights. In particular, they claimed that requiring Americans to purchase health insurance or pay a penalty reaches beyond the federal government's power under the U.S. Constitution's commerce clause. Since the law's passage, several lawsuits were filed in various federal district courts. Eleven noteworthy court rulings revealed a split regarding the legality of this law. Among them, only five upheld the law. The division on the legality of the PPACA can be defined largely by the political orientation of the court judges. The judges who found the law unconstitutional were appointed by Republican presidents, and those upholding it were appointed by Democratic presidents.

The next steps in these legal challenges typically would have involved appeals in various U.S. Courts of Appeals; however, Republicans successfully bypassed these courts by having the U.S. Supreme Court hear the arguments against PPACA. They convinced the U.S. Supreme Court that the resolution of the overhaul's constitutionality is "a matter of imperative public importance," which is the only grounds for skipping the appellate courts.

The U.S. Supreme Court heard arguments in 2012 and ruled that the individual mandate of PPACA does not violate citizens' constitutional rights under Congress' taxation power. Five of the U.S. Supreme Court's nine justices made the ruling on the taxation issue. They reasoned that paying a tax in lieu of purchasing health insurance does not impose health insurance on an individual: An individual has the right to choose between carrying health insurance or paying a tax penalty. The justices could not come to an agreement on the original argument that the individual mandate requirement extends beyond the federal government's power under the U.S. Constitution's commerce clause.

A second challenge to the health-care law was brought to the Supreme Court, which focused on the legality of the federal government providing tax subsidies to individuals who purchased health insurance through federal health care exchanges. (Note that health-care exchanges are so-called markets where individuals can purchase reasonably priced health insurance, though there has been much controversy about whether lower costs have been achieved.) Much of the challenge was based on wording of the law that specified subsidies for insurance purchased through state health-care exchanges. In 2015, six of the court's nine justices ruled that tax subsidies through federal exchanges are permissible, arguing that the law was created to be inclusive rather than exclusive. Are there more challenges on the horizon?

At least through the publication of this edition of the book, the PPACA remains intact. However, a vigorous policy debate in Washington, D.C., continues, and the possibility remains that future challenges to the law will be brought forward.

Thus far, the focus of the legal challenges has been on the individual mandate. Even though the rulings have focused on elements of the individual mandate, employers should take away that the complexity of the law has caused much confusion in companies. Benefits professionals must stay abreast of new developments that help clarify how to achieve and maintain compliance. Finally, growing legal practices focus exclusively on this law because of its complexity.

State Regulations

Every state has laws regulating health insurers' practices that apply to fully insured plans, but typically not self-funded plans. State laws mandating health benefits require that insurance companies include certain health benefits in the insurance policies that they offer or make particular optional health benefits available upon request. Overall, these laws address four areas of responsibility:

- Extending coverage to particular services, treatments, and health conditions (e.g., substance abuse treatment).
- Reimbursing recognized health-care providers for health care services.
- Individuals who must be covered by health-care policies (e.g., adopted children).
- Length of time coverage must be available to employees who are terminating their employment.

Laws vary from state to state. Every state includes a department that oversees insurance regulations, with data being available to the public upon request. Also, the **National Association of Insurance Commissioners (NAIC),**[12] a nonprofit organization, addresses issues concerning the supervision of insurance within each state (www.naic.org).

In the next sections, various types of health-care plans are reviewed. As noted earlier, the following ways to provide health-care coverage include fee-for-service plans, alternative managed care plans, and any of those plans associated with the consumer-driven approach. The U.S. Bureau of Labor Statistics uses several criteria to help distinguish between fee-for-service plans and managed care plans. which are shown in Exhibit 5.3. The primary criterion centers on whether the plan is prepaid or an indemnity plan. A **prepaid plan** pays health-care providers a fixed amount according to the number of individuals covered by the plan. An **indemnity plan** reimburses either the health-care provider or patient. Following is a discussion of these approaches to health-care plan design, as well as a review of other health-related benefits including dental, vision, and mental health, and substance abuse.

HEALTH PLAN DESIGN ALTERNATIVES

There is a variety of health-care plan design alternatives. The U.S. Bureau of Labor Statistics provides four questions to help distinguish among them:

- Is the plan an indemnity or prepaid plan? Indemnity plans reimburse the patient or the provider as medical expenses occur or afterward. Prepaid plans pay medical service providers a fixed amount based on the number of people enrolled, regardless of services received.

EXHIBIT 5.3   How the National Compensation Survey Determines the Type of Medical Plan Employers Offer

Source: U.S. Bureau of Labor Statistics, "Understanding Health Plan Types: What's In a Name?" *Pay and Benefits* (Volume 4, No. 2), January 2015.

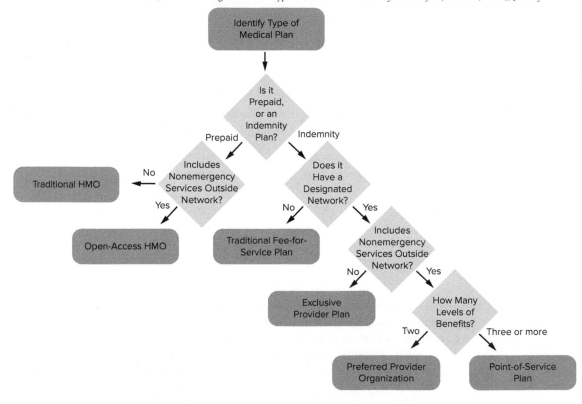

- Does the plan have a network? A network is a specific group of doctors, hospitals, suppliers, and clinics who have contracted to provide services for an agreed rate.
- Does the plan allow people to receive nonemergency care outside the network? This question identifies how restrictive the plan is regarding choice of medical providers.
- Does the plan have more than two levels of coverage? This question determines if the plan is a point-of-service plan, which typically has several reimbursement levels depending on where enrollees receive services.

We review the alternative plan designs shown in Exhibit 5.3.

FEE-FOR-SERVICE PLANS

Fee-for-service plans provide protection against health care expenses in the form of a cash benefit paid to the employee or directly to the health care provider after receiving health-care services. These plans pay benefits on a *reimbursement basis.* Three types of eligible health expenses are hospital expenses, surgical expenses, and physician charges. Under fee-for-service plans, participants may generally select any licensed physician, surgeon, or medical facility for treatment, and the insurer reimburses the participants after medical services are rendered. These plans generally do not rely on networks of health-care providers.

MANAGED CARE PLANS

Managed care plans emphasize cost control by limiting an employee's choice of doctors and hospitals. Three common forms of managed care include health maintenance organizations (HMOs), exclusive provider plans (EPOs), preferred provider organizations (PPOs), and point-of-service (POS) plans.

Health Maintenance Organizations

HMOs are sometimes described as providing prepaid medical services, because fixed periodic enrollment fees cover HMO members for all medically necessary services only if the services are delivered by health-care providers in the designated network and, approved by the HMO. HMOs generally provide inpatient and outpatient care, emergency room care, as well as services from physicians, surgeons, and other health-care professionals. Most medical services are either fully covered or, in the case of some HMOs, participants are required to make copayments, which we take up later in the chapter. Another type of HMO is the **open-access HMO**. These are prepaid plans and require the use of network health-care providers with one exception. In open-access HMO plans, emergency care outside the network is covered, which is not the case for traditional HMO plans. HMOs generally do not cover expenses incurred in emergency rooms outside the designated network unless deemed by medical experts as a life-or-death matter.

EXHIBIT 5.4
Role of
Primary Care
Physicians

- Make an initial diagnosis and evaluation of the patient's condition.
- Identify applicable treatment protocols and practice guidelines.
- Decide whether treatment is warranted and, if warranted, specify the treatment.
- Approve referrals to medical specialists.
- Evaluate patient's health following treatment.

HMOs designate some of their physicians, usually general or family practitioners, as primary care physicians. HMOs assign each member to a primary care physician or require each member to choose one. **Primary care physicians** determine when patients need the care of specialists. HMOs use primary care physicians to control costs by significantly reducing the number of unnecessary visits to specialists. As primary care physicians, doctors perform several duties. Exhibit 5.4 lists the major duties of primary care physicians.

HMOs require that patients make copayments. The most common HMO copayments apply to physician office visits, hospital admissions, prescription drugs, and emergency room services. Office visits are nominal amounts, usually $10 to $15 per visit. Hospital admissions and emergency room services are higher, ranging between $50 and $150 for each occurrence. Mental health services and substance abuse treatment require copayments as well. Inpatient services require copayments that are not higher in amount than copayments for hospital admissions for medical treatment. As flat dollar amounts, copayments generally average between 15 and 20 percent of the service provider (e.g., surgeon) charge for the service (e.g., surgical procedure).

Types of Health Maintenance Organizations

HMOs differ based on where service is rendered, how medical care is delivered, and how contractual relationships between medical providers and the HMOs are structured.

Prepaid Group Practice Model

Prepaid group practices provide medical care for a set amount. Group HMOs typically operate around the clock, with phone coverage for emergencies and emergency room treatment. Prepaid group practices may take one of three specific forms.

Staff model HMOs own the medical facilities, and these organizations employ medical and support staff on these premises. These practices compensate physicians on a salary basis. Staff physicians treat only members of their HMO. Occasionally, staff model HMOs establish contracts with specialists to provide services not covered by staff members. Contract physicians are compensated according to a capped fee schedule. This means that the HMO establishes the amount it will reimburse physicians for each procedure. If contract physicians charge more than the fee set by the HMO, then they must bill the difference to the patients. For example, an HMO sets a cap of $100 for an annual physical examination. If the physician charges $120 for the annual examination, then the physician bills the HMO for $100 and the patient for the remaining $20.

Group model HMOs primarily use contracts with established practices of physicians that cover multiple specialties. Unlike staff model HMOs, group model HMOs do not directly employ physicians. These HMOs compensate physicians according to a pre-established schedule of fees for each service, or by setting monthly amounts per patient.

Network model HMOs and group model HMOs are similar except for one feature. **Network model HMOs** contract with two or more independent practices of physicians. These HMOs usually compensate physicians according to a capped fee schedule.

Individual Practice Associations

Individual practice associations (IPAs) are partnerships of independent physicians, health professionals, and group practices. IPAs charge lower fees to designated populations of employees (e.g., Company A's workforce) than fees charged to others. Physicians who participate in this type of HMO practice from their own facilities and continue to see HMO enrollees and patients who are not HMO enrollees.

Preferred Provider Organizations

Under a **preferred provider organization (PPO),** a select group of health-care providers agrees to furnish health-care services to a given population at a lower level of reimbursement than is the case for fee-for-service plans. Physicians qualify as preferred providers by meeting quality standards, agreeing to follow cost-containment procedures implemented by the PPO, and accepting the PPO's reimbursement structure. In return, the employer, insurance company, or third-party administrator helps guarantee provider physicians minimum patient loads by furnishing employees with financial incentives to use the preferred providers. PPOs provide lower reimbursements for services outside preferred networks. Exhibit 5.5 summarizes the main features of a PPO plan.

An **exclusive provider organization (EPO)** is a variation of a PPO. EPOs operate similarly to PPOs, but these systems differ. EPOs are more restrictive than PPO plans. EPOs offer reimbursement for services provided within the established network. Exceptions to this rule include medical emergencies or the need for a medical specialty not contained in the provider network. Compared to HMOs, EPOs do not require having a primary care physician.

Point-of-Service Plans

A **point-of-service (POS) plan** combines features of fee-for-service systems and health maintenance organizations. Specifically, POS plans are almost identical to PPOs, except, like HMOs, POS plans require the selection of a primary care physician. Employees pay a nominal copayment for each visit to a designated network of physicians. In this regard, POS plans are similar to HMOs. Unlike HMOs, however, POS plans provide employees with the option to receive care

EXHIBIT 5.5 PPO Plan Coverage

Inpatient Hospital Services	
Preferred provider organization hospital	90% after annual plan deductible. No admission deductible.
Nonpreferred provider organization hospital	$300 per admission deductible. The plan pays 65% after annual plan deductible if member voluntarily chooses to use a non-PPO, or voluntarily travels in excess of 25 miles when a PPO hospital is available within the same travel distance. Coverage will be at 80% after annual plan deductible if a PPO hospital within 25 miles of a member's residence is not medically qualified to perform the required services, if no PPO exists within 25 miles of the member's residence, or if a member utilizes a non-PPO for emergency services.
Outpatient Services	
Lab/X-ray	100% of usual and customary (U&C) after annual plan deductible.
Approved durable medical equipment and prosthetics	80% of U&C after annual plan deductible. Contact the plan administrator for approval prior to obtaining items.
Facility charges	90% after annual plan deductible for PPOs and licensed, free-standing surgical facilities. (Note: Outpatient facility charges will be covered at 65% after annual plan deductible if member voluntarily chooses to use a non-PPO, or voluntarily travels in excess of 25 miles when a PPO hospital is available within the same travel distance. Coverage will be at 80% after annual plan deductible if a PPO hospital within 25 miles of a member's residence is not medically qualified to perform the required services, if no PPO exists within 25 miles of the member's residence, or if a member utilizes a non-PPO for emergency services.)
Professional and Other Services	
Physician and surgeon services	80% of U&C after annual plan deductible for inpatient, outpatient, and office visits.
Preventive services	Well baby care (through age 6), pap smears (includes office visit), mammograms, prostate screening, routine adult physicals, and school health exams (grades 5 and 9) are covered per the applicable coverages. No deductibles apply.
Physician Network	
Physician and surgeon services (where available)	90% of billed charges. U&C charges do not apply.

from health-care providers outside the designated network of physicians, but employees pay somewhat more for this choice. This choice feature is common to fee-for-service plans. Exhibit 5.6 describes the features of a POS plan. In summary,

EXHIBIT 5.6 POS Benefits

POS Plan Design	In-Network Benefit	Out-of-Network Benefit
Plan year maximum benefit	Unlimited	Unlimited
Lifetime maximum benefit	Unlimited	Unlimited
Annual out-of-pocket maximum	Individual $6,600 Family $13,200	Not Applicable
Annual plan deductible	Individual $0 Family $0	Individual $300 Family $600
POS Services Covered		
Inpatient hospitalizations	100% after $350 copayment	60% of covered charges after $500 copayment
Psychiatric admission (*maximum of 30 visits per calendar year*)	100% after $350 copayment	No out-of-network benefit, covered in-network only
Inpatient alcohol and/or substance abuse treatment (*maximum of 30 visits per calendar year*)	100% after $350 copayment	No out-of-network benefit, covered in-network only
Emergency room services	100% after $250 copayment per occurrence	60% after lesser of $500 copayment or 50% of usual and customary (U&C)
Outpatient surgeries	100%	60% of U&C after plan deductible
Diagnostic lab and X-ray	100%	60% of U&C after plan deductible
Physician visits	100% after $20 copayment	60% of U&C after plan deductible
Preventive services (*including immunizations*)	100% after $20 copayment	No out-of-network benefit, covered in-network only
Well baby care	100%	No out-of-network benefit, covered in-network only
Outpatient psychiatric (*maximum of 30 visits per calendar year*)	100% after $30 copayment	No out-of-network benefit, covered in-network only
Outpatient substance abuse (*maximum of 20 visits per calendar year*)	100% after $30 copayment	No out-of-network benefit, covered in-network only
Prescription drugs (*generic incentive and formulary restrictions may apply. Formulary is subject to change during the plan year.*)	Generic: $12 copayment Brand: $30 copayment Nonformulary: $50 copayment	Emergency drugs only. In-network copayment applies
Durable medical equipment	100%	60% of U&C after plan deductible

we reviewed fee-for-service and alternative managed care plans. Four questions put forth by the U.S. Bureau of Labor Statistics help distinguish among specific health-care plans. Exhibit 5.7 provides a summary of these plans based on the Bureau's questions.

EXHIBIT 5.7 Health-Care Plan Types and Features Based on the U.S. Bureau of Labor Statistics Criteria

Source: Adapted from the U.S. Bureau of Labor Statistics, "Understanding Health Plan Types: What's In a Name?" *Pay and Benefits* (Volume 4, No. 2), January 2015.

Type of plan	Is the plan reimbursement or prepaid?	Does the plan have a network?	Does the plan cover nonemergency care outside the network?	Does the plan have more than two levels of benefits?
Fee-for-service plan	Reimbursement	No	Yes	No
Preferred provider organization (PPO)	Reimbursement	Yes	Yes	Yes
Exclusive provider organization (EPO)	Reimbursement	Yes	No	No
Point-of-service plan	Reimbursement	Yes	Yes	Yes
Health maintenance organization (HMO)	Prepaid	Yes	No	No
Open-access health maintenance organization	Prepaid	Yes	Yes	No

FEATURES OF HEALTH–CARE PLANS

Health-care plans share a number of features in common. These include:

- Deductible
- Coinsurance
- Out-of-Pocket Maximum
- Preexisting Condition Clauses
- Preadmission Certification
- Second Surgical Opinion
- Lifetime and Yearly Limits

HMO plans share several features in common with fee-for-service plans, including out-of-pocket maximums, preexisting condition clauses, preadmission certification, second surgical opinions, and lifetime and yearly limits. HMOs differ from fee-for-service plans in three important ways. First, HMOs offer prepaid services, while fee-for-service plans operate on a reimbursement basis. Second, HMOs include the use of primary care physicians as a cost-control measure. Third, coinsurance rates are generally lower in HMO plans than in fee-for-service plans. Exhibit 5.8 illustrates the features of an HMO.

PPO plans include features that resemble fee-for-service plans or HMO plans. Features most similar to fee-for-service plans are out-of-pocket maximums and coinsurance, and those most similar to HMOs include the use of copayments. Preexisting condition clauses, preadmission certification, second surgical

EXHIBIT 5.8
HMO Benefits

HMO Plan Design	
Plan year maximum benefit	Unlimited
Lifetime maximum benefit	Unlimited
Hospital Services	
Inpatient hospitalization	100% after $350 copayment per admission
Alcohol and substance abuse* *(maximum number of days determined by the plan)*	100% after $150 copayment per admission
Psychiatric admission* *(maximum number of days determined by the plan)*	100% after $350 copayment per admission
Outpatient surgery	100%
Diagnostic lab and X-ray	100%
Emergency room hospital services	100% after $250 copayment
Professional and Other Services	
Physician visits	100%, $30 copayment may apply *(including physical exams and immunizations)*
Well baby care	100%
Psychiatric care* *(maximum number of days determined by the plan)*	100% after $30 copayment per visit
Alcohol and substance abuse care* *(maximum number of days determined by the plan)*	100% after $30 copayment per visit
Prescription drugs	$15 copayment, generic incentive, and formulary restrictions may apply. Formulary is subject to change during the plan year.
Durable medical equipment	80%

*HMOs determine the maximum number of inpatient days and outpatient visits for psychiatric and alcohol/substance abuse treatment. Each plan must provide for a minimum of 10 inpatient days and 20 outpatient visits per plan year. These are in addition to detoxification benefits, which include diagnosis and treatment of medical complications. Some HMOs may provide benefit limitations on a calendar year.

opinions, and lifetime and yearly limits are similar to those in fee-for-service and HMO plans. PPOs contain deductible and coinsurance provisions that differ somewhat from other plans.

Deductible

A common feature of fee-for-service plans is the deductible. Over a designated period, employees must pay for services (i.e., meet a deductible) before the plan pays benefits. The deductible amount ranges anywhere between $3,000 for care received within the network of approved providers and $5,800 for care provide outside the network. Alternatively, deductible amounts may depend on annual earnings, expressed as a fixed amount. Fee-for-service plans usually apply separate deductible amounts for each type of coverage (i.e., hospitalization, surgical expenses, and physician expenses). In other words, insured individuals must pay a specified amount for hospitalization, surgical expenses, and physician expenses, respectively. Exhibit 5.9 illustrates deductibles based on annual salary. The deductible feature applies to a designated period, usually a one-year period that corresponds with the calendar year or the company's benefit plan year.

Coinsurance

Insurance plans feature coinsurance, which becomes relevant after the insured pays the annual deductible. Coinsurance refers to the percentage of covered expenses paid by the insured. The insurance company pays the difference between the total covered expenses amount and the coinsurance amount. Most plans stipulate 20 percent coinsurance. This means that the plan will pay 80 percent of covered expenses, while the policyholder is responsible for the difference—in this case, 20 percent.

Out-of-Pocket Maximum

As discussed above, health-care costs are on the rise. Despite generous coinsurance rates, the expense amounts for which individuals are responsible can be staggering. Oftentimes, these amounts are beyond the financial means of most individuals. Thus, most plans specify the maximum amount a policyholder must pay per calendar year or plan year, known as the out-of-pocket maximum provision.

The purpose of the out-of-pocket maximum provision is to protect individuals from catastrophic medical expenses or expenses associated with recurring episodes of the same illness. Out-of-pocket maximums are usually stated as a fixed

EXHIBIT 5.9
Plan Year
Deductibles

The benefits described in this summary represent the major areas of coverage. The plan year is July 1 through June 30 of the following year.		
Plan year deductible	The plan year deductible is indexed to salary for employees. See the following table for current plan year information.	
Additional deductibles	Each emergency room visit:	$450
	Non-PPO hospital admission:	$100
	Transplant deductible:	$500

Employee's Annual Salary (Based on each employee's annual salary as of April 1)	**Member Plan Year Deductible**	**Family Plan Year Deductible Cap**
$52,700 or less	$375	$ 950
$52,701–$66,000	$475	$1,250
$66,001 or more	$525	$1,350
Retiree/annuitant/survivor	$375	$ 950
Dependents	$375	NA

dollar amount and apply to expenses beyond the deductible amount. Unmarried individuals often have an annual out-of-pocket maximum as high as $4,500, and family out-of-pocket maximums are as high as $9,000. For example, an insurance plan specifies a $200 deductible. An unmarried person is responsible for the first $200 of expenses plus additional expenses up to $800 per year—that is, the out-of-pocket maximum—for a total of $1,000.

Exhibit 5.10 shows an example of an out-of-pocket maximum, as well as coinsurance rates and deductible amounts for specific services.

Preexisting Condition Clauses

A **preexisting condition** is a condition for which medical advice, diagnosis, care, or treatment was received or recommended during a designated period preceding the beginning of coverage and for which coverage is excluded. Preexisting condition clauses were created to limit their liabilities for serious medical conditions that predate an individual's coverage. The PPACA prohibits the inclusion of preexisting clauses in any employer-sponsored plan, that is, even grandfathered plans can no longer impose a preexisting condition clause. One exception pertains to grandfathered plans bought by an individual. In that case, grandfathered plans can impose preexisting condition clauses.

Preadmission Certification

Many insurance plans require **preadmission certification** of medical necessity for hospitalization. Specifically, physicians must receive approval from a registered nurse or medical doctor employed by an insurance company before admitting patients to the hospital on a nonemergency basis—that is, when a patient's life is not in imminent danger. Insurance company doctors and nurses judge whether hospitalization or alternative care is necessary. In addition, they determine the length of stay appropriate for the medical condition. Precertification requirements

EXHIBIT 5.10
Deductibles and Out-of-Pocket Maximums

General Deductibles: $3,500 per Individual; $6,000 per Family per Plan Year
Professional and physician coinsurance: 20%
Physician network, where available: 10%
PPO inpatient coinsurance: 10%
Transplant deductible: $100
Transplant inpatient and outpatient coinsurance: 20%
Standard hospital coinsurance: 20%
Standard hospital admission deductible: $350
All emergency room deductibles: $250
Emergency room coinsurance: 20%
Charges That Apply toward Out-of-Pocket Maximums:
• Prescription drug deductible and copayments.
• Mental health substance abuse benefits, coinsurance, or copayments.
• Medical coinsurance.

reserve the right for insurance companies not to pay for unauthorized admissions or hospital stays that extend beyond the approved period.

Second Surgical Opinion

Second surgical opinion reduces unnecessary surgical procedures (and costs) by encouraging an individual to seek an independent opinion from another doctor. Following a recommendation of surgery from a physician, many individuals are inclined to seek an independent opinion to avoid the risks associated with surgery. With second surgical opinion provisions, insurance companies cover the cost of this consultation. Some insurance companies require second surgical opinions before authorizing surgery, while others offer second surgical opinion consultations as an option to each individual.

Lifetime and Yearly Limits

At one time, most health-care plans specified *lifetime limits* and *yearly limits*. **Lifetime limits** refers to the maximum amount a plan would for as long as a person receives coverage. **Yearly limits** refer to the maximum amount a plan would cover each year. Neither is permitted under PPACA for either grandfathered or nongrandfathered plans.

Until the passage of the PPACA, employers could purchase health plans with lower lifetime and yearly limits at correspondingly lower costs. The PPACA prohibits limits on essential benefits.

CONSUMER-DRIVEN HEALTH CARE

Managed care plans became popular alternatives to fee-for-service plans mainly to help control the costs of health care. As has been discussed, managed care plans by design impose substantial restrictions on an employee's ability to make choices about from whom they could receive medical treatment, the gatekeeper role of primary care physicians, and the level of benefits they could receive based on designated in- and non-network providers. Despite these cost-control objectives, health-care costs have continued to rise dramatically over the years while also restricting employee choice. The average cost to provide employer-sponsored health insurance increased nearly 107 percent between 2001 and 2016.

According to the U.S. Bureau of Labor Statistics, companies further sought ways to control the costs of health insurance. Increasingly, companies are adopting a **consumer-driven health-care plan (CDHP)** approach. This approach refers to the objective of helping companies maintain control over costs while also enabling employees to make wise choices about their health care. CDHPs combine a pretax payment account with a high-deductible health plan. **High-deductible health insurance plans (HDHPs)** require substantially higher deductibles compared to managed care plans and traditional fee-for-service plans. What exactly distinguishes an HDHP from traditional health-care plans? For individual coverage, the minimum annual deductible is $1,300 with a maximum out-of-pocket limit at or below $6,550 in 2017. For family coverage, the deductible is $2,600 with a maximum out-of-pocket limit at or below $13,100. Generally, deductibles and copayments count toward the maximum out-of-pocket limit.

Oftentimes, CDHPs are referred to as three-tier payment systems. The first tier is an account that allows employees to pay for services using pretax dollars. Either the employer or the employee funds the account based on the type of account. The second tier, referred to as the coverage gap, is the difference between the amount of money in the individual's pretax account and the health plan's deductible. The amount not covered by the account is the employee's responsibility. In the third tier, an HDHP covers expense amounts above the deductible. Two examples illustrate these principles.

EXAMPLE 1: *Medical expenses ($4,000) are greater than the insurance plan's deductible amount ($1,500).*

> **Tier 1:** *Use of money held in a pretax account to cover up to the health plan deductible amount, and necessary coinsurance and copayments. John has a pretax savings account (one of the three types noted in the next section).* The available balance in his account is $1,000 in 2016. John may use the money in this pretax account to pay for eligible medical expenses in 2016. In most circumstances, he will use it to cover up to the deductible amount in his health plan as well as any required coinsurance or copayments. Let's assume that John's deductible amount is $1,500 in 2016. He may apply the entire balance in his pretax account to cover $1,000 of the $1,500 insurance deductible.
>
> **Tier 2:** *Coverage Gap: Difference between the pretax account balance and the insurance plan deductible amount (when the pretax account balance is lower than the insurance deductible amount).* For John, the difference is –$500. The negative balance indicates that his pretax account balance ($1,000) is less than his insurance plan's deductible amount ($1,500) by $500. Therefore, John is responsible for paying this $500 coverage gap between the balance of his pretax account and the deductible amount.
>
> **Tier 3:** *Insurance plan covers the costs of medical care for amounts greater than the insurance plan deductible amount.* As noted previously, John incurs medical expenses equal to $4,000 in 2016. Both his pretax account balance ($1,000) and additional out-of-pocket expense ($500) equals the insurance plan's deductible amount of $1,500. The difference between John's total medical expenses ($4,000) and deductible amount ($1,500) equals $3,000. The health insurance plan pays this amount ($3,000).

EXAMPLE 2: *Medical expenses ($1,200) are less than the insurance plan's deductible amount ($1,500).*

> **Tier 1:** *Use of money held in a pretax account to cover up to the health insurance plan deductible amount.* Sally has a pretax savings account (one of the three types noted in the next section). The available balance in her account is

$1,000 in 2016. Sally may use the money in this pretax account to pay for eligible medical expenses in 2016. In most circumstances, she will use it to cover up to the deductible amount in her health plan. Let's assume that Sally's deductible amount is $1,500 in 2016. She may apply the entire balance in her pretax account to cover $1,000 of the $1,500 insurance deductible.

Tier 2: *Coverage gap: Difference between the pretax account balance and the insurance plan deductible amount (when the pretax account balance is less than the insurance deductible amount).* For Sally, the difference is –$500. The negative balance indicates that her pretax account balance ($1,000) is less than her insurance plan's deductible amount ($1,500). *However*, Sally's out-of-pocket expense is just $200, because her medical expenses for the year ($1,200) are more than the balance in her pretax account ($1,000).

Tier 3: *Insurance plan covers the costs of medical care for amounts greater than the insurance plan deductible amount.* Tier 3 is not relevant in this particular example. The insurance plan does not pay any of Sally's medical expenses in 2016 because her total medical expenses ($1,200) did not reach the plan's deductible amount ($1,500).

The idea of consumer-driven health care received substantially greater attention than ever before under the Bush administration (President George W. Bush) and the Republican-led Congress, who favored greater employee involvement in their medical care and reductions in the cost burden for companies to help maintain competitiveness in the global market. The **Medicare Prescription Drug, Improvement and Modernization Act of 2003** added section 223 to the IRC, effective January 1, 2004, to permit eligible individuals to establish **health savings accounts (HSAs)** for employees who are enrolled in an HDHP to help pay for medical expenses. It is important to note that HSAs are not available for any other type of health-care plan.

The sum of an employer's and employee's contribution to an HSA cannot exceed the high-deductible health plan's annual deductible or $3,400 for individual coverage ($6,750 in the case of family coverage), whichever is less. In 2017, an employer, an employee, or both, could contribute as much as $3,400 annually for unmarried employees without dependent children or as much as $6,750 for married or unmarried employees with dependent children. Employers may require employees to contribute to these limits. An unused balance at the end of the year carries over to the next year and the employee owns the account and its holdings following termination or retirement from the company. Beginning at age 65, HSA holders may use these funds for retirement income.

Employers may consider using two other health accounts to help defray the costs of medical care: health reimbursement arrangements and flexible spending accounts. Employers establish **health reimbursement arrangements (HRAs)** that reimburse employees for health-care expenses. Only the employer is permitted to fund HRAs and there is no allowable maximum contribution limit. As with HSAs, employees can carry over unused balances into subsequent years.

The establishment of flexible spending accounts preceded the era of consumer-driven health care by decades. The IRS established flexible spending accounts in the 1970s as part of cafeteria benefit plans (Chapter 10) because employers were increasing the annual deductibles amounts and coinsurance rates in response to higher health plan premiums. These increases were proving to be particularly burdensome to employees. **Flexible spending accounts (FSAs)** permit employees to pay for specified health-care costs that are not covered by an employer's insurance plan. Prior to each plan year, employees elect the amount of pay they wish to allocate to this kind of plan. Employers then use these moneys to reimburse employees for expenses incurred during the plan year that qualify for repayment.

Qualifying expenses include an individual's out-of-pocket costs for medical treatments, products, or services related to a mental or physical defect or disease, along with certain associated costs, such as health plan deductibles or transportation to get medical care. However, health, life, and long-term care (e.g., nursing home or in-home assistance) premiums paid for by an employer or through an employee's pretax salary reductions generally do not qualify for reimbursement under a health FSA. Other exclusions include medical expenses reimbursed through health insurance plans and the costs of purely cosmetic procedures that enhance appearance but are not related to treating a disease or defect. Over-the-counter products are qualified expenses if they are used to diagnose, treat, alleviate, or prevent a disease or ailment, such as blood sugar monitoring kits for diabetic patients or crutches and bandages for someone with a serious leg injury.

A noteworthy drawback of FSAs is the "use it or lose it" provision. FSAs require employees to estimate the amount of money they think they will need for eligible medical expenses in the coming year, but that is often challenging because it is difficult to predict medical needs and to estimate the costs of health care. Employees lose contributions to their FSAs when they overestimate the cost of medical needs, because employees are not permitted to carry balances nor be reimbursed for unused balances remaining at the end of the year.

Employers also bear some risk from offering FSAs to employees. The maximum amount of expenses an employee can contribute to an FSA each year is $2,550 (in 2016), indexed for inflation. Although there is no statutory limit on the amount of reimbursement employees can receive under a medical FSA at a particular time, employers usually set a maximum limit—perhaps $2,000—to protect themselves against major losses under the **risk-of-loss rules** or **uniform coverage requirement.** Under this requirement, employers are obligated to make the full amount of benefits and coverage elected under an FSA plan available to employees from the first day the plan becomes effective, regardless of how much money an employee has actually contributed.

Let's assume that an employee plans to contribute $1,500 per year to her employer's FSA plan, based on monthly contributions of $125. In this case, $125 per month equals the $1,500 total annual contribution divided by 12 months per year. Continuing with this example, assume that this employee has a minor illness after making only three monthly contributions to the account ($375), and the medical and prescription costs to treat this minor illness are $1,275. The employer must allow this employee to withdraw $1,275 even though she has contributed only $375 thus far. This situation places demands on employer cash resources. Also, if this employee were to leave the company after this three-month period, the employer would have paid $900 out of its own funds toward this employee's treatment (i.e., $1,275 for the treatment cost, less $375, this employee's contribution to the FSA)

In summary, we reviewed consumer-driven health-care approaches, including high-deductible health plans. We also described savings accounts or arrangements that are often associated with consumer-driven approaches. Exhibit 5.11 summarizes the key features of HSA, HRA, and FSA plans.

EXHIBIT 5.11 **Comparison of Various Pretax Savings Accounts and Relationship to High-Deductible Health Plan**

Adapted from S. G. Yi, "Consumer-Driven Health Care: What Is IT, and What Does It Mean for Employees and Employers?" *Compensation and Working Conditions* (online), U.S. Bureau of Labor Statistics, October 25, 2010, http://www.bls.gov/opub/mlr/cwc/consumer-driven-health-care-what-is-it-and-what-does-it-mean-for-employees-and-employers.pdf.

Type of account	Pretax employee contribution allowed	Employer contribution allowed	Rollover allowed	May the assets in the fund be used for investing purposes?		Must the account be linked with a HDHP?	
				Yes/ No	If yes, what investments are allowed?	Yes/ No	If yes, what plan limits constitute a Qualified HDHP?
Health savings account (HSA)	Yes	Yes	Yes	Yes	The individual may use the assets in the fund to invest in any individual retirement account.	Yes	Minimum deductible: Self – $3,400 Family – $6,750 Max. annual out-of-pocket amount: Self – $6,550 Family – $13,100 Based on Internal Revenue Service limits for 2017
Health reimbursement arrangement (HRA)	No	Yes	Yes	No	The funds may only be used for qualified medical expenses.	No	---
Flexible spending account (FSA)	Yes	Yes	No	No	The funds may only be used for qualified medical expenses.	No	---

OTHER HEALTH-CARE-RELATED BENEFITS

Nowadays, the majority of health-care plans cover other health-care benefits. Oftentimes, employers use separate plans to provide specific kinds of benefits usually to cover dental care, vision care, prescription drugs, and mental health and substance abuse care. Sometimes, employers rely on **carve-out plans**, which refer to a contract agreement entered between an insurance company and another company to provide special services such as prescription drugs or cancer treatment to its members or beneficiaries. Sometimes, carve-out plans are purchased to cover dental care, vision care, or mental and substance abuse services. Usually, specialty HMOs or PPOs manage carve-out plans based on the expectation that single-specialty practices may control costs more effectively than multispecialty organizations. Prescription benefits and mental health benefits are PPACA-defined essential benefits.

Dental Insurance

Dental insurance benefits may cover routine preventative procedures (e.g., cleanings once every six months) and necessary procedures to promote the health of teeth and gums. Most dental plans do not include procedures for cosmetic improvements. Employers have several options from which to choose for providing dental benefits, including fee-for-service plans and various managed care systems.

Types of Dental Plans

Three main types of dental plans are available: dental fee-for-service plans, dental service corporation plans, and dental maintenance organization plans. Dental service corporations and dental maintenance organizations represent managed care options. Increasingly, companies are choosing to offer employees managed care options because of the anticipated cost savings.

Dental fee-for-service plans have features similar to those of medical fee-for-service plans. These plans specify covered dental services based on a usual, customary, and reasonable charge. Dental fee-for-service plans also include deductibles (similar in amount to medical plans), coinsurance, and maximum benefits. Coinsurance rates often vary between 20 and 40 percent of usual, customary, and reasonable charges after the insured pays the deductible. Dental fee-for-service plans usually set limits to the dollar amount of benefits over a subscriber's lifetime. These limits generally vary by procedure.

Dental service corporations are nonprofit organizations that are owned and administered by state dental associations. Like HMOs, dental service corporations offer prepaid benefits and require copayments for services received within the designated network of providers, usually equal to 20 to 30 percent of fees. The basis for reimbursement is either usual, customary, and reasonable fees or a negotiated schedule of fees for specific dental treatments and procedures. It is not uncommon for fees to exceed the amounts that dental service corporations are willing to pay. In this case, patients pay the difference, but this excess amount does not count toward annual deductibles.

Dental maintenance organizations, or **dental HMOs,** are most similar to HMOs for medical care. Dental HMOs provide prepaid dental services. Participants are required to seek treatment from an approved provider, and they pay a nominal copayment. Sometimes, managed care providers offer members a choice between a dentist within the network of approved providers and a dentist outside the network. In this case, the level of prepaid benefits is significantly less for nonnetwork dentists, creating an incentive for members to seek treatment from an approved provider.

Vision Insurance

Vision insurance plans usually cover eye examinations, lenses, frames, and the fitting of glasses. Similar to dental protection, vision insurance benefits may be delivered through indemnity plans or managed care arrangements. All forms of delivery limit the frequency and types of services. Typically, benefits are limited to eye examinations, basic prescription lenses, and frames once every one to two years. Vision plan benefits are relatively limited because they exclude coverage of specialty prescription eyeglass lenses (e.g., sunglasses, lightweight plastic lenses, and photosensitive lenses), and these plans restrict the coverage amount for frames. These plans generally do not cover any of the costs of contact lenses unless a vision care provider deems their usage a medical necessity.

Prescription Drug Benefits

Prescription drug plans cover the costs of drugs. These plans apply exclusively to drugs that state or federal laws require to be dispensed by licensed pharmacists. Prescription drugs dispensed to individuals during hospitalization or treatment in long-term care facilities are not covered by prescription drug plans. Insurers specify which prescription drugs are covered, how much they will pay, and the basis for paying for drugs.

Currently, three kinds of prescription drug plans are available to companies that choose to provide these benefits to employees. The first, **medical reimbursement plans,** reimburse employees for some or all of the cost of prescription drugs. These plans are usually associated with self-funded or independent indemnity plans. Similar to indemnity plans, medical reimbursement plans pay benefits after an employee has met an annual deductible for the plan. After an employee has met the deductible, these plans offer coinsurance, usually 80 percent of the prescription drug cost, and the employee pays the difference. Maximum annual and lifetime benefits amounts vary based on the provisions set forth in the plan.

The second kind of plan, often referred to as a **prescription card program,** operates similarly to managed care plans because it offers prepaid benefits with nominal copayments. The name arose from the common practice of pharmacies requiring the presentation of an identification card. Prescription card programs limit benefits to prescriptions filled at participating pharmacies, similar to managed care arrangements for medical treatment. Copayment amounts vary from $5 to $50 per prescription. The amount depends upon whether the prescriptions meet criteria set by the plan, including the use of generic alternatives and the categorization of prescription drugs on formularies. **Formularies** are lists of drugs proven to be clinically appropriate and cost effective. Participants pay lower copayments for prescription drugs that meet the established criteria. Prescription card programs may be associated with an independent insurer or as part of an established HMO.

The third type of plan, a **mail-order prescription drug program,** dispenses expensive medications used to treat chronic health conditions such high blood pressure or high cholesterol. Typically, mail-order programs are offered in combination with prescription card programs. The copay is typically much less for mail-order purchases. A single mail-order program supplies medication to participants of many health insurance plans nationwide. Local pharmacies do not enjoy this advantage, because their patronage is much smaller and is limited to people who live in close proximity.

The costs of these prescription drug plans vary. Reimbursement plans tend to be most expensive because pharmacies charge full retail price. Also, reimbursement plans entail substantial administrative costs because an administrator evaluates each claim, applies deductibles, and prepares an explanation of benefits. Prescription card and mail-order programs are usually less expensive, because insurance companies have negotiated lower prices in exchange for providing a significant volume of individuals who will need prescription medications. In addition, costs are lower because participants make copayments when they order prescriptions and then the pharmacy bills the insurance company at a set interval for all the prescriptions filled during this interval (e.g., every week or every two weeks).

Increasingly, many prescription drug plans contain two cost-control features: formularies and multiple tiers. Many plans establish formularies to manage costs. The basis for setting formularies varies from plan to plan. For example, some plans prescribe drugs that are therapeutically equivalent to more-expensive drugs and use lower levels of coinsurance or copayments to encourage usage. Other plans are more restrictive by limiting coverage only to a specified set of prescription drugs.

Multiple tiers specify copayment amounts that an individual will pay for a specific prescription. Usually, multitier prescription drug plans specify three tiers, from least copayment amount to highest copayment amount: generic medication ($10 to $20 per prescription), formulary brand-name medication ($25 to $40 per prescription), and nonformulary brand-name medication ($40 to full price per prescription). The idea behind multiple-tier prescription plans is that employees will choose less-expensive and equally effective alternatives to nonformulary medications. For example, bupropion hydrochloride (used to relieve symptoms of clinical depression or to aid in smoking cessation) may be obtained as a generic of the brand name Wellbutrin, manufactured by GlaxoSmithKline.

Presumably, multitier prescription plans should save employers considerable costs while also providing effective treatments based on less-expensive alternative prescription medication. However, one study suggests that attaining the intended goals of multitier prescription plans may be more challenging.

A study by Medco Health Solutions Inc. and Harvard Medical School, published in the December 2003 issue of *New England Journal of Medicine,* examined how a move to a three-tier plan affects drug spending and utilization. The study also provided information for health plan providers that are considering increasing member cost sharing as a strategy for reducing their spending on drugs.

The study found that for two employers who implemented multitier plan designs, this change led a significant proportion of patients who were taking brand-name drugs (with the highest copayment) to choose more cost-effective alternatives. Depending on the particular drug class, at least 18 percent, and as much as 49 percent, of plan members switched to lower-cost medication. However, the survey also found that an aggressive approach to plan changes can have the unintended result of causing some patients to stop taking their medications altogether.

Mental Health and Substance Abuse

Approximately 25 percent of Americans experience some form of mental illness, such as clinical depression, at least once during their lifetimes. Psychiatrists define *mental disorder* as "a behavioral or psychological syndrome or pattern . . . associated with present distress (a painful symptom) or disability (impairment in one or more important areas of functioning) or with a significantly increased risk of suffering death, pain, disability, or an important loss of freedom."[13] Nearly 20 percent of Americans develop a substance abuse problem. As a result, insurance plans provide mental health and substance abuse benefits designed to cover treatment of mental illness and chemical dependence on alcohol and legal and illegal drugs. Delivery methods include fee-for-service plans and managed care options. As will be discussed in Chapter 9, employee assistance programs (EAPs) represent a portal to taking advantage of employer-sponsored mental health and substance abuse treatment options. EAPs help employees cope with personal problems that may impair their personal lives or job performance. Examples of these problems are alcohol or drug abuse, domestic violence, the emotional impact of AIDS and other diseases, clinical depression, and eating disorders. EAPs also assist employers in helping troubled employees identify and solve problems that may be interfering with their jobs or personal lives.

Features of Mental Health and Substance Abuse Plans

Mental health and substance abuse plans cover the costs of a variety of treatments, including prescription psychiatric drugs (e.g., antidepressant medication), psychological testing, inpatient hospital care, and outpatient care (individual or group therapy).

Mental health benefits amounts vary by the type of disorder. Psychiatrists and psychologists rely on the *Diagnostic and Statistical Manual of Mental Disorders* (*DSM-5*) to diagnose mental disorders based on symptoms, and both fee-for-service and managed care plans rely on the *DSM-5* to authorize payment of benefits.

Regulation of Mental Health and Substance Abuse Plans

Various federal and state laws apply to the operation of mental health and substance abuse plans. At the federal level, the **Mental Health Parity and Addiction Equity Act of 2008**[14] plays a prominent role in establishing parity requirements for mental health plans offered in conjunction with a group health plan that contains medical and surgical benefits. Mental health and substance abuse plans cannot impose more restrictive limits than the limits provided for in medical plans. The Mental Health Parity and Addiction Equity Act of 2008 requires that any group health plan that includes mental health and substance use disorder benefits along with standard medical and surgical coverage must treat them equally in terms of out-of-pocket costs, benefit limits, and practices such as prior authorization and utilization review. (Utilization review as a cost-control method is discussed in Chapter 10.) These practices must be based on the same level of scientific evidence used by the insurer for medical and surgical benefits. For example, a plan may not apply separate deductibles for treatment related to mental health or substance abuse disorders and medical or surgical benefits—they must be calculated as one limit.

State laws also play a role in mental health and substance abuse plans. The specific provisions vary from state to state, but, in general, state laws specify minimum standards for coverage, including the minimum number of days of inpatient treatment and the minimum number of outpatient counseling sessions.

Maternity Care

Maternity care benefits cover all or a portion of the costs during pregnancy and for a short period after giving birth. Most maternity care benefits apply to physicians' fees, laboratory work (e.g., blood work, amniocentesis), and hospitalization during and following the time of delivery. Federal and state laws influence maternity care benefits. Federal law does not require that employers provide maternity care benefits. However, some federal laws do influence how companies design and implement maternity care benefits. As will be discussed shortly, some state laws mandate the inclusion of maternity care benefits in employee-benefits plans.

At the federal level, the Pregnancy Discrimination Act of 1978 (Chapter 3) prohibits employers from treating pregnancy less favorably than other medical conditions covered under employee-benefits plans. In addition, employers must treat pregnancy and childbirth the same way they treat other causes of disability. The **Family and Medical Leave Act of 1993** entitles most male and female employees of private-sector companies with 50 or more employees and government organizations up to 12 unpaid workweeks of leave during any 12-month period because of the birth of a child (and other family-related reasons that are discussed in Chapter 8). The **Newborns' and Mothers' Health Protection Act of 1996**[15] sets minimum standards for the length of hospital stays for mothers and newborn children; it prohibits employers and all insurers (independent and self-funded indemnity plans, as well as managed care plans) from using financial incentives to shorten hospital stays. At the state level, some states require that employers offer maternity care benefits to employees if other health-care benefits are provided. These mandates exclude employers that offer health benefits through self-funded plans.

RETIREE HEALTH-CARE BENEFITS

According to the U.S. Bureau of Labor Statistics, a relatively small percentage of retirees receive employer-sponsored health care: 16 percent for those under age 65, and 14 percent for those age 65 and over. In recent decades companies have encountered a strong financial disincentive to provide health-care benefits to retired employees for two reasons. First, the substantial increases in health-care costs and costs of medical plans have created a tremendous financial strain on companies that choose to offer them. As noted earlier in this chapter, the cost of medical services has increased dramatically through recent decades. The financial pressure on companies intensifies with coverage of retirees because older individuals are more likely to need expensive prescription medication and are more likely to require hospitalization because of serious health problems than younger individuals are. Of course, the lasting effects of a sharp economic slowdown, particularly since late 2007, intensified global competition, and higher energy costs have made it more difficult for companies to support full workforces. As a result, many employees have experienced small pay increases relative to increases in the cost of living, reductions in benefits offerings, higher contributions for benefits such as health coverage, and layoffs.

Second, changes in company accounting practices have made offering health-care benefits to retirees less appealing. The **Financial Accounting Standards Board (FASB),** a nonprofit company responsible for improving standards of financial accounting and reporting in companies, implemented FAS 106 in 1990 and FAS 158 in 2005. **Financial Accounting Standard (FAS) 106** is a rule that changed the method of how companies recognize the costs of nonpension retirement benefits, including health insurance, on financial balance sheets. This rule effectively reduces the amount of a company's net profit amount listed on the balance sheet by listing the costs of these benefits as an expense. The FASB's view is that benefits such as health-care coverage establish an exchange between the employer and the employee. In exchange for the current services provided by the employee, the employer promises to provide, in addition to current wages and other benefits, health and welfare benefits after the employee retires. In other words, postretirement benefits are part of an employee's compensation for services rendered. Since payment is deferred, the benefits are a type of deferred compensation. The employer's obligation for that compensation is incurred as employees render the services necessary to earn their postretirement benefits.

In 2003, FASB instituted **FAS 132,** which requires that companies disclose substantial information about the economic value and costs of retiree health-care plans. The FASB maintains that health-care benefits are probably as significant to current employees and retirees as are defined benefit plans. Other FAS rules require clear disclosure of economic resources and obligations related to defined benefit plans. Thus, FAS 132 requires similar disclosure. As a result, companies without sufficient current assets to maintain retiree health-care plans are less likely to continue offering these benefits.

For example, FASB established 132(R), Employers' Disclosures about Postretirement Benefit Plan Assets. The FASB decided to amend FASB Statement No. 132 (revised in 2003), Employers' Disclosures about Pensions and Other Postretirement Benefits, to include additional reporting requirements:

1. The entity's objective in disclosing information about plan assets, which is to provide users of financial statements with an understanding of:

    a. The major categories of assets held in an employer's plan(s).

    b. How management makes investment allocation decisions, including the factors that are pertinent to an investor's understanding of investment policies or strategies.

    c. Significant concentrations of risk within plan assets.

2. A list of examples of detailed categories of plan assets that would include a category for investment funds (e.g., mutual funds, hedge funds, and commingled funds).

3. A requirement that an entity disclose the significant investment strategies for investment funds as major categories of plan assets.[16]

In 2005, **FAS 158** established requirements to enhance further transparency through accounting practices for other postretirement employee benefits. Further updates may be found on the FASB Web site (www.fasb.org). In sum, nowadays, there is the sobering realization that the soaring costs of retiree health-care benefits may be pushing some companies to the financial limit. Current forces may lead companies to stand down from such offerings in the future.

Summary

This chapter reviews the fundamental concepts of company-sponsored health-care plans, starting with basic definitions and a perusal of the origins of employer-sponsored health benefits and the prevalence and cost of these plans in private industry. Also reviewed are the government regulation of health plans, with distinctions between federal and state laws. Further, a variety of approaches to providing health care were discussed, including fee-for-service plans, alternative managed care plans, and any of those plans associated with the consumer-driven approach. Finally, this chapter discussed retiree health care. FAS 106 and 132 have created a disincentive to companies that offer retiree health-care benefits, and the mounting pressures companies face to meet these obligations.

Key Terms

health-care plans, *128*
fully insured plans, *128*
individual coverage, *128*
group coverage, *128*
insurance policy, *129*
premium, *129*
underwriting, *129*
mortality tables, *129*
morbidity tables, *129*
experience ratings, *129*
self-funded plans, *129*
single coverage, *129*
family coverage, *129*
multiple-payer system, *129*
single-payer system, *130*
universal health care systems, *130*
Health Maintenance Organization Act of 1973 (HMO Act), *131*

hospitalization benefits, *133*
inpatient benefits, *133*
outpatient benefits, *133*
usual, customary, and reasonable charges, *133*
Women's Health and Cancer Rights Act of 1998, *137*
Patient Protection and Affordable Care Act (PPACA), *138*
individual mandate, *138*
employer mandate, *138*
grandfathered plans, *138*
non-grandfathered plans, *138*
coinsurance, *139*
copayments, *139*
deductible, *139*
out-of-pocket maximum, *139*
essential benefits, *139*
Cadillac tax, *140*

National Association of Insurance Commissioners (NAIC), *141*
prepaid plan, *142*
indemnity plan, *142*
fee-for-service plans, *143*
managed care plans, *143*
open-access HMOs, *143*
primary care physicians, *143*
staff model HMOs, *144*
group model HMOs, *145*
network model HMOs, *145*
individual practice associations (IPAs), *145*
preferred provider organization (PPO), *145*
exclusive provider organization (EPO), *145*
point-of-service (POS) plan, *145*

Discussion Questions

1. Discuss the differences between individual coverage and group coverage, fully insured plans and self-funded plans, and single coverage and family coverage.
2. Summarize the main requirements of the PPACA. Do you think that the government should require that every person has health insurance? Explain your answer.
3. Summarize three broad health-care plan design alternatives.
4. Describe the principles of fee-for-service plans and managed care plans. What are the similarities and differences?
5. Briefly describe the consumer-driven approach and explain the role that spending accounts or arrangements play in this approach.

Cases

1. Understanding Your Employee Benefits: Health Insurance Options

After attending an informational session on your company's health-care plan offerings, you are still unsure about the right plan to select. Your company offers employees the choice to participate in a preferred provider organization (PPO) plan or a health maintenance organization (HMO) plan. You are currently enrolled in the PPO plan, but after learning more about the HMO at the session, you are considering changing to the HMO plan. This is an important decision, as the plan you select will provide the health coverage for you and your family. While you are satisfied with the PPO, it seems that selecting the HMO could lower your health-care expenses.

Under the company's current PPO plan, you have access to a network of doctors and pay a lower copayment and deductible if you go to doctors within the network. However, if you do need to see a doctor who is not in the network, you are still covered by the plan, but at a higher cost to you. You have enjoyed the flexibility of the PPO option and have developed relationships with some specific doctors within the network. For example, you see an allergist who treats your allergy problems. Further, you have taken your children to the same pediatrician since they were born. While the children do not have any chronic health issues, you have a trusted relationship with the doctor and are hesitant to make a change.

Now, as you examine your options, you find that the HMO offers some features that could provide you with a cost savings. The cost of the monthly premium that you would pay for the HMO to cover you and your family is lower than the premium that you pay for the PPO. Further, while you would still pay copayments for office visits and other services, you would not have the deductible and coinsurance that you currently pay with the PPO. However, with the staff model HMO option that your employer is offering, you could only see the doctors employed by the HMO. Further, you would need to select a primary care physician whom you would need to see before you could see a doctor who is a specialist, such as an allergist.

The flexibility of the PPO was very attractive to you, and you are unsure if you are comfortable with the limits of the HMO. However, the cost savings may make it worthwhile to pursue the HMO. You have to make your decision next month, during the company's annual open enrollment period. As you sit down to review the materials, you are not sure what you should do.

1. What are some advantages and disadvantages of the HMO to you?
2. What should you do? What are factors that will influence your decision?

2. Managing Employee Benefits: Considering Consumer-Driven Health Care

As Classics Architects recovers from an economic downturn, the multilocation architecture and interior design firm is examining costs in all areas of the business. Nigel Duncan, Director of Human Resources, knows that the company must lower the costs of its health insurance in particular. With a few months to go before the company's annual open-enrollment period for benefits, Nigel is starting to think that giving employees more control in their health decisions may just be the path to lowering health-care insurance costs.

As Nigel examines reports on employee claims under the current health insurance plan, he questions whether employees are making the right choices for their health care. For example, there has been a spike in the number of emergency room claims over the last year. This concerns Nigel, as the cost of expensive emergency room visits impact Classics Architects' overall health insurance premium costs. Nigel suspects that these emergency room visits may be made out of convenience instead of necessity. The employees pay only a slightly higher copayment to use the emergency room instead of a doctor's office visit. Thus, employees may be using the emergency room immediately instead of waiting to schedule appointments with their own doctors, even if their illnesses do not require immediate care. This is just one example of employee behavior that is driving up Classic Achitects' health-care costs.

Nigel believes that it might be best to take a consumer-driven health-care approach by selecting a health insurance plan with higher deductibles, which will lower the cost of premiums for the company. As employees will bear more of the cost of their own health care, Nigel believes they will make better health-care choices. To make this shift, Nigel is comparing the use of a flexible spending account (FSA) to a health savings account (HSA) to help employees manage the increased costs by setting aside funds on a pretax basis to pay for medical expenses, such as the deductibles.

Nigel wants to determine if an FSA or an HSA will help control costs more at Classic Architects. An FSA would allow employees to set aside pretax earnings to pay for medical expenses not covered by insurance. The FSA would be paired with a health insurance plan that has a higher deductible than the company's current plan. However, Nigel thinks that adding the HSA might have a more significant impact on the company's health-care costs. The HSA would be coupled with a high-deductible health insurance plan, which would cost a significantly less amount to the company than the plan offered with the FSA. The company would allow the employees to set aside pretax earnings to spend on medical expenses, similar to the FSA, but the expenses would be higher for the employees due to the high deductible. Thus, the HSA would permit the company to contribute to the account as well. With each of these options, employees would be more aware of the costs of their health care and should make better health-care choices.

As Nigel reviews the utilization reports and the premiums that the company is paying for health insurance, he thinks that moving to a more consumer-driven approach is likely a good idea for the company. However, he is also concerned with employee acceptance of such a change. Before making his final recommendation, he knows that he needs to thoroughly explore the pros and cons of each option.

1. What are some overall advantages and disadvantages of pursuing consumer-driven health-care options?
2. Should Classic Architects select a flexible spending account or a health savings account?

Endnotes

1. U.S. Bureau of Labor Statistics, "Welfare Work for Employees in Industrial Establishments in the United States," Bulletin No. 250, 1919: 119–23.
2. U.S. Bureau of Labor Statistics, *Employee Benefits in the United States, March 2015* (Bulletin 2782).
3. *Ibid.*
4. *Ibid.*
5. *Ibid.*
6. U.S. Bureau of Labor Statistics, *Consumer Price Index,* (CPI-U) database. Accessed May 11, 2016, www.bls.gov/cpi.
7. 42 U.S.C. 300(e)e–330(e)-17.
8. ERISA §3(1), 29 U.S.C. §1002(1).
9. Added to the Omnibus Consolidated Emergency Supplemental Act on October 21, 1998, P.L. No. 105-277.
10. 42 U.S.C. §12101.
11. U.S. Equal Employment Opportunity Commission, "Justifications for Disability-Based Distinctions," *EEOC Compliance Manual.* Washington, DC: EEOC, October 3, 2000. Accessed May 6, 2016, https://www.eeoc.gov/policy/docs/benefits.html#III. Disability-Based Distinctions.
12. National Association of Insurance Commissioners. Accessed May 5, 2016, www.naic.org.
13. American Psychiatric Association, *Diagnostic and Statistical Manual of Mental Disorders (DSM-5).* Washington, DC: American Psychiatric Association, 2015.
14. Mental Health Parity Act, P.L. No. 110-460, December 23, 2008.
15. 42 U.S.C. §300(g)(g)-(4)-(51).
16. Financial Accounting Standards Board, 2008. *Employers' Disclosures about Postretirement Benefit Plan Assets.* 2008. Accessed May 3, 2016, www.fasb.org.

Chapter Six

Employer-Sponsored Disability Insurance, Life Insurance, and Workers' Compensation

In this chapter, we will explore three types of benefits that provide financial support for disabled or deceased workers' families. Two of these benefits are offered on a discretionary basis (employer-sponsored disability insurance and life insurance). The third, workers' compensation, is mostly required by law. The similarities and differences between this legally required insurance program and discretionary employer-sponsored programs will be examined.

DISABILITY INSURANCE

Disability insurance replaces income for employees who become unable to work on a regular basis because of an illness or injury. Employer-sponsored disability insurance is more encompassing than workers' compensation, because its benefits generally apply to both work-related and nonwork-related illnesses and injuries, whereas workers' compensation insurance applies only to work-related illnesses and injuries. Unfortunately, employees need this kind of protection. At all working ages, the probability of a worker's being disabled for at least 90 consecutive days is much greater than the chance of dying while performing on the job; one of every three employees will have a disability that lasts at least 90 days.[1]

Much as they do for company-sponsored health-care plans, employers usually enter into a contractual relationship with one or more insurance companies to provide disability benefits for their employees and, if specified, their dependents. The contractual relationship, or **insurance policy,** specifies the conditions under which it will pay benefits and the amount of money it will pay for particular disabilities. Employers pay insurance companies a negotiated amount, or **premium,** to establish and maintain insurance policies. The term *insured* refers to an employee covered by an insurance policy.

Disability insurance typically takes two forms. The first, **short-term disability insurance,** provides benefits for limited periods of time, usually less than one year. The second, **long-term disability insurance,** provides benefits for extended periods of time—anywhere between six months and life. Disability criteria differ between short-term and long-term plans. Short-term plans usually consider a disability to be an inability to perform any and every duty of a disabled person's occupation. Long-term plans use a more stringent definition, typically specifying an inability to engage in any occupation for which the individual is qualified by reason of training, education, or experience. These definitions will be further discussed.

Both discretionary short-term and long-term disability plans sometimes duplicate public disability benefits mandated by state workers' compensation laws and the Social Security Act (discussed later in this chapter and in Chapter 7, respectively). The discretionary plans generally supplement legally required benefits and do not replace disability benefits mandated by law.

It is worthwhile to note that sick leave policies (Chapter 8) are separate from disability leave. Sick leave policies compensate employees when they are absent due to occasional minor illnesses or injuries, such as a stomach flu or sprained ankle. Employers pay sick leave benefits from the regular payroll. In contrast, employers provide disability benefits from disability insurance policies or self-insurance.

Origins of Disability Insurance and Workers' Compensation Insurance

Instances of company-sponsored and individual disability insurance appeared in the 1800s as the United States shifted from an agrarian economy to an industrialized economy. The agrarian economy was largely based on self-employment and the employment of family members. The industrialized economy, in contrast, mainly entailed ownership of manufacturing facilities that employed scores of workers. Many workers became seriously ill or injured while performing their jobs due to the absence of health and safety regulations. (The Occupational Safety and Health Act (OSHA) was passed in the early 1970s.) In the 1800s and early 1900s, seriously injured and ill workers were left with virtually no recourse, because social insurance programs to protect injured and ill workers were nonexistent.[2] As a result, these workers faced impoverishment.

Workers' compensation insurance came into existence during this early period. State governments, rather than the federal government, were responsible for creating workers' compensation programs. At the time, the U.S. Supreme Court interpreted the Constitution to preclude federal legislation of private-sector employers. The first constitutionally acceptable workers' compensation laws were enacted in New Jersey and Wisconsin in 1911. By 1948, every state had a workers' compensation law.

State workers' compensation laws are based on two ideas: the principle of liability without fault—that is, an employer is absolutely liable for providing benefits to employees for occupational disabilities or injuries that result, regardless of fault;[3] and employers should assume the costs of occupational injuries and accidents. Presumably, these expenses represent costs of production that employers are able to recoup by setting higher prices.

Prior to the enactment of workers' compensation laws, injured employees could choose not to pursue compensation from employers, or they could file a lawsuit in court for compensation. Employers could mount one of three common-law defenses against liability:[4]

1. *Assumption of risk* (showing the injury resulted from an ordinary hazard of employment of which the worker should have been aware).

2. *Fellow worker rule* (showing the injury was caused by a fellow worker's negligence).
3. *Contributory negligence* (showing the worker's own negligence contributed to the injury, regardless of any fault of the employer).

The cost of litigation often proved to be out of the reach of injured workers, which made it difficult to pursue any remedies.

After the introduction of social insurance programs (including workers' compensation and Social Security in the 1910s and 1930s, respectively), private disability insurance was still necessary because the government programs were not designed to provide substantial income replacement as the result of illness or injury.

Prior to the 1960s, there were three relatively primitive employer-sponsored insurance forms that had emerged. First, employers created **establishment funds** to provide minimal cash payments to workers who became occupationally ill or injured. Second, insurance companies sold individual disability insurance policies to workers. Third, greater awareness following state workers' compensation laws in the early 20th century led employers to purchase group disability insurance policies. These initial forms were primitive because lump sum benefits were paid following occurrences of disability and the amounts were generally the same regardless of age or the severity of illness or injury. This approach left the youngest and more seriously disabled workers with insufficient funds to help cover their lost incomes over longer periods of time than the oldest and least seriously ill or injured disabled workers.

During the 1960s, insurance companies began to manage liability more effectively by offering benefits on an income replacement basis to avoid the above-noted shortcomings of earlier disability insurance approaches.

Coverage and Costs of Disability Programs

In 2015, 38 percent of private-sector workers had access to an employer-sponsored short-term disability plan and 32 percent had access to a long-term disability plan.[5] Among full-time workers, 49 percent and 44 percent had access to a long-term or short-term disability plan, respectively. Among part-time workers, only 14 percent and 5 percent had access to a long-term or short-term disability plan, respectively. On average, employers spent about $125 annually per employee to provide short-term disability insurance, and about $104 for long-term disability insurance.[6]

Short-Term Disability Insurance Programs

Short-term disability plans classify **short-term disability** as an inability to perform the duties of one's regular job. Manifestations of short-term disability include the following temporary (short-term) conditions:

- Recovery from injuries.
- Recovery from surgery.

- Treatment of an illness requiring any hospitalization.
- Pregnancy—the Pregnancy Discrimination Act of 1978 mandates that employers treat pregnancy and childbirth the same way they treat other causes of disability (Chapter 3).

Most short-term disability plans pay employees 50 to 66.67 percent of their pay either on a monthly or weekly basis; some pay as much as 100 percent. Short-term disability plans pay benefits for a limited period, usually no more than one year. Many companies set a monthly maximum benefit amount, which could be less for highly paid employees. For example, a company pays employees 66.67 percent, subject to a monthly maximum benefit totaling $5,000. Let's assume that an employee's annual pay equals $130,000 ($10,833 per month). Without the maximum cap, the employee would earn $7,225 a month (0.667 × $10,833). The cap results in a monthly loss of income totaling $2,225 (that is, $7,225 − $5,000).

Three additional features of short-term disability plans include:

- A preexisting condition clause.
- Waiting periods—a pre-eligibility period and an elimination period.
- Exclusion provisions for designated health conditions.

Preexisting Condition

A **preexisting condition** is a mental or physical disability for which medical advice, diagnosis, care, or treatment was received during a designated period preceding the beginning of disability insurance coverage. The designated period usually is any time prior to employment and enrollment in a company's disability insurance plan. Insurance companies impose exclusions for preexisting conditions to limit their liabilities that predate an individual's coverage.

Waiting Periods

The **pre-eligibility period** spans from the initial date of hire to the time of eligibility for coverage in a disability insurance program. Once the pre-eligibility period has expired, an **elimination period** refers to the minimum amount of time an employee must wait after becoming disabled before disability insurance payments begin. Employees are responsible for paying a limited amount to cover the costs of treating illness or injury. Employers prefer disability insurance policies with longer elimination periods because the premiums are lower. Insurance companies charge less for policies with longer elimination periods because longer periods reduce the amount the insurance policy will have to pay in claims. The most common elimination period for short-term disability plans is three months, but it can range anywhere between one month and a year.

Exclusion Provisions

Short-term disability plans often contain exclusion provisions. **Exclusion provisions** list the particular health conditions that are ineligible for coverage. Disabilities that result from self-inflicted injuries are almost always excluded. Short-term disability plans often exclude most mental illnesses or disabilities due to chemical dependencies (e.g., addictions to alcohol or illegal drugs). Employers support addicted workers through separate programs known as employee assistance programs (Chapter 9).

Long-Term Disability Insurance Programs

Long-term disability insurance carriers use a two-stage definition for long-term disability. At the first stage, **long-term disability** refers to illnesses or accidents that prevent an employee from performing his or her "own occupation" over a designated period, oftentimes up to two years. The term *own occupation* refers to education, training, or experience necessary to perform work in one's occupation, such as that of a pipefitter or crane operator. After the designated period elapses, the second-stage definition adds the phrase inability to perform work in *any occupation* or paid employment. The second-stage definition is consistent with the concept of total disability in the Social Security disability benefits program.

Traditionally, long-term disability plans covered only total disabilities. More recently, many long-term disability insurance carriers have also added partial disabilities for the following reason: Including partial disabilities results in cost savings to insurance companies because, in most cases, totally disabled individuals avoid paid employment as this would cause them to forfeit future disability benefits. With the **partial disabilities inclusion,** insurance companies cover a portion of income loss associated with paid part-time employment while a disabled person works on a part-time basis in any job. For example, long-term disability plans become effective when part-time employment falls below a designated level expressed as a percentage of income (adjusted for cost-of-living increases) prior to the qualifying event—for example, below 75 or 80 percent.

Maximum benefits usually equal 50 to 70 percent of monthly pay, subject to a maximum dollar amount. Similar to short-term plans, the maximum benefit may be as high as $5,000 per month. Generally, long-term benefits are subject to an elimination period of anywhere between six months and one year. Long-term disability benefits usually become active only after an employee's sick leave and short-term disability benefits have been exhausted. Long-term disability benefits continue until retirement or for a specified period.

Funding Disability Insurance Programs

Employers may fund disability programs in three ways. First, employers may use an independent insurance company to provide disability benefits. Similar to the terms of health-care programs, companies pay premiums to one or more insurance companies to insure against the costs of disabilities. Second, employers may support disability benefits through partial self-funding. This option applies mainly to long-term disability insurance programs. Under partial self-funding, employers pay claims from their assets invested in a trust fund for a limited period (e.g., two or three years) or up to a maximum dollar amount. Additionally, employers purchase stop-loss insurance from an independent insurance company to cover the claims that exceed the self-funding limits. Third, full self-funding arrangements may provide all disability benefits from company assets. Self-funded plans may be handled internally or through a third-party claims management company. When handled by a third party, full self-funded plans are described as administrative-services-only (ASO) plans.

Employers often factor two considerations into their decisions to partially or fully self-fund disability insurance plans. First, the size of the employee group helps employers predict the probability of disability occurrences. Statistically, larger employee groups enable more accurate predictions than do smaller groups. Predictions of tolerable disability events support partial or full self-funding. Second, estimating exposure or liability for disability claims is essential. *Exposure* refers to the anticipated amount of annual disability claims under partial and full self-funding. Employers consider their tolerance for risk and pursue either approach.

Relationships between Company-Sponsored Disability Plans and Benefits Laws

Four benefits laws influence the design and implementation of company-sponsored disability plans:

- The Age Discrimination in Employment Act of 1967.
- The Americans with Disabilities Act of 1990.
- The Employee Retirement Income Security Act of 1974.
- State workers' compensation and Social Security disability regulations.

The Age Discrimination in Employment Act (ADEA) of 1967

The **Older Workers Benefit Protection Act (OWBPA),** which is the 1990 amendment to the Age Discrimination in Employment Act of 1967 (ADEA), generally bans the termination of an employee's long-term disability benefits for active employees based on age.[7] When employers require that all employees contribute toward coverage of benefits, under particular circumstances, they can also require older employees to pay more for health care, disability, or life insurance than younger employees. This is the case because these benefits generally become more costly with age (e.g., older workers may be more likely to incur serious illnesses, thus insurance companies may charge employers higher rates to provide coverage for older workers than for younger ones). However, an older employee may not be required to pay more for the benefit *as a condition of employment*. Where the premium has increased for an older employee, the employer must provide three options to older workers. First, the employee has the option of withdrawing from the benefit plan altogether. Second, the employee has the option of reducing his or her benefit coverage in order to keep his or her premium cost the same. Third, an older employee may be offered the option of paying more for the benefit in order to avoid otherwise justified reductions in coverage. Employers can legally reduce the coverage of older workers for benefits that typically become more costly as employees further age *only if* the costs for providing those benefits are significantly greater than the cost for younger workers. When costs differ significantly, the employer may reduce the benefit for older workers only to the point where it is paying just as much per older worker (with lower coverage) as it is for younger workers (with higher coverage). This practice is referred to as the equal benefit or equal cost principle.

The Americans with Disabilities Act of 1990

The **Americans with Disabilities Act** of 1990 prohibits discriminatory employment practices against qualified individuals with disabilities. A **qualified individual with a disability** is a person who possesses the necessary skills, experience, education, and other job-related requirements and, regardless of reasonable accommodation, can perform the essential functions of a job. Two federal courts, the Sixth and Seventh Circuits, have maintained that recipients of long-term disability benefits are not qualified individuals with the rights to raise ADA claims.[8]

In addition, the U.S. Equal Employment Opportunity Commission (EEOC), the government entity that oversees the administration and enforcement of the ADA, has ruled that employers may lawfully offer different benefits under disability retirement plans. According to the EEOC, disability retirement plans "provide lifetime income for an employee unable to work because of illness or injury, without regard to the employee's age."[9] For example, it is permissible not to provide cost-of-living adjustments for disability benefits. It is also acceptable to include offset provisions in disability plans that reduce disability benefits to compensate for other insured income benefits. Employers violate the ADA when they do not extend coverage to qualified individuals with disabilities or when they provide less-favorable treatment. Examples of less favorable treatment include exclusion of eligible qualified employees from participation in disability retirement plans and requiring a longer pre-eligibility period for qualified individuals with disabilities than for nondisabled employees.

The Employee Retirement Income Security Act of 1974

The Employee Retirement Income Security Act (ERISA) of 1974 regulates the establishment and implementation of company-sponsored welfare benefits practices, including disability insurance and life insurance.

State Workers' Compensation and Social Security Disability Regulations

Employees may receive long-term disability benefits from public disability programs and company-sponsored programs. Company-sponsored insurance plans may include an offset provision.

Offset provisions reduce company-sponsored disability benefits by subtracting a particular percentage of the amount that an employee is eligible to receive from workers' compensation or Social Security. Offset provisions limit the total disability benefits amount that an individual receives. Without offset provisions, a disabled individual stands to earn as much or more than his or her income prior to becoming disabled. The combined Social Security disability and workers' compensation benefits amount may not exceed 80 percent of average current earnings prior to disability.

LIFE INSURANCE

Employer-sponsored **life insurance** protects family members by paying a specified amount to an employee's beneficiaries upon the employee's death. Most policies pay some multiple of the employee's salary—for instance, benefits paid at twice the employee's annual salary. Employees usually have the option of purchasing additional coverage. Frequently, employer-sponsored life insurance plans also include accidental death and dismemberment claims, which pay additional benefits if death was the result of an accident or if the insured experienced the accidental loss of a limb.

An individual can purchase life insurance on an individual basis. Alternatively, an employee can subscribe to the employer's group life insurance plan, which has clear benefits for both them and their employers. Group plans allow all participants to benefit from coverage, while employers assume the cost of financing the plan either partly or entirely. Also, group policies permit a larger set of employees to participate in a plan at a lower per-employee cost than if each employee purchased life insurance on an individual basis.

Origins of Life Insurance

Many of the social forces that gave rise to Social Security survivors' insurance (Chapter 7), workers' compensation, and private disability insurance apply to the advent of private life insurance. As previously noted, the major factors include the era of industrialization in the United States, government-imposed wage freezes during World War II, and favorable tax treatment for employers and employees.

Coverage and Costs of Life Insurance

In 2015, approximately 72 percent of full-time employees and 13 percent of part-time employees had access to employer-sponsored life insurance.[10] On average, employers spent about $83 annually per employee to provide life insurance coverage.[11]

Types of Life Insurance Programs

Three kinds of life insurance plan designs are: term life insurance, whole life insurance, and universal life insurance. **Term life insurance,** the most common type offered by companies, provides protection to employees' beneficiaries only during a limited period based on a specified number of years (e.g., five years) subject to a maximum age (usually 65 or 70). After that, the insurance automatically expires. Neither the employee nor beneficiaries receive a benefit upon expiration of the plan. To continue coverage under a term life plan, an employee must renew the policy and make premium payments until reaching the maximum allowed age for coverage.

Whole life insurance pays an amount to beneficiaries, but unlike term policies, whole life plans do not terminate until payment is made to beneficiaries. As a result, whole life insurance policies are substantially more expensive than term life insurance, making the whole life insurance approach an uncommon feature of employer-sponsored insurance programs. From an employee's or beneficiary's perspective, whole life insurance policies combine insurance protection with a savings feature (or cash accumulation plan): A portion of the money toward the policy's premium will be available in the future, plus interest earned on this amount. Fixed annual interest rates of 2 or 3 percent are fairly common.

Universal life insurance provides protection to employees' beneficiaries based on the insurance feature of term life insurance and a more flexible savings or cash accumulation plan than those offered by whole life insurance plans. The focus in the following discussion will be on employer-sponsored group term life insurance and universal life insurance.

Group Term Life Insurance

Offering term life insurance to a group of employees does not constitute a group term life insurance plan. This designation generally rests on providing term life insurance to at least 10 full-time employees. Employers may offer group term life insurance on a contributory or noncontributory basis. Under **contributory plans,** employees pay the entire insurance premium or they share the cost with their employer. Under **noncontributory plans,** the employer pays the entire premium for coverage within designated limits (e.g., up to twice an employee's annual salary). Most group term life insurance is offered on a noncontributory basis mainly because the employer receives substantially higher tax benefits with non-contributory plans than with contributory plans.

Costs of Group Term Life Insurance

Employers' costs do not refer to the actual annual premium amounts. Rather, employers' costs are based on a regulation established by the U.S. Code in a table titled "Uniform Premiums for $1,000 of Group Term Life Insurance Protection."[12] This expresses the monthly cost for group term life insurance based on sex and age (in five-year brackets). Exhibit 6.1 contains the Uniform Premiums table for age only.

The cost amounts listed in the current version of the table in Exhibit 6.1 represent mortality experiences for group term life insurance subscribers. Insurance providers

EXHIBIT 6.1
Uniform
Premiums for
$1,000 of
Group Term
Life Insurance
Protection

Source: Table I,
Treas. Regs. §1.79-
3(d)(2).

Five-Year Age Bracket	Cost per $1,000 of Protection for One Month
Under 25	$0.05
25 to 29	0.06
30 to 34	0.08
35 to 39	0.09
40 to 44	0.10
45 to 49	0.15
50 to 54	0.23
55 to 59	0.43
60 to 64	0.66
65 to 69	1.27
70 and above	2.06

use mortality tables to decide whether to offer insurance and, if so, to determine the terms and premium amount. This decision-making process is known as **underwriting. Mortality tables** indicate yearly probabilities of death based on factors such as age and sex, established by the Society of Actuaries. The Uniform Table combines probabilities for men and women. The values in the current Uniform Premiums table were adjusted to reflect lower rates of mortality between 1988 and 2000.

Universal Life Insurance

As previously noted, universal life insurance combines features of term life insurance and whole life insurance. Universal life insurance was created to provide more flexibility than whole life insurance by allowing a policy owner to shift money between the insurance and savings components of the policy. The insurance company initially breaks down the premium into insurance and savings. The policy owner may make adjustments to the amounts of the premium that are directed to insurance and savings. For example, if the savings portion is earning a low return, it can be used instead of external funds to pay the premiums. Also, unlike whole life insurance, universal life policies permit the cash value of investments to grow at a variable rate that is tied to market rates. As a result, the premium, benefits, and payment schedules may change.

Accidental Death and Dismemberment Insurance

Accidental death and dismemberment insurance (AD&D) covers death or dismemberment as a result of an accident. *Dismemberment* refers to the loss of two limbs or the complete loss of sight (i.e., blindness). Compared to life insurance, AD&D generally does not pay survivor benefits in the case of death by illness. AD&D premiums are generally lower than life insurance premiums because the incidences of death by accident are lower than death by natural causes.

At one time, AD&D protection was provided as an extra provision in companies' group life insurance programs. However, as more and more workplaces contain fewer hazards as a result of the decline of the manufacturing and mining business sectors but heavily emphasize safety training when relevant, accidental death at work has become less of a concern. Also, as the cost of providing mandatory workers' compensation coverage has risen substantially over the years, companies have found that including AD&D coverage was becoming cost prohibitive. In many workplaces, companies offer voluntary AD&D coverage, which means that employees who wish to have this coverage may pay the premium under the company's group contract. However, most companies shy away from AD&D because an employee older than age 40 is more likely to die from natural causes than from an accident. This statistic is important, considering that a large proportion of the workplace is older than age 40. Companies are more inclined to spend their benefits dollars on health insurance, or to increase contributions to 401(k) retirement accounts, because most employees stand to benefit more from those benefits than from AD&D coverage. Nevertheless, many companies do include AD&D coverage to employees on a voluntary basis. Offering voluntary AD&D coverage to employees has been a reasonable compromise between balancing employers' costs and the limitations of workers' compensation insurance in some states that pay relatively small benefits for accidental death or dismemberment.

STATE COMPULSORY DISABILITY LAWS (WORKERS' COMPENSATION)

State compulsory disability laws created **workers' compensation** programs. Workers' compensation insurance programs, run by the states individually, are designed to cover expenses incurred in employee work-related accidents and injuries. Six basic objectives underlie workers' compensation:[13]

- To provide sure, prompt, and reasonable income and medical benefits to work-accident victims, or income benefits to their dependents, regardless of fault.
- To provide a single remedy and reduce court delays, costs, and workloads arising out of personal injury litigation.
- To relieve public and private charities of financial drains.
- To eliminate payment of fees to lawyers and witnesses, as well as time-consuming trials and appeals.
- To encourage maximum employer interest in safety and rehabilitation through appropriate experience-rating mechanisms.
- To promote the transparent study of causes of accidents (rather than concealment of fault), reducing preventable accidents and human suffering.

The National Commission on State Workmen's Compensation Laws specified six primary obligations of state workers' compensation programs. This commission has established these obligations to ensure prompt and just remedies for workers injured on the job.[14] Exhibit 6.2 lists these obligations.

Workers' compensation differs from Social Security disability insurance in a number of important ways. Workers' compensation pays for:

- Medical care for work-related injuries beginning immediately after the injury occurs.
- Temporary disability benefits after a waiting period of three to seven days.

EXHIBIT 6.2
Primary Obligations of State Workers' Compensation Programs

Source: J. V. Nackley, *Primer on Workers' Compensation.* Washington, DC: Bureau of National Affairs, 1987.

1. Take initiative in administering the law.
2. Continually review program performance and be willing to change procedures and to request the state legislature to make needed amendments.
3. Advise workers of their rights and obligations and assure that they receive the benefits to which they are entitled.
4. Apprise employers and insurance carriers of their rights and obligations; inform other parties in the delivery system, such as health-care providers, of their obligations and privileges.
5. Assist in voluntary and informal resolution of disputes that are consistent with law.
6. Adjudicate claims that cannot be resolved voluntarily.

- Permanent partial and permanent total disability benefits to workers who have lasting consequences of disabilities caused on the job.
- In most states, rehabilitation and training benefits for those unable to return to pre-injury careers.
- Benefits to survivors of workers who die of work-related causes.

Social Security, in contrast, pays benefits:

- To workers with long-term disabilities from any cause, but only when the disabilities preclude work.
- For rehabilitation services.
- For survivor benefits to families of deceased workers.

Coverage of Workers' Compensation Programs

Employers must fund workers' compensation programs according to state guidelines. Participation in workers' compensation programs is compulsory in all states except for Texas, where private-sector employers are not required to provide workers' compensation protection. Compulsory laws require every employer to accept the state workers' compensation regulations. Elective laws permit employers the option of accepting or rejecting state workers' compensation regulations.

Rejecting these laws causes employers to lose the common law defense of contributory negligence, which was described earlier in the chapter.

Maritime workers within U.S. borders and federal civilian employees are covered by their own workers' compensation programs. The maritime workers' compensation program is mandated by the **Longshore and Harborworkers' Compensation Act,**[15] and federal civilian employees receive workers' compensation protection under the **Federal Employees' Compensation Act.**[16] Workers' compensation laws cover virtually all employees in the United States, except for domestic workers, some agricultural workers, and workers in small businesses with fewer than a stipulated number of employees based on state regulations.[17]

Cost of Workers' Compensation Insurance

In 2015, private-sector employers paid nearly $940 per employee annually for workers' compensation protection.[18] The annual amount was substantially higher for workers in the construction industry, at $2,630, and substantially lower for employees in the leisure and hospitality industry, at $582. Additionally, the cost of workers' compensation varies widely from state to state.

Financing Workers' Compensation Programs

Workers' compensation laws specify three permissible methods of funding. First, employers generally subscribe to workers' compensation insurance through private carriers. Second, employers may subscribe through state funds. Third, the self-insurance approach requires companies to deposit surety bonds, thus enabling them to pay their own workers' claims directly.[19] Many employers select self-insurance when it is available because it gives them greater discretion in administering their own risks. Nevertheless, self-insured companies must pay their workers the same benefits paid by state funds or private insurance carriers.

In most states, the insurance commissioner sets the maximum allowable workers' compensation insurance premium rates for private insurance carriers. Rates are based on each $100 of a payroll. Increasingly, some states permit insurance carriers to set rates on a competitive basis.

States rely on ratemaking service organizations to set initial rates, and these rates are influenced by historical injury and illness data. **Ratemaking service organizations** collect data on workplace accidents and put together rating manuals. **Rating manuals** specify insurance rates based on classifications of businesses. A few states employ independent rating organizations such as A.M. Best, a for-profit company that specializes in collecting insurance data and rating insurance companies. The remainder of states consult with the National Council on Compensation Insurance, another for-profit company which prepares three separate manuals for state insurance agencies. Independent rating bureaus used by a few states compile manuals that correspond to the National Council on Compensation Insurance's manuals. The U.S. Department of Labor collects data.

Sometimes, extenuating circumstances require payment of workers' compensation benefits from special funds for self-insured employers or private insurance companies become insolvent. Also, **second-injury funds** represent an important funding element of workers' compensation programs where claims are associated with pre-existing conditions from a work-related injury during prior employment elsewhere.

Workers' Compensation Claims

Employees can make three kinds of claims for workers' compensation benefits: injury claims, occupational disease claims, and death claims. First, an **injury claim** is usually defined as a claim for a disability that has resulted from an accident during the course of fulfilling work duties, such as a fall, an injury from equipment use, or a physical strain from heavy lifting. Also, employees who work long hours at computer keyboards or assembly lines, performing the same task over and over again, frequently complain of numbness in the fingers and neck as well as severe wrist pain. This type of injury is known as repetitive strain injury.

Second, an **occupational disease claim** results from a disability caused by an ailment associated with a particular industrial trade or process. For example, black lung, a chronic respiratory disease, is a common ailment among coal miners. In older office buildings, lung disease from prolonged exposure to asbestos is another kind of ailment. Generally, the following occupational diseases are covered under workers' compensation programs:

- Pneumoconioses, which are associated with exposure to dusts.
- Silicosis from exposure to silica.
- Asbestosis.
- Radiation illness.

Third, a **death claim** applies to a death that occurs in the course of employment or is caused by compensable injuries or occupational diseases. The injuries and illnesses covered by workers' compensation programs vary from state to state.

Workers file claims to the state commission charged with administering the workers' compensation program. The names of these agencies vary by state, and a directory of these state agencies are available on the U.S. Department of Labor Web site's (www.dol.gov) Office of Workers' Compensation Programs. Typically, one state agency oversees the administration of the program and disburses benefits to the individuals whose claims have been deemed meritorious. Another agency within a state, such as the board of workers' compensation appeals, resolves conflicts such as claim denials that may arise when claimants are dissatisfied with the outcome.

Types and Amounts of Workers' Compensation Benefits

Depending upon the claim, workers' compensation laws specify four kinds of benefits: unlimited medical care, disability income, death benefits, and rehabilitation services.

Unlimited Medical Care

The first type of workers' compensation benefits, medical care benefits, are usually provided without regard to the amount or time over which the benefits will be paid. Medical fee schedules in most states specify the maximum amount paid for particular medical procedures.

Disability Income

The second kind of benefit, disability income, compensates individuals whose work-related accidents or illnesses have at least partially limited their ability to perform the regular duties of their jobs. Benefit amounts depend on the nature of the disability. Workers' compensation programs recognize four types of disabilities: (1) temporary total, (2) permanent total, (3) temporary partial, and (4) permanent partial.

Temporary total disabilities preclude individuals from performing meaningful work for a limited period. Individuals with temporary total disabilities eventually make full recoveries. **Permanent total disabilities** prevent individuals from ever performing any work. Individuals with **temporary partial disabilities** may perform limited amounts of work until making a full recovery. **Permanent partial disabilities** limit the kind of work that individuals perform on an enduring basis. The duration of benefits varies by the type of disability and is determined by each state. Typically, benefits last for up to 500 weeks.

Permanent partial disabilities fall into one of two categories: Workers' compensation programs list specific **scheduled injuries** that involve the loss of a member of the body, including an arm, leg, finger, hand, or eye. Each state specifies an amount for scheduled injuries. For instance, Alabama pays about $37,000 for the loss of a hand, while Illinois pays nearly $280,000. **Nonscheduled injuries** refer to general injuries of the body that make working difficult or impossible. Examples of nonscheduled injuries include back and head damage. States rely on one of three approaches to pay benefits for permanent partial disabilities classified as unscheduled: (1) impairment approach, (2) wage-loss approach, and (3) loss of wage-earning capacity.

The **impairment approach** bases benefit amounts on the physical or mental loss associated with an injury to a bodily function. This approach does not account for loss of future earnings because it ignores the physical and mental capacities necessary to perform the essential functions of one's job. For instance, the impairment approach designates the same benefit for the loss of an arm to college professors and to concert pianists. Clearly, the loss of an arm will prevent a pianist from performing, but this should have lesser impact on a college professor's job to lecture students.

The **wage-loss approach** bases benefits on the actual loss of earnings that results directly from nonscheduled injuries. Application of this approach requires monitoring of an individual's income following an injury. The objective is to replace a part or all of the earnings loss due to the injury. Issues of fairness do arise. For example, the wage-loss approach does not provide any compensation for nonscheduled injuries when wages remain the same or increase. Also, calculating wage loss is not always straightforward: It is entirely possible that wage loss may actually be coincidental to an injury, with poor economic conditions or faltering company performance as the true causes.

The **loss of wage earning capacity approach** factors in two important issues that are likely to affect an injured worker's ability to compete for employment: human capital (e.g., work experience, age, and education) and the type of permanent impairment. This approach has the potential to control costs because it recognizes the importance of human capital variables. Many injured workers may have the necessary education and work experience to perform different jobs without any compromise in earnings. However, this approach is the most subjective method for determining nonscheduled benefit amounts.

Death Benefits

Third, **death benefits** are awarded in two forms: burial allowances and survivors' benefits. Burial allowances reflect a fixed amount, varying by state. In 2015, maximum burial allowances ranged from $3,000 to about $15,000. Survivors' benefits are paid to the spouses of deceased employees and to any dependent children. The amounts vary widely by state, based on different criteria. For example, for a spouse in 2015, the minimum allowable weekly payment to a spouse could be as little as $20 to slightly more than $500. States usually limit the duration of spousal benefits to a designated number of weeks or until remarriage, whichever comes first. Benefits for children typically equal two-thirds of the deceased parent's wages each year until a designated maximum age. The maximum age increases for children in college.

Rehabilitative Services

The fourth benefit, **rehabilitative services,** covers physical and vocational rehabilitation. Rehabilitative services are available in all states. Claims for this benefit must usually be made within six months to two years after the accident. In most states, the employer covers the costs of physical and vocational rehabilitation. A minority of state governments cover the costs of physical and vocational rehabilitation.

Employers' Rights under Workers' Compensation Programs

Participation in workers' compensation programs and compliance with applicable regulations protect employers from legal action initiated by injured workers based on the no-fault principles of these programs. However, there are four possible exceptions to immunity from legal action:

- An employer's intentional acts.
- Lawsuits alleging employer retaliation for filing a workers' compensation claim.
- Lawsuits against noncomplying employers.
- Lawsuits relating to "dual capacity" relationships.

An Employer's Intentional Acts

Most state courts consider intentional actions to harm employees as reasonable cause for holding an employer liable. Two kinds of lawsuits allege an employer's intentional acts to harm employees. The first, **deliberate and knowing torts,** entails an employer's deliberate and knowing intent to harm at least one employee. The second, **violations of an affirmative duty,** takes place when an employer fails to reveal the exposure of one or more workers to harmful substances, or when the employer does not disclose a medical condition typically caused by exposure. In particular, failure to notify violates an employer's affirmative duty when the illness is either correctable at the point of discovery or its progress may be stopped by removing employees from further exposure.

Retaliation against Workers Who Filed Workers' Compensation Claims

In most states, employees possess the right to sue employers who retaliate against them for either filing workers' compensation claims or pursuing their rights established in workers' compensation programs. Retaliation usually entails an adverse effect upon a worker's status (e.g., a demotion or pay cut) or termination of a worker's employment. Employees may initiate these lawsuits by claiming retaliatory action. Employers then possess the burden of proof to establish their actions as a legally sanctioned business necessity.

Employer Noncompliance

Workers' compensation laws oblige employers to comply with applicable state laws. Employers begin to fulfill their obligations by purchasing insurance from state funds or private insurance carriers, or through self-insurance. Failure to carry workers' compensation insurance may lead to one or more consequences:

- Lost immunity, making violators susceptible to common-law charges (of contributory negligence or other torts).
- Monetary penalties, including fines and payment of unpaid premiums.
- Criminal penalties.
- Liability for the full cost of workers' compensation claims.

Most states recognize two acceptable alternatives for employees to receive remedy. First, they gain the right to initiate legal action against noncompliant employers, as just described. Second, most states extend workers' compensation protection to employees regardless of an employer's compliance status.

Dual Capacity

Dual capacity is a legal doctrine that applies to the relationship between employers and employees. Specifically, a company may fulfill a role for an employee that is completely different from its role as employer. Even though an employer meets its obligations under workers' compensation laws, it may be susceptible to common-law actions. An employer's immunity does not protect it from common-law actions by employees when the company also serves a dual capacity that confers duties unrelated to, and independent of, those imposed upon it as an employer. A Supreme Court of Pennsylvania decision offers a clear illustration of the dual capacity doctrine:

> A hospital employee who became ill while performing his job received injuries during medical treatment of the illness (by the same hospital). The hospital's role as an employer was completely unrelated to its role as a medical services provider. The court ruled that Presbyterian University Hospital fulfilled a dual capacity role as an employer and provider of medical treatment to this employee. Specifically, the court concluded that the employee's injuries were sustained because of its role as medical services provider rather than as employer—(a) the purpose of the emergency room visit was to treat the illness, (b) the immediate purpose of seeking treatment was personal, and (c) the hospital billed the employee's insurance carrier for the treatment as it would have for any patient. As a result, this employee gained the right to sue the hospital for injuries sustained during treatment because an X-ray table harness broke, causing the employee to fall onto the floor and sustain injuries.[20]

Becoming injured while using an employer's product to perform work is another instance of dual capacity. For instance, a door-to-door salesperson for Company X, a manufacturer of vacuum cleaners, becomes injured while demonstrating the use of her employer's products. A defective vacuum cleaner exploded during the demonstration, causing serious burns and the loss of the salesperson's left eye. The salesperson is eligible to file a workers' compensation claim because she was injured while performing her job. She may also have the right to initiate a products liability lawsuit as the user of her employer's defective product.

Typical Employers' Defenses When Employees Challenge Immunity

As discussed above, employers maintain immunity from worker-initiated legal action when they are in full compliance with workers' compensation regulations. Employers lose immunity when they fail to comply. Most state courts usually recognize four acceptable defenses against employee lawsuits for premeditated acts. Premeditation excludes an employee's unwarrantable ignorance, bad judgment, or dishonesty. Employer defenses rely on assertions that the causes of injuries or illnesses were unrelated to work-related activities:

- Preexisting conditions (illnesses or injuries that occurred prior to participation in an employer's workers' compensation program, except for work-related illnesses or injuries that worsen the preexisting conditions).
- Employee negligence (e.g., injuries sustained due to noncompliance with clearly communicated safety procedures).
- Employee misconduct (e.g., injuries sustained from acts of aggression against other employees).
- Safety violations by the employee.

In general, employers must continue to provide workers' compensation payments even if an employee is discharged because he or she willfully violates work rules in the course of employment after sustaining an injury. For example, a Maine Court of Appeals required that the employer restore workers' compensation payments notwithstanding an employee's intentional dishonesty:

> An injured employee began to receive workers' compensation payments for a work-related incident that led to the loss of three fingers and serious injuries to a hand, an arm, and a shoulder. After returning to work on a light-duty basis, this employee misrepresented his use of a paid sick day. In actuality, the employer learned that the employee missed work to participate in a golf tournament. The employer discharged this employee and terminated his workers' compensation benefits because the employee willfully misused the paid time off for illness. Ultimately, the court based its decision on the irrelevance of the employee's dishonesty to the negative impact of the injuries on earnings capacity.[21]

Summary

This chapter reviews the fundamental concepts of these protection programs. The social maladies of the late 19th and early 20th centuries eventually gave rise to two discretionary employer benefits, employer-sponsored disability and life insurance programs, as well as workers' compensation protection, which is mandatory in all but three states. These programs provide the backup to workers and their dependents for work-related and nonwork-related injuries, illnesses, or death. The next chapter will review various Social Security programs, of which one is disability insurance. A comparison will be made between workers' compensation benefits and the Social Security disability and survivor benefits.

Key Terms

insurance policy, *168*
premium, *168*
short-term disability insurance, *168*
long-term disability insurance, *168*
establishment funds, *170*
short-term disability, *170*
preexisting condition, *171*
pre-eligibility period, *171*
elimination period, *171*
exclusion provisions, *171*
long-term disability, *172*
partial disabilities inclusion, *172*
Older Workers Benefit Protection Act (OWBPA), *173*
Americans with Disabilities Act, *174*
qualified individual with a disability, *174*
offset provisions, *174*
life insurance, *175*

term life insurance, *175*
whole life insurance, *175*
universal life insurance, *176*
contributory plans, *176*
noncontributory plans, *176*
underwriting, *177*
mortality tables, *177*
accidental death and dismemberment insurance (AD&D), *177*
state compulsory disability laws, *178*
workers' compensation, *178*
Longshore and Harbor-workers' Compensation Act, *179*
Federal Employees' Compensation Act, *179*
ratemaking service organizations, *180*
rating manuals, *180*
second-injury funds, *180*
injury claim, *180*

occupational disease claim, *180*
death claim, *181*
temporary total disabilities, *181*
permanent total disabilities, *181*
temporary partial disabilities, *181*
permanent partial disabilities, *181*
scheduled injuries, *181*
nonscheduled injuries, *181*
impairment approach, *182*
wage-loss approach, *182*
loss of wage earning capacity approach, *182*
death benefits, *182*
rehabilitative services, *182*
deliberate and knowing torts, *183*
violations of an affirmative duty, *183*
dual capacity, *184*

Discussion Questions

1. Discuss the basic concept of insurance. How does this concept apply to disabilities and life?

2. Identify three types of life insurance plans. Briefly describe the differences among them.

3. Compare the main objectives of state regulation of workers' compensation programs and employer-sponsored disability and life insurance plans.

4. List and describe the types of claims in state workers' compensation programs. Is there redundancy with employer-sponsored private insurance? Explain your answer.

5. Under what circumstances should employees be ineligible for public or private disability and life benefits? Discuss the rationale for your answer. Are the expenses associated with providing public and private programs serving the best interests of society?

Cases

1. Understanding Your Employee Benefits: A Workers' Compensation Claim

Before you leave the store at the end of your shift, your supervisor asks you to restock the shelves. As you reach for a box from the top of a ladder in the storage room, you suddenly realize that there is a problem. The ladder shakes, and the next thing you know is that you are on the floor and your leg is in a tangle. A few hours later at the hospital, you learn that your leg is broken and you will need surgery. Further, you can expect to be off work for at least the next six weeks.

Like most people, you depend on your weekly paycheck to pay your bills, and you will have significant financial challenges if you can't work. The cost of the medical care related to your injury is also going to be significant. While you have health insurance, you know that with deductibles and co-payment requirements, you will still need to pay quite a bit. You feel some relief, however, when the doctor tells you that the accident should be covered by workers' compensation. She tells you to speak to your supervisor to report the accident and start the process of applying for workers' compensation, which will cover your medical expenses and provide you with continuing income while you are out recovering from the surgery.

However, your supervisor tells you in a phone call that the doctor has misled you and that you won't qualify for workers' compensation because the accident was your fault. He suggests that you do not file a report about the injury. He assures you that your health insurance will cover the medical expenses and that you will have time off available under the Family Medical Leave Act (FMLA). He also tells you that he will have the HR manager send you the FMLA paperwork and ends the call by reminding you not to mention workers' compensation to the HR manager. He says that if you do, you aren't going to be working for him again.

Now you are unsure of what to do. You call a coworker who witnessed the accident to see if she agrees that it was your fault. She tells you that the accident was not your fault because the ladder you were using was broken the previous week and your supervisor forgot to have it fixed. Your company has strict safety guidelines, and if the store manager learns that he was neglectful, your supervisor could lose his job. You have always liked your supervisor and don't want to cause him any trouble, but you don't think it is right that he has threatened you about reporting this accident, which wasn't even your fault. You decide that you should call the HR manager yourself for advice.

1. Are you eligible for workers' compensation? Does it matter if the accident was your fault?
2. What are your rights in this situation? What should you do?

2. Managing Employee Benefits: Adding a Long-Term Disability Benefit

It is time for the annual review of benefit offerings at Medfirst Pharmaceuticals. With more than 1,500 employees and growth on the horizon, Director of Compensation Harold Jones knows that he must ensure that the benefit package is attractive to potential new employees while still meeting the needs of current employees. Medfirst has a diverse workforce that includes scientists, administrators, support staff, and field sales employees. Harold thinks that the current package is attractive but that more options might add overall value.

The company currently offers a health insurance plan, a retirement savings plan, a generous paid time-off allowance, life insurance, and short-term disability insurance. Harold has reviewed benefit utilization reports and also an employee satisfaction survey and finds that, overall, employees are satisfied with their benefits. Medfirst is focused on retaining employees over the long term, and several questions on the employee satisfaction survey ask about their concerns related to their employment at Medfirst. While employees seem confident that the company is on the right track to remaining successful, employees noted that they were concerned about their financial security and long-term opportunities at Medfirst. Harold thinks that these feelings may be a result of external forces, such as the recent downturn in the economy, coupled with excessive media coverage of health problems that continue to plague the public in general.

As Harold reflects on these employee concerns, he considers some employees over the last several years who have had to take extended leaves of absence due to medical problems. One employee in particular had to have back surgery that left him out of work for almost a year. Harold knows that the absence of income and the high medical expenses caused a toll on this employee, who had to borrow from his retirement account in order to pay his home mortgage during that time period. Harold knows that stories such as this are becoming more common and that giving employees some relief from such concern would be welcomed. Thus, he is considering offering a long-term disability insurance option for employees.

A long-term disability insurance benefit would provide employees with income continuation in the event of an illness or injury that leaves an employee unable to work for a period of greater than six months. Harold learns that there are some options such as partial disabilities coverage, which provides employees some payments if they are able to continue working only in a part-time capacity due to their illnesses or injuries. Such an option hadn't occurred to Harold, and he realizes that he needs to learn more to determine if Medfirst should offer long-term disability insurance.

1. How do disability insurance benefits differ from workers' compensation?

2. If a company already offers short-term disability insurance, why should the company consider long-term disability insurance?

3. Do you think the long-term disability insurance benefit would be a valuable addition to Medfirst's benefit offerings? Should the company include the partial disabilities coverage?

Endnotes

1. Society of Actuaries, *Experience Studies in Individual Disability.* 2006. Accessed February 12, 2016, www.soa.org.

2. F. R. Dulles and M. Dubofsky, *Labor in America: A History.* Arlington Heights, IL: Harlan Davidson, 1993.

3. U.S. Chamber of Commerce, *2015 Analysis of Workers' Compensation Laws.* Washington, DC: U.S. Chamber of Commerce, 2015.

4. I. Sengupta and M. L. Baldwin, *Workers Compensation: Benefits, Coverage, and Costs, 2013.* Washington, DC: National Academy of Social Insurance, August 2015.

5. U.S. Department of Labor, *Employee Benefits in the United States—March 2015.* Bulletin No. 2782, 2015.

6. U.S. Department of Labor, *Employer Costs for Employee Compensation—September 2015.* (USDL 15-2329), 2015.

7. I.R.C. §104(a)(3).

8. U.S. Equal Employment Opportunity Commission, *Interpretive Guidance on Title I of ADA,* 29 C.F.R. §1630. June 8, 2000. Accessed April 4, 2009, www.eeoc.gov/policy/regs/1630-mitigating-qanda.html; Equal Employment Opportunity Commission, *Technical Assistance Manual on Title I of ADA.* January 27, 1992. Accessed July 26, 2001, www.eeoc.gov.

9. Bureau of Labor Statistics, *Employee Benefits in Medium and Large Private Establishments, 1997.* Washington, DC: U.S. Government Printing Office, 1999.

10. U.S. Department of Labor, *Employee Benefits in the United States—March 2015.* (USDL 2782), 2015.

11. U.S. Department of Labor, *Employer Costs for Employee Compensation—September 2015.* (USDL 15-2329), 2015.

12. I.R.C. §79; Treas. Regs. §§1.79-1, 1.79-3(d)(2).

13. U.S. Chamber of Commerce, *2015 Analysis of Workers' Compensation Laws.* 2015.

14. J. V. Nackley, *Primer on Workers' Compensation.* Washington, DC: Bureau of National Affairs, 1987.

15. 33 U.S.C. §§ 901–950.

16. 5 U.S.C. §§8101–8193.

17. U.S. Chamber of Commerce, *2015 Analysis of Workers' Compensation Laws.* 2015.

18. U.S. Department of Labor, *Employer Costs for Employee Compensation—September 2015.* (USDL 15-2329), 2015.

19. Nackley, *Primer on Workers' Compensation.*

20. *Tatrai v. Presbyterian University Hospital*, 439 A.2d 1162 (PA 1982).

21. *Cousins v. Georgia-Pacific Corp.*, 599 A.2d 73 (ME 1991).

Chapter Seven

Government-Mandated Social Security Programs

Learning Objectives

In this chapter, you will gain an understanding of:

1. Origins and introduction of Social Security programs.

2. Structure of the OASDI program.

3. Structure of Medicare programs.

4. Financing of OASDI and Medicare programs.

5. Unemployment insurance programs.

The U.S. government established Social Security and workers' compensation insurance programs because of social maladies associated with events of the early 20th century. Without government assistance, many people would have become destitute. These programs were geared toward promoting the social good. The **social good** refers to a booming economy, low levels of unemployment, progressive wages and benefits, and safe and healthful working conditions. We will review the Social Security programs in this chapter.

ORIGINS OF SOCIAL SECURITY

Early social security programs helped minimize **income discontinuity** caused by the Great Depression, protecting families from financial devastation during long unemployment spells. During the **Great Depression** of the 1930s, scores of businesses failed and masses of employees became chronically unemployed. Companies shifted their focus from exclusively maximizing profits to staying in business. Overall, ensuring the financial solvency of employees during periods of temporary unemployment and following work-related injuries promoted the well-being of the economy and contributed to the ability of some companies to remain in business. By providing subsistence payments to the unemployed, injured workers, and the elderly, social security programs made it possible for those individuals to by food, clothing, and other necessities. As we will see, amendments to the Social Security Act established health-care protection to individuals aged 65 or older.

INTRODUCTION TO THE SOCIAL SECURITY PROGRAMS

The Social Security Act of 1935 and subsequent amendments to the act established four public social insurance programs:

- Old-Age, Survivor, and Disability Insurance (OASDI)
- Medicare
- Unemployment insurance
- Supplemental Security Income benefits

The economic devastation of the Great Depression era prompted the federal government into action because most Americans had used up any life savings to meet essential expenses, and opportunities for gainful employment were scarce.

The passage of the Social Security Act set up two programs: a federal system of income benefits for retired workers and a system of unemployment insurance administered by the federal government and state governments. Amendments to the Social Security Act in 1939 established the survivors' insurance benefit, and in 1965 established the disability insurance program and the Medicare program. The term **Old-Age, Survivor, and Disability Insurance (OASDI)** refers to the programs that provide retirement income, income to the survivors of deceased workers, and income to disabled workers and their family members. The **Medicare** program serves nearly all U.S. citizens of at least age 65, and disabled Social Security beneficiaries, by providing insurance coverage for hospitalization, convalescent care, and major doctor bills.

In this chapter, the fundamentals of OASDI, as well as Medicare and unemployment insurance as employee benefits, will be reviewed. Supplemental Security Income (SSI) is a federal income supplement program funded by general tax revenues, which serves two purposes. First, the SSI program assists the aged, blind, and disabled people, who have little or no income. Second, this program provides cash to help these individuals to meet basic needs for food, clothing, and shelter. The SSI program will not be covered because it is unrelated to employee benefits programs.

Employers Required to Participate in Social Security Programs

Coverage rules differ somewhat for the OASDI, Medicare, and the unemployment insurance programs.

OASDI and Medicare

Millions of Americans receive Social Security OASDI and Medicare benefits every year. In 2015, more than 64 million Americans received Social Security benefits.[1] Three exempt groups include civilian employees of the federal government and railroad employees with at least 10 years of service (excluding the Medicare program); state and local government employees who are already covered under other retirement plans unless these government organizations choose to participate in this program; and children under age 21, except children aged 18 or older employed in their parents' businesses.

Unemployment Insurance

Most employers are required to make contributions to the unemployment insurance program. State unemployment insurance programs provide benefits to millions of unemployed individuals every year. A worker files an initial claim with its state's unemployment insurance office. The names for these organizations vary by state and can be identified on the U.S. Department of Labor Web site (www.dol.gov). For example, in California, the name of this office is the State of California Employment Development Department.

Administration of Social Security Programs

Federal agencies possess primary responsibilities for OASDI and Medicare programs. The federal government and each state share the responsibility for the administration of the unemployment insurance programs.

OASDI and Medicare Administration

Two federal agencies primarily oversee Social Security programs: the **Social Security Administration** and the **Centers for Medicare & Medicaid Services.** The Social Security Administration (SSA) "administers the federal retirement, survivors, and disability insurance programs, as well as the program of supplemental security income (SSI) for the aged, blind, and disabled, and performs certain functions with respect to the black lung benefits program. SSA also directs the aid to the aged, blind, and disabled in Guam, Puerto Rico, and the Virgin Islands."[2]

Unemployment Insurance Administration

Titles III and IX of the Social Security Act authorized the federal government to grant money to states to administer unemployment compensation, and it also established a federal unemployment insurance trust fund. The Federal Unemployment Tax Act (FUTA), which we discuss later in this chapter, authorized the collection of both federal and state payroll taxes from employers and specified how these funds were to be used. The federal share of these taxes covers the cost of administering the unemployment insurance and employment service programs. The state share of these taxes may be used only for benefit costs. Each state sets its own rules and oversees program administration. State laws vary regarding eligibility for benefits, the amount of benefits, and the number of weeks for which they may be paid.

At the federal level, the **Employment and Training Administration** in the U.S. Department of Labor oversees unemployment insurance programs. The Employment and Training Administration strives "to contribute to the more efficient and effective functioning of the U.S. labor market by providing high-quality job training, employment, labor market information, and income maintenance services primarily through state and local workforce development systems."[3]

Employment security agencies in state labor departments, or independent agencies or commissions, oversee the administration of unemployment insurance programs at the state level. Each state maintains records, collects taxes, determines the eligibility of individuals for benefits, processes claims, and disburses unemployment benefits.

Social Security Numbers

Originally, the Social Security Act authorized the creation of a recordkeeping system to keep track of employees' wages for determining the amount of employee benefits under the original OASDI and unemployment insurance programs. This authorization led to the creation of the nine-digit **Social Security number system** in the late 1930s. Since then, the Social Security Administration issues Social Security numbers to U.S. citizens, foreign students, and resident aliens for a variety of reasons.

OLD-AGE, SURVIVOR, AND DISABILITY INSURANCE (OASDI)

OASDI contains two additional benefits that were established by amendments to the Social Security Act following its enactment in 1935. Besides providing retirement income, the amendments include survivors' insurance (1939) and disability insurance (1965). The phrase *old-age* refers to retirement income benefits.

Qualifying for OASDI Benefits

As mentioned above, employees from a wide variety of employers are eligible to receive Social Security program benefits. The Social Security Administration uses a system of **Social Security credits** to determine whether eligible individuals qualify for OASDI and Medicare benefits. Employees accumulate credits based on their payment of Social Security taxes, which employers withhold from earnings.

Employees earn one Social Security credit, also known as a quarter of coverage, for a specified earnings amount earned in a calendar quarter (three months). The designated earnings amount increases every year based on the increase in average earnings in the United States. In 2016, an employee earned one credit for each $1,260 of pay, subject to a maximum of four credits per calendar year. Credits accumulate over the course of employment. An employee must earn at least 40 credits to be eligible to receive retirement benefits (fewer than this amount for a disabled individual, as we will describe shortly). Earned benefits are recognized on an individual's Social Security record. Employees do not forfeit credits when they change jobs or become unemployed.

Determining Benefit Amounts

The Social Security Administration pays monthly benefits to recipients of the OASDI program. The **primary insurance amount (PIA)** equals the monthly benefit amount paid to a retired worker at full retirement age or to a disabled worker. As will be discussed later, survivor benefit amounts depend on several additional criteria. A person's average indexed monthly earnings (AIME) determine the initial PIA. Automatic cost-of-living adjustments (COLAs) are applied to guard against inflation. The formulas used to determine OASDI benefits are complex. Chapter 7 of the *Social Security Handbook*,[4] published by the Social Security Administration, provides a detailed description of these complex computations. Nevertheless, let's look at the basic concepts.

Average Indexed Monthly Earnings

Average indexed monthly earnings (AIME) represent a person's earnings prior to age 62, disability, or death, adjusted for changes in the person's earnings over the course of his or her employment, and for changes in average wages in the economy over the same period. The Social Security Administration uses the AIME to ensure that the proportion of benefits to past earnings is about the same for all OASDI recipients. In other words, using AIME to determine the primary insurance amount (PIA) helps ensure that every beneficiary will have the same proportion of discontinued income (due to retirement, disability, or death) replaced by OASDI benefits.

Automatic Cost-of-Living Adjustments

The Social Security Administration considers applying **automatic cost-of living adjustments (COLAs)** to annual benefits each December to account for changes in the cost of living based on the Consumer Price Index. Social Security benefits were not increased in 2016 because on average, the cost of living did not increase during the previous year. The **Consumer Price Index (CPI)** is the most commonly used method for tracking changes in the costs of goods and services throughout the United States. According to the U.S. Bureau of Labor Statistics (BLS):

> The Consumer Price Index for Urban Wage Earners and Clerical Workers (CPI-W) is based on the expenditures of households included in the CPI-U definition that also meet two requirements: more than one-half of the household's income must come from clerical or wage occupations, and at least one of the household's earners must have been employed for at least 37 weeks during the previous 12 months. The CPI-W population represents about 32 percent of the total U.S. population.[5]

Old-Age Benefits

The Social Security Administration uses several criteria to determine an individual's eligibility for retirement benefits and uses formulas to calculate monthly benefits.

Eligibility Criteria

The number of credits needed to participate in the old-age program depends on the year of birth. Everyone born in 1929 or later needs 40 credits. Individuals born prior to 1929 require fewer credits. Individuals become **fully insured** for life when they have earned the minimum number of credits.

Year of Birth	Credits Needed
1929 or later	40
1928	39
1927	38
1926	37
1925	36
1924	35

Once an individual has become fully insured, he or she must meet an age criterion before receiving retirement benefits. Individuals may begin receiving retirement benefits as early as age 62, but their benefits will be permanently reduced prior to reaching **full retirement age.** Benefits are reduced to account for the longer period over which benefits will be paid. The year of birth determines the full retirement age for the purposes of these benefits. Fully insured individuals born prior to 1938 meet the full retirement age criterion at age 65. Congress increased the full retirement age for people born in 1938 or later because of higher life expectancies of 65-year-old individuals—for men and women born in 1940, at age 65, life expectancy is expected to be an additional 11.9 and 13.4 years, respectively. For men and women born in 2014, at age 65, life expectancy is projected to be an additional 18.1

and 20.6 years, respectively.[6] The age for collecting full Social Security retirement benefits is gradually increasing from 65 to 67 over a 22-year period ending in 2022. Exhibit 7.1 shows the changes in full retirement age based on year of birth and the reduction in benefits received before full retirement age.

For example, Mary was born in 1941, which means she will be entitled to full Social Security retirement benefits when she turns 65 years and 8 months (full retirement age). She has decided to retire at age 62, making her eligible to receive reduced Social Security retirement benefits. Let's assume that her annual Social Security retirement benefit will be $15,000 at full retirement age. At age 62, Mary falls three years and eight months short of full retirement age. As a result, her benefits will be reduced by 22.5 percent until full retirement age. Look carefully at Exhibit 7.1. The instructions direct individuals to select the "total percentage reduction" that corresponds to the year before birth. In Mary's case, she selected the total percentage reduction for 1940, the year before her birth, in 1941. If this reduction did not apply, Mary would have earned $55,005 until full retirement age—that is, ($15,000 × 3 years) + ($15,000 × 0.667 year). The amount by which Mary's benefit will be reduced is $12,375 (i.e., $55,005 × 22.5%), yielding an annual benefit of $42,628 (i.e., $55,005 − $12,375).

The retirement program contains incentives to encourage individuals to delay their retirement after reaching full retirement age. Specifically, the Social Security Administration increases retirement benefits by a designated percent age for each month worked beyond full retirement until age 70, subject to a maximum percentage increase. The percentage increase depends upon the year of birth. Why does Social Security pay reduced monthly benefits for those who claim them

EXHIBIT 7.1
Social Security Full Retirement and Reductions by Age

Source: Social Security Full Retirement and Reductions by Age. Accessed January 31, 2016, www.socialsecurity.gov.

No matter what a person's full retirement age is, he or she may start receiving benefits as early as age 62; the earliest a person can start receiving Social Security retirement benefits will remain at age 62.

Year of Birth*	Full Retirement Age	Total % Reduction
1937 or earlier	65	20.00
1938	65 and 2 months	20.83
1939	65 and 4 months	21.67
1940	65 and 6 months	22.50
1941	65 and 8 months	23.33
1942	65 and 10 months	24.17
1943–1954	66	25.00
1955	66 and 2 months	25.84
1956	66 and 4 months	26.66
1957	66 and 6 months	27.50
1958	66 and 8 months	28.33
1959	66 and 10 months	29.17
1960 and later	67	30.00

*Persons born on January 1 of any year should refer to the previous year.

before their specified full retirement age? Younger retirees are predicted to have a longer life expectancy than older retirees. Complex statistical analyses suggest that, based on average life expectancy, taking a *lower monthly benefit* sooner would lead to earning about the same *total benefit* over one's lifetime as an individual who put off retirement to claim a *higher monthly benefit*. Exhibit 7.2 lists the monthly and annual increases based on year of birth.

For instance, Exhibit 7.1 shows that the full retirement age for individuals born in 1937 or earlier is 65 years. John, born in 1937, turned age 65 in 2002. Let's assume that John would earn an annual benefit of $13,200 at full retirement age. However, John decides to postpone his retirement an additional three years. Exhibit 7.2 shows that individuals born in 1937 may increase their annual benefits by 6.5 percent for each year beyond full retirement age. John's annual benefits will be substantially greater because he will work until age 68. Specifically, John's annual benefit will be about $15,945 when he retires—that is:

$$\$13,200 + [(\$13,200 \times 6.5\%) + (\$14,058 \times 6.5\%) + (\$14,972 \times 6.5\%)]$$

When the Social Security Act was passed in the 1930s, it was based on the common model of the single-earner family—a married couple with or without children. Only one of the adults, typically the husband, worked. The OASDI benefits program was designed to compensate spouses who stayed at home to raise a family

EXHIBIT 7.2
Delayed
Retirement
Credits

Source: Social Security Administration. Accessed February 12, 2016, www .socialsecurity.gov.

The Social Security Amendments of 1983 (H.R. 1900, Public Law 98-21) contained two provisions that may have an impact on when an individual decides to retire. The two provisions are an increase in the retirement age that first affected individuals retiring in 2000 and an increase in the delayed retirement credit for those who work beyond full retirement age.

Delayed Retirement Credits

- Social Security benefits are increased (by a certain percentage depending on a person's date of birth) if retirement is delayed beyond full retirement age.
- The benefit increase stops when a person reaches age 70, even if the person continues to delay taking benefits.

Increase for Delayed Retirement		
Year of Birth	**Yearly Rate of Increase (%)**	**Monthly Rate of Increase (%)**
1930	4.5%	3/8 of 1%
1931–1932	5.0	5/12 of 1
1933–1934	5.5	11/24 of 1
1935–1936	6.0	1/2 of 1
1937–1938	6.5	13/24 of 1
1939–1940	7.0	7/12 of 1
1941–1942	7.5	5/8 of 1
1943 or later	8.0	2/3 of 1

and who were financially dependent on the working spouse. Under this traditional model, the stay-at-home spouse did not have any income from employment or retirement income. Nowadays, both spouses in a married couple typically work, with both earning their own Social Security retirement benefit as well as possible additional income from employer-sponsored retirement plans. On June 26, 2015, the U.S. Supreme Court issued a decision in *Obergefell v. Hodges*, holding that same-sex couples have a constitutional right to marry in all states. The court's decision opened the door for same-sex couples to be recognized as married for purposes of determining entitlement to Social Security benefits or eligibility.[7]

Retirement Benefit Amount Determination

The formulas to determine retirement benefits were reviewed above. In general, a person's retirement benefit equals the primary insurance amount (PIA). Exhibit 7.3 shows an example of how the Social Security Administration calculates PIAs. Family benefits usually equal 50 percent of the PIA. In 2015, the annual monthly benefit for all retired workers was $1,335.

Survivor Benefits

The Social Security Administration pays benefits to eligible family members of a deceased worker.

Eligibility

In general, a worker needs to have accumulated at least 40 credits to qualify family members for survivor benefits. Family members include:

- Nondisabled widow or widower at the full retirement age or older.
- Disabled widow or widower as young as age 50.
- Nondisabled widow or widower at any age if he or she takes care of the worker's children under age 16 or disabled children at any age.
- Divorced spouse as young as age 60.
- Unmarried children under 18, or up to age 19 if attending elementary or secondary school on a full-time basis.
- Disabled children at any age if disability began before age 22 and the parent was unmarried at the time.
- Stepchildren, grandchildren, or adopted children (in most cases).
- Dependent parents at age 62 or older.

Survivor Benefit Amount Determination

Survivor benefits are usually less than a worker's PIA. The Social Security Administration pays monthly survivor benefits at a level ranging from 71.5 to 100 percent of the PIA, depending upon the survivor's status. In addition, the Social Security Administration pays a lump sum benefit to the surviving spouse, subject to two criteria. First, the worker must have earned at least 6 credits of the last 13 calendar quarters just before death. Second, the surviving spouse must have lived with the worker at the time of death. Surviving children receive this

EXHIBIT 7.3   Calculating the Primary Insurance Amount (PIA)

Source: Social Security Administration, *Primary Insurance Amount*. Accessed January 29, 2016, www.ssa.gov.

PIA definition	The "primary insurance amount" (PIA) is the benefit (before rounding down to the next-lower whole dollar) that a person would receive if he or she elects to begin receiving retirement benefits at his or her normal retirement age. At this age, the benefit is neither reduced for early retirement nor increased for delayed retirement.
PIA Formula Bend Points	The PIA is the sum of three separate percentages of portions of average indexed monthly earnings. The portions depend on the *year* in which a worker attains age 62, becomes disabled before age 62, or dies before attaining age 62.
	For 2016, these portions are the first $856, the amount between $856 and $5,157, and the amount over $5,157, respectively. These dollar amounts are the "bend points" of the 2016 PIA formula. A table shows bend points, for years beginning with 1979, for both the PIA and maximum family benefit formulas.
PIA Formula	For an individual who first becomes eligible for old-age insurance benefits or disability insurance benefits in 2016, or who dies in 2016 before becoming eligible for benefits, his or her PIA will be the sum of:
	(a) 90 percent of the first $856 of his or her average indexed monthly earnings, plus
	(b) 32 percent of his or her average indexed monthly earnings over $856 and through $5,157, plus
	(c) 15 percent of his or her average indexed monthly earnings over $5,157.
	This amount is rounded to the next lower multiple of $0.10 if it is not already a multiple of $0.10.

Determination of the PIA Bend Points for 2016

Amounts in Formula	Average Wage Indices	Bend Points for 1979
	For 1977: $9,779.44	First: $180
	For 2014: $46.481.52	Second: $1,085
Computation of Bend Points for 2016	*First bend point* $180 times $46,481.52 divided by 9,779.44 equals $855.54, which rounds to $856	*Second bend point* $1,085 times 46,481.52 divided by 9,779.44 equals $5,156.99, which rounds to $5,157

benefit if there is no eligible spouse. In 2016, the average monthly survivor benefit for a widowed mother and two children was $2,680, and a widow or widower alone was $1,285.

Disability Benefits

The Social Security Administration pays benefits to seriously disabled workers and family members, paying only for total disability. The Social Security Administration defines disability as an inability to engage in any substantial gainful activity (SGA) because of a medically determinable physical or mental impairment(s):

- That is expected to result in death, or
- That has lasted or is expected to last for a continuous period of at least 12 months.

Work is "substantial" if it involves doing significant physical or mental activities or a combination of both. For work activity to be substantial, it does not need to be performed on a full-time basis. Work activity performed on a part-time basis may also be SGA. "Gainful" work activity is:

- Work performed for pay or profit; or
- Work of a nature generally performed for pay or profit; or
- Work intended for profit, whether or not a profit is realized.

Eligibility

Individuals who meet the definition of disability are eligible to receive benefits after meeting two criteria. The first is the **recent work test**, and the second is the **duration of work test**. The recent work test considers the age at which an individual becomes disabled. Exhibit 7.4 displays the criteria for the recent work test.

EXHIBIT 7.4   Recent Work Test

The following table shows the rules for how much work you need for the recent work test, based on your age when your disability began. We base the rules in this table on the *calendar quarter* in which you turned or will turn a certain age.

The calendar quarters are
First Quarter: January 1 through March 31
Second Quarter: April 1 through June 30
Third Quarter: July 1 through September 30
Fourth Quarter: October 1 through December 31

Rules for work needed for the recent work test

If you become disabled...	*Then, you generally need:*
In or before the quarter you turn age 24	1.5 years of work during the three-year period ending with the quarter your disability began.
In the quarter after you turn age 24 but before the quarter you turn age 31	Work during half the time for the period beginning with the quarter after you turned 21 and ending with the quarter you became disabled. Example: If you become disabled in the quarter you turned age 27, then you would need three years of work out of the six-year period ending with the quarter you became disabled.
In the quarter you turn age 31 or later	Work during five years out of the 10-year period ending with the quarter your disability began.

Source: U.S. Social Security Administration. *Disability Benefits.* Accessed January 29, 2016, www.socialsecurity.gov.

EXHIBIT 7.5
Duration of
Work Test

Source: U.S. Social
Security Administra-
tion. *Disability Bene-
fits.* Accessed January
29, 2016, www.
socialsecurity.gov.

Examples of work needed for the duration of work test

If you become disabled...	Then, you generally need:
Before age 28	1.5 years of work
Age 30	2 years
Age 34	3 years
Age 38	4 years
Age 42	5 years
Age 44	5.5 years
Age 46	6 years
Age 48	6.5 years
Age 50	7 years
Age 52	7.5 years
Age 54	8 years
Age 56	8.5 years
Age 58	9 years
Age 60	9.5 years

The duration of work test considers whether an individual has worked sufficiently long enough (and has contributed to Social Security). Exhibit 7.5 provides examples of the work need for the duration of the work test. As shown in Exhibits 7.4 and 7.5, younger workers need fewer quarters of coverage because they have fewer years to accumulate them.

Disability Benefit Amount Determination

Disability benefits equal the full primary insurance amount. Disability payments to eligible family members usually equal half of the PIA. In 2016, the average monthly disability benefit for all disabled workers was $1,166. The benefit for a disabled worker, spouse, and one or more children was $1,983.

Comparing Workers' Compensation with Social Security Disability and Survivors' Benefits

Workers' compensation differs from Social Security disability and survivor insurance in important ways. Workers' compensation pays for medical care for *work-related injuries* after a brief waiting period of 3–7 days. It also pays permanent partial and permanent total disability benefits to workers who have lasting consequences of work-related disabilities. The waiting period could be several weeks before these income benefits become effective. Further, in most states, workers' compensation pays rehabilitation and training benefits for those unable to return to preinjury careers (in most states, for a limited duration). Finally, workers' compensation pays benefits to survivors of workers who die of work-related causes. In comparison, Social Security pays benefits to workers with long-term or permanent disabilities from *any cause*, but only when the disabilities preclude the ability to work. Payments for permanent disability are made throughout the person's life. In addition, Social Security pays survivor benefits to families of deceased workers. Finally, Social Security benefits begin after a five-month waiting period.

MEDICARE

The Medicare program serves nearly all U.S. citizens aged 65 or older by providing insurance coverage for hospitalization, convalescent care, and major doctor bills. The Medicare program includes five separate features:

- *Medicare Part A*—Hospital insurance.
- *Medicare Part B*—Medical insurance.
- *Medigap*—Voluntary supplemental insurance to pay for services not covered in Parts A and B.
- *Medicare Part C: Medicare Advantage*—Choices in health-care providers, such as through HMOs and PPOs (Chapter 5).
- *Medicare Part D: Medicare Prescription Drug Benefit*—Prescription drug coverage.

Most individuals who are eligible to receive protection under Medicare may choose to receive coverage in one of two ways, as shown in Exhibit 7.6. As this exhibit shows, a person may receive coverage under the original Medicare plan or Medicare Advantage plans.

In a nutshell, the original Medicare plan is a fee-for-service plan that is managed by the federal government. As discussed in Chapter 5, fee-for-service plans include many health-care services, medical supplies, and certain prescription drugs. Participants in fee-for-service plans have the choice to receive care from virtually any licensed health-care provider or facility. On the other hand, Medicare Advantage plans include a variety of insurance options, including health maintenance organizations, preferred provider organizations, Medicare special needs plans, and Medicare medical savings account (MSA) plans. Medicare Advantage plans are run by private companies and are subject to strict regulations specified in the Medicare program. Some of the restrictions pertain to the pricing of the different plans. The key features will be reviewed in subsequent sections of this chapter.

Eligibility Criteria for Medicare Benefits

Individuals aged 65 or older who have earned at least 40 credits are eligible to receive Medicare benefits, and coverage automatically extends to spouses of eligible individuals. In addition, family members with disabilities are eligible to receive Medicare benefits, and younger individuals qualify for Medicare protection if they are seriously disabled for at least 24 months or suffering from permanent kidney failure requiring dialysis or a transplant. Meeting at least one of these criteria provides Part A coverage without paying a premium. Having fewer than 40 credits requires that an individual

EXHIBIT 7.6
Medicare
Basics

Source: Medicare,
www.medicare.gov.

Original Medicare Plan	OR	Medicare Advantage Plans like HMOs and PPOs

Part A (Hospital)	**Part B (Medical)**

Medicare provides this coverage. Part B is optional. You have your choice of doctors. Your costs may be higher than in Medicare Advantage plans.

Called "Part C," this option combines your Part A (Hospital) and Part B (Medical)

Private insurance companies approved by Medicare provide this coverage. Generally, you must see doctors in the plan. Your costs may be lower than in the original Medicare plan, and you may get extra benefits.

+

Part D (Prescription Drug Coverage)

You can choose this coverage. Private companies approved by Medicare run these plans. Plans cover different drugs. Medically necessary drugs must be covered.

Part D (Prescription Drug Coverage)

Most Part C plans cover prescription drugs. If they don't, you may be able to choose this coverage. Plans cover different drugs. Medically necessary drugs must be covered.

+

Medigap (Medicare Supplemental Insurance)

You can choose to buy this private coverage (or an employer/union may offer similar coverage) to fill in gaps in Part A and Part B coverage. Costs vary by policy and company.

pay a monthly premium to receive coverage. In 2016, the monthly Part A premium was $226 with 30–39 credits, and $411 with fewer than 30 credits.

Part A coverage automatically qualifies an individual to enroll in Part B coverage for a monthly premium. In 2016, typical monthly Part B premiums were $104.90. Costlier rates apply to some individuals with higher income.

Medicare Part A Coverage

This compulsory hospitalization insurance covers both inpatient and outpatient hospital care and services. Examples of Part A coverage include:

- Inpatient hospital care in a semiprivate room, meals, general nursing, and other hospital supplies and services.
- Home health services limited to reasonable and essential part-time or intermittent skilled nursing care and home health aide services; and physical therapy, occupational therapy, and speech-language therapy ordered by a doctor.

- Hospice care for people with terminal illness (i.e., illness that is expected to lead to death within six months), including pharmaceutical products for symptom control and pain relief, medical and support services from a Medicare-approved hospice provider, and other services not otherwise covered by Medicare (e.g., grief counseling).
- Skilled nursing facility care, including semiprivate room, meals, skilled nursing and rehabilitative services, and supplies for up to 100 days per year. An example of skilled care is physical therapy after a stroke or serious accident.

Medicare Part B Coverage

This voluntary supplementary medical insurance helps pay for medical services not covered by Part A, such as doctors' services, outpatient care, clinical laboratory services (e.g., blood tests, urinalysis), and some preventative health services (e.g., cardiovascular screenings, bone mass measurement). Part B also provides ambulance services to a hospital or skilled nursing facility when transportation in any other vehicle would endanger a person's health.

This plan is structured similarly to indemnity medical insurance (fee-for-service), which was discussed in Chapter 5. Part B typically covers 80 percent of medical services and supplies after the enrolled individual pays an annual deductible for services furnished under this plan. As discussed in Chapter 5, the deductible is the amount an individual pays for services before insurance benefits become active.

Medigap Insurance

Medigap insurance supplements Part A and Part B coverage, and it is available to Medicare recipients in most states from private insurance companies for an extra fee. Most Medigap plans help cover the costs of coinsurance, copayments, and deductibles. Federal and state laws limit the sale of these plans to up to 10 different standardized choices, which vary in terms of the level of protection. For example, some policies cover costs not covered by the original Medicare plan.

Some insurers offer Medicare Select plans. **Medicare Select plans** are Medigap policies that offer lower premiums in exchange for limiting the choice of health-care providers. Three states—Massachusetts, Minnesota, and Wisconsin—do not subscribe to this system for offering Medigap insurance. Separate rules apply in these states.

Medicare Part C: Medicare Advantage

The Balanced Budget Act of 1997 established Medicare Choice—renamed to **Medicare Advantage** in 2004—a third Medicare program, as an alternative to the original program (Parts A and B). The Medicare Advantage program, informally referred to as Part C, provides beneficiaries the opportunity to receive health care from a variety of options, including private fee-for-service plans, managed care plans, or medical savings accounts. Fee-for-service plans provide protection against health-care expenses in the form of cash benefits paid to the insured or directly to the health-care provider after receiving health-care services. These plans pay benefits on a reimbursement basis. Medicare Parts A and B are based on fee-for-service arrangements. Managed care plans often pay a higher level of benefits if health care is received from approved providers.

Medicare Prescription Drug Benefit

The passage of the Medicare Prescription Drug, Improvement, and Modernization Act of 2003 (also known as the Medicare Modernization Act) instituted a prescription drug benefit for Medicare program participants. Commonly referred to as Part D, the drug benefit was first offered in 2006. A participant pays the deductible—$360 in 2016—before Medicare begins to provide coverage. For expenses above $360 through $3,310, the participant pays a copayment for each prescription. For expenses above $3,310 through $4,850, the participant pays 45 percent of the cost of brand-name drugs and 58 percent for generic drugs in 2016. This expense range ($3,310 to $4,850) is known as the coverage gap. Once outside the coverage gap, the participant pays a small copayment equal to 5 percent of the cost for each prescription. These dollar amounts were valid in 2016 and are subject to change from year to year. The coverage gap will be eliminated by 2020 following a provision in the Patient Protection and Affordable Care Act.

Medicare as the Primary or Secondary Payer

Individuals who have Medicare coverage may also simultaneously receive benefits from another health-care plan, including an employer's group health plan, a retiree health insurance plan sponsored by a former employer, or an employed spouse's group health plan. An important question arises regarding which plan—Medicare or the other health plan—pays benefits first.

The following guidelines describe when Medicare or the other health plan is the primary provider.

Who Pays First If You Have Other Health Coverage?	
Your situation	**Who pays first?**
I have Medicare and more than one other type of insurance or coverage.	Check your insurance policy or coverage—it may include the rules about who pays first.
I have Medicare and group health plan coverage. Who pays first?	If your employer has less than 20 employees, Medicare generally pays first. Generally, your group health plan pays first if both of these are true: 1. You're 65 or older and covered by a group health plan through your current employer or the current employer of a spouse of any age. 2. The employer has 20 or more employees and covers any of the same services as Medicare (this means the group health plan pays first on your hospital and medical bills.)

I have Medicare and I work for a small company that has a group health plan.

But if your employer joins with other employers or employee organizations (like unions) to sponsor a group health plan (called a multi-employer plan), and any of the other employers have 20 or more employees, Medicare would generally pay second. Your plan might also ask for an exception, so even if your employer has fewer than 20 employees, you'll need to find out from your employer whether Medicare pays first or second.

I'm under 65, disabled and have Medicare and group health plan coverage based on current employment.

Generally, if your employer has less than 100 employees, Medicare pays first if you're under 65 or you have Medicare because of a disability.

Sometimes employers with fewer than 100 employees join with other employers to form a multi-employer plan. If at least one employer in the multi-employer plan has 100 employees or more, Medicare pays second.

If the employer has 100 employees or more, the health plan is called a large group health plan. If you're covered by a multi-employer plan large group health plan because of your current employment or the current employment of a family member, Medicare pays second.

Medicare pays first if a domestic partner is entitled to Medicare on the basis of age and has group health plan coverage based on the current employment status of his/her partner.

My Employer participates in a multi-employer plan or a multiple employer plan. Who pays first?

Multi-employer and multiple employer group health plans are plans sponsored by or contributed to by 2 or more employers. If your employer joins with other employers or employee organizations (like unions) to sponsor or contribute to a multi-employer or a multiple employer plan, and any of the other employers has 20 or more employees, Medicare would generally pay second.

I'm in a Health Maintenance Organization (HMO) Plan or an employer Preferred Provider Organization (PPO) Plan that pays first. Who pays if I go outside the employer plan's network?

If you go outside your employer plan's network, you might not get any payment from the plan or Medicare. Call your employer plan before you go outside the network to find out if the service will be covered.

I'm retired and have Medicare and group health plan coverage from my former employer.

Generally, Medicare pays first for your health-care bills and your group health plan (retiree) coverage pays second.

If the employer has more than 20 employees, the group health plan generally pays first.

Note: "Spouse" includes both opposite-sex and same-sex marriages where either
1) you're entitled to Medicare as a spouse based on Social Security's rules; or
2) the marriage was legally entered into in a U.S. jurisdiction that recognizes the marriage—including one of the 50 states, the District of Columbia, or a U.S. territory—or a foreign country, so long as that marriage would also be recognized by a U.S. jurisdiction.

Source: U.S. Official Government Site for Medicare, "Your Guide to Who Pays First if You Have Other Health Coverage?" August 2015 (CMS Product No. 02179). Accessed January 19, 2016, www.medicare.gov.

FINANCING OASDI AND MEDICARE PROGRAMS

Funding for OASDI and Medicare programs requires equal employer and employee contributions under the **Federal Insurance Contributions Act (FICA).**[8] FICA requires that an employer pay tax based on its payroll; employees contribute tax based on earnings, which is withheld from each paycheck. The **Self-Employment Contributions Act (SECA)**[9] requires that self-employed individuals contribute to the OASDI and Medicare programs, but at a different tax rate. In either case, the tax rate is subject to an increase each year to sufficiently fund OASDI programs. FICA requires employers and employees to contribute 7.65 percent each; for self-employed individuals, it is generally double that amount, or 15.3 percent. This tax amount is apportioned between OASDI and Medicare programs, as discussed next.

OASDI Programs

The largest share of the FICA tax funds OASDI programs. In 2017, 6.20 percent of the contributions of employers and employees were set aside. Self-employed individuals contributed 12.40 percent.

OASDI taxes are subject to a **taxable wage base.** A taxable wage base limits the amount of annual wages or payroll cost per employee subject to taxation. The taxable wage base may also increase over time to account for increases in the cost of living. In 2017, the taxable wage base was $127,200 for everyone. Annual wages, payroll costs per employee, and self-employed earnings above this level were not taxed.

Medicare Programs

The **Medicare tax,** or **hospital insurance tax,** supports the Medicare Part A program. Employers, employees, and self-employed individuals contribute 1.45 percent. Self-employed individuals contribute double that amount, or 2.9 percent. The Medicare tax is not subject to a taxable wage base. All payroll amounts and wages are taxed.

Financial Status of the OASDI and Medicare Programs

For years, concerns about the long-term financial viability of the OASDI and Medicare programs have been expressed in political arenas and outcries from the public. The viability of these programs relies on sufficient funding to cover current beneficiaries and future beneficiaries. One way to ensure viability is to increase the FICA tax rates for these programs based on complex statistical estimates of usage over the long term. Alternatively, viability could be ensured by substantially reducing the level of benefits. The viability of these programs is the subject of ongoing political debate over the methods for ensuring long-term success.

According to the Social Security Administration, many people believe that the Social Security taxes they pay are held in interest-bearing accounts, set aside by the federal government, to meet their own future retirement income and health-care needs. However, to the contrary, all employee and employer contributions are deposited into three separate trust funds: old-age and survivor, disability, and Medicare funds. These Social Security programs represent a pay-as-you-go benefit system. In other words, money in the trust funds deposited today by employees and employers is used to pay the benefits for today's retirees and other beneficiaries. There is no guarantee that benefits will be available in the future as employees become disabled, reach retirement age, and require medical insurance at age 65.

One can get an idea about the financial condition of the Social Security programs from annual reports prepared by the Social Security Board of Trustees. In the 2015 fiscal year report,[10] the trustees announced that the OASI (retirement and survivor insurance programs) and the DI (disability insurance) program paid more in benefits and expenses than it collected in taxes and other income sources. The deficit for 2015 was projected to be an additional $46 billion. Deficits are expected to grow rapidly as the number of individuals receiving Social Security benefits exceeds the number of employees who are contributing to the Social Security program. By the year 2034, resources in the Social Security trust fund are expected to be depleted.[11]

The Medicare trust fund faces a more immediate shortfall than does the OASDI trust funds. The Medicare program is expected to pay out more in benefits than it receives in income in all future years. Based on the 2015 report on the status of Medicare, the projected date of the Medicare trust fund exhaustion is 2030.[12]

The combination of three factors is believed to have hastened the deterioration of the Social Security programs. First, individuals are living longer than ever before, which means that they are receiving retirement and medical benefits for an extended period. Note that once retired, an individual no longer contributes to the programs' trust funds. Second, immigration is accounting for some growth in the labor force. Immigrant workers' income tends to be quite low compared to nonimmigrant workers; thus, their FICA tax amounts are substantially less. Finally, as discussed earlier in this chapter, unemployment leaves millions of individuals who are not contributing to the Social Security system. Similarly, these factors are hindering the financial viability of Medicare. Also, specific to Medicare, new medical technology and pharmacological products continue to raise the costs of medical care, placing greater strains on the Medicare trust fund.

UNEMPLOYMENT INSURANCE

The national federal–state unemployment insurance program provides weekly income to individuals who become unemployed through no fault of their own. Each state administers its own program and develops guidelines within parameters set by the federal government. States pay into a central unemployment tax fund administered by the federal government, which then invests these payments and disburses funds to the states as needed.

Eligibility Criteria for Unemployment Insurance Benefits

Individuals must meet several criteria to qualify for unemployment benefits. Unemployment itself does not necessarily qualify an individual for these benefits, although this criterion varies somewhat by state. In general, unemployed workers must meet several eligibility criteria, including:

- Limited voluntary employment, and involuntary unemployment except for disqualifying causes.
- Minimum earnings and employment requirements.
- A waiting period in most states.
- A capacity to work and an availability for work.
- An active seeking of suitable work.

Limited Voluntary Employment and Involuntary Unemployment

Workers who become unemployed through no fault of their own are eligible to receive unemployment insurance. Specifically, voluntary termination usually disqualifies workers from receiving unemployment insurance benefits unless they chose to quit their jobs for reasonable cause. *Reasonable cause* refers to the creation of working conditions that cannot be tolerated by any sensible person. Involuntary termination does not guarantee eligibility for benefits; most states stipulate disqualifying events. These include termination for misconduct, refusal of suitable work, and participation in some labor disputes. Some states will pay benefits for participation in labor disputes that result from a lockout by the employer or if the employer violates the terms of either a contract or labor laws. Additional disqualifying events include regular breaks between school terms for educators and deliberate misrepresentation used to receive benefits.

Minimum Earnings and Employment Requirements

Every state requires an employee to have sufficient earnings or to have worked at least a specified minimum period of time. The minimum employment period to qualify for unemployment insurance benefits is the **base period**. Many states require both a minimum earnings amount and fulfillment of a designated base period. The three most common methods are multiple of high-quarter wages, multiple of weekly benefit amount, and flat qualifying amount. These methods will be described next, and the descriptions are based on the U.S. federal government's Congressional Research Service.[13]

Multiple of High-Quarter Wages

Under this method, workers are required to earn a certain dollar amount in the calendar quarter (consecutive three-month period) with the highest earnings of their base period. In addition, workers must earn total base period wages that are a multiple—typically 1.5—of the high-quarter wages. For example, in Arizona, the base period is first four of the last five completed calendar quarters before filing a claim for unemployment insurance benefits. If a worker earns $5,000 in the high quarter, the worker must earn at least another $2,500 in the rest of the base period.

Multiple of Weekly Benefit Amount

Under this method, the state first computes the worker's weekly benefit amount. The worker must have earned a multiple—often 40—of this amount during the base period. For example, if a worker's weekly benefit amount equals $100, then the worker will need base period earnings of 40 times $100, or $4,000, before any unemployment insurance benefit would be paid. In Texas, the multiple is 37 times of the weekly benefit amount. Most states also require wages in at least two calendar quarters. Some states have weighted schedules that require varying multiples for varying weekly benefits. Some states allow a reduced weekly benefit amount to meet the multiple requirement.

Flat Qualifying Amount

States using this method require a certain dollar amount of total wages to be earned during the base period. This method is used by most states with an annual-wage requirement for determining the weekly benefit. Illinois' amount is $1,600. Also, this approach is used by some states with a high-quarter wage/weekly benefit requirement such as Oregon.

Waiting Period

Most states impose a **waiting period,** usually one week following submission of a claim, prior to paying benefits. States impose waiting periods for a variety of reasons, including time needed to process claims. Other states use waiting periods to limit total costs. Aggregating a week's worth of benefits over the total number of eligible individuals adds up to substantial amounts.

Capacity to Work and Availability for Work

Unemployed workers must be mentally and physically capable of performing work. Availability for work refers to a person's willingness and readiness to work. The former requirement can be thought of as ability, and the latter as motivation.

Actively Seeking Suitable Work

Unemployed workers must demonstrate that they are actively seeking work. The requirements vary by state. Usually, going on job interviews provides sufficient evidence. The term **suitable work** contains two elements. First, suitable work refers to jobs that require skills, knowledge, and ability similar to a person's customary work. Second, suitable work offers employment terms and conditions that do not violate relevant laws (e.g., violation of the minimum wage requirement of the Fair Labor Standards Act of 1938).

Unemployment Insurance Benefit Amounts

Individuals who meet the eligibility criteria receive weekly benefits. Because the federal government places no limits on a maximum allowable amount, the benefit amount varies widely from state to state. Most states calculate the weekly benefits as a specified fraction of an employee's average wages during the highest calendar quarter of the base period. Most unemployment insurance programs provide benefits that amount to 50 to 67 percent of previous earnings. The calculation typically excludes some income, including holidays, vacation, back pay, workers' compensation, and retirement earned from another employer. States use one of three methods to calculate **weekly benefit amounts (WBAs):**

- A fraction of the highest wages for a calendar quarter earned during the base period.
- A percentage of the average weekly wage earned during the base period.
- A percentage of annual wages.

States determine WBAs subject to minimum and maximum amounts. For example, Hawaii's minimum WBA was $5 in 2015, which was the lowest amount. Massachusetts' WBA was $698, representing the highest in the nation.

Duration of Unemployment Insurance Benefits

The federal government took extra steps to temporally extend the duration of unemployment insurance benefits during the deep economic recession that began in late 2007. During that time, millions of jobs left several millions of newly unemployed workers unable to secure work within the scope of state unemployment insurance programs. As a result, Congress approved the **Emergency Unemployment Insurance (EUC)** program in June 2008 in the **Supplemental Appropriations Act of 2008**. The EUC program provided 13 additional weeks of federally funded unemployment insurance benefits to unemployed workers who had exhausted all state unemployment insurance benefits for which they were eligible. As the economic recession deepened, particularly in states such as Michigan and Nevada where unemployment rates were about 15 percent, it became apparent to the federal government that the EUC program extensions were not sufficient to bridge the lengthening gap between periods of employment. In response, Congress enacted the **Unemployment Compensation Act of 2008** on November 21, 2008. This law expanded the EUC benefits to 20 weeks nationwide (from 13 weeks), and it provided for 13 more weeks of EUC. The EUC expired at the end of 2013. Unemployment insurance benefits information for each of the 50 states and U.S. territories, including Puerto Rico and the Virgin Islands, may be obtained from the U.S. Department of Labor Web site (www.workforcesecurity .doleta.gov).

Financing Unemployment Insurance Benefits

Unemployment insurance benefits are financed by federal and, sometimes, state taxes levied on employers. Federal tax is levied on employers under the **Federal Unemployment Tax Act (FUTA)**.[14] Employer contributions amount to 6.2 percent of the first $7,000 earned by each employee (i.e., the taxable wage base). FUTA specifies $7,000 as the minimum allowable taxable wage base. Relatively few states' taxable wage bases are as low as the FUTA-specified minimum. States typically set the taxable wage base according to the average wage level. In 2015, states' taxable wage bases ranged from $7,000, in Arizona and California, to $40,900 in Hawaii.

The federal government deposits 5.4 percent of the taxes levied on employers to the Federal Unemployment Trust Fund, which is administered by the Treasury Department. The Treasury Department invests this money in government securities, crediting the principal amount contributed by each state and investment income to an account. The federal government retains 0.8 percent to cover administrative costs and to maintain a reserve to bail out states with very low balances in their accounts.

States also impose taxes on employers to fund their unemployment insurance programs permitted by state unemployment tax acts (SUTA taxes). The state unemployment employer tax rate varies according to an experience rating system. Every state applies different tax rates to companies, subject to statutory minimum and maximum rates. In 2015, Iowa's SUTA rate ranged between 0 and 7.50 percent. Wisconsin's rate ranged between 0.27 and 12 percent, representing the highest state rate at the time. Each company's tax rate depends upon its prior experience with unemployment. Accordingly, a company that lays off a large percentage of employees will have a higher tax rate than a company that lays off relatively few or none of its employees.

Summary

This chapter reviews the fundamental concepts of Social Security and workers' compensation programs. The social maladies of the late 19th and early 20th centuries gave rise to these protection programs. The programs examined in this chapter interface with a variety of tax regulations and employment laws and require mandatory employee contributions, employer contributions, or both.

Key Terms

Federal Insurance Contributions Act (FICA), *208*
Self-Employment Contributions Act (SECA), *208*
taxable wage base, *208*
Medicare tax, *208*
hospital insurance tax, *208*

base period, *210*
waiting period, *211*
suitable work, *211*
weekly benefit amounts (WBAs), *212*
Emergency Unemployment Insurance (EUC), *212*

Supplemental Appropriations Act of 2008, *212*
Unemployment Compensation Act of 2008, *212*
Federal Unemployment Tax Act (FUTA), *212*

Discussion Questions

1. Name the three broad categories of programs established under the Social Security Act of 1935. Briefly describe each one.
2. Name and briefly describe the specific benefits in the OASDI program.
3. Define the purpose of Medicare, and briefly contrast the two options an eligible person has for receiving Medicare benefits.
4. How are the OASDI and Medicare programs financed?
5. Explain the criteria to qualify for unemployment insurance benefits.

Cases

1. Understanding Your Employee Benefits: Qualifying for Unemployment Benefits

During the three years that you have worked at your current company, the company has had some success, but mostly, it has not done well. The most recent downturn in business has made you concerned about the future of the company. Several employees who work in your department were laid off in the past six months due to lack of work, and you are concerned that you may be next on the list. It seems that others feel the same way, as company morale is at an all-time low. In fact, the overall company morale, coupled with the poor attitude of your supervisor, is making your job miserable. You aren't sure if it is worthwhile at this point to try to stick it out.

Every day you dread getting up and going to work. Your supervisor is frustrated about trying to get work done with a lean staff, and you feel that he is taking it out on you. He criticizes you constantly and sometimes makes it seem that it is your fault that things are going so poorly. He has mentioned several times that the department will likely be closed within the year. You know that he is under a great deal of stress, given the impending lay offs, but the situation is becoming unbearable. You still show up to work and do your best, but you're not sure how much longer you can do it. It seems inevitable that you will lose your job, so you are starting to think that it might be a better idea to resign your position now.

You know that you are going to need to look for a new job soon, regardless of what you do, but it is hard to even think about a job search while you are working full time. You are thinking that maybe quitting your job now will relieve some stress and give you the time you need to conduct a job search. However, you rely on your weekly paycheck, and you aren't sure what you will do if it takes you very long to find a new job. A former coworker who was laid off last year told you that the unemployment insurance payment that he received helped bridge the gap between the lay off and finding a new job. After a one-week waiting period, he received a weekly benefit that helped him pay his bills until he found another job. As the job market is uncertain, you think that you need the support of unemployment insurance to sustain yourself until you find another job.

You are pretty sure that you will be eligible for unemployment insurance if your company does ultimately lay you off. However, you're not sure if you can still qualify for unemployment insurance if you resign. If you are able to collect unemployment insurance, you would like to quit soon so that you can move on with your job search, and you must do some research to understand the unemployment insurance benefit.

1. Are you eligible to receive unemployment if you resign?
2. Should you resign or wait to find out if and when you are laid off?

2. Managing Employee Benefits: Social Security and Retirement Planning at Taylor Foods

As Gavin Jackson leaves the monthly professional luncheon for human resource executives in his area, he starts to consider how the information he learned will affect his company, Taylor Foods. The program speaker provided an update on the Social Security system and how challenges in financing the system may affect organizations. As the director of human resources at this large food-processing and distribution company, Gavin must plan the retirement benefits for the organization's employees. Gavin had been aware that the Social Security system is in trouble, but now has some clear ideas about how it will affect both the retirement benefits offered by Taylor Foods and the retirement plans of its employees.

Gavin learned that the current Social Security system is unstable and that the future of benefits to be provided is uncertain. In particular, the Old-Age, Survivor, and Disability Insurance (OASDI), which provides retirement benefit payments to retired workers, is under a strain. Retirement benefits comprise a majority of the payments made by the Social Security system, and the instability of the system suggests that current workers may not be able to rely on the Social Security system as it exists today to support them in retirement. Gavin knows that this information affects the retirement benefit planning at Taylor Foods.

The speaker also noted that employees retiring in the relatively near future may base their retirement decisions to some extent on the Social Security benefits available to them. While employees may receive their retirement benefits from Social Security starting at age 62, the amount is reduced if they haven't reached the full retirement age, which is determined based on year of birth. For example, the age for full retirement is 67 for anyone born in 1960 or later. Further, the system contains other incentives to encourage individuals to delay retirement. This is important to Taylor Foods, as the age at which employees plan to retire affects the company's human resource planning process. Annually, Gavin creates staffing plans that include estimates for turnover of employees, and employee retirements are included in those estimates. This information, coupled with a current downturn in the economy, leads Gavin to believe that Taylor Foods may experience a lower level of turnover as employees delay retirement.

Gavin is considering both of these issues as he considers retirement benefits, as well as staffing planning at Taylor Foods. While the company currently offers a competitive retirement plan, he knows that he needs to reexamine the benefits in the context of his new understanding of the Social Security system. He also needs to consider how employees planning to delay retirement will affect the organization and the human resource planning process.

1. How does the instability of the Social Security system affect retirement benefit planning at Taylor Foods?
2. Should Gavin consider the possibility of employees delaying retirement in the company's human resource planning process?

Endnotes

1. U.S. Social Security Administration, *Fact Sheet on the Old-Age, Survivors, and Disability Insurance Program.* Accessed January 29, 2016, www.ssa.gov.
2. U.S. Social Security Administration, *Organization Manual*, "Chapter S: Social Security Administration." Accessed February 16, 2016, www.ssa.gov.

3. U.S. Department of Labor, "ETA Mission, Values, Strategies, and Goals." Accessed March 18, 2012, www.doleta.gov/etainfo/mission.cfm.

4. U.S. Social Security Administration, 2016. *Social Security Handbook*. Accessed March 4, 2016, www.socialsecurity.gov.

5. U.S. Bureau of Labor Statistics. "Frequently Asked Questions," *Consumer Price Index*. Accessed January 31, 2016, www.bls.gov/cpi/cpifaq.htm.

6. U.S. Social Security Administration. *Periodic Life Expectancy—2015 OASDI Trustees Report* (Table V.A3). Accessed January 31, 2016, www.ssa.gov.

7. *Obergefell v. Hodges*, 135 S. Ct. 2584 (June 26, 2015).

8. 26 U.S.C. §§3101–3125.

9. 26 U.S.C. §§1401–1403.

10. U.S. Social Security Commission. *The 2015 Annual Report of the Board of Trustees of the Federal Old-Age and Survivors Insurance and Federal Disability Insurance Trust Funds*. 2015. Accessed January 15, 2016, www.ssa.gov.

11. Ibid.

12. *2015 Annual Report of the Boards of Trustees of the Federal Hospital Insurance and Federal Supplementary Medical Insurance Trust Funds*. July 22, 2015. Accessed January 28, 2016, www.cms.gov.

13. J. M. Whittaker and K. P. Isaacs, *Unemployment Insurance: Programs and Benefits*. Congressional Research Service, December 9, 2015. Accessed January 30, 2016, www.crs.gov.

14. I.R.C. §3121(d); Treas. Reg. §§31.3121(d)-2; 31.3121(d)-1.

Services

Part Three

Chapter Eight

Paid Time-Off and Flexible Work Schedule Benefits

Learning Objectives

In this chapter, you will gain an understanding of:

1. Various types of paid time-off practices.
2. Design elements of paid time-off practices.
3. Leave under the Family and Medical Leave Act of 1993.
4. Various types of flexible work arrangements.

With limited exceptions, employers offer paid time off and flexible work schedules on a discretionary basis. Both employees and employers benefit from these offerings. For employees, paid time-off benefits and flexible work arrangements facilitate the pursuit of leisure activities, rest and relaxation, or holidays without financial strain. Flexible work arrangements make it possible to balance ongoing work and family demands. Increasingly, employers have come to value paid time-off and flexible work arrangements for employees. These benefits help with recruitment and employee retention as well as giving the opportunity to "charge their batteries," making them more productive over the long run. Paid time-off benefits and flexible work arrangements are important elements of the psychological contract, which we discussed in Chapter 2.

DEFINING AND EXPLORING PAID TIME-OFF PROGRAMS

Paid time-off policies compensate employees when they are not performing their primary work duties. Private-sector U.S. companies offer most paid time-off benefits to employees, who are working in the United States, on a discretionary basis. In nonunion settings, companies offer most paid time off as a matter of custom, particularly paid holidays. In unionized settings, the collective bargaining agreement or contract details employee entitlements to paid time-off benefits. Exhibit 8.1 shows the percentage of private-sector workers who have access to paid time-off benefits (unpaid family leave is one exception to all types of paid leave listed in this exhibit). Notice the differences between full- and part-time employees as well as between union and nonunion employees. In most cases, about twice as many full-time employees enjoy paid time-off benefits compared to part-time employees. Exhibit 8.1 also illustrates the union advantage because more union workers have access to paid time-off benefits compared to nonunion employees (for all but paid family leave).

According to the U.S. Bureau of Labor Statistics, the cost of paid leave for workers in the private sector is as follows:[1]

Private industry employer costs for paid leave benefits in September 2015 averaged $2.17 per hour worked, or 6.9 percent of total compensation. Paid leave benefit costs were highest for management, professional, and related occupations, $4.69 per hour, or 8.4 percent of total compensation. Costs were lowest among service occupations, 56 cents, or 3.9 percent of total compensation. Vacation benefit costs averaged $1.13 per hour (3.6 percent of total compensation) while holiday benefit costs were 66 cents per hour (2.1 percent), sick leave costs were 26 cents per hour (0.8 percent), and personal leave costs were 12 cents per hour (0.4 percent). Paid leave costs varied by economic sector. In goods-producing establishments, paid

EXHIBIT 8.1   **Percent of Workers with Access to Selected Leave Benefits, by Worker Characteristics: Private Industry National Compensation Survey, March 2015**

Source: U.S. Bureau of Labor Statistics. *Employee Benefits in the United States, March 2015* (BLS 15-2782).

Characteristics	Leave Benefits (All workers = 100 percent)							
	Paid Holidays	Paid Vacations	Paid Personal Leave	Paid Funeral Leave	Paid Jury Duty Leave	Paid Military Leave	Family Leave*	
							Paid	Unpaid
All workers	77	76	38	59	60	32	12	87
Full time	90	91	47	70	71	38	15	89
Part time	37	34	15	27	29	13	5	79
Union	90	89	50	77	79	40	11	91
Nonunion	75	75	37	57	58	31	12	86

*The sum of paid and unpaid family leave may exceed 100 percent because some workers have access to both types of plans.

leave amounted to $2.46 per hour (6.5 percent of total compensation) versus $2.11 (7.0 percent) for service-providing establishments.

Included in the paid leave amounts are employer costs for vacations, holidays, sick leave, and personal leave. Paid leave benefit costs are often directly linked to wages; therefore, higher paid occupations or industries will typically show higher costs. The percentages are based on total compensation costs for the reference group.

PAID TIME-OFF PRACTICES

In this chapter, the following paid time-off practices are reviewed:

- Holidays
- Vacation
- Sick leave
- Personal leave
- Integrated paid time-off policies (paid time-off banks)
- Parental leave
- Bereavement or funeral leave
- Jury duty and witness duty leaves
- Military leave
- Nonproduction time
- On-call time
- Sabbatical leave
- Volunteerism

Holidays

Private-sector employers usually follow the holiday time-off practices for federal government employees. Federal law established 12 paid holidays for federal government employees (Exhibit 8.2).[2] Most federal government employees work five days a week—Monday through Friday. When holidays fall on a weekend day, employees receive a day off during the workweek to observe the holiday. Most state workers observe holidays based on state laws.

Some companies add one or two days off with pay to the list of regularly scheduled holidays. **Floating holidays** allow employees to take paid time off to observe any holiday not included on the employer's list of recognized paid holidays. Companies do not limit floating holidays to federal or state holidays. Alternatively, some employers permit employees to use floating holidays to extend the number of allotted paid vacation days.

Companies must pay attention to the treatment of religious holidays, which, except for Christmas, are not included on any list of federal or state public holidays. Title VII of the Civil Rights Act prohibits illegal discrimination in employment practices on the basis of sex, religion, color, race, and national origin. The Equal Employment Opportunity Commission (EEOC) established guidelines that encourage companies to honor employee wishes to observe religious holidays, unless doing so would cause undue hardship to both the company and some employees.[3] It is imperative that companies treat the observance of religious holidays uniformly as paid or unpaid time off. Employees who feel that they are being discriminated against on religious grounds may file a complaint at the nearest EEOC field office (www.eeoc.gov/offices.html).

It is not uncommon for holidays to overlap with scheduled vacation time or sick leave time. Companies must decide whether to count such instances of paid holidays as a paid vacation day or sickness day. Most often, companies choose to recognize holidays as separate from vacation or sick leave. Thus, when overlap occurs, the employer provides an additional day of paid time off.

EXHIBIT 8.2
U.S. Office of Personnel Management: Federal Holidays

Source: U.S. Office of Personnel Management, *2016 Federal Holidays*. Accessed January 8, 2016, www.opm.gov.

Friday, January 1, 2016	New Year's Day
Monday, January 15	Birthday of Martin Luther King, Jr.
Monday, February 15†	Washington's Birthday
Monday, May 30	Memorial Day
Monday, July 4	Independence Day
Monday, September 5	Labor Day
Monday, October 10	Columbus Day
Friday, November 11	Veterans Day
Thursday, November 24	Thanksgiving Day
Monday, December 26	Christmas Day

†This holiday is designated as "Washington's Birthday," the law that specifies holidays for federal employees. Though other institutions such as state and local governments and private businesses may use other names, it is our policy to always refer to holidays by the names designated in the law.

Some companies extend paid holidays by granting one or two additional paid days preceding or following the holiday. Quite common is extending the Thursday Thanksgiving holiday by granting the next day as paid time off. Another custom grants Christmas Eve as paid time off to extend the Christmas holiday.

Vacation

Some employers view paid vacation as a reward. Does paying employees for rest and relaxation seem like a good investment? Increasingly, researchers believe so. An emerging sentiment is that companies provide employees additional paid days off because occasional rest and relaxation promotes good health and long-term productivity.

The design of vacation policies varies widely based on five important considerations.

- Eligibility for vacation leave.
- Single or multiple vacation policies for different occupational groups.
- Rules for determining the amount of available vacation time per year.
- Avoiding conflicts between vacation time and pressing work deadlines.
- Handling unused vacation time at the end of the year.

First, who is eligible to receive vacation benefits? Employees generally become eligible for vacation benefits after maintaining employment for a period ranging between six months and one year of full-time employment. Many companies often exclude part-time employees from receiving vacation benefits but, when they do, limit paid vacation in proportion to hours worked.

Second, companies must decide whether to set up a single vacation policy for all employees or separate ones for different employee groups. The choice to use separate policies usually provides more vacation benefits to managerial, professional, and executive-level employees to recognize their greater direct impact on company performance.

Third, vacation policies specify rules for vacation day allotment per calendar or fiscal year. Some companies allot the same number of vacation each calendar or fiscal year. More often, companies recognize employee seniority. For example:

Employment	Vacation Earned
Less than 1 year	Ineligible for vacation benefits
1–5 years	5 days
6–9 years	10 days
10–19 years	15 days

In March 2015, private-sector employees received a higher number of paid vacation days based on seniority. The mean numbers were as follows: 10 (after 1 year), 14 (after 5 years), 17 (after 10 years), and 19 (after 20 years).[4] Companies may also choose to increase vacation benefits by a smaller increment for each additional year of employment; for instance:

Employment	Vacation Earned
Less than 1 year	Ineligible for vacation benefits
1 year but less than 2	5 days
2 years but less than 3	6 days
3 years but less than 4	7 days

Alternatively, companies may determine vacation benefits according to hours worked. Usually, this approach applies to nonexempt workers, as designated by the overtime pay provision of the Fair Labor Standards Act of 1938 (FLSA). Generally, administrative, professional, and executive employees are exempt from the FLSA overtime pay provision. Most other jobs are nonexempt. Nonexempt jobs are subject to the FLSA overtime pay provision. The following is an example of a vacation policy for nonexempt employees:

Years of Service	Hours of Vacation Earned per Biweekly Pay Period	Maximum Hours Earned per Year
Less than 1 year Ineligible for vacation benefits		
1–4	4.00	104 hours or 13 days
5–9	4.62	120 hours or 15 days
10–14	5.52	144 hours or 18 days
15–19	6.46	168 hours or 21 days
20 or more	7.04	184 hours or 23 days

Fourth, employers must decide the rules for scheduling when business activity is substantial, such as the case for retail workers during the holiday period. Another consideration is how to handle multiple requests for the same days off. Most policies require that employees request approval for time off. Requests should indicate the start and return-to-work dates. When two or more employees request the same days off, priority is usually given to employees with greater seniority.

Fifth, vacation policies should specify carryover and cash-out provisions. **Carryover provisions** permit employees to take unused vacation time at a later time. Alternatively, vacation policies require the use of allotted vacation days during the designated year, forfeiting any unused vacation days. Many employees refer to this choice as a **"use it or lose it" provision.** Policies that prohibit carryover may include a cash-out provision. **Cash-out provisions** pay employees an amount equal to the unused vacation days based on regular daily earnings. In general, federal law does not require private-sector companies to pay employees for the accrual of unused vacation time. However, in 24 states, employers are required to pay employees for accrued vacation upon termination.

Sick Leave

Sick leave benefits compensate employees for a specified number of days absent due to personal illness. Sick leave policies are separate from disability leave policies (Chapter 6) because the focus is on occasional minor illness or injury. Sometimes, these policies permit employees paid time off to care for an ill child, spouse, or parent. Although beneficial to employees, sick leave plans can be disruptive when other employees are off from work.

Some companies require that employees provide evidence of illness (e.g., a note from a physician) while others do not. The decision to require medical certification often rests on the incidence of unscheduled absenteeism in the workforce. For our purposes, unscheduled absences occur when an employee does not report to work at the scheduled time. Illness is perhaps the most socially acceptable reason for an unscheduled absence, and employees are probably more likely to attribute unscheduled absences to illness than to other reasons (e.g., a day at the beach). Unscheduled absences can easily impair productivity and push up costs. When unscheduled absences create hardship, companies will require medical certification.

Not all companies choose to offer paid time off for illness. For ones that do, the U.S. Bureau of Labor Statistics indicates that the majority of companies offering sick leave benefits provide between five and nine days. Approximately half of the workers employed in small companies, defined as having fewer than 100 workers, have access to paid sick leave as an employee benefit, compared to more than 70 percent employed in larger companies. This fact has contributed to a debate over paid sick leave that is emerging across the United States. This debate has been prompted by concerns that employees will attend work even when they are ill. Oftentimes, sick employees will attend work because either they cannot afford to take time off without pay or they fear that they will be fired. Having sick workers report to work can create problems for employers when healthy employees become ill. In small companies, just a few employees could cause major disruptions to operations. Notwithstanding concerns, paid sick leave has recently become a required benefit in some settings. In 2015, President Barack Obama issued Executive Order 13706, which requires that government contractors and subcontractors offer paid sick leave to their employees.

In addition, state laws governing paid sick leave specify the criteria for what constitutes illness as well as other features such as carryover provisions. California law mandates how employees accrue and use paid sick leave benefits. Employers must include a carryover provision for unused sick leave from one calendar year to the next. As of October 2016, four additional states—Connecticut, Massachusetts, Oregon, and Vermont—have joined California.

Some cities have joined in. For instance, Seattle requires that employers with 5 to 49 employees provide five paid sick days per year, and additional days for larger employers. In San Francisco, employers with 10 or more employees must provide 9 paid sick days and 5 sick days in smaller companies.

Personal Leave

Personal leave policies grant paid time off for virtually any reason, usually not more than two or three consecutive days. Companies may choose to limit the scope of personal leave policies by specifying acceptable reasons. Common uses of personal leave include the proverbial mental health day, which allows employees the opportunity to "recharge their batteries"; for example, employees might spend a day at the beach, catch up on personal errands, or simply relax at home. Alternatively, employees may use personal leave to extend a vacation period or sick leave. Companies allot a fixed number of personal days each year, or they award this benefit based on employee seniority. Annual allotments commonly range between 1 and 10 days.

Integrated Paid Time-Off Policies, or Paid Time-Off Banks

Integrated paid time-off policies have become an increasingly popular alternative to separate holiday, vacation, sick leave, and personal leave plans because they are more effective in controlling unscheduled absenteeism than are other types of absence control policies.[5] These **integrated paid time-off policies,** or **paid time-off banks,** do not distinguish among reasons for absence, as specific policies do. The idea is to provide individuals the freedom to schedule time off without justifying the reasons. Employers benefit from integrated policies by reducing the burden of administering separate plans and eliminating the need for processing medical certifications.

Paid time-off banks do not incorporate all types of time off with pay. Bereavement or funeral leave is a stand-alone policy because the death of a friend or relative is typically an unanticipated event beyond an employee's control. Also, integrating funeral leave into paid time-off banks would likely create dissatisfaction among workers because it would signal that grieving for a deceased friend or relative is equivalent to a casual day off. Jury duty and witness leave, military leave, and nonproduction time are influenced by law, and nonproduction time is negotiated as part of collective bargaining agreements. Sabbatical leaves are also excluded from paid time-off banks because sabbaticals are extended leaves used to reward valued, long-service employees.

Effective paid time-off bank policies slowly increase the number of days an employee may use for time off. For example, an employee may accumulate as many as 12 paid days off at the rate of one day per month during the first year of employment. That number may increase to 16 paid days off at the rate of 1.25 days per month during the second through fifth years of employment. Patterns such as these may extend to longer-service employees. Companies structure paid time-off banks in this fashion to reward longer-service employees who have proven their worth to the companies. According to the U.S. Bureau of Labor Statistics, the average annual number of paid days off range from 15 days (1 year of service to 24 days (20 years of service).

Effective paid time-off bank policies include a carryover provision rather than a use-it-or-lose-it provision. Carryover policies limit the likely flood of absences that would occur toward the end of the year because employees then do not feel compelled to take days off so that they do not lose a valuable unused benefit.

Parental Leave

As we discuss shortly, the Family and Medical Leave Act of 1993 mandates that most companies provide employees up to 12 weeks of *unpaid* leave for family reasons. In recent years, many companies voluntarily instituted paid parental leave policies, including Amazon.com Inc., Microsoft Corp., Netflix Inc., and Blackstone Group LP. Netflix offers one of the most generous family benefits, where employees may take up to one year of paid leave to care for a child.

Paid family leave traditionally benefited female workers because they played the role of primary caregiver. Increasingly, companies are working diligently to legitimize paternity leave. There continues to be a social stigma that is associated with fathers who choose to take time off (paid or unpaid) following the birth or adoption of a child. Unfortunately, a prevalent corporate norm devalues men who take such time off, in part, characterizing those men as not being committed to their careers or interested in advancement. Facebook's CEO Mark Zuckerberg set an example to legitimize paternity leave by taking extended leave after the birth of his first child. Currently, Facebook offers its employees up to four weeks of paid parental leave. Overall, there appears to be a trend toward offering paid parental leave programs, and, most recently, well-known companies are giving legitimacy to paternity leave.

Bereavement or Funeral Leave

Bereavement leave or **funeral leave** provides paid time off for employees, usually following the death of a relative. Bereavement policies specify the maximum allowable days off based on the employee's relationship with the deceased person. Companies grant a limited number of days off ranging anywhere between one and five days. Some companies designate maximum allowable amounts, depending on the relationship between the employee and the deceased, offering longer periods for immediate relatives (e.g., a parent or spouse) and shorter periods for less-immediate relatives (e.g., a cousin) or friends.

Jury Duty and Witness Duty Leaves

Most employers choose to pay nonexempt employees while they are serving on a jury or as witnesses in a court of law. Jury duty policies are guided by federal and state laws; witness duty policies are guided by state law in only about half of all states. At the federal level, the **Jury Systems Improvement Act of 1978** recognizes that participation on a jury in federal court is a protected right of an individual. Employers can neither prohibit employees from exercising this right nor treat employees who exercise this right less favorably. Unfavorable treatment includes intimidation of employees with threats of discharge or actual termination for participating on juries. Violations of this law come with penalties ranging from significant monetary penalties to payment of lost wages and reinstatement with credit for lost seniority. Restoration of seniority is important for many benefits as we have discussed throughout this book. In this chapter, we learned that some companies award more paid time off to employees with higher seniority. State laws regarding jury participation in state courts are similar to federal laws applicable to jury participation in federal courts. In sum, these laws prohibit employers from treating employees who serve on state court juries unfavorably. Violations can lead to monetary fines.

The Fair Labor Standards Act prohibits employers from reducing the salaries of exempt-status employees while they are participating on a jury, with two exceptions. For example, the U.S. government paid jurors a nominal amount—$40 to $50 daily in 2016. First, employers can reduce salary only by the government's payment amount for jury duty that lasts less than one regular workweek. Second, for jury duty lasting one week or more, employers may reduce pay only if the employee does not perform *any* work. For example, responding to work-related e-mails is considered to be work.

In some cases, an individual may be summoned by the court to serve as a witness in a trial. Witness duty laws are currently limited to approximately 20 states, Puerto Rico, and the District of Columbia. These laws usually specify the criteria of witness status (e.g., victim of a crime, subpoena by a court of law), provisions regarding prohibition of employer retaliation, the employee's duty to provide reasonable notice, and penalties for companies in violation.

Military Leave

Military leave policy is guided by federal and state laws, focusing on an employer's obligation to reemploy previously employed individuals following the completion of military service. At the federal level, the **Uniformed Services Employment and Reemployment Rights Act of 1994 (USERRA)**[6] extends reemployment rights to persons who have been absent from a position of employment because of service in the uniformed services on a voluntary or involuntary basis, including active duty, inactive duty training, full-time National Guard duty, time for a fitness-for-duty examination, and whose cumulative service in the uniformed services while employed with a particular company does not exceed five years. Employers may not discriminate or retaliate against a past or present member of a uniformed service who has applied for membership in the uniformed service or is obligated to serve in the uniformed service. USERRA offers protection against denial of initial employment, reemployment, retention in employment, promotion, or any benefit of employment because of this status. Protected individuals possess the right to elect to continue their existing employer-based health plan coverage for them and their dependents for up to 24 months while in the military. When reemployed following the completion of military service, employers are required to reinstate covered employees in the health plan. And, benefits that would have been attained (e.g., seniority in a retirement plan) if there were no interruption in service are restored.

Nonproduction Time

Nonproduction time refers to time uses related to, but not in actual performance of, the main job duties. Or, nonproduction time can refer to nonwork periods during a work shift. Examples of nonproduction time related to the performance of job duties include cleanup, preparation, and travel between job locations. Examples of nonwork time during a work shift include rest periods or breaks, and periods to eat a meal.

According to the Fair Labor Standards Act of 1938, employees must be paid for time devoted to principal work activities—that is, performing the tasks and duties described in their job descriptions. In addition, employers must compensate employees for duties and activities that are indispensable to performing principal activities. Examples include preparatory and concluding activities, regardless of whether these activities occur outside the regular work shift. Typical examples of compensable nonproduction time include:

- Cleanup.
- Preparation.
- Travel time between job locations within the scope of the regular work shift.
- Rest periods shorter than 20 minutes.
- Meal periods at least 30 minutes in duration when employees must take their lunch at their workstation.

In 2014, the U.S. Supreme Court ruled on the issue of whether security screenings at the workplace constitutes a compensable work activity (*Integrity Staffing Solutions, Inc. v. Busk et al.*). The Supreme Court heard this case on appeal from the company after a lower court ruled that workplace screening constitutes a compensable work activity. Integrity Staffing Solutions employs workers (paid on an hourly basis) whose job is to retrieve products from warehouse shelves and package them for delivery to Amazon.com customers. The company mandated these workers to undergo a security screening before leaving the warehouse each day. Security screenings were conducted to prevent employee theft for the sole benefit of the employers and their customers. Former employees claimed that they were entitled to compensation under the FLSA for the roughly 25 minutes each day that they spent waiting to undergo those screenings. They also claimed that the company could have substantially reduced wait times by adding more screeners or staggering shift terminations.

The court concluded that the security screenings at issue here are not compensable activities because the screenings were not the principal activity that the employee is employed to perform. Integrity Staffing employed individuals to retrieve products from warehouse shelves and package those products for shipment to Amazon.com customers, not to undergo security screenings. In addition, the court ruled that the security screenings were not integral and indispensable to the employees' duties as warehouse workers. In other words, the screenings were not a necessary step for retrieving products from warehouse shelves or packaging them for shipment.[7]

On-Call Time

According to the U.S. Department of Labor, employers must compensate nonexempt employees for on-call time. **On-call time** requires spending time on or close to the employer's premises so that employees cannot use the time effectively for their own purposes. Most employers can demand that nonexempt employees be available on an as-needed basis. For example, medical technologists and nursing staff members must be available to report to work outside normal shifts when there are major medical emergencies. Also, companies may place some of their maintenance staff on call to respond to major emergencies, such as chemical spills or the breakdown of assembly lines during off hours.

Nonexempt employees subject to on-call time must be compensated according to the minimum wage provisions of the Fair Labor Standards Act of 1938 (FLSA; see Chapter 3). Employers may require that exempt-status employees fulfill on-call time. However, the FLSA does not require that employers offer additional compensation for time while on call.

A multitude of court cases have addressed whether employers are obligated to compensate employees while they are on call. Naturally, employers tend to resist compensating employees when circumstances do not require them to report to work. For instance, in *Owens v. Local No. 169,* a federal appeals court judge ruled that the time pulp-mill mechanics spent on call was not compensable under FLSA because the on-call policy of the employer, while giving on-call employees the option of wearing a beeper, did not significantly restrict them from engaging in personal activities. Under the employer's policy, the mechanics were not required to remain at home or respond to specific calls. They only had to accept a "fair share" of calls, averaging six calls a year. Based on these facts, the court held that the mechanics were not entitled to compensation while on call.[8]

Sabbatical Leave

Sabbatical leave has its origins in college and university settings and applies most often to faculty members. Sabbatical leaves are usually, but not always, paid time off to undertake professional development activities including the completion of research projects and curriculum development. Universities grant sabbatical leaves to faculty members who meet minimum service requirements, usually three years of full-time service, with partial or full pay for up to an entire year. The service requirement is applied each time following the completion of a sabbatical, limiting the number of leaves taken per faculty member.

Some employers outside the academic world have begun offering paid sabbatical leaves of absence to employees to further professional development. Increasingly, companies that offer sabbatical leave benefits focus on rejuvenation, helping employees "recharge their batteries" and return to work as refreshed and poised to be highly productive. According to Marla Kaplowitz, the North America CEO of media agency MEC, "A sabbatical is a way of recognizing that everyone needs a break at a certain point."[9] Companies consider the costs and benefits. According to Capterra's CEO, the cost of a sabbatical equals a 10 percent reduction in productivity on an annual basis, but only 2 percent over a five-year period.[10] He maintains that the benefit to the company and the employee's health and personal growth is a worthwhile expense. According to WorldatWork, approximately 18 percent of companies offer a sabbatical leave program. About half are paid. Previously, only large companies were known for offering employees sabbatical leaves. Among them are General

Mills, which provides a sabbatical leave after serving the company for seven years. Upon returning from a sabbatical, a 25-year veteran of General Mills said, "I had all the energy and strength and endurance that I wanted."[11] Nowadays, smaller companies have begun offering sabbatical leaves. According to the WorldatWork survey, about 20 percent of companies with an employee base of up to 2,500 offer sabbatical leave benefits. For example, law firm Perkins Cole offers a two-month sabbatical after 10 years for exempt staff and after 13 years for nonexempt staff.

Companies establish guidelines regarding qualification, length of leave, and level of pay. An important guideline pertains to minimum length of employment following completion of a sabbatical. For example, companies require employees to remain employed for a minimum of one year following the sabbatical or else repay part or all of the salary received during the sabbatical. This provision is necessary to protect a company's investment and to limit moves by employees to competitors.

Not all sabbaticals are alike. A survey of U.S. companies identified five different types of sabbatical leave programs:[12]

1. *Traditional Sabbaticals.* Provide employees an opportunity to renew or retool themselves in work-related areas.

2. *Personal Growth Leaves.* Allow employees to further their education or acquire new competencies that will benefit themselves and the company.

3. *Social Service Leaves.* Provide employees with the opportunity to undertake significant public service, either in the local community or in other areas important to the company. Social service leaves enhance personal growth and company image as a responsible corporate citizen.

4. *Extended Personal Leaves.* Provide unpaid leave of two or more years with return-to-work guarantees. These leaves are commonly taken by employees with significant family obligations such as raising young children or caring for elderly relatives.

5. *Voluntary Leaves to Meet Business Needs.* Serve the company in times of downsizing or low production by offering extended unpaid time off.

Volunteerism

Volunteerism refers to giving one's time to support charitable causes. Traditionally, volunteer activities were almost always a personal choice outside the scope of employment. That's changing. More and more companies have included paid time off for volunteering as an employee benefit. From a company's standpoint, a meaningful cause is associated with the work of nonprofit, charitable organizations, such as United Way, to help improve the well-being of people. A multitude of meaningful causes exist throughout the world, such as improving literacy, providing comfort to terminally ill patients, serving food at homeless shelters, serving as a mentor to children who are from broken homes, and spending time with elderly or disabled residents of nursing homes.

More and more companies are providing employees with paid time off to contribute to causes of their choice. In 2013, approximately 20 percent of companies offered paid time off for volunteer activities, trending up since 2007.[13] Companies favor providing paid time off for volunteer work for three reasons. First, volunteer opportunities allow employees to balance work and life demands. In many instances, companies tout this benefit as a form of work-life balance and a mechanism for the betterment of the community. Brokerage company Charles Schwab provides employees with eight paid hours per year for this purpose. Managers have the discretion to provide additional paid time off for volunteer activities.[14] Second, giving employees the opportunity to contribute time to charitable causes on company time shows a company's commitment to social responsibility, thus enhancing the company's overall image in the public eye.

Paid-time off amounts vary considerably. It is not uncommon for companies to offer up to two weeks per year. In some cases, companies will make a monetary donation to the employee's charity such as health-care company Novo Nordisk. Others may hold fund-raising events. For example, energy company NuStar hosts a golf tournament and Casting for a Cause, which engaged employees in fishing to raise money for the homeless.[15] The concept of *social responsibility* has been described in different ways. For instance, it's been called "profit making only," "going beyond profit making," "any discretionary corporate activity intended to further social welfare," and "improving social or environmental conditions." Third, paid time off to volunteer is believed to help promote retention. Employees are likely to feel that the employer shares similar values, possibly boosting commitment to the company. For younger employees, company-sponsored volunteer benefits can help with recruitment. According to Sales Foundation's Suzanne DiBiana, "In Silicon Valley young graduates and employees are accepting jobs depending upon whether a company has a CSR [corporate social responsibility initiative] in place."[16] It's not surprising that companies with volunteer benefits regularly appear on the *Fortune* magazine annual rankings of the 100 best companies to work for.

LEAVE UNDER THE FAMILY AND MEDICAL LEAVE ACT OF 1993

The Family and Medical Leave Act (FMLA) bestows rights upon workers to take substantial unpaid time off from work to attend to serious personal illness or qualifying family events, and it created return-to-work protections. Prior to this act, most employees were forced to quit their jobs. Or, in the best-case scenario, employers might welcome them back only if a replacement were not hired. As we will see, societal changes have led to important revision, strengthening protections under the act. In recent years, some cities and states have passed legislation, which builds upon existing FMLA protections by expanding eligibility criteria or providing for paid leave. Let's take a look at the FMLA.

Key Provisions

The **Family and Medical Leave Act (FMLA)** provides employees with job protection in cases of family or medical emergencies.[17] Employees may take up to 12 weeks of unpaid time off for personal illness that extends beyond three work-days. The FMLA guaranteed unpaid leave with the right of the employee to return either to the position he or she left when the leave began or to an equivalent position with the same benefits, pay, and other terms and conditions of employment. This *job restoration* clause has certain provisions to be discussed later in this chapter.

The FMLA does not require that employers pay employees while on family leave; most companies choose not to pay them unless state or local law requires paid leave. However, the FMLA does require employers to maintain group health insurance coverage for an employee while on FMLA leave whenever such insurance was provided before the leave was taken. In addition, employers must provide insurance protection on the same terms as if the employee had continued to work.

Under certain circumstances, employees may choose to substitute paid leave for unpaid FMLA leave. When an employee has earned or accrued paid vacation, personal, or family leave, it may be substituted for all or part of any otherwise unpaid FMLA. This provision is important to many employees who cannot afford to take an unpaid leave.

For example, let's assume that an employee named John Smith has just learned that his spouse has become critically ill and will need extensive care at home. John has accumulated 13 days of paid vacation and 12 days of paid personal sick leave. Under FMLA, John may take up to 12 weeks of unpaid leave. Because John has accumulated 25 days of paid leave time, he will be paid for up to five weeks (based on 40-hour workweeks).

Administered by the U.S. Department of Labor Wage and Hour Division, the FMLA applies to all local, state, and federal government employers. The FMLA also applies to private-sector companies with 50 or more workers employed during 20 or more weeks in the preceding or current calendar year. Further, the FMLA applies to all public or private elementary or secondary schools, regardless of the number employed. Regardless, employees qualify for FMLA leave when they have worked at least 1,250 hours over the previous 12 months and they live within 75 miles of their place of employment.

Employees who qualify for FMLA leave may take it for one or more of the following reasons:

- Birth and care of a newborn child of the employee.
- Placement with the employee of a son or daughter for adoption or foster care and to care for the newly placed child.
- Care for an immediate family member (spouse, child, or parent) with a serious health condition.
- When the employee is unable to work because of a serious health condition.

Spouses employed by the same employer are jointly entitled to a combined total of 12 workweeks of family leave for the birth and care of a newborn child, placement of a child for adoption or foster care, and care for a parent who has a serious health condition.

Circumstances warranting the leave determine whether employees may take the entire 12-week leave on a consecutive basis or intermittently. Employers give approval for intermittent leave for the birth and care of a child or placement for adoption or foster care. Medical circumstances trigger intermittent leave to care for a seriously ill family member or in the event of personal illness. Employees must give employers a minimum 30-day advance notification of leave when the event is expected (e.g., the birth of a child).

Returning from FMLA Leave

Upon return from FMLA leave, an employee must be restored to his or her original job, or to an equivalent job with equal pay, benefits, and other terms and conditions of employment. The FMLA also guarantees that employees retain all their benefits (e.g., seniority in the retirement system) earned prior to the leave. Employers possess the right not to grant leave or restore employment if doing so would cause considerable and severe economic burden. This exception applies to the highest-paid 10 percent of employees only when the employer fulfills the following obligations:

- Notifies the employee of his or her ineligibility in response to the employee's notice of intent to take FMLA leave.
- Notifies the employee as soon as the employer decides that it will deny job restoration, and explain the reasons for this decision.
- Offers the employee a reasonable opportunity to return to work from FMLA leave after giving this notice.
- Makes a final determination regarding whether reinstatement will be denied at the end of the leave period if the employee requests restoration.

Revisions to the FMLA

Three major revisions to the FMLA were instituted since its passage in 1993. The first two changes apply to qualified family members of individuals in military service. The first change is referred to as *military caregiver leave*, adding protections for a family member who is the spouse, son, daughter, parent, or next of kin of a service member with a serious injury or illness. An eligible relative may take up to 26 weeks off to care for their injured military family members. The second change is referred to as *qualifying exigency leave*. Qualified family members of National Guard or reserves members who are called to active duty or active duty status qualify for leave. The U.S. Department of Labor considers nine broad categories of qualifying exigencies:

- Issues arising from the military member's short notice deployment (i.e., deployment within seven or fewer days' notice). For a period of up to seven days from the day the military member receives notice of deployment, an employee may take qualifying exigency leave to address any issue that arises from the short-notice deployment.
- Attending military events and related activities, such as official ceremonies, programs, events and informational briefings, or family support or assistance programs sponsored by the military, military service organizations, or the American Red Cross that are related to the member's deployment.

- Certain childcare and related activities arising from the military member's covered active duty, including arranging for alternative childcare, providing child care on a nonroutine, urgent, immediate-need basis, enrolling in or transferring a child to a new school or day-care facility.

- Certain activities arising from the military member's covered active duty related to care of the military member's parent who is incapable of self-care, such as arranging for alternative care, providing care on a nonroutine, urgent, immediate-need basis, admitting or transferring a parent to a new care facility, and attending certain meetings with staff at a care facility, such as meetings with hospice or social service providers.

- Making or updating financial and legal arrangements to address a military member's absence while on covered active duty, including preparing and executing financial and health-care powers of attorney, enrolling in the Defense Enrollment Eligibility Reporting System (DEERS), or obtaining military identification cards.

- Attending counseling for the employee, the military member, or the child of the military member when the need for that counseling arises from the covered active duty of the military member and is provided by someone other than a health-care provider.

- Taking up to 15 calendar days of leave to spend time with a military member who is on short-term, temporary Rest and Recuperation leave during deployment. The employee's leave for this reason must be taken while the military member is on Rest and Recuperation leave.

- Certain post-deployment activities within 90 days of the end of the military member's covered active duty, including attending arrival ceremonies, reintegration briefings and events, and other official ceremonies or programs sponsored by the military, and addressing issues arising from the death of a military member, including attending the funeral.

- Any other event that the employee and employer agree is a qualifying exigency.

The third change, effective March 27, 2015, incorporates a broader definition of spouse. Eligible employees in legal same-sex marriages qualify to take FMLA leave to care for their spouse or family member, regardless of where they live. This will ensure that the FMLA will give spouses in same-sex marriages the same ability as all other spouses to fully exercise their FMLA rights.

State and Local Family Leave Laws

Since the passage of the FMLA, some states and local governments have instituted laws which mandate that employers furnish paid family leave. As of October 2016, four states—California, New Jersey, New York, and Rhode Island—possess paid family leave laws. For instance, the New Jersey Family Leave Act permits up to six weeks of paid leave amounting to two-thirds of wages (subject to a cap). The Rhode Island Temporary Caregiver Insurance Program established 4 weeks of paid leave to care for a family member and up to 30 weeks of paid leave for a worker's own disability. In recent years, a multitude of local governments have enacted paid family leave benefits. For instance, New York City's law provides up to six weeks of fully paid family leave for nonunion workers employed by the city.

FLEXIBLE WORK ARRANGEMENTS

Flexible work arrangements create the flexibility for employees to balance work and nonwork demands or interests.[18] More than 80 percent of companies offer some type of flexibility to its employees. Telework and flextime schedules are by far the most commonly used practices. Numerous benefits of flexible work arrangements include enhanced recruitment and retention, job satisfaction, and employee engagement. Lower stress, unscheduled absenteeism, and voluntary turnover are also advantages to providing flexible work arrangements. Flexible work arrangements have downsides as well. For instance, flexible work arrangements could hamper collaboration because work schedules do not align.[19]

There are many variations of flexible work arrangements. We will review three of the more common practices:

- Flextime schedules.
- Compressed workweek schedules.
- Telecommuting.

Flextime Schedules

Flextime schedules allow employees to modify work schedules within specified limits set by the employer. Employees adjust when they will start work and when they will leave. However, flextime generally does not lead to reduced work hours. For instance, an employee may choose to work between 10 a.m. and 6 p.m., 9 a.m. and 5 p.m., or 8 a.m. and 4 p.m.

All workers must be present during **core hours**—certain workday hours when business activity is regularly high. The number of core hours may vary from company to company, by departments within companies, or by season. Although employees are relatively free to choose start and completion times that fall outside core hours, management must carefully coordinate these times to avoid understaffing. Some flextime programs incorporate a **banking hours** feature. The banking hours feature enables employees to vary the number of daily work hours, as long as they maintain the regular number of work hours on a weekly basis.

How do flextime schedules create benefits in the employment relationship? Let's consider three potential benefits. First, flextime schedules lead to lower tardiness and absenteeism. Flexibly defining the workweek better enables employees to schedule medical and other appointments outside work hours. As a result, workers are less likely to be late or miss work altogether.

Second, flexible work schedules should lead to higher work productivity. Employees have greater choice about when to work during the day. Individuals who work best during the morning hours may schedule morning hours, while individuals who work best during the afternoons or evenings will choose those times. In addition, possessing the flexibility to attend to personal matters outside work should help employees focus on doing their jobs better.

Third, flexible work schedules benefit employers by creating longer business hours and better service. Staggering employee schedules should enable businesses to stay open longer hours without incurring overtime pay expenses. Also, customers should perceive better service because of expanded business hours. Companies that conduct business by telephone on a national and international basis will more likely be open during the normal operating hours of customers in other time zones.

Compressed Workweek Schedules

Compressed workweek schedules enable employees to perform their work in fewer days than a regular five-day workweek. Thus, employees may work four 10-hour days or three 12-hour days. For example, these schedules can promote a company's recruitment and retention successes by:

- Reducing the number of times employees must commute between home and work.
- Providing more time together for dual-career couples who live in different cities.

However, employers may face challenges when implementing compressed workweek benefits. More employees than can feasibly be accommodated may request compressed schedules. For example, parents of young children may favor schedules that allow them to be at home before the end of the school day.

Employers and employees often wonder whether the Fair Labor Standards Act (Chapter 3) addresses overtime pay issues for employees who work on flexible schedules. The FLSA does not regulate flexible work schedules. Alternative work arrangements, such as flexible work schedules, are a matter of agreement between the employer and the employee (or the employee's union representative).

Telecommuting

Telecommuting represents alternative work arrangements in which employees perform work at home or some other location besides the office. Nearly 4 million people telecommute.[20] Telecommuters generally spend part of their time working in the office and other times working at home. This alternative work arrangement is appropriate for work that does not require regular, direct interpersonal interactions with other workers. Examples include accounting, systems analysis, and telephone sales. Telecommuters stay in touch with coworkers and superiors via e-mail, phone, and fax. Exhibit 8.3 lists a variety of possible telecommuting arrangements.

Potential benefits for employers include increased productivity and lower overhead costs for office space and supplies. Telecommuting also serves as an effective recruiting and retention practice for employees who strongly desire to perform their jobs away from the office. Employers may also increase the retention of valued employees who choose not to move when their companies relocate.

Employees find telecommuting beneficial for a number of reasons. Telecommuting enables parents to be near their infants or preschool-age children, and to

EXHIBIT 8.3 Alternative Telecommuting Arrangements

Source: Adapted from Bureau of National Affairs, "Telecommuting," *Compensation & Benefits.* (Washington, DC: Bureau of National Affairs, 2001). CD-ROM.

- *Satellite work center:* Employees work from a remote extension of the employer's office, which includes clerical staff and a full-time manager.
- *Neighborhood work center:* Employees work from a satellite office shared by several employers.
- *Nomadic executive office:* Executives who travel extensively maintain control over projects via e-mail, phone, and fax.

In addition:

- Employees sometimes work entirely outside the office. Others might work off-site only once a month, or two to three days a week.
- Telecommuters can be full- or part-time employees.
- Telecommuting arrangements can be temporary or permanent. A temporarily disabled employee may work at home until fully recovered. A permanently disabled employee may work at home exclusively.

be home when older children finish their school days. In addition, telecommuting arrangements minimize commuting time and expenses, which are exceptional in such congested metropolitan areas as Boston, Los Angeles, and New York City where travel time may increase threefold during peak rush-hour traffic periods. Parking and toll costs may also lead to some disadvantages for employers and employees. Notwithstanding these concerns, often times, employers are concerned about not having direct contact with employees, which makes conducting performance appraisals more difficult. Employees have concerns, too. They sometimes feel that work-at-home arrangements are disruptive to their personal lives. Other employees feel isolated because they do not interact personally as often with coworkers and superiors.

Summary

This chapter reviews the fundamental concepts of paid time-off policies and flexible work schedules. Most paid time-off benefits and flexible work schedules are offered on a discretionary basis. Federal and state laws play a role in some of these discretionary offerings, as do mandates for family and medical leave. In more recent years, many states and cities have issued mandates for paid family or sick leave.

Key Terms

paid time off, *220*
floating holidays, *222*
carryover provisions, *224*
use-it-or-lose-it provision, *224*
cash-out provisions, *224*
sick leave, *225*
integrated paid time-off policies, *236*
paid time-off banks, *236*
bereavement leave, *227*

funeral leave, *227*
Jury Systems Improvement Act of 1978, *227*
Uniformed Services Employment and Reemployment Rights Act of 1994 (USERRA), *228*
nonproduction time, *228*
on-call time, *229*
sabbatical leave, *230*

volunteerism, *231*
Family and Medical Leave Act (FMLA), *232*
flexible work arrangements, *236*
flextime schedules, *236*
core hours, *236*
banking hours, *236*
compressed workweek schedules, *237*
telecommuting, *237*

Discussion Questions

1. Discuss the pros and cons of choosing an integrated paid time-off policy instead of multiple specific paid time-off policies—for example, sick leave, vacation, and so forth.

2. Most companies award vacation and sick-leave time according to seniority. Should companies base the allocation of these benefits on employee performance? Discuss the rationale for your answer.

3. Some cities and states have passed laws that provide paid family or medical leave. Should the Family and Medical Leave Act be revised to require paid leave? Explain why or why not.

4. Explain the pros and cons of flexible work arrangements.

Cases

1. Understanding Your Employee Benefits: The Decision to Work from Home

As you make the nearly hour-long commute home from your job at your company's downtown office, you think about today's announcement with some excitement. The director of human resources introduced a new company policy that permits employees to apply to telecommute. The company is doing well and is hiring new workers. As a result, management recently reviewed company policies and practices to accommodate the needs of the growing workforce. The company is looking to save some facility costs and also respond to employee requests for more flexible work options. The company will allow people in certain positions, including yours, to work from home either full time or a just a few days each week.

With high gas prices, daily parking expenses, and the logistics challenges that the two hours a day you spend commuting causes, you see this as a great opportunity. You have two children, and, although they are in school full time, it is almost impossible for you to attend your children's special events at school without taking a full day off and using one of your limited vacation days. Further, when your children get sick, you have to use a sick day to stay at home taking care of them and not working.

The new company policy states that employees who telecommute must use their own computers and provide evidence that they have a safe and quiet work environment. The company will provide you with any other work supplies that you need. All of the information you need to do your job is available to you via an online connection, so the transition to working at home should be fairly easy. You already have an office at home with a computer, so you could begin telecommuting as soon as your request is approved.

It seems like the perfect solution to your daily challenges, but you worry about how telecommuting will affect your career. You've heard from others that old adage, "out of sight, out of mind" and have concerns about your chances for future promotions if you aren't in the office every day. Further, you have high productivity expectations and you consider whether working at home alone will allow you to work harder, as you would not have the typical office distractions, or whether you would be distracted by work that needs to be done around the house. You also think that you might feel somewhat isolated, as you generally are a social person and enjoy seeing your coworkers each day. As you consider some of the negatives of telecommuting, your excitement wears off, and you aren't sure what you should do.

1. Should you apply to telecommute? If so, should you pursue a part-time or full-time work-at-home arrangement?
2. If you do telecommute, what can you do to make sure that the arrangement does not negatively impact your career? Are there any other concerns you should have?

2. Managing Employee Benefits: Transitioning to a Paid Time-Off Bank

Human Resources Manager Stan Gomez finds that he is spending a lot of time talking with supervisors about employee absences. Stan is the Human Resource Manager works for Custom Call Services, a contract customer service-call center that provides year-round online and telephone service to the customers of a wide variety of clients. Staffing levels are essential to meet the demanding level of calls and inquiries the center receives each day. The company offers paid time-off options to its employees to allow them to balance work and nonwork interests. A goal of the time-off program is to keep unscheduled absences to a minimum in order to keep productivity and service quality high. Unscheduled absences create a problem, as the company has to cover the workload of the absent employee with little advance notice.

Custom Call Center offers a generous paid time-off program to allow employees to have time off to rest and relax, to meet personal obligations, and to manage unexpected illnesses. Currently, employees receive 10 vacation days, 3 personal days, and 5 sick days per year. Due to the nature of the business and the need to provide service to clients every day, the company does not close on any holidays. Thus, in addition to other time-off benefits, the company provides seven floating holidays and encourages employees to take these on or near traditional holidays.

The time-off program currently creates some challenges for the company. While the company uses an automated system to track employees' time off, supervisors still need to record and properly allocate time off as it is taken. This requires the supervisors to know the reasons for each absence and the scheduling policy for each type of absence. For example, employees must schedule vacation and floating holidays in advance. They are encouraged to schedule personal days in advance, but personal days may be taken without advance notice if necessary. Finally, sick days do not require advance notice, but they may require a doctor's note if an employee uses a few days in a row, or if the supervisor questions the need for the absence.

The sick days create the most challenges for supervisors, as sick days are typically taken without advance notice. Many supervisors suspect that not all last-minute call-offs are necessary. Some employees have admitted that they use sick days even if they are not sick when they have exhausted all of their other time-off options. Essentially, they plan to take a day off, but because the policy does not allow them to schedule sick days in advance, they call off shortly before they are scheduled to work. As a result, supervisors must quickly arrange to cover those shifts.

To overcome these challenges, Stan is considering transitioning the company to an integrated paid time-off (PTO) policy in which all time off is grouped into one bank. Instead of the current time-off allotments, the company would offer 25 PTO days each year. Under this policy, employees could still call off on the same day due to illness, but they would be encouraged to schedule most of their time off in advance. Further, supervisors would not need to know the reasons for the absences; they only would need to track the number of days taken off by employees. Stan thinks that the PTO bank would eliminate many unscheduled absences and ease the administrative burden of the company's current time-off policies.

1. Should Custom Call Services switch to a PTO policy? What are the pros and cons of doing so?

2. If Custom Call Services does transition to a PTO policy, what are some things that Stan should consider including in the policy to address concerns about absenteeism?

Endnotes

1. U.S. Bureau of Labor Statistics, *Employer Costs for Employee Compensation—September 2015.* USDL 15-2329. Accessed January 22, 2016, www.bls.gov.

2. 5 U.S.C. §6103(a).

3. 29 C.F.R. §1605.1.

4. U.S. Bureau of Labor Statistics. *Employee Benefits in the United States, March 2015* (BLS 15-2782).

5. M. M. Markowich, *Paid Time-Off Banks.* Phoenix, AZ: WorldatWork Press, 2007.

6. 38 U.S.C. §4301.

7. *Integrity Staffing Solutions, Inc., v. Busk et al.,* No. 13-433 (U.S. Supreme Court, December 9, 2014).

8. *Owens v. Local No. 169,* 30 WH Cases 1634, Cal. 9, July 29, 1992.

9. R. Feintzeig, "Cure for Office Burnout: Mini Sabbaticals," *Fortune,* October 28, 2014. Accessed January 10, 2016, www.fortune.com.

10. K. Harrison, "The Most Popular Employee Perks of 2014," *Fortune,* February 19, 2014. Accessed January 4, 2016, www.fortune.com.

11. C. Kane, "Go Ahead, Take That Long Vacation," *Fortune,* March 16, 2015. Accessed January 21, 2016, www.fortune.com.

12. H. Helen Axel, "Redefining Corporate Sabbaticals for the 1990s," *The Conference Board,* Report No. 1005, 1992.

13. Society for Human Resource Management, *2013 Employee Benefits: An Overview of Employee Benefits Offerings in the U.S.,* 2013. Accessed January 20, 2016, www.shrm.org.

14. S. Halzack, "Paid Time Off for Volunteering Gains Traction as a Way to Retain Employees," *Washington Post,* August 11, 2013. Accessed January 15, 2016, www.washingtonpost.com.

15. M. L. Barnett, "Stakeholder Influence Capacity and the Variability of Financial Returns to Corporate Social Responsibility," *Academy of Management Review,* July 2007: 794–816; A. Mackey, T. B. Mackey, and J. B. Barney, "Corporate Social Responsibility and Firm Performance: Investor Preferences and Corporate Strategies," *Academy of Management Review,* July 2007: 817–835; and A. B. Carroll, "A Three-Dimensional Conceptual Model of Corporate Performance," *Academy of Management Review,* October 1979: 499.

16. R. Scott, "The Best Volunteer Programs Do This," *Forbes,* June 15, 2015. Accessed January 21, 2016, www.forbes.com.

17. 29 C.F.R. §825.

18. U.S. Bureau of Labor Statistics, *American Time Use Survey—2010 Results.* USDL 11-0919, 2011. Accessed August 14, 2012, www.bls.gov/news.release/archives/atus_06222011.pdf.

19. S. Dominus and J. Graham, "Rethining the Work-Life Equation," *New York Times*, February 16, 2016, accessed March 25, 2016, www.nytimes.com; WorldatWork and FlexJobs, "Trends in Workplace Flexibility," *WorldatWork*, September 2015; R. D. Richards, "The 2015 Workplace Flexibility Study," February 3, 2015; N. Bloom, "To Raise Productivity, Let More Employees Work from Home," *Harvard Business Review* (online), January–February 2014. Accessed March 2, 2016, www.hbr.org.

20. K. Lister, "Latest Telecommuting Statistics," Global Workplace Analytics, January 2016. Accessed March 25, 2016, www.workplaceanalytics.com.

Chapter Nine

Accommodation and Enhancement Benefits

Learning Objectives

In this chapter, you will gain an understanding of:

1. Accommodation and enhancement benefits and why companies offer them.

2. How companies promote the mental and physical well-being of employees and family members.

3. Various family assistance programs.

4. Different types of educational benefits.

5. Support programs for daily living, including transportation services and physical fitness.

Increasingly, more employees are facing greater challenges as they strive to fulfill work and family obligations while others seek to further their education to minimize skills obsolescence and earnings potential. All the while, pressures to perform well at work intensify particularly when economic conditions decline and companies contemplate reducing staffing levels. All of these considerations and pressures oftentimes challenge workers' abilities to effectively cope with them.

Many companies offer accommodation and enhancement benefits to promote effective coping skills, as well as educational opportunities for employees and, sometimes, family members. Accommodation and enhancement benefits are more recent additions to employee-benefits packages (compared to health care and retirement benefits). Now more than ever, more and more companies consider offering such benefits a business necessity.

DEFINING ACCOMMODATION AND ENHANCEMENT BENEFITS

As discretionary benefits, **accommodation benefits** and **enhancement benefits** promote one or more of the following four objectives:

- The mental and physical well-being of employees and family members.
- Family assistance.
- Educational benefits for employees.
- Support for daily living.

Following a discussion of the rationale for these benefits, a variety of accommodation and enhancement benefits associated with each objective is reviewed.

Rationale for Accommodation and Enhancement Benefits

The decision to provide accommodation and enhancement benefits is based on three considerations. First, in the long run, the cost of absenteeism and tardiness is usually less with the inclusion of accommodation and enhancement benefits in the employee-benefits package. Programs that promote two particular objectives— the mental and physical well-being of employees and family members, and other family assistance programs—contribute to this attendance imperative. After all, ill or dependent family members often rely on other family members (most of whom are also employees) to care for them, necessitating absence from work. Support programs for daily living also promote regular attendance. For example, commute times in congested areas vary considerably, based on the occurrence of accidents and traffic volume. In addition, employers may choose to offer transportation services such as vanpooling or discounted public transportation passes.

Second, many employees are not sufficiently productive for a variety of health-related reasons. For example, excessive smoking tends to limit physical capacity because of impaired lung function. Excessive alcohol consumption may inhibit an employee's ability to make sound decisions or impair physical coordination. Excess body weight may reduce an employee's stamina, leading to lower job performance. Employers may sponsor smoking cessation programs, alcohol treatment programs, or weight-control programs to promote better health.

Third, promoting educational opportunities, including tuition reimbursement and scholarships, yields benefits for both employers and employees. For example, scholarships and tuition reimbursement programs reduce the financial barriers to education by sponsoring employees' pursuit of general equivalency diplomas, college courses, or college degrees. Employees benefit from acquiring greater credentials to compete for higher-level jobs in the company. And, employers benefit from staffing flexibility because employees possess a wider range and depth of knowledge and skills. As technology changes the nature of work, skills, and knowledge updates minimize the problem of obsolescence.

Origins of Accommodation and Enhancement Benefits

Widespread alcohol use on the job was generally socially acceptable during the early part of the 20th century. However, in the era of industrialization, serious concerns emerged among many business owners about low worker productivity and inefficiencies, which they attributed to problem drinking. In addition, alcohol consumption in the workplace was seen as a contributor to accidents.

Forerunners to current alcohol treatment programs such as Alcoholics Anonymous sprouted up in response to the deleterious effects of excessive alcohol consumption in the workplace, as well as on the welfare of alcoholic individuals and their families. In the 1940s, during and following World War II, companies adopted a rehabilitative rather than punitive stance toward alcohol consumption. Three factors during this period prompted this approach. First, during World War II, private businesses refocused their work on efforts to support the war, which required additional hiring to replace workers who were drafted into the military and to bolster staffing beyond typical levels. The need for efficiencies was perhaps never greater, creating highly stressful working conditions. Alcohol consumption, in part, was a coping mechanism, albeit a dysfunctional one. Second, the additional staffing needs required the employment of those who would not otherwise be hired for a variety of reasons, including insufficient skills to perform adequately in the workplace. Oftentimes, the limited supply of workers included those with problems, including excessive alcohol consumption. Third, upon returning from the war, workers were reemployed. Many of them suffered from the effects of the extreme stress of the war experience, and they attempted to cope through alcohol consumption. These factors gave rise to formal alcohol intervention programs, which focused on rehabilitation. Alcohol intervention programs laid the foundation of contemporary employee assistance programs, which are discussed in this chapter.

Indeed, the scope of various wellness-type benefits has increased dramatically through the recent decades as the stigma of mental health problems has diminished and companies have realized that promoting good health can lead to lower costs of health and workers' compensation insurance. Nowadays, many companies offer a variety of accommodation and enhancement programs to facilitate worker productivity and welfare. The rationale and features of these programs are discussed in the remainder of the chapter.

THE MENTAL AND PHYSICAL WELL-BEING OF EMPLOYEES AND FAMILY MEMBERS

Companies may choose to offer one or more programs to promote the mental and physical well-being of employees and family members: employee assistance programs (EAPs) and wellness programs.

Employee Assistance Programs

Employee assistance programs (EAPs) help employees cope with personal problems that may impair their personal lives or job performance. Examples of such problems include alcohol or drug abuse, domestic violence, the emotional impact of AIDS and other chronic diseases, clinical depression, and eating disorders. EAPs also assist employers in helping troubled employees identify and solve problems that may be interfering with their jobs.

Informed companies offer EAPs because, at any given time, an estimated 20 percent of employees experience difficulties that interfere with job performance, estimated to cost more than $44 billion in lost work productivity each year.[1] In 2015, 51 percent of workers in private industry were eligible for an EAP.[2] More full-time employees had access to an EAP (56 percent) than did part-time employees (36 percent). Similarly, more union workers had access (73 percent) compared to nonunion workers (49 percent). Although EAP costs are substantial, the possible benefits are expected to outweigh the costs of increased employee turnover, absenteeism, health-care premiums costs, unemployment insurance rates, workers' compensation rates, accident costs, and disability insurance costs. For instance, the hotel chain Marriott International realized an estimated payback of $2.60 for every $1 invested into EAP services.[3] While anecdotal information suggests the effectiveness of programs such as EAPs, unfortunately, current large-scale evaluation studies are virtually nonexistent. Perhaps more companies would add EAPs to their employee-benefits programs if there were large-scale studies rather than a variety of anecdotal or company-specific evidence.

The federal government has contributed to the rise in EAPs with the **Drug-Free Workplace Act of 1988.**[4] This act mandates that companies holding federal contracts worth at least $100,000 promote a drug-free workplace. Exhibit 9.1 lists the main requirements of the Drug-Free Workplace Act, which appears to have made a difference. The percentage of American workers who use illegal drugs has dropped from 13.6 percent in 2008 to 4.7 percent in 2014. Still, there is a long way to go to eradicate the problem of illegal drug use, and the use of EAPs may contribute to further reductions.[5]

EXHIBIT 9.1
Drug-Free
Workplace
Act:
Requirements
for Employers

The Drug-Free Workplace Act of 1988 requires some federal contractors and all federal grantees to agree that they will provide drug-free workplaces as a condition of receiving a contract or grant from a federal agency.

Organizations, with contracts from any U.S. federal agency, must comply with the provisions of the act if the contract is in the amount of $100,000 or more. Organizations must do the following:

(A) Publish a statement notifying employees that the unlawful manufacture, distribution, dispensation, possession, or use of a controlled substance is prohibited in the person's workplace. The statement should also notify employees of any punitive actions that will be taken.

(B) Establish a drug-free awareness program to inform employees about:
   (i) The dangers of drug abuse in the workplace.
   (ii) The policy of maintaining a drug-free workplace.
   (iii) Any available drug counseling, rehabilitation, and employee assistance programs.
   (iv) The penalties that many be imposed on employees for drug abuse violations.

(C) Make it a requirement that each employee be given a copy of the workplace substance abuse policy.

If a contractor is found not to have a drug-free workplace, each contract awarded by any federal agency shall be subject to suspension of payments under the contract or termination of the contract, or both. The contractor may also be ineligible for award of any contract by any federal agency, and for participation in any future procurement by any federal agency, for a period not to exceed five years.

EAP Services

Employee assistance programs include a variety of services; the specific services contained in any EAP depend on an employer's choice. If a company is unionized, collective bargaining determines some of the EAP services. Employers rely on staff members to develop and implement EAPs, or they establish contracts with third-party providers. Sometimes, employers use a combination of these methods. The choice rests on keeping costs to acceptable amounts. Exhibit 9.2 lists the most common types of EAP services.

The inclusion of outplacement assistance programs in EAPs represents a relatively recent phenomenon because of ever-changing business conditions. Many companies use outplacement assistance programs to provide technical and emotional support to employees who are being laid off or terminated. Companies assist through a variety of career and personal programs designed to develop an employee's job-searching skills and self-confidence. A variety of factors lead to employee termination—factors to which outplacement assistance programs are best suited:

- Elimination of specific positions, often the result of changes in technology.
- Layoffs eliminating hundreds of thousands of jobs across industry sectors since the deep economic recession began in 2007.
- Changes in management.
- Mergers and acquisitions.
- Plant closings.

EXHIBIT 9.2
Typical
Services of
Employee
Assistance
Programs

- Orientation meetings and educational materials to familiarize managers and employees with EAP services and procedures for supervisory referrals or employee self-referrals.
- Problem identification and assessment by interviewing an apparently troubled employee.
- Short-term counseling when appropriate, instead of long-term, intensive therapy.
- Referrals to health professionals and community resources when short-term counseling is insufficient to address a troubled employee's problems.
- Follow-up meetings to determine the effectiveness of treatment and make additional plans (e.g., weekly counseling sessions for six months).
- Usually, staff crisis hotlines to help employees in urgent situations that require immediate attention.

- Outsourcing manufacturing, customer service, and professional services (for example, information technology and accounting) to countries with lower pay scales and fewer labor protection laws.

Outplacement assistance provides such services as personal counseling, career assessment and evaluation, training in job-search techniques, résumé and cover letter preparation, interviewing techniques, and training in the use of basic workplace technology such as computers.[6] Employers also receive benefits from offering outplacement assistance to employees. Outplacement assistance programs may promote a positive image of the company among those being terminated, their families, and friends by assisting these employees as they prepare for new employment opportunities.

EAP Delivery Options

Employers may choose from two main delivery options when establishing EAPs. The first option, **referral EAPs,** lists the names and contact information for a variety of professional help services, ranging from crisis hotlines to alcohol and substance abuse treatment programs. Under this arrangement, the employer usually does not have a contractual relationship with service providers. Sometimes, large employers negotiate a reduced rate with service providers because of the volume of referrals.

The second option, **full-service EAPs,** includes service providers such as alcohol treatment programs. Employers offer full-service EAPs through in-house services, third-party providers, or participation in a consortium EAP. Staff members of **in-house EAPs** are employees of the company. Employers decide between offering in-house EAPs within work facilities (in-house) or somewhere outside these facilities through an independent EAP provider. Oftentimes, employers establish in-house EAPs outside the work facilities to enhance employees' willingness to use them. Employees may be more likely to use EAPs when they generally cannot be seen doing so by coworkers.

Employers establish contracts with third-party providers for full-service EAPs. **Third-party providers** are independent companies that offer EAP services to one or more employers. Contracts specify the services and the cost for each one.

Consortium EAPs establish contracts with sets of numerous smaller employers. Smaller companies combine limited resources to establish a contract with a third-party provider. Compared to larger companies, a smaller company alone generally pays a substantially higher fee per employee. Consortium EAP arrangements reduce this amount by increasing the number of employees who may take advantage of the EAP services.

Procedures for Employee Participation in EAPs

An employee participates in an EAP based on self-initiative or a referral by someone else. Employees initiate participation in an EAP when they recognize a problem and possess a desire to remedy it. Oftentimes, employees either do not recognize how problems adversely affect their work and personal lives or do not subscribe to the view that EAPs are appropriate and worthwhile. Some employees may mistrust employer sponsorship of EAPs. For example, they may view EAPs as a method to gather evidence for termination of employment. A number of employees may hold the view that personal problems are just that—problems not to be shared in the workplace. Some employees may simply feel strong shame about their problems to the point of denial.

Referrals direct troubled employees to EAPs. Before making a referral, a supervisor should engage in constructive confrontation. **Constructive confrontation** entails discussing incidents of poor performance with the troubled employee, citing the necessity of improving job performance within a designated period. In many instances, employees recognize that personal problems are responsible for poor performance; these employees voluntarily seek help through an EAP. In an informal letter, the U.S. Equal Employment Opportunity Commission (EEOC) made the following statement:

> When employees do not take the initiative to seek help, submitting a formal referral to the EAP on behalf of an employee should be made under extenuating circumstances. These circumstances include concern that the employee is suicidal or the employee has made threats of violence in the workplace. Beyond those circumstances, employers should make referrals as a matter of agreement with the employee. Mandatory referrals could result in a violation of the Americans with Disabilities Act.[7]

When making a referral, supervisors are responsible for describing the signs of trouble—for example, describing excessive absenteeism and the frequency of these occurrences during the previous three months. Their responsibilities do not extend to making diagnoses. For instance, it is inappropriate to conclude that a troubled employee is an alcoholic because supervisors do not possess the necessary training to make diagnoses of medical or psychological problems.

Confidentiality

Confidentiality of information is essential to the success of EAPs. Employees are not likely to seek help from EAPs when they believe that information about their status will be shared with supervisors and coworkers. The greatest concern is possible job loss, loss of opportunities for promotion and pay increases, and damage to both personal and professional reputation.

These concerns require that employers take measures to protect confidentiality and communicate these procedures to employees. Troubled employees must feel confident that there will be no oral or written disclosure of information to anyone outside the EAP staff.

Release of Confidential Information

Protecting confidentiality does not necessarily mean that EAPs always conceal information from employers and coworkers. In most cases, EAP service providers must obtain the employee's written consent before they release information to supervisors, treatment facilities, or family members. Some situations require EAPs to disclose confidential information about participants to legal entities. However, most situations require signed consent for information disclosure from employees. In any event, sound policy includes a promise of confidentiality, except when employees provide written consent, granting permission to release information to designated individuals or when required by law.

Every state includes laws that enforce the release of confidential information to the appropriate authorities without written consent. EAPs must universally release information about reports of child abuse and neglect. Also, EAPS are obligated to release confidential information about evidence or strong professional judgments that troubled individuals pose a risk to the health and welfare of themselves or others.

Evaluating Employee Assistance Programs

Are EAPs effective? What does EAP effectivness mean? Employers seek information to evaluate the effectiveness of these programs by seeking answers to several questions:

- Are troubled employees aware of their employer's EAP?
- Do coworkers and supervisors understand the importance of, and procedures for, referring troubled employees to EAPs?
- Do the benefits of EAPs (e.g., helping troubled employees, achieving higher productivity and lower absenteeism) outweigh the costs? Of course, it is difficult to ascribe monetary value to helping others.
- Based on available information, should the EAP be modified in any particular ways, offered as is, or dropped altogether?

Evaluating EAPs requires a variety of complex tasks—for example, survey development and implementation. A significant part of the challenge centers on knowing the right questions to ask and how to reliably measure EAP outcomes. Companies may rely on a professional association for advice about EAPs. The **International Employee Assistance Professionals Association (EAPA)** has developed an evaluation system for EAPs (www.eapassn.org). Methods of evaluation include interviews, peer review, and case analysis.

Employer Liability

Employers may be legally responsible for inappropriate actions of EAPs, just as health-care professionals may be held liable for similar inappropriate actions. Possible trouble spots for employers include:

- Misdiagnosis of a condition that refers an employee to the wrong facility.
- Negligent referral to a provider who does not have proper credentials.
- Abandonment, either because a provider stops treatment prematurely or a worker's employment is terminated during the course of treatment, making him or her ineligible for further treatment.
- Inappropriate relationships with a client. The ethics code of health and social service professional organization prohibits sexual involvement with clients, and in some jurisdictions, it also is illegal. Most ethics codes also prohibit social relationships and business relationships between therapists and clients.
- Defaming an employee's character with libelous or slanderous statements due to participation in an EAP.

Relationship with Employee Benefits Laws

The Employee Retirement Income Security Act of 1974 (ERISA), the Consolidated Omnibus Budget Reconciliation Act of 1985 (COBRA), and the Patient Protection and Affordable Care Act of 2010 (PPACA) may influence EAP practices.

ERISA   The essence of ERISA is to provide protection of employee-benefits rights in retirement plans and welfare plans. As described in Chapter 3, ERISA defines a welfare plan as:

> any plan, fund or program which was heretofore or is hereafter established or maintained by an employer or by an employee organization, or by both, to the extent that such plan, fund, or program established or is maintained *for the purpose of providing for its participants or their beneficiaries through the purchase of insurance or otherwise* [emphasis added].[8]

The italicized phrase above means that not all EAPs are subject to ERISA's reporting and disclosure requirements for welfare plans. As discussed earlier, some EAPs are referral services only. In this case, employers neither fund EAP services directly nor fund these services indirectly through the purchase of insurance, exempting referral services from ERISA requirements.

COBRA   COBRA amended ERISA by providing employees and beneficiaries the right to elect continuation coverage under group health plans if they would lose coverage due to a qualifying event. COBRA usually applies to EAPs under two circumstances: (1) the EAP qualifies as a welfare benefit plan under ERISA, and (2) the EAP qualifies as a health-care plan by providing counseling for a medical condition.

PPACA   Recently, the Departments of Labor, the Treasury, and Health and Human Services published regulations about when EAPs qualify as "excepted benefits."

Excepted benefits are not subject to requirements of the PPACA that apply to group health plans, which we discussed in Chapter 5, that include restrictions on annual and lifetime limits or the requirement that health coverage cover preventive services without cost sharing. For instance, if an EAP provides referral services only, then the applicable group health plan mandates will not apply to it. However, comprehensive EAPs that provides medical care would qualify it as health coverage subject to PPACA requirements unless it qualifies as excepted benefit. An EAP is considered an excepted benefit if it meets four criteria:[9]

- No significant benefits in the nature of medical care.
- Not coordinated with benefits under another group health plan so that, specifically there is (1) no need to exhaust EAP before using the group health plan benefits, and (2) no need to elect group health plan for coverage under the EAP.
- No employee premiums are required for the EAP.
- No cost sharing (coinsurance or copayments) under the EAP.

Wellness Programs

Companies sponsor **wellness programs** to promote and maintain the physical and psychological health of employees. Wellness programs vary in scope. They may emphasize weight loss only, or they may emphasize a range of activities, including:

- Back care.
- Smoking cessation.
- Stress management.
- Weight control and nutrition.
- Health risk appraisals.

Employers may choose to offer wellness programs on site or off site. While some companies may invest in staffing professionals for wellness programs, others contract with external vendors such as community health agencies or private health clubs.

Wellness programs are becoming more widespread as more employers become conscious of the impact employee health has on performance. Employers that start wellness programs not only help lower health-related costs, but also find that employees are more engaged and productive at work. A recent study found that medical costs fall by about $3.27 for every dollar spent on wellness programs, and that the costs of absenteeism declined by $2.73 for every dollar spent.[10] Further program growth is being prompted by the shift toward wellness and prevention in the design of employer-sponsored health-care benefits and by federal health-care reform legislation. Barry Hall, global wellness research leader at Buck Consultants LLC's Boston office, said, "Wellness is currently the biggest area of growth in benefits, and it's primarily fueled by employer demand."[11] The EEOC permits employers to offer employees substantial monetary incentives or discounts on their health insurance contributions if they are willing to answer health-related questions that is part of a voluntary wellness program. Employees are eligible to receive an incentive of up to

30 percent of the cost of individual health insurance coverage. Spouses who participate also qualify for an equal incentive. Employers may offer incentives of up to 50 percent for participation in tobacco prevention and reduction programs.

Back Care

Employers sponsor **back care programs** to reduce back injuries through worker training, exercise programs, ergonomic evaluations of the work environment, and relaxation techniques. Apart from containing health-care and workers' compensation claims, back care programs presumably reduce frequent absenteeism. The prevalence of injuries to the shoulders and back and their links to absence are substantial. In 2014, there were 1.1 million occupational injuries and illnesses within U.S. private industries that required recuperation away from work beyond the day of the incident.[12] The median number of missed workdays associated with back injuries was eight.

Smoking Cessation Programs

One poll revealed that smoking can be both disruptive and costly to companies. It estimated that the cost of absenteeism attributed to smoking-related health conditions amounted to $218.5 billion, and companies incurred an additional $59.4 billion in health-care costs.[13] Employers may invest in **smoking cessation** programs ranging from simply informational campaigns that emphasize the negative aspects of smoking to intensive programs geared toward helping individuals stop smoking. Many employers offer courses and treatment to help and encourage smokers to quit. For example, employers may sponsor the participation of employees in the SmokEnders education program. Other options include offering nicotine replacement therapy, such as nicotine gum and patches, and self-help services. Also, many companies endorse antismoking events, such as the American Cancer Society's "Great American Smokeout," during which companies distribute T-shirts, buttons, and literature that discredit smoking, with slogans such as "Commit to Quit."

Employer-sponsored smoking cessation programs usually operate on a reimbursement basis. Employees pay a fee for the program. Upon successful completion of the program, they reimburse employees for part or all of the cost. Employees are not reimbursed if they fail to complete the program.

Employers deduct contributions to smoking cessation programs as a normal business expense. Employees generally enjoy tax benefits as well. For example, they may deduct the costs of smoking cessation programs and prescription drugs for nicotine withdrawal, unless they are reimbursed by the employer or health-care plan.[14] Employees may pay for nonprescription drugs to assist with smoking cessation with money from a flexible spending account (FSA, Chapter 5). Also, an individual who does not have an FSA may not deduct the cost of nonprescription smoking-cessation drugs from his or her income taxes.[15]

Stress Management Programs

An alarming statistic indicates that workplace stress contributes to 120,000 deaths per year.[16] Another is that the health-care costs related to stress were estimated to be $48 billion due to significant work demands and $24 billion due to work-family conflict. **Stress management** programs can help employees cope with many factors inside and outside of the work environment that contribute to stress. For instance, job conditions, health and personal problems, and personal and professional relationships can make employees anxious and thus less productive. Symptoms of stressful workplaces include low morale, chronic absenteeism, low productivity, and high turnover rates. Stress management techniques may include seminars that focus on recognizing signs of stress and burnout. Stress reduction techniques can improve the quality of life inside and outside the workplace. Employers benefit from increased employee productivity, reduced absenteeism, and lower health-care costs.

Weight-Control and Nutrition Programs

Weight-control and nutrition programs educate employees about proper nutrition and weight loss to promote sound health. Information from the medical community has clearly indicated that excess weight and poor nutrition are significant risk factors in cardiovascular disease, diabetes, high blood pressure, and cholesterol levels. Over time, these employee programs should yield better health, increased morale, and improved appearance. For employers, these programs should result in improved employee productivity and lower health-care costs.

Companies can contribute to employees' weight control and proper nutrition in different ways. For example, some employers sponsor memberships in weight-loss programs such as Weight Watchers. Employers may also reinforce the positive results of weight-loss programs through support groups, counseling, and competitions. In addition, companies sometimes actively attempt to influence employee food choices by including nutritional foods and beverages as options in vending machines. Further, companies may occasionally offer health screenings on location for diabetes, high blood pressure, and cholesterol level. Employers treat the costs of wellness programs as a normal business expense; however, employees do not receive any tax benefits for costs (e.g., fees to participate in a weight-control program). Finally, as discussed later, employers may offer physical fitness opportunities on site or off site.

Health Risk Appraisals

Employer-sponsored **health risk appraisals** inform employees of potential health risks based on a physical examination, responses to questions about certain habits (e.g., diet, amount of exercise), and review of family members' health histories.

In many cases, the results of health risk appraisals help employees minimize risks whenever possible. Exhibit 9.3 lists common elements of health risk appraisals. Follow-through helps employers control health insurance claims. When wellness programs and EAPs are integrated with each other, the results of health risk appraisals can encourage employees to utilize EAP services on a confidential basis. For example, it is not uncommon for many individuals who are overweight to recognize this fact; however, recognizing the issue is often easier than resolving it. The use of such appraisals can remind employees of the health risks associated with excess body weight and, when combined with recommendations for an

EXHIBIT 9.3
Elements of
Health Risk
Appraisals

- Analysis of blood chemicals, such as cholesterol, triglycerides, glucose, and uric acid levels.
- Blood pressure check.
- Body measurements: height, weight, percentage of body fat.
- Colorectal cancer screening.
- Diabetes screening.
- Electrocardiogram.
- Examination for breast cancer.
- Glaucoma screening.
- Hearing tests.
- Kidney and liver functions.
- Lung function.
- Medical history.
- Physical capacity.
- Physical fitness.
- Stress tests.

action plan and referrals to EAP resources, the employee is more likely to seek resolution.

Wellness Programs and the Law

In 2016, the EEOC issued rulings to clarify the relationship between wellness programs and Title I of the Americans with Disabilities Act (ADA) as well as between wellness programs and the Genetic Information and Nondiscrimination Act (GINA).[17] The ADA-related ruling is based on an exception to the law that allows employers to make inquiries about employees' health or do medical examinations that are part of a voluntary employee health program, including a wellness program. Three points of confusion arose. First, the ADA did not define the meaning of "voluntary" or what makes up a "health program." Second, the ADA did not address whether employers could offer incentives to encourage employees to participate in such programs. Third, the EEOC issued the rule to help explain the differences between the ADA's requirements for voluntary health programs and other federal laws, such as the Health Insurance Portability and Accountability Act (HIPAA), as amended by the Patient Protection and Affordable Care Act (PPACA), which regulates wellness programs that are part of a group health plan.

The GINA-related ruling is based on an exception to GINA's prohibition against acquiring genetic information of job applicants or employees where employers offer voluntary health or genetic services to them or their family members. As noted earlier, employers may offer employees an incentive in exchange for providing information about current or previous health conditions. (In some cases, employers levy penalties against those who refuse to provide such information.) The EEOC ruling clarifies that inducements or penalties are permitted under two conditions. First, the wellness program must be designed to provide a reasonable chance of improving health or preventing disease. Second, employers are prohibited from using wellness programs as a cover to violate GINA, ensure that the program participation is not too time-consuming or invasive, and use medically acceptable methods for improving health or preventing disease.

Both rulings are highly complex. Benefits professionals should invest time in studying the details of these rulings, and consult legal experts for advice.

FAMILY ASSISTANCE PROGRAMS

Family assistance programs help employees provide care to young children and dependent elderly relatives. Presumably, employees are likely to attend work regularly and work productively when these family members receive the necessary attention. A variety of employer programs and benefits can help employees cope with their family assistance responsibilities. These programs range from making referrals to on-site child or elder care centers, to company-sponsored day care programs, and the programs vary in the amount of financial and human resources needed to administer them. Generally, the least expensive and least labor-intensive programs are referral services. Referral services are designed to help workers identify and take advantage of available community resources, conveyed through media, such as educational workshops, videos, employee newsletters and magazines, and EAPs.

Elder care programs provide physical, emotional, or financial assistance for aging parents, spouses, or other relatives who are not fully self-sufficient because they are too frail or disabled. According to the U.S. Bureau of Labor Statistics, **child care** is "A workplace program that provides for either the full or partial cost of caring for an employee's children in a nursery, day care center, or a baby sitter in facilities either on or off the employer's premises." Child care programs focus on supervising preschool-age dependent children whose parents work outside the home. Many employees now rely on elder care and child care programs due to the increasing longevity of their parents.[18] Child care needs arise from the growing number of single parents and dual-career households with children.[19] Still, only 10 percent of private-sector companies offer child care benefits.[20] According to the U.S. Bureau of Labor Statistics, child care is "A workplace program that provides for either the full or partial cost of caring for an employee's children in a nursery, day care center, or a baby sitter in facilities either on or off the employer's premises."

Day care is another possible benefit. Some companies subsidize child or elder day care in community-based centers. Elder care programs usually provide self-help, meals, and entertainment activities for the participants. Child care programs typically offer supervision, preschool preparation, and meals. Facilities must usually maintain state or local licenses. Other companies choose to sponsor on-site day care centers, offering services that are similar to community-based centers.

ADOPTION ASSISTANCE PROGRAMS

Adoption benefits can be placed into three categories: Information resources, financial assistance, and parental leave policies that extend mandatory leave under the Family and Medical Leave Act.[21] A recent study revealed that there has been steady growth in the number of large employers willing to provide financial adoption benefits.[22] Among the primary reasons that employers provide adoption benefits are to offer competitive work-life benefits packages, to provide a family-friendly image, and to establish equity for adoptive parents on par with what is available for biological parents at companies.

According to the Child Welfare Information Gateway, *information sources* may entail referrals to licensed adoption agencies, support groups, and experts who can educate employees about the adoption process. For instance, the Dave Thomas Foundation for Adoption (www.davethomasfoundation.org) is a well-known resource. Each year, it publishes a list of the top 100 companies that offer adoption-friendly employee benefits. *Financial assistance* benefits vary widely. Some companies provide a lump sum payment for an adoption, ranging widely between $1,000 and 15,000. Other companies reimburse employees for up to 80 percent of adoption fees, amounting to approximately $4,000. As discussed in Chapter 8, *parental leave* policies are becoming increasingly more common and apply to both biological and adoptive children. At the extreme, Netflix offers unlimited paid parental leave, but, the norm ranges between one and three months.

Employers and employees receive tax benefits through employer-sponsored programs up to designated limits. For purposes of both the tax credit and the employer-sponsored programs, IRC Section 23(a) defines **qualified adoption expenses** as reasonable and necessary adoption fees, court costs, attorneys' fees, and other expenses, which:

- Are directly related to, and the principal purpose of which is for, the legal adoption of an eligible child by the taxpayer.
- Are not incurred in violation of state or federal law or in carrying out any surrogate parenting arrangement.
- Are not expenses in connection with the adoption by an individual of a child who is the child of such individual's spouse.
- Are not reimbursed under another program.

Some additional notes: Eligible children are those who are younger than age 18 or who are physically or mentally incapable of caring for themselves regardless of age. Also, qualified adoption expenses do not include foreign adoptions, unless such adoptions become final.

EDUCATIONAL BENEFITS FOR EMPLOYEES

Many companies offer educational benefits to employees and, sometimes, their children. A recent survey revealed that 83 percent of companies offer some type of educational benefits.[23] Of those that do, virtually all full-time workers are eligible to participate, while only about one-third of part-time workers qualify. Educational benefits enable employees to pursue educational opportunities that they would otherwise be unable to afford or be unwilling to pay for. Also, educational benefits assist employees by providing them with a college education or advanced degree such as an MBA or executive MBA, particularly at a time when tuition costs are rising rapidly.

Companies stand to benefit from sponsoring employee education. Many companies, however, do not benefit because they often fail to develop and implement career development programs that allow employees to seek promotions with greater responsibility and compensation. The lack of follow-up may lead educated employees to seek promotions by taking jobs elsewhere.

There are three types of educational benefits:

- IRC Section 127 educational assistance.
- Tuition reimbursement.
- Scholarship programs.

Educational Assistance

The IRS currently offers two definitions of educational assistance, based on amendments to IRC Section 127.[24] These are *educational assistance benefits* and *educational assistance programs*. **Educational assistance benefits** include payments for tuition, fees and similar expenses, books, supplies, and equipment. The payments may be for either undergraduate- or graduate-level courses and do not have to be for work-related classes. Educational assistance benefits do not include payments for the following items: meals, lodging, or transportation; tools or supplies (other than textbooks) that may be kept after completing the course of instruction; and courses involving sports, games, or hobbies unless these are related to the business of the employer or are required as part of a degree program. Starbucks Coffee is an example of a company that offers generous educational assistance, which is named the "College Achievement Program." In 2015, the company announced that it would pay for most employees (currently, about 140,000 out of 238,000) to earn a bachelor's degree from Arizona State University's online course offerings.

Alternatively, the IRS permits employers to establish an **educational assistance program** under which every eligible employee can exclude as much as $5,250 a year of educational assistance from gross income, regardless of whether the courses are job-related. Educational assistance programs may qualify for tax benefits. Besides conforming to educational assistance program definitions, an employer must meet three additional requirements:

- Describe an educational assistance program in a separate written document.
- Offer the program exclusively for the benefit of employees.
- Satisfy nondiscrimination requirements.

In general, employees pay taxes on educational amounts that exceed $5,250. There is one exception to this limit: Educational benefits that qualify as working condition fringe benefits are not subject to this limit. A **working condition fringe benefit** is:

> Any property or services provided to an employee of the employer to the extent that, if the employee paid for such property or services, such payment would be

allowable as a deduction under section 162 [trade or business expenses] or 167 [depreciation of the property used in the trade or business].[25]

Tuition Reimbursement

Tuition reimbursement programs fully or partially reimburse an employee for expenses incurred for education or training. Tuition reimbursement programs fall under the category of employee benefits. Under these programs, employees usually choose the courses they wish to take and when they want to take them. Many employers allow employees to enroll in courses that are not directly related to their work. It is not uncommon to confuse tuition reimbursement programs with pay-for-knowledge programs. Pay-for-knowledge is one kind of direct or monetary compensation. Companies establish set curricula that employees should take, and they generally award pay increases to employees upon successful completion of courses within the curricula. The main goal of pay-for-knowledge programs is to train employees to meet changing job requirements resulting from new technology and global competitive pressures. Pay increases are not directly associated with tuition reimbursement programs.

Tuition reimbursement plans qualify as working condition fringe benefits either when instruction or training must maintain or improve essential job skills or when instruction or training is required by employers, by law, for employees to work in their jobs or to keep their same status or rate of compensation.

Scholarships

Employer-sponsored **scholarship programs** cover some or all of the tuition and related expenses for employees or family members pursuing undergraduate degrees in two- or four-year colleges. In most cases, these programs extend only to the children of employees. Employer-sponsored scholarship programs are the least-common educational benefit, perhaps because companies are less likely to benefit directly from educating the children of employees than from educating the employees themselves.

Employers treat the cost of scholarships as a normal business expense. In some cases, employees receive tax benefits for the scholarship amounts. Section 117 of the IRC describes **qualified scholarship programs** that grant tax benefits to employees for their own, or their children's, education below graduate-level work. The tax benefit equals the amount of qualified tuition reduction plus related expenses (e.g., fees, books, supplies). **Qualified tuition reductions** include the reduction in tuition granted by an employer's program. However, not all tuition reductions and related expenses qualify for tax benefits. For instance, tuition reductions that discriminate in favor of highly compensated employees* do not qualify for favorable tax treatment.

---

*See Chapter 11 for the definition of *highly compensated employees.*

SUPPORT PROGRAMS FOR DAILY LIVING

Employers may choose to offer one or more support programs designed to help employees manage common daily challenges. Two common examples include transportation services and opportunities either to become fit or to maintain physical fitness.

Transportation Services

Some employers sponsor **transportation services** to facilitate travel from home to work and back. Employers provide transit subsidies to employees working in metropolitan and suburban areas served by various forms of mass transportation such as buses, subways, and trains. Companies may offer transit passes, tokens, or vouchers. Practices vary from partial subsidies to full subsidies. They may sponsor public transportation subsidies, vanpools, or employer-sponsored vans or buses that transport employees between their homes and the workplace.

Many employers must offer transportation services to comply with the Clean Air Act of 1990.[26] Increasingly, local and state governments request that companies reduce the number of single-passenger automobiles commuting to their workplaces each day because of government mandates for cleaner air. The **Clean Air Act Amendments of 1990** require employers in smoggy metropolitan areas such as Los Angeles to comply with state and local laws concerning commuter trip reduction. Employers may also offer transportation services to recruit individuals who do not care to drive themselves in rush-hour traffic. Further, transportation services enable companies to offset for deficits in parking space availability, particularly in congested metropolitan areas.

The IRC distinguishes between two categories of transportation benefits: *De Minimis transportation benefits* and *qualified transportation benefits*. A **de minimis transportation benefit** is any local transportation benefit provided to an employee if it has so little value that accounting for it would be administratively impracticable. The IRC defines **qualified transportation benefits** as transit passes, vanpooling, bicycling, and parking associated with these things. The cost of these benefits are excluded from income in calculating income taxes. In 2016, employees could deduct a monthly maximum of $130 for employer-subsidized transit passes or vanpools. For employer-subsidized parking, the maximum amount was $255.

Physical Fitness

Some employers support physical fitness activities by incorporating on-site fitness centers or by sponsoring memberships in nearby health clubs. Presumably, employees who take advantage of these benefits tend to be absent less often, manage stress more effectively, and control their weight. Employers benefit from lower absenteeism and lower health insurance claims.

Employers deduct the cost of these benefits as a normal business expense. Employees may exclude the value of facility usage from income under the IRC certain benefits section for on-premises athletic facilities under the control of the employer.[27] Qualified physical fitness facilities include any gym or other athletic facility (e.g., swimming pool, tennis court, golf course) that is located on the premises of the employer, is operated by the employer, and is used almost entirely by employees of the employer, their spouses, and their dependent children.

The term *on-premises* is somewhat misleading. An on-premises facility must be a gym or other athletic facility located on an employer's property. An employer's property is not restricted to business locations (e.g., field offices, corporate headquarters, manufacturing facilities). The concept of employer control refers to either of the following: The employer operates the facility or has a contract with a facility, but the operation is still under the employer's control.[28]

Summary

This chapter reviews the fundamental concepts of company-sponsored accommodation and enhancement benefits. The chapter began with a review of the objectives of accommodation and enhancement benefits, followed by a description of several benefits. Tax regulations and various laws have a significant impact on the design of most accommodation and enhancement benefits. Changing pressures often justify the expense of these benefits to promote a stable and productive workforce.

Key Terms

accommodation benefits, 244

enhancement benefits, 244

employee assistance programs (EAPs), 246

Drug-Free Workplace Act of 1988, 246

outplacement assistance, 248

referral EAPs, 248

full-service EAPs, 248

in-house EAPs, 248

third-party providers, 248

consortium EAPs, 249

constructive confrontation, 249

International Employee Assistance Professionals Association (EAPA), 250

excepted benefits, 252

wellness programs, 252

back care programs, 253

smoking cessation, 253

stress management, 254

weight control and nutrition programs, 254

health risk appraisals, 254

family assistance programs, 256

elder care, 256

child care, 256

day care, 256

adoption benefits, 256

qualified adoption expenses, 257

educational assistance benefits, 258

educational assistance program, 258

working condition fringe benefit, 258

tuition reimbursement programs, 259

scholarship programs, 259

qualified scholarship programs, 259

qualified tuition reductions, 259

transportation services, 260

Clean Air Act Amendments of 1990, 260

de minimis transportation benefit, 260

qualified transportation benefits, 260

Discussion Questions

1. In which ways do accommodation and enhancement programs benefit employers? In which ways do they benefit employees?
2. Discuss the differences between EAPs and wellness benefits.
3. Do you think it is ethical to offer financial incentives to employees who participate in a wellness program? How about penalties for choosing not to participate? Explain your answers.
4. Some companies do not include educational benefits in their benefits plans. Discuss reasons why this may be the case.
5. Companies always face budget constraints, preventing them from offering every possible benefit. Identify one accommodation and enhancement benefit that you believe is most important and another that you believe is least important. Explain your answer.

Cases

1. Understanding Your Employee Benefits: Reaching Out for Help

As you walk out of your annual performance review meeting, you think that you might need some help. You've just received a generally poor review of your work by your manager, and while you are disappointed, you are not surprised. You have had a particularly difficult year, and you don't even feel motivated to work anymore. In fact, you have missed quite a few days of work and are worried about keeping your job if you miss many more days. Your manager knows that your decline is due to some personal problems, and she gave you a brochure about the company's EAP. As you return to your desk, you consider calling the toll-free telephone number on the brochure.

You mother passed away last year, which is when your problems started. You and your mother were close, and in addition to your suffering from the loss, she left behind some burdensome debts that you are now responsible for. At the same time, you made some unwise investments. All of these problems have been weighing heavily on you and distracting you from your work. You do like your job, but the distractions have made it difficult for you to feel motivated at work, and you have lost focus. Your performance review reflects your decline, and you know that something needs to change soon.

The brochure explains that your company offers a full-service EAP as a company benefit. The EAP is available to you at no charge and seems to be easy to use. The brochure explains that the EAP can help you understand and manage a wide variety of personal problems, such as depression, relationship problems, parenting challenges, and financial problems. The brochure notes that the program is confidential and that you will be able to talk with a counselor over the telephone to first understand your problem. The counselor may then continue to work with you or refer you to other services to get you the help you need.

While you think that the EAP may be able to help you, you are hesitant to call. Your manager knows your mother passed away, but she is not aware of your financial troubles. You are concerned that if she knew about your financial situation, she might think even more negatively about you. Further, during the performance review, your manager mentioned that if your performance does not improve in the future, you could eventually lose your job. You are concerned that if she learns more about your problems from the EAP, she may use some of the information to terminate your employment.

Even though your manager asked you to call the EAP, you think it might be better to just deal with your problems on your own. In addition to your concerns about the confidentiality of what you might share with a counselor, you just don't think that you are the type of person who needs to talk to a counselor. You set the brochure on your desk and try to get back to work as you consider whether you should make the call.

1. Are your concerns about the confidentiality of the service valid?
2. Do you think it would help you to call the EAP? Why or why not?

2. Managing Employee Benefits: Employee Wellness at Premier Financial Services

Shelly Austin is frustrated as she conducts the company's annual analysis of employee benefits. As the Director of Compensation and Benefits at Premier Financial Services, she is charged with ensuring that the company's benefit offerings provide value for the organization. This means that the benefits must be cost effective and also meet the needs of employees. Shelley's goal is for the employees to appreciate the benefits and also for the benefits to have a positive impact on the organization. As she reviews a collection of reports, it seems clear that the company has room for improvement in both cost-effectiveness and employee satisfaction.

Premier Financial Services provides a variety of financial products and services to high-income clients across the country. The company operates in a fast-paced, competitive, and high-stress environment. A majority of the employees are in sales positions and receive commission-based pay; thus, many employees work long hours to make more sales and increase their pay. These long working hours seem to lead many employees to neglect their health, as Shelly observes increasing premium costs associated with a high number of claims under the company's health insurance plan.

In addition to increasing health insurance costs, a recent employee satisfaction survey suggests that Premier Financial Services has some room to improve in creating a welcoming and engaging work environment. Among other things, employees report that they find their daily work days stressful and feel that it is challenging to manage their time on a daily basis. A surprising percentage of employees reported in the survey that they have considered looking for another job within the last six months. This generally negative mood is reflected by company profits, as Premier Financial has experienced a decline in overall sales over the past year. Further, Shelly has noted that there has been a higher rate of absenteeism over the last few months. In examining information from past years, the decline seems to be an ongoing trend.

In researching solutions to the challenge of lowering health insurance costs and improving the overall well-being of employees, Shelly has determined that Premier Financial should consider implementing a wellness program. The company currently does not offer any kind of wellness program benefits, and Shelly believes that even though there would be a cost to add a wellness program, in the long run, it could positively impact overall benefit costs and employee satisfaction. However, her research has uncovered many options for wellness programs, so she is not sure where to begin.

1. Would a wellness program benefit Premier Financial Services?
2. What components of a wellness program would be appropriate for this company?
3. If a wellness program is started, how can Shelly encourage employees to participate in the program?

Endnotes

1. "Why HMSA: ROI-HMSA," Health Management Systems of America. Accessed May 15, 2016, www.hmsanet.com/why-hmsa-roi.html.
2. U.S. Department of Labor, *Employee Benefits in the United States—March 2015*. Bulletin 2782, September 2015.
3. J. Ferguson, "EAP ROI: Getting the Most Bang for Your Buck." ESI Group, January 9, 2016, www.theeap.com.

4. 41 U.S.C. §701.

5. J. Calmes, "Hiring Hurdle: Finding Workers Who Can Pass a Drug Test." *New York Times* (online), May 17, 2016, www.nytimes.com.

6. V. M. Gibson, "The Ins and Outs of Outplacement," 80 *Management Review,* 1991: 59–61.

7. U.S. Equal Employment Opportunity Commission, "ADA: Disability Defined—in General." July 19, 2000, www.eeoc.gov.

8. ERISA §3(1); 29 U.S.C. §1002(1).

9. "Amendments to Excepted Benefits," 79 *Federal Register* 190, October 1, 2014: 59130–59137.

10. K. Baicker, D. Cutler, and Z. Song, "Workplace Wellness Programs Can Generate Savings," 29 *Health Affairs* 2, 2010: 304–311.

11. S. J. Wells, "Navigating the Expanding Wellness Industry," 56 *HR Magazine,* March 2011: 45–50.

12. U.S. Bureau of Labor Statistics, *Nonfatal Occupational Injuries and Illnesses Requiring Days Away from Work, 2014* (USDL-15-2205).

13. D. Witters and S. Agrawal, "Smoking Linked to $278 Billion in Losses for U.S. Employers." *Gallup* (online), September 26, 2013, www.gallup.com.

14. I.R.C. §213; I.R.S. Ruling 99–28, June 21, 1999.

15. I.R.S. Information Release 2003-103, September 3, 2003.

16. M. Blanding, "Workplace Stress Responsible for Up to $190B in Annual U.S. Healthcare Costs." *Forbes* (online), January 26, 2015, www.forbes.com.

17. U.S. Equal Employment Opportunity Commission, "EEOC's Final Rule on Employer Wellness Programs and Title I of the Americans with Disabilities Act," May 17, 2016, www.eeoc.gov; U.S. Equal Employment Opportunity Commission, "EEOC's Final Rule on Employer Wellness Programs and the Genetic Information Nondiscrimination Act," May 17, 2016, www.eeoc.gov.

18. G. Spencer, Nov. "Projection of the Population of the United States, by Age, Sex, Race, and Hispanic Origin: 1992 to 2050. *Current Population Reports* P-25, No. 1092. Washington, DC: U.S. Government Printing Office, November 1992.

19. U.S. Census Bureau, *Statistical Abstracts of the United States: 2012.* 2011. Accessed March 22, 2012, www.census.gov.

20. U.S. Department of Labor, *Employee Benefits in the United States—March 2015.* Bulletin 2782, September 2015.

21. *Ibid.*

22. Child Welfare Information Gateway, "Employer-Provided Adoption Benefits." February 2011, https://www.childwelfare.gov/pubs/f-benefi/.

23. J. Held, N. Mrkvicka, and J. Stich, "Educational Assistance Benefits: 2015 Survey Results," International Foundation of Employee Benefit Plans (IFEBP), 2015. Brookfield, WI: IFEBP.

24. I.R.C. §127(c)(1), amended by P.L. 107–16, §411(b).

25. I.R.C. §132(d).

26. 42 U.S.C. §85.

27. I.R.C. §132(j)(4)(B).

28. *Ibid.*

Part Four

Extending Employee Benefits: Design and Global Issues

Managing the Employee-Benefits System

Learning Objectives

In this chapter, you will gain an understanding of:

1. Differences between the traditional and flexible approaches to benefits designs.
2. Essentials of communicating the benefits program.
3. Methods for managing benefits costs.
4. Outsourcing employee benefits.

We have spent considerable time reviewing the rationale and context for offering employee benefits as well as the most typical employee-benefits offerings in U.S. companies. In this chapter, we will consider alternative structures of employee-benefits plans and methods for communicating benefits to employees. In addition, we will review various cost-control methods, which are important as the costs of employee benefits rise. Finally, we will give consideration to whether companies should manage employee-benefits programs internally or outsource this activity to third-party administrators.

A COMPARISON OF TRADITIONAL BENEFITS PLANS AND FLEXIBLE BENEFITS PLANS

Traditional benefits plans contain the same set of benefits for each employee. Offering the same benefits to all employees creates administrative ease and represents a one-size-fits-all approach. Increasingly, companies are replacing fixed benefits plans with flexible benefits plans, which give employees a choice of benefits. These two approaches to benefits design will be discussed. Exhibits 10.1 and 10.2 illustrate the typical structures of traditional and flexible benefits plans. A cafeteria plan design represents one type of flexible benefits plans. Cafeteria plans meet requirements set in the Internal Revenue Code (IRC) Section 125, which we discuss shortly.

A One-Size-Fits-All Approach

Traditionally, a company offered its employees a predetermined set and level of benefits, based largely on cost considerations. For example, every employee of Company A received the same set of benefits, including health care and life insurance. In addition, every employee received the same level of benefits regardless of need or preferences—for instance, all employees of Company A received life insurance coverage equal to their annual salaries or wages (computed over a one-year period). From the employee's perspective, life insurance benefits in any amount are better than no life insurance benefits at all.

Differences in employee needs and preferences strongly influence the adequacy of this company-sponsored benefit. Oftentimes, relatively young employees without dependent children or a spouse (or life partner) do not see the value in purchasing life insurance because they do not have responsibility for ensuring the financial welfare of family members. However, employees with dependents usually deem life insurance as an essential benefit. Other employees do not elect to enroll in a company's health-care plan because they receive coverage under a spouse's plan. Most companies use cafeteria plan designs to help ensure that

EXHIBIT 10.1
Traditional
Benefit Plan
Structure

Source: J.S. Rosen-
bloom, *Handbook of*
Employee Benefits.
New York: McGraw-
Hill, 2001.

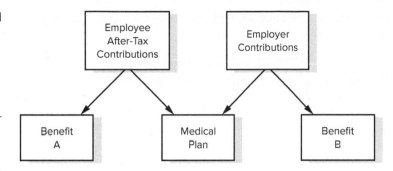

EXHIBIT 10.2
Comprehensive
Cafeteria Plan

Source: J.S. Rosen-
bloom, *Handbook of*
Employee Benefits.
New York: McGraw-
Hill, 2001.

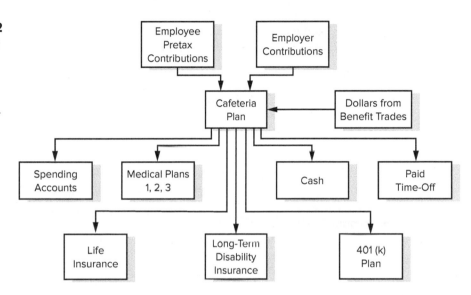

employees' needs and preferences are being met. Employers are most likely to see a return on investment by offering choices. Relevant benefit alternatives should help with recruitment and retention.

Employer Choice to Customize Benefits

Companies can customize employee benefits offerings by offering **flexible bene-fits** or **cafeteria plans.** Employees can choose from among a set of designated benefits and different levels of these benefits. Under these plans, employers grant employees the opportunity to accept or reject certain benefits. For instance, an employee may pass over day care benefits in favor of life insurance. The choice of life insurance provides the option of accepting the basic insurance coverage (an amount equal to annual salary) or to pay for additional coverage (an amount equal to three times annual salary). Companies implement cafeteria plans to meet the challenges of diversity. Limited evidence suggests positive reactions to flexible plans, including benefits satisfaction, overall job satisfaction, pay satisfaction, and understanding of benefits, which increases after the implementation of a flexible benefits plan.

Cafeteria Plans under Section 125

IRC Section 125 offers participants certain benefits on a pretax basis. Participants in a cafeteria plan must be given the choice between at least one taxable benefit (such as cash) and one qualified benefit. A plan offering only a choice between taxable benefits is not a Section 125 plan. **Qualified benefits** refer to employer-sponsored benefits for which an employee may exclude the cost from federal income tax calculation. Throughout this book, we have considered many employee benefits. For the purposes of Section 125 cafeteria plans, some choices are not considered a qualified benefit. It is important to distinguish between allowable and prohibited qualified benefits. Exhibit 10.3 lists the allowable qualified benefits and the prohibited qualified benefits in Section 125 plans.

Additional Guidelines for Section 125 Plans

Employers must follow several guidelines to maintain a Section 125 cafeteria plan. Specifically, the plan must:

- Be in writing.
- Allow employees the opportunity to choose between two or more benefits, consisting of at least one nontaxable benefit and at least one taxable benefit, such as cash.
- Permit only current and former employees to participate, as long as the plan is not established principally for the benefit of former employees.
- Require participants to make yearly benefit choices before the beginning of the plan year, except for making changes in benefit choices necessitated by changes in life circumstances, such as electing additional health-care coverage immediately following the birth or adoption of a child.
- Prohibit any benefit that defers an employee's receipt of compensation from year to year.
- Meet nondiscrimination requirements.

EXHIBIT 10.3
Allowable and
Prohibited
Qualified
Employee
Benefits in
Section 125
Cafeteria Plans

Allowable Qualified Benefits

- Employer-provided accident and health plan.
- Group term life insurance.
- Health savings accounts, including distributions to pay long-term care services.
- Dependent care assistance.
- Adoption assistance.

Prohibited Qualified Benefits

- Medical savings accounts.
- Scholarships.
- Educational assistance programs or scholarships.
- Fringe benefits such as employer-sponsored transportation services.

The first five requirements are relatively straightforward. However, the last requirement is more complex, warranting further discussion. **Nondiscrimination rules** prohibit employers from giving preferential treatment to highly compensated participants and key employees. For example, employer contributions to retirement plans that amount to 15 percent of highly compensated or key employees' annual salaries (as defined in Chapter 11) violate nondiscrimination rules when employer contributions to other employees are only 6 percent of salaries. Satisfying nondiscrimination rules permits plan participants to take tax deductions for qualified benefits. Failure to meet nondiscrimination rules eliminates tax benefits for one or both groups of employees: (a) highly compensated or key employees, and (b) employees who are classified neither as highly compensated employees nor as key employees. The nature of the violation determines which group forfeits tax benefits. Three possible violations relate to eligibility, benefits, and concentration:

- *Eligibility.* Companies have at least some nonkey employees in the plan.
- *Benefits.* All employees should receive the same amount of employeer contributions, the same eligibility rules should be the same for all employees, and the same benefits must be provided to all employees.
- *Concentration.* The value of nontaxable benfits provided to key employees cannont exceed 25 percent of the total nontaxable benefits provided under the plan.

Types of Flexible Benefit Plan Arrangements

Employers design flexible benefits plans in a variety of ways. The four most common types of these arrangements include salary reduction plans, modular plans, core-plus-option plans, and mix-and-match plans. Exhibit 10.4 summarizes these four plans and displays their relative flexibility and cost.

Pretax Salary Reduction Plans

Pretax salary reduction plans permit employees to set aside a portion of wages or salary each year on a pretax basis for qualified benefits expenses. In other words, employees exclude allocated wages or salaries from the calculation of annual federal income taxes or state income taxes. As we discussed in Chapter 2, this exclusion creates a strong incentive for participation. Employees enter into annual salary reduction agreements before the start of each benefits plan year.

Two well-known versions of salary reduction agreements are available: flexible spending accounts and premium-only plans. **Flexible spending accounts** permit employees to pay for certain benefits expenses (e.g., dental, medical, vision, or day care expenses) or to pay the premium or cost for at least one of these benefits. Usually, flexible spending accounts apply to expenses that exceed regular benefits limits. Prior to each plan year, employees elect the amount of salary-reduction dollars they wish to allocate to this kind of plan. Employers then use this money to reimburse employees for eligible expenses

EXHIBIT 10.4 Flexible Benefit Plans

Source: M.W. Barringer and G.T. Milkovich, "A Theoretical Explanation of the Adoption and Design of Flexible Benefits Plans," 23 *Academy of Management Review* 2, 1998, 305–324.

← Low Flexibility ———————————————————————————————————— High Flexibility →

Low Cost			High Cost
Salary Reduction Only	**Modular Options**	**Core Plus Options**	**Mix and Match**
Premium conversion	The employee can choose from among several different combinations of benefits (usually the same types of benefits but different levels of benefits).	*Core*	Flexible credits are provided, and the employee can purchase any type and level of coverage of offered.
The employee pays a premium for insurance with a pretax salary reduction.		The employee receives basic coverage in certain areas (e.g., health, life, and/or disability insurance).	
Flexible spending account Pretax salary reductions fund an account for paying uncovered medical or dependent care bills.		*Plus* The employee has flexible credits to purchase additional coverage in the core area or in supplemental areas, such as child care, vacation days, or a trade-in for cash.	

Notes: Flexible spending accounts may be included in any of the plans described. Medical plan options may include multiple types (HMOs, fee for service) and levels (e.g., high/medium/low deductible and coinsurance rates), or they may be limited to a choice between a single fee-for-service plan and an HMO.

incurred during the plan year. Exhibit 10.5 illustrates the features typical of flexible spending accounts. **Premium-only plans** enable employees to pay their share of the cost to receive health care, dental care, and other company-sponsored health plans.

Modular Plans

With **modular plans,** an employer offers numerous fixed benefits packages to meet the lifecycle needs and priorities of different employee groups. Examples of groups include single employees with no dependents, single parents, married workers with dependents, and employees nearing retirement.

Under this arrangement, the costs of these benefits packages vary, based on which benefits are included and their prices. An employer decides upon a fixed amount of money it will spend each year to provide a benefits package. Usually, the fixed amount equals the lowest cost among the available modular packages. Employees contribute the cost difference between a more extensive benefits package and the lowest-cost package.

EXHIBIT 10.5 Flexible Spending Account (FSA) Program

The Flexible Spending Account (FSA) program is an optional benefit that gives employees the opportunity to use tax-free dollars to pay eligible dependent and/or medical care expenses. The FSA program offers two plans:

- **The Medical Care Assistance Program (MCAP)** allows you to use pretax dollars to pay eligible, medically necessary expenses that you, your spouse, and your dependents incur during the plan year.
- **The Dependent Care Assistance Program (DCAP)** enables you to use pretax dollars to pay eligible dependent care expenses you incur during the plan year.

How Flexible Spending Works

Employees may contribute up to a maximum of $2,550 in 2016 with pretax dollars for each program. Contributions are deducted from your paycheck and deposited into your FSA account before state, federal, and Social Security taxes are withheld. This amount does not appear on your W-2 Form as taxable income, so it lowers your taxable income, leaving more money to spend and fewer taxes to pay.

How to Enroll

Read the FSA booklet to ensure your expenses meet the IRS/FSA requirements and are eligible for MCAP/DCAP. During the benefit choice period, enroll in MCAP/DCAP by completing the appropriate forms and submitting them to your group insurance representative. New employees, or employees who have an eligible change in status, may enroll within 60 days of their date of hire or change in status. Eligible changes in status (or, qualifying event) include:

- Marriage, divorce, or legal separation.
- Birth or adoption of a child.
- Death of a spouse or child.
- Change in residence or work location that affects benefits eligibility for you or your covered dependent(s).
- Your child(ren) meets (or fails to meet) the plan's eligibility rules (e.g., student status changes).
- You or one of your covered dependents gain or lose other benefits coverage due to a change in employment status (e.g., beginning or ending a job).

FSA Savings Example

The following is an example of how FSA works:

	Participating in FSA	Not Participating in FSA
Annual pay	$35,000	$35,000
Pre-tax contribution to reimbursement account	($1,500)[a]	$0
Taxable income	$33,500	$35,000
Federal income and social security taxes	($7,107)[b]	($7,597)[c]
After-tax dollars spent on eligible expenses	$0	($1,500)[d]
Spendable income	$26,393	$25,903
Tax savings with the FSA	$490	$0

[a]This value is subtracted from annual pay.
[b,c,d]These values are subtracted from taxable income.

EXHIBIT 10.6
A Sample
Core-Plus-
Option Plan

The core-plus-option plan contains two sets of benefits: *core benefits* and *optional benefits*. All employees receive a minimum level of *core benefits*:

- Term life insurance equal to annual salary.
- Health protection coverage (fee-for-service plan, HMO, PPO, high-deductible plan) for the employee and dependents.
- Disability insurance.

All employees receive credits equal to 4 to 7 percent of salary, which can be used to purchase *optional benefits*:

- Dental insurance for the employee and dependents.
- Vision insurance for the employee and dependents.
- Additional life insurance coverage.
- Paid vacation time up to 10 days per year.

Core-Plus-Option Plans

Core-plus-option plans extend a pre-established set of benefits such as health-care and retirement plans as a program core. More often than not, core benefits are mandatory for all employees. Beyond the core, employees may choose from a collection of optional benefits that suit their personal needs. Companies establish upper limits of benefits values available to each employee. If employees do not choose the maximum amount of benefits, employers may offer an option of trading extra benefits credits for cash. Exhibit 10.6 illustrates the choices of a typical core-plus plan.

Mix-and-Match Plans

An employer decides the annual amount it will spend to fund each employee's benefits package. **Mix-and-match plans** permit employees to purchase any benefit (and benefit level). Companies award flexible credits to purchase these plans. Each credit equals $1.00, and the costs of each benefit are clearly communicated to employees. For instance, a company grants each employee 3,500 flexible credits. An employee chooses to purchase health-care coverage for the year (1,800 credits) with additional coverage for his spouse and child (750 credits), totaling 2,550 credits. This employee may use the remaining 950 credits to purchase additional benefits or trade the credits for dollars.

COMMUNICATING THE EMPLOYEE-BENEFITS PROGRAM

Benefits communication is an essential feature of effective plans. The law and good business sense establish the necessity for benefits communication. Sound communication programs facilitate these objectives. It is obvious that employees who are not aware of particular discretionary benefits will not gain from these offerings, and employers would be needlessly spending money. Moreover, simply communicating the existence of these benefits is insufficient. There are two broad considerations of sound benefits communication programs, which include:

- Meeting legally mandated requirements.
- "Good business sense" communication issues.

Legal Considerations in Benefits Communication

Legally, employers must satisfy disclosure written requirements set forth in the Employee Retirement Income Security Act of 1974 (ERISA). Employers satisfy these requirements by providing employees with *summary plan descriptions* and *summaries of material modifications.* These documents should not presume expert knowledge about design features. ERISA specifies that written notices be written so the "average" participant can understand them.

Summary Plan Description

A **summary plan description** describes the following information:

- Names and addresses of the employees responsible for developing and administering the benefits plan.
- A description and explanation of the benefits such as health-care and retirement plans.
- Disclosure of employee rights under ERISA.
- Eligibility criteria for participating in the benefits program.
- Conditions under which an employee becomes disqualified for benefits or is suspended.
- Claims procedures for receiving payments (e.g., reimbursement for medical expenses) and for appealing denial of claims.
- Whether a retirement plan is insured by the Pension Benefit Guarantee Corporation (PBGC). The PBGC issues insurance to protect an employee's vested retirement savings when the retirement plan becomes insolvent or the retirement plan is terminated (Chapter 3).

Summary plan descriptions may be very lengthy, depending on the number of benefits. Exhibit 10.7 shows an excerpt from a company's summary plan description of its health-care plans.

Employers are obligated to distribute summary plan descriptions to employees and the U.S. Department of Labor within 120 days of the plan becoming subject to ERISA's reporting and disclosure requirements (Chapter 3). In addition, ERISA requires that employees or their beneficiaries receive a summary plan description within 90 days of becoming a plan participant. Finally, employers must supply participants with completely updated summary plan descriptions no later than 210 days following every fifth plan year even when the benefits remain unchanged.

EXHIBIT 10.7 Health Plan Overview

Source: Illinois Central Management Services, *State of Illinois Benefits Handbook: Fiscal Year July, 2007–June, 2008.* 2007.

Depending on residence, there may be several types of health plans from which to choose. The offerings change each year. Refer to the benefit choice options booklet for the current offerings.

Types of Health Plans

- Managed care plans
  Health Maintenance Organizations (HMOs)
  Point-of-Service (POS) plans

Each plan provides medical, pharmaceutical, and mental health/substance abuse treatment benefits. However, the covered services, benefit levels, exclusions, and restrictions on service providers differ.

In making choices, consider the following: health status, coverage needs, and service preferences. Premiums differ among the various plans, too. Dependents must have the same health and dental plan as the member under whom they are covered.

Managed Care Plans

Over the years, as health-care costs continue to rise, more and more employers offer managed health-care plans. Individuals receiving medical care under a managed care plan are encouraged to have annual preventive physicals and seek early treatment if they become ill.

Managed care plans negotiate rates with participating network physicians, hospitals, and pharmacies. In turn, the plans offer cost-effective medical care with lower out-of-pocket costs.

HMO plan participants choose a doctor or provider location from those participating in the plan's provider network. This doctor or location becomes the primary care provider (PCP). HMO plans provide a comprehensive network for care. All routine medical care, hospitalizations, and referrals for specialized medical care must be coordinated under the direction of the PCP. Services provided without approval/referral from a PCP will not be covered. Plan participants are responsible for 100 percent of the cost of out-of-network care. Coverage outside the HMO area is limited to emergency services only.

A point-of-service plan combines HMO-like benefits and traditional health coverage. POS plan participants choose a PCP from those participating in the plan's provider network. Care received in-network under the direction of the PCP is provided at maximum benefits. A POS plan participant also has the option to go out of network for eligible services and receive reduced benefits with deductibles and coinsurance. Managed care plans contract with a network of physicians and hospitals to deliver or arrange for the delivery of covered services.

Summary of Material Modification

A **summary of material modification** describes important (i.e., material) changes to the benefits plan. Material information applies to changes in the benefits program, including plan administrators, claims procedures, eligibility rules, and vesting provisions of retirement plans. ERISA obligates employers to distribute summaries of material modifications within 210 days after the end of the plan year in which the material change occurred. Summaries of material modifications go to employees and the Department of Labor.

The "Good Business Sense" of Benefits Communication

An effective communication program should have three primary objectives:

- To create an awareness of, and appreciation for, the way current benefits improve the financial security as well as the physical and mental well-being of employees.
- To provide a high level of understanding about available benefits.
- To encourage the wise use of benefits.

A variety of media can be used to communicate such information to employees. Printed brochures that abstract the key features of the benefits program are useful for conveying the "big picture" and help potential employees compare benefits offerings with those offered by other companies they may be considering. Once employees join the company, initial group meetings with benefits administrators or audiovisual presentations can detail the elements of the company's benefits program. Shortly after group meetings or the audiovisual presentations (usually within a month), new employees should meet individually with benefits administrators, sometimes known as counselors, to select benefits options. Increasingly, companies are moving away from this approach by eliminating group or individual meetings with benefits counselors. Instead, they expect new employees to make their choices based on written explanations of benefits. In any event, after selecting benefits, the company should provide personal benefits statements that detail the scope of coverage and value of each component for the current year. Exhibit 10.8 illustrates a personal statement of benefits.

More recent communications methods include a company's intranet and social media. A company intranet is a useful way to communicate benefits information to employees on an ongoing basis beyond the legally required written documents. In an era of the paperless office, employees are less likely to have written materials readily available. Employees can review general information about the benefits program whenever they want. Exhibit 10.9 lists general information about the kinds of available information.

Social media tools are currently less common methods for communicating benefits information. However, Facebook, podcasts, and Twitter may become an increasingly popular tool for the younger generations of employees. Here are some examples of possible social media use in benefits communication. For instance, employees could use Facebook to post questions about coworkers' experiences with different savings accounts, including FSA and HSA accounts. Experience with particular benefits choices can be a useful supplement to formal descriptions. Companies could use Twitter as one method for making employees aware of changes in employee benefits features or offerings.

EXHIBIT 10.8 Employee-Benefits Statement

Source: University of Illinois, Office of Human Resources, Urbana–Champaign, 2001.

Benefits Statement
Employee Name: Brown, Michael
Date Employed: 05–21–1995

The following benefit information is based on the pay period from 10–21–2016 through 11–20–2017.

Health Section
Medical: Personal Care HMO
(Includes vision care plan)

	Monthly Cost Breakdown				
For You Only	**For 0 Dependent(s)**	**Total You Pay**	**State Pays**	**Total Cost**
243.14	0	35.50	207.64	243.14

Dental: Quality Care Dental (Employee Only)

	Monthly Cost Breakdown				
For You Only	**For 0 Dependent(s)**	**Total You Pay**	**State Pays**	**Total Cost**
16.32	0	7.50	8.82	16.32

Insurance Section
State Basic Life: Minnesota Life Insurance

	Monthly Cost Breakdown		
Coverage Amount	**Total You Pay**	**State Pays**	**Total Cost**
105,000.00	0	43.06	43.06

State Optional Life: Minnesota Life Insurance 3 × Salary

	Monthly Cost Breakdown		
Coverage Amount	**Total You Pay**	**State Pays**	**Total Cost**
315,000.00	28.35	0.00	28.35

Disability: Employee Retirement System

	Monthly Cost Breakdown		
Coverage Amount	**Total You Pay**	**State Pays**	**Total Cost**
50% of salary (52,500.00)	0.00	87.50	87.50

Defined Benefit Retirement Plan			
8% of salary (105,000.00)	700.00	700.00	1,400.00

EXHIBIT 10.9   Employee-Benefits Overview

Source: University Office of Human Resources, University of Illinois, Urbana–Champaign, 2001.

This section is designed to provide detailed information regarding your benefits as a University of Illinois employee. It will give you a comprehensive explanation of each benefit and the resources you will need to initiate enrollment, make changes, or find answers to questions regarding your benefits.

Please select from the following categories:

- *Announcements.* Provides announcements of upcoming sign-up periods or events and updated information relating to your benefits.
- *Benefits Directory.* Provides a listing of staff members, including addresses, phone numbers, and e-mail addresses for the Benefits Service Center and each campus.
- *Benefit Choice.* Benefit Choice is an annual open enrollment period that allows employees to make changes to their State of Illinois health, dental, and life insurance coverages and enroll or reenroll in flexible spending accounts.
- *Benefit Forms.* Provides links to printable and online benefit forms.
- *Benefits Statement.* Provides a statement outlining your current benefit enrollments and instructions for accessing that information.
- *Benefits Summary.* Provides a detailed, comprehensive description of each benefit plan and its provisions.
- *Frequently Asked Questions.* Provides a list of commonly asked questions relating to your benefits.
- *Leave Information.* Provides time-off related information for benefits such as family medical leave, sick leave, and vacation leave.
- *Retirement Planning Seminars.* Provides dates and sign-up information.
- *SURS Information.* Provides links to information on the State University Retirement System.

MANAGING THE COSTS OF EMPLOYEE BENEFITS

As has been discussed throughout this book, managing the costs of benefits programs is essential because the already high costs continually increase. In this section, alternative methods to assist companies in managing benefits costs are introduced:

- Employee contributions
- Waiting periods
- High-deductible plans
- Employee education
- Utilization reviews
- Case management
- Provider payment systems
- Lifestyle interventions

Employee Contributions

Employee contributions help companies save money by requiring that employees pay a nominal amount of the total costs to provide particular benefits. Employees typically share the cost of benefits with pretax contributions or after-tax contributions. As we have seen throughout the book, various tax regulations permit employees to exclude contributions from annual income before calculating income tax obligations. For review, these are called **pretax contributions. After-tax contributions** do not reduce the amount of annual income subject to income tax. For instance, companies expect employees to share the cost of health-care coverage with pretax contributions; these companies base employee contributions on their total annual earnings, as shown in the following example.

Annual Pay	Monthly Employee Contribution
Less than $20,000	$35.00
$20,000–$29,999	$45.00
$30,000–$44,999	$55.00
$45,000–$59,999	$65.00
$60,000 or more	$70.00

Waiting Periods

Companies impose one or more waiting periods to limit participation in the benefits program. **Waiting periods** specify the minimum number of months or years an employee must remain employed before becoming eligible for one or more benefits. Waiting periods often correspond to the length of probationary periods. Companies impose probationary periods to judge a newcomer's job performance, and they explicitly reserve the right to terminate employees who demonstrate low job performance. The use of waiting periods helps companies control costs. Companies might consider extending waiting periods for as long as possible for maximum cost savings. However, there are limits. The Affordable Care Act limits waiting periods before participation in employer-sponsored health-care programs to a maximum of 90 days.

High-Deductible Plans

In Chapter 5, we discussed the role of high-deductible health-care plans in cost control, which shift more responsibility for the costs of health care from employers to employees in terms of higher deductibles. High-deductible plans result in immediate cost savings to companies through lower premiums.

Some companies have adopted high-deductible workers' compensation plans. Traditionally, companies purchased guaranteed coverage, which means that the insurance company would administer the program, undertake all risk, and be responsible for all financial obligations. Under this approach, companies would not have significant deductible costs. Companies pay substantially lower premiums in exchange for agreeing to pay up to a predetermined deductible amount. The guaranteed approach ensures a substantial expenditure regardless of whether any workers become injured or ill. Under the same scenario, a company's expenditures for workers' compensation stand to be substantially less with high-deductible programs.

Employee Education

Educating employees about the cost of health care is essential to controlling the rising costs of health-care programs, because past employer tendency not to educate employees about costs may have inadvertently led to overuse for two reasons. First, since the 1940s and 1950s, most medium- and large-scale employers have offered health-care coverage to employees. Offering health-care coverage provided companies with lucrative tax breaks, and including health care in the benefits package helped companies recruit and retain valued employees. Most employees viewed health-care coverage along with other benefits as a privilege because these were included as standard benefits, and in years past, employees often did not pay much for these benefits. Second, fee-for-service plans were quite common decades ago. By design, these plans provided individuals with substantial freedom to go directly to doctors of their choice, oftentimes to very expensive medical specialists even when unnecessary.

Even as costs rose, employers continued to offer generous coverage while also absorbing higher costs. Since the U.S. economy experienced economic recessions in the 2000s and competitive pressures forced more companies to carefully audit their costs, employers shift more costs to employees by having them pay a greater share for the benefits. Educating employees about health-care costs and the reasons for rising costs should promote cost containment, particularly when coupled with higher required employee contributions. Moreover, educating employees about the costs of health care, as well as the benefits of preventive wellness programs, should help employers get better control of their costs.

Utilization Reviews

Health-care providers conduct **utilization reviews** to evaluate the quality of specific health-care services. Employers offering group health benefits and insurers consult utilization reviews to ensure that medical treatments are medically appropriate. Sponsors of these reviews hire medical doctors and registered nurses to carry out utilization reviews. These medical professionals rely on professional practice standards established by medical associations to judge the medical appropriateness of treatment and quality of patient care.

Three types of utilization reviews may be considered. The first, **prospective reviews** or **precertification reviews,** evaluate the appropriateness of proposed medical treatment as a condition for authorizing payment. Prospective reviews entail:

- Verifying a patient's coverage.
- Determining whether the health plan covers the treatment.

- Judging whether the proposed treatment is medically appropriate.
- Specifying whether a second surgical opinion is necessary.

Second, **concurrent reviews** focus on current hospital patients. Insurers conduct concurrent reviews to judge whether additional inpatient hospitalization is medically necessary. Oftentimes, these reviews take place approximately one day before a patient is scheduled to be discharged from the hospital. Alternatively, insurers conduct utilization reviews shortly after hospital admission.

Third, **retrospective reviews** take place prior to an insurance company's disbursement of benefits. Retrospective reviews have two main objectives, starting with a determination of whether the health-care program covers the patient, the medical conditions, and the medical treatment. These reviews also judge whether claims are fraudulent by confirming that medical treatments were administered and were appropriate for the medical condition.

Case Management

Many health-care plans use independent **case management** companies to ensure participants receive essential medical attention on a cost-effective basis. Usually, registered nurses or social workers collaborate with physicians to balance the medical needs of the patient and cost containment. Serious health problems arising from injuries or illnesses may be acute (possibly life threatening) or chronic (ongoing). Exhibit 10.10 lists examples of serious health conditions that may warrant case management.

Provider Payment Systems

Provider payment systems refer to payment arrangements between managed care insurers and health-care providers. Managed care plans establish provider payment systems to control the costs of health care. Fee-for-service plans generally do not include this feature because health-care providers seek reimbursement after rendering services.

EXHIBIT 10.10 **Serious Health** **Conditions** **Warranting Case** **Management**	Acquired immune deficiency syndrome	Multiple sclerosis
	Alzheimer's disease	Muscular dystrophy
	Amputations	Neurological disorders
	Cancer	Organ transplants
	Cardiovascular conditions	Paralysis
	Cerebral palsy	Pregnancy complications
	Cerebral vascular accident (stroke)	Premature birth
	Chemical dependency	Psychiatric disorders
	Congenital anomaly	Renal failure
	Head injuries	Respiratory ailments
	Major burns	Spinal cord injuries

Provider payment systems negotiate acceptable payment amounts to participating physicians, health-care facilities, and pharmacies for the duration of the contract, (oftentimes, up to a few years). Agreements may include one or more cost-saving features, including percentage discounts, capped fee schedules, partial capitation, and full capitation.

As the term implies, **percentage discounts** reduce the amounts of health-care providers' usual charges. Under this arrangement, health-care providers agree to the percentage of discounts. Percentage discounts are not always the most cost-effective methods for two reasons. First, managed care plans do not enforce a limit on the number of services, making it difficult to anticipate total costs. Second, health-care providers are free to increase their "regular" fees, adding to total costs.

Capped fee schedules set maximum dollar amounts for each service. Similar to percentage discounts, capped fee schedules do not limit the volume of services, making it difficult to anticipate total costs. Managed care plans use usual, customary, and reasonable fees as a starting point for establishing capped fee schedules. From there, they set maximums by limiting payments to a percentage of usual, customary, and reasonable fees.

Partial capitation systems apply to primary care physicians. These systems pay primary care physicians a fixed dollar amount for each patient assigned to them. It is not uncommon for current patients to change primary care physicians or to leave the managed care plan altogether, or for new patients to join managed care plans. As a result, the number of patients associated with each primary care physician varies over time. Partial capitation systems render payments to primary care physicians monthly to account for variability in patient load. These payment systems make it easier to anticipate total costs because physicians are rewarded for the total number of assigned patients.

Full capitation systems also pay primary care physicians a fixed amount for each assigned patient; however, the actual amount may vary from patient to patient. Under this system, managed care plans hold primary care physicians accountable for the cost of services rendered to each assigned patient. Managed care plans deduct all, or a percentage of, the costs from the allotted maximum amount. Full capitation systems effectively control costs because total outlay does not increase with the volume of services. Unlike percentage discount systems and capped fee schedules, full capitation systems create financial disincentives for primary care physicians to authorize treatments and referrals to specialists.

Lifestyle Interventions

Lifestyle interventions refer to any activity that changes how a person lives life. For example, stopping cigarette smoking is an example of a lifestyle change that can be brought on by participation in a smoking cessation program. Chapter 9 discussed a variety of wellness programs, which, if followed by employees, should lead to lifestyle changes and fit with the idea of lifestyle intervention. In most companies, employees *choose* whether to participate in wellness programs, thus initiating a lifestyle intervention. However, some companies believe that it is their responsibility to decide whether such intervention is mandatory.

For example, Scotts Miracle-Gro Company made controversial headlines by setting a policy to terminate employees who did not quit smoking on or off the job. The company offered resources necessary to help employees quit smoking. Problems arose when a newly hired employee, Scott Rodrigues, was fired when a drug test identified nicotine in his urine. The presence of nicotine in his system established that he violated the company's no-smoking policy. Rodrigues challenged the company's policy in the U.S. District Court (Massachusetts), alleging that he was fired because he smoked cigarettes in private, off-duty, away from work. In addition, Rodrigues claimed that his right to privacy was violated when the company required him to submit to a urinalysis for nonmedical reasons. Further, he alleged that the Scotts Company's policy violated his rights under the Massachusetts Privacy Statute and constituted a violation of his civil rights. Finally, Rodrigues maintained that the company's antismoking policy violated ERISA because it interfered with receipt of medical benefits. In more general terms, this case challenged the employer right to control employees' personal lives and activities by prohibiting legal private conduct the employer finds to be dangerous, distasteful, or disagreeable. The judge ruled against Rodrigues on all counts, indicating that his privacy rights were not violated because he was seen smoking in public.

Except in states where it is unlawful to terminate employees who smoke off the job, the court's ruling set the stage for employers to consider, possibly implement, policies similar to the Scotts Company's nonsmoking policy. Employers may follow the Scotts Company's example with the goal of reducing employee absences due to smoking-related illnesses and the cost of health care. Employers may also consider similar policies against behaviors such as unhealthy eating, which may cause excessive weight gain.

OUTSOURCING THE BENEFITS FUNCTION

Until now, the discussions in this chapter have been based on the presumption that employers manage and administer the entire benefits function internally with a staff of benefits professionals, including managers and support staff. However, some employers chose to outsource some or all of the benefits functions (and other HR functions, for that matter). **Outsourcing** refers to a contractual agreement by which an employer transfers responsibility to a third-party provider to manage one or more benefits. In the case of benefits, third-party providers are independent companies with expertise in benefits design and administration. Outsourcing agreements remain in effect from a few months to a few years.

Outsourcing some or all benefits administration is on the rise. On average, companies outsource roughly two-fifths of all their benefits functions, and more than one-third of companies have increased outsourcing in the past two years, and the top reason companies outsource benefits functions is for expertise.[1] Other less-common reasons for outsourcing include technology, costs, and risk. Some of the most common fully outsourced benefit services include the administration of employee assistance programs (EAPs), flexible spending accounts (FSAs), and continuation of health-care coverage mandated by COBRA.

Outsourcing some or all benefits administration can be very expensive in the short run because most or all contract fees are due up front. Over time, efficient arrangements can be less costly than devoting several employees' time to benefits administration, especially when flexibility allows companies to invest in critical activities that don't lend themselves well to outsourcing as is the case with product design.

Summary

This chapter describes the importance of considering whether to implement fixed benefits programs or flexible benefits programs. Making this choice, in part, requires a review and interpretation of internal information (e.g., the needs and preferences of the workforce) and external information (e.g., how competitors choose benefits offerings and the structure of those programs). Companies continually balance the needs and preferences of employees with cost considerations, requiring consideration of cost-control methods. The treatment of benefits communications in this chapter emphasizes legal mandates for what and how to communicate benefit plans as well as the good business sense that goes along with offering benefits. Finally, the chapter concludes with a review of outsourcing and points out some of the broad issues that companies will have to face when designing employee-benefits programs.

Key Terms

flexible benefits, 269
cafeteria plans, 269
qualified benefits, 270
nondiscrimination rules, 271
pretax salary reduction plans, 271
flexible spending accounts, 271
premium-only plans, 272
modular plans, 272
core-plus-option plans, 274

mix-and-match plans, 274
summary plan description, 275
summary of material modification, 276
pretax contributions, 280
after-tax contributions, 280
waiting periods, 280
utilization reviews, 281
prospective reviews, 281
precertification reviews, 281

concurrent reviews, 282
retrospective reviews, 282
case management, 282
provider payment systems, 282
percentage discounts, 283
capped fee schedules, 283
partial capitation, 283
full capitation, 283
outsourcing, 284

Discussion Questions

1. Respond to the following statement: "Flexible benefits plans are more trouble than they are worth." Do you agree or disagree with this statement? Provide a rationale for your answer.

2. Discuss how IRC Section 125 plans create advantages for employees and employers.

3. What is the "good business sense" of benefits communications?

4. List and describe three specific benefits cost-control methods. What are some of the drawbacks to using one or more of these methods?

5. Should companies dictate what employees can do after work hours? Explain your answer.

Cases

1. Understanding Your Employee Benefits: Managing Your Health-Care Expenses

It is currently the annual open enrollment period for employee benefits at your company, and you have several decisions ahead of you. You are reviewing the benefits offered by your company and note the flexible spending account (FSA) option. The information states that you are able to set aside up to $2,550 of your income on a pretax basis and use that money to pay for specific medical expenses. You have not participated in the past, but as you read more, you think that this option could save you some money. However, if you were to chose to participate in the FSA, you aren't sure how much income would be appropriate to set aside.

Under the plan, you would designate a monthly payroll deduction. These funds would be deducted from your pay before taxes are calculated. The funds would be held in an account for you, and as you incurred medical expenses, you would submit a request for reimbursement. Since you would contribute the funds on a pretax basis, you would gain savings as you would not pay taxes on the income you set aside. The more you set aside, the more you would save in reduced tax liability. However, the rules of the FSA state that, at the end of the year, you would lose any money that you set aside but didn't use. This makes the decision to participate a little more complex. In order to gain the tax advantage, you should set aside as much as possible, up to the maximum allowed. However, if you estimate incorrectly, you could end up with a loss if you don't submit enough expenses to receive reimbursement of all of the funds you set aside.

You recently started a family, and thus your medical expenses have increased, suggesting that the FSA is something you should consider. As you look at the enrollment information, you see that you must decide on the monthly deduction that you will make in order to enroll, so you start thinking about your medical expenses. You know that your health insurance plan has a deductible, coinsurance, and copayments for every doctor's visit. However, you have been surprised at how quickly your medical expenses have added up. While you are aware of the plan features such as the deductible, you aren't really sure how it works. Every time you receive a statement from your doctor that shows what your health insurance covered and what you owe, you aren't really sure how the charges are determined. For this reason, you aren't sure how to even start estimating your medical expenses.

The enrollment forms are due in a few weeks. The potential tax savings are attractive, but the need to make an accurate estimate of your medical expenses concerns you. You know that you will need to do some research before you make a decision, but at this point, you just aren't sure how to get started.

1. Should you participate in the flexible spending account?
2. How should you determine how much to set aside?

2. Managing Employee Benefits: Cutting Costs at Reading Publishing

The rising cost of health care is leading many companies to examine opportunities to control costs of health insurance as well as other benefit programs they offer. Reading Publishing is no exception. Director of Compensation and Benefits Jake Holston faces this challenge. The company is successful and continuing to grow, but Jake knows that his role in controlling costs while providing benefits that meet employee needs is essential to the success of the company.

Jake's focus on cost control has resulted in several changes over the last several years. The company has already increased the employee contribution to health insurance premiums twice in the last five years. The company also renegotiated its health insurance plan last year, and with slightly higher deductibles, overall premium costs were reduced. Jake is convinced that he has lowered the cost of the company's health-care insurance as much as possible at this point. His focus now is to try to reduce costs by lowering the number of claims made by employees.

To lower the number of claims, Reading Publishing has recently started using case managers to work with employees who have chronic health problems. While this step has helped control the number of claims by those with chronic health problems, this is only a small number of Reading Publishing's overall employee population. Jake knows that a problem still exists as he reviews a utilization report provided by the company's insurer, which shows a higher-than-average number of claims. With only a few employees with chronic health problems, the high number of claims is clearly coming from the broader employee population.

Jake suspects that many of the claims may be a result of unhealthy behavior by employees. He knows that employees at Reading Publishing are under a great deal of stress. Many employees travel frequently, and editors face overwhelming deadlines. Jake knows that many employees smoke and that frequent alcohol consumption is part of the culture of the industry. Finally, given their highly demanding schedules, few employees take time to exercise or engage in other healthy behaviors. Jake is sure that their health insurance claims have been influenced by these behaviors, leading to the overall higher costs for coverage.

Given some of the indicators in the utilization reports and his knowledge of typical employee behavior, Jake believes that there is some opportunity for change. As his challenge now is to think creatively about strategies to control health insurance costs, as well as the costs of other benefits, he starts to consider how to influence employees to change some of their behaviors.

1. What are some examples of steps that Jake could take to lower the cost of Reading Publishing's health insurance?
2. What are some other areas that Jake should explore to reduce the overall costs of benefits?

Endnote

1. International Foundation of Employee Benefit Plans, "Corporate Benefits Departments: Staffing and Operations: 2015 Survey Results." Accessed March 1, 2016, www.ifebp.org.

Chapter Eleven

Nonqualified Deferred Compensation Plans for Executives

Establishing executive compensation and benefits requires knowledge of additional principles and practices that usually do not apply to nonexecutive employees. This area of compensation and benefits has drawn a lot of attention in the press, usually because executives' compensation rises even when company profitability is down, or they leave with lucrative benefits after termination for poor performance or scandal. We start this chapter by distinguishing between executive and nonexecutive employees, which is based on regulations rather than titles.

DEFINING EXECUTIVE EMPLOYMENT STATUS

Who Are Executives?

Who are executives? We can all agree that executives play a central role in setting competitive strategy. But, we have to look at some provisions of the Internal Revenue Code (IRC), administered by the Internal Revenue Service (IRS), which helps answer this question. The IRC recognizes two groups of employees who operate in this capacity: highly compensated employees and key employees. The IRS uses the term "key employees" to determine the necessity of including top-heavy provisions in qualified retirement plans. The IRS uses the term "highly compensated employees" for nondiscrimination rules in employer-sponsored benefits. Although these two designations were created for federal tax rule applications, employees in both groups are typically the ones who serve in executive leadership roles and participate in executive compensation and benefits plans.

Key Employees

The term **key employee** means any employee who at any time during the year is:

1. An officer having annual pay of more than $175,000, *OR*
2. An individual who for 2017 was either of the following:
   a. A 5 percent owner of the employer's business.
   b. A 1 percent owner of the employer's business whose annual pay was more than $150,000.

U.S. Treasury Regulations define the term *officer* in this definition of key employees:

> Generally, the term officer means an administrative executive who is in regular and continued service. The term officer implies continuity of service and excludes those employed for a special and single transaction. An employee who merely has the title of an officer but not the authority of an officer is not considered an officer for purposes of the key employee test. Similarly, an employee who does not have the title of an officer but has the authority of an officer is an officer for purposes of the key employee test. In the case of one or more employers treated as a single employer under sections 414(b), (c), or (m), whether or not an individual is an officer shall be determined based upon his responsibilities with respect to the employer or employers for which he is directly employed, and not with respect to the controlled group of corporations, employers under common control, or an affiliated service group.

A partner of a partnership will not be treated as an officer for purposes of the key employee test merely because she owns a capital or profits interest in the partnership; exercises her voting rights as a partner; and may, for limited purposes, be authorized and does in fact act as an agent of the partnership.

Highly Compensated Employees

The IRC defines a **highly compensated employee** as one of the following during the current year or preceding year:

- A 5 percent owner at any time during the year or the preceding year, *OR*
- For the preceding year:
  a. The employee had compensation from the employer in excess of $120,000 in 2017, *AND*
  b. If the employer so chooses, the employee was in the top-paid group of employees where top-paid employees are the top 20 percent most highly compensated employees.

DEFINING NONQUALIFIED DEFERRED COMPENSATION PLANS (NQDC)

Nonqualified deferred compensation (NQDC) plans are the hallmark of executive compensation. According to the IRS, a **nonqualified deferred compensation (NQDC)** plan is an agreement between an employer and an employee to pay compensation in the future. Executives recognize that NQDC plans allow them to accumulate substantially more money for retirement than allowed by qualified plan limits (Chapter 4). According to the IRS, employers typically deduct expenses only when the employee receives income from the plan well into the future. This rule differs from tax treatment for qualified plans under which employers earn tax benefits when contributions are made rather than when employees receive income in the future.

Companies use nonqualified retirement plans to achieve either of two objectives: restoration and supplemental retirement benefits. *Restoration* addresses the gap between the maximum retirement benefits allowed by the IRS for qualified plans and the more-substantial retirement income benefit amounts that result from typically lofty annual pay amounts. In Chapter 4, we discovered limits to the amount of annual earnings that could be included in the determination of qualified plan benefits—$270,000 in 2017 (indexed for inflation, in $5,000 increments). Most executives' annual pay exceeds that limit. As a general rule for defined benefit plans, annual earnings above this level cannot be included in benefits calculations. Also, the IRS limits the annual benefit for defined benefit plans to the lesser of $215,000 in 2017 (indexed for inflation, or highest average compensation for three consecutive years). For defined contribution plans, annual additions were limited to $54,000 in 2017 (indexed for inflation, or 100 percent of the participant's compensation). In Chapter 4, we defined annual additions as the sum of contributions to a participant's defined contribution plan account based on employee contributions, employer contributions, and forfeitures allocated to the participant's account.

For example, a company offers a qualified defined benefit plan. An executive earned $300,000 in annual compensation during 2017. The IRS limits the amount of annual income for benefits determination to $270,000. This regulation requires the company to exclude $50,000 of the executive's annual compensation from the defined benefit formula. Companies may choose to establish a nonqualified deferred compensation plan for its executives to restore benefits based on the difference (in this example, $30,000) between actual earnings ($300,000) and legal limits ($270,000).

Second, companies offer nonqualified plans to provide *supplemental retirement benefits*, increasing total retirement benefits to a sum substantially greater than benefits provided by restoration plans. Supplemental executive retirement plans (SERPs) generate higher retirement benefits in a variety of ways. For instance, nonexecutive employees earn an annual retirement benefit equal to 60 percent of the highest average annual salary for a consecutive three-year period. Executives receive a substantially higher percentage of the restored annual benefit.

Characteristics Distinguishing between Nonqualified Plans and Qualified Plans

Nonqualified plans differ from qualified plans in three important ways: ERISA qualification criteria, funding status, and mandatory retirement age. Each is addressed in turn.

ERISA Qualification Criteria

NQDC plans fail to meet at least one of the ERISA criteria necessary to qualify for favorable tax treatment. In comparison, plans that meet all the ERISA minimum standards are qualified plans (a detailed discussion of ERISA minimum standards is in Chapters 3 and 4). Some of the ERISA Title I and Title II provisions set the minimum standards required to qualify pension plans for favorable tax treatment. Title I specifies a variety of protections for participants and beneficiaries:

1. Reporting and disclosure.
2. Minimum standards for participation and vesting.
3. Funding.
4. Fiduciary responsibilities.
5. Administration and enforcement.
6. Continuation coverage and additional standards for group health plans.
7. Group health plan portability, access, and renewability requirements.

Which minimum standards are usually not met? First, as previously discussed, executives' annual pay often far exceeds the IRC limits for qualified plans. Limiting executives to qualified plans would make ineligible a substantial amount of compensation. Second, plans for executives will invariably fail to meet ERISA's coverage requirements which prohibit employers from disproportionately favoring highly compensated employees, described in Chapter 4. There, we discussed that companies use the ratio percentage test or average benefit test to demonstrate whether plans meet the coverage requirement by maintaining a nondiscriminatory ratio of non–highly compensated employees to highly compensated employees. Third, executive retirement plans violate **nondiscrimination rules**, which prohibit employers from discriminating in favor of highly compensated employees in contributions or benefits, availability of benefits, rights, or plan features.

Funding Status

Companies decide whether to establish executive plans as funded or unfunded. **Funded plans** place money or property, such as company stock in trust funds or to purchase insurance company contracts in an executive's name without risk of forfeiture. That is, trust funds and insurance contracts secure an employer's promise to make future payments. Neither a company nor its creditors may withdraw from a trust fund or redeem an insurance policy. **Unfunded plans** only contain the promise to pay deferred compensation benefits in the future. There are no dedicated funds to honor the promise. For example, executives may forfeit retirement benefits when a company becomes bankrupt or financially insolvent. Or, they may lose retirement benefits following a change of company ownership.

Companies consider several factors in deciding whether to fund nonqualified plans of which we consider three that promote decisions to fund these plans. Managing liabilities, costs, and shareholder expectations. First, liability management speaks to adequate preparation to honor financial obligations made to executives as set forth in nonqualified plans. Funding compels companies to set aside resources. Second, cost is a noteworthy consideration. Funding nonqualified plans represents a significant opportunity cost. For instance, money devoted to nonqualified plans means that fewer resources are available for research and development and for marketing initiatives. Ultimately, companies decide whether the investment in nonqualified plans promotes longer-term opportunities such as profits or corporate reputation. Third, shareholders' expectations may lead companies not to fund nonqualified plans. Similar to the previous explanation, shareholders may view funding as a detrimental cost. Shareholders are sensitive to public debate about excessive executive compensation packages. Diverting substantial resources to promote lucrative retirement income is often seen as a less-productive compensation expenditure than are long-term incentives that presumably align the interests of executives with those of shareholders.

Mandatory Retirement Age

Normal retirement age is the lowest age at which an employee who retires may begin receiving retirement benefits. This requirement is clearly specified in company documents. Upon attaining this age, an employee gains the right to receive full retirement benefits. It is worth noting that the Age Discrimination in Employment Act forbids employers from setting a **mandatory retirement age** for virtually all employees, *except for*:

> Any employee who has attained 65 years of age and who, for the two-year period immediately before retirement, is employed in a bona fide executive or a high policymaking position, if such employee is entitled to an immediate nonforfeitable annual retirement benefit from a pension, profit-sharing, savings, or deferred compensation plan, or any combination of such plans, of the employer of such employee, which equals, in the aggregate, at least $44,000.[1*]

A **bona fide executive** primarily manages the overall company and directs the work of two or more people. An employee in a **high policymaking position** plays a significant role in the development of company policy but does not have direct line control, as, for example, over business functions such as accounting, finance, human resources, and so forth.

NONQUALIFIED RETIREMENT PLANS FOR EXECUTIVES

Benefits professionals distinguish among four broad classes of nonqualified executive retirement plans: excess benefit plans, supplemental executive retirement plans (SERPs), salary reduction arrangements, and bonus deferral plans. Our focus is on the first two types. Companies offer excess plans to restore retirement

---

*Other exceptions apply, such as in cases of public safety; for example, airline pilots generally may work until age 65.

income disallowed by qualification rules, while SERPs award benefits at substantially higher levels than restoration levels.

Excess Benefit Plans

Excess benefit plans increase retirement benefits by the amount lost due to limits set by the IRS. Companies design excess benefit plans as extensions to qualified defined benefit or defined contribution plans. As discussed in Chapter 4, defined benefit plans guarantee retirement benefits, usually expressed as a monthly sum equal to a percentage of a participant's preretirement pay, multiplied by the number of years of service for the employer. Under defined contribution plans, employers and employees can make annual contributions to separate accounts established for each participating employee, based on a formula contained in the plan document. In many plans, formulas call for employers to contribute a percentage of their compensation annually.

Companies may offer excess benefit plans on a funded or an unfunded basis. Funded excess benefit plans are subject to ERISA's reporting and disclosure, fiduciary requirements, and administration and enforcement. These ERISA requirements do not apply to unfunded plans.

Supplemental Executive Retirement Plans (SERPs)

Supplemental executive retirement plans (SERPs) provide executives with supplemental retirement benefits and increase an total retirement benefits to a substantially greater sum than do restoration plans. SERPs include a variety of objectives that distinguish them from excess benefit plans:

- *Inclusion of other types of monetary pay in the calculation of retirement benefits.* Qualified plans and excess plans use only base pay or salary to calculate retirement benefits. SERPs include additional monetary compensation, such as annual bonuses or incentive payments, for determining benefit amounts.
- *Use of SERPs as a tool in executive-level succession planning.* Companies may grant full retirement benefits to employees at an earlier age or with fewer years of service than required in qualified plans.
- *Rewarding substantially higher retirement benefits.* Companies may establish SERPs by using alternative methods for calculating benefits that generate higher income than standard formulas used in qualified plans. For example, a qualified defined benefit plan may use an employee's career average pay to determine retirement benefits, while a SERP may rely on the average of the employee's highest three years of salary. A qualified defined contribution plan may entail annual employer contributions equaling up to 25 percent of salary; alternatively, a SERP may specify higher contributions up to 35 percent.
- *Compensating for short-term employment or older new hires.* Qualified plans follow strict regulations for contribution amounts and service requirements to determine retirement income. SERPs provide more flexibility by offering accelerated vesting schedules or waiving the vesting requirement, granting additional years of service, or guaranteeing a minimum level of retirement benefits. Companies

may offer SERPs on a funded or an unfunded basis. Of course, funded SERPs are subject to ERISA requirements. Unfunded SERPs are not subject to similar restrictions.

A well-known unfunded SERP is the **top hat plan.** Companies maintain top hat plans "primarily for the purpose of providing deferred compensation for a select group of management or highly compensated employees."[2] Practitioners have adopted the term *top hat* as a convention to reference unfunded plans. It was not created in any tax regulation or legal definition.

Companies use discretion when designing top hat plans for restoration or supplemental income objectives. By design, top hat plans are exempt from three parts of ERISA's Title I:

- Minimum standards for participation and vesting.
- Funding.
- Fiduciary responsibilities.

Exemption requires that employers maintain unfunded top hat plans and offer them exclusively to a "select group of management or highly compensated employees."[3] For example, the U.S. Department of Labor interprets "select groups" as employees who, "by virtue of their position or compensation level," possess the power to negotiate the terms of their deferred compensation arrangement, and thus do not need protections provided by ERISA. Meeting these criteria can be challenging, because ERISA does not unequivocally define *unfunded* or *select group*. Instead, companies currently rely on Department of Labor Advisory Opinion letters or on often-conflicting court rulings for guidance.

Contrasting Excess Benefit Plans and SERPs

Excess benefit plans and SERPs differ in two additional ways. First, companies choose to bestow vesting rights on participants of both types, but there is a notable difference. Lengthier vesting schedules are more characteristic of SERPs than of excess benefit plans. Increasing the vesting period promotes retention by providing incentives to achieve nonforfeitable rights to lucrative retirement benefits. Alternatively, companies may promote retention by setting a specific age at which executives become vested in the SERP benefits. Second, companies may include offset provisions to reduce contributions to and benefits from SERPs when executives participate in unrelated company-sponsored retirement programs.

FUNDING MECHANISMS

Companies may choose from a variety of mechanisms to fund excess benefit plans or SERPs. It is essential to recognize that the term *funding mechanism* is not synonymous with *funded plans.* **Funding mechanisms** provide the financial resources for funded or unfunded plans. As discussed earlier, unfunded plans provide the least amount of security to executives. Overall, funding mechanisms vary according to the level of security, listed below from the least amount of security to the greatest amount:

- General-asset approach (unfunded).
- Corporate-owned life insurance (unfunded).
- Split-dollar life insurance (unfunded).
- Rabbi trusts (unfunded).
- Secular trusts (funded).
- Employee-owned annuities (funded).

Funded and unfunded plans impose federal tax obligations on both employees and employers. The concept of **constructive receipt** guides the timing of an executive's obligation to pay income taxes. Under this doctrine, the plan is subject to taxation if the assets are available to the employee without substantial restrictions, limitations, or risk of forfeiture.[4]

Until funded or vested, the contributions are not deductible as a business expense. Once vested, the employer can deduct all related expenses associated with the compensation together with the executive paying annual federal taxes based on contributions to and earnings from the plan. For unfunded plans, executives generally pay federal income taxes when they begin to receive payments. Employers usually are responsible for federal taxes when executives receive benefits. It is important to note that the rules for NQDC taxation are quite complex. A variety of other criteria comes into play for guiding the timing of taxation of both executives and employers. Stated here are some of the general rules.

General Assets

Companies may fund NQDC plans with general assets of the company. General assets include cash and company stock. This funding method provides the least amount of security to executives for two reasons. First, companies are typically required to turn assets over to creditors in the event of bankruptcy or insolvency. Second, the agreement to compensate executives from general assets is not protected by ERISA. Employers may choose not to honor any agreement to pay executives. In such cases, the only remedy is to initiate a costly lawsuit against the employer for breach of contract.

Corporate-Owned Life Insurance

Corporate-owned life insurance is based on whole life insurance policies. As discussed in Chapter 6, whole life insurance policies pay a designated amount to the designated beneficiaries of the deceased. In the case of corporate-owned life insurance, employers purchase whole life insurance policies on the lives of executives and they name themselves as beneficiaries. The goal is to match deferred compensation amounts promised to executives. Employers use the insurance benefit to recover the costs of nonqualified deferred compensation following the executive's death.

Selecting the necessary policy amounts is difficult because companies cannot easily anticipate possible decisions to terminate executives or the timing of their deaths. The use of corporate-owned life insurance does not create a funded plan because companies rely on general assets to pay executives.

Split-Dollar Life Insurance

Split-dollar life insurance policies provide separate life benefits and death benefits. The employer and executive share the premium payment, and an agreement between the employer and executive determines the relative share of the premium. Classifying split-dollar life insurance as a funded or an unfunded plan is not straightforward. It is generally unfunded when employers maintain ownership of the policy, in which case the designated owner usually pays the larger share of the premium cost. Benefits professionals use the term *collateral approach* when the executive maintains ownership. The *endorsement approach* designates the employer as the owner.

Under the collateral approach, the executive reimburses the employer for its contribution upon retirement or termination for gross violation of terms of the employment agreement. The policy's named beneficiary receives a benefit following the executive's death. If an executive dies before repayment, the employer recoups the balance from the death benefit.

Under the endorsement approach, the employer pays for most or all of the premium. In such cases, the employer has the right to borrow against the cash value of the policy for business purposes, and the executive reimburses the employer for the portion of the premium cost that exceeds the annual increase in the policy's cash value. The employer names itself as beneficiary for the exact amount of its cumulative premium payments, and the employee names a beneficiary to receive the difference—that is, the amount that exceeds the policy's cash value.

Rabbi Trusts

Named after an IRS ruling that created it, a **rabbi trust** is an irrevocable grantor trust. In the field of finance, trusts are a way of holding assets with a specific objective.* The grantor of the trust, in this case, is the employer, who maintains ownership. Companies establish rabbi trusts to provide executives and key employees or beneficiaries with deferred compensation upon retirement or termination without cause. Rabbi trusts may also provide income to designated beneficiaries following the death of an employee. Starting at the time of retirement, termination, or death, a company makes payments directly from its general assets.

Financial lending institutions usually serve as the trustees. Most often, companies select financial institutions with which they regularly engage in business transactions. Trustees possess fiduciary responsibilities to ensure the solvency of the trust's assets.

Rabbi trusts do not offer the greatest security for executives. In the event of company bankruptcy, it must release assets to creditors after filing for insolvency or bankruptcy making rabbi trusts an unfunded option.

---

*An irrevocable trust cannot be changed or canceled once it is established unless the beneficiary grants permission. In this case, the beneficiary is the employee for whom the trust was established.

Secular Trusts

A **secular trust** is similar to a rabbi trust with one exception. Secular trusts are not subject to a company's creditors in the event of bankruptcy or insolvency. As such, secular trusts are funded plans that meet ERISA provisions.

Employee-Owned Annuities

Employee-owned annuities offer executives the greatest degree of financial security because they own the annuities. An executive sets up annuity arrangements with a third-party vendor such as a mutual fund company or an insurance company. The employer then pays the cost for the annuity. An executive's vested retirement benefit usually determines the annuity amount. Employee-owned annuities are funded, requiring compliance with ERISA. However, this type of deferred compensation plan is not subject to ERISA's provisions because executives set up annuity contracts, not the companies. ERISA applies only to company-sponsored pension and welfare plans, which we defined in Chapter 3.

STOCK OPTIONS AND STOCK PURCHASE PLANS

Basic terminology regarding stock options will be reviewed next, followed by a discussion of five alternative stock option plans commonly used in nonqualified deferred compensation plans:

1. Stock options
2. Restricted stock plans and restricted stock units
3. Stock appreciation rights
4. Phantom stock plans
5. Employee stock purchase plans

Basic Terminology

Company stock represents equity, that is, ownership interest in the company. **Company stock shares** represent equity segments of equal value. Equity interest increases positively with the number of stock shares. Stocks are bought and sold every business day in public stock exchanges; the New York Stock Exchange is perhaps the best-known stock exchange. Additional relevant terminology for this discussion includes:

- **Stock option:** A right granted by a company to an employee to purchase a number of shares of stocks at a designated price within a specified period of time.
- **Stock grant:** A company's offering of stock to an employee.
- **Exercise of stock option:** An employee's purchase of stock using stock options.
- **Disposition:** Sale of stock by the stockholder.
- **Fair market value:** The average value between the highest and lowest reported sales price of a stock on the New York Stock Exchange on any given date.

Stock Options

Broadly, there are two particular types of stock options–incentive stock options and nonstatutory stock options. **Incentive stock options** entitle executives to purchase their companies' stock in the future at a predetermined price. The predetermined price usually equals the stock price at the time an executive is granted the stock option. In effect, executives are purchasing the stocks at a discounted price. Executives generally exercise their option to purchase the stock after the price has increased dramatically. An executive receives **capital gains** as the difference between the stock price at the time of purchase and the lower stock price at the time an executive receives the stock option. Executives receive income tax benefits by participating in incentive stock option plans. They are not required to pay tax on the capital gains until they sell their stock shares. The tax rate for such transactions is called the capital gains rate. It is typically substantially lower than the executive's ordinary income tax rate, further adding incentive value to incentive stock options. If stock price at the time of disposition were lower than at the price of the stock option grant, the executive would experience a **capital loss**.

Much like incentive stock options, companies award stock options to executives at discounted prices. In contrast to incentive stock options, **nonstatutory stock options** do not qualify for favorable tax treatment. Executives pay income taxes on the difference between the discounted price and the stock's fair market value at the time of the stock grant, not at the time of disposition, and they do so at their ordinary income tax rate. They do not pay taxes in the future when they choose to exercise their nonstatutory stock options.

Nonstatutory stock options do provide executives an advantage. Executives' tax liability is ultimately lower over the long term: Stock prices generally increase over time. As a result, the capital gains will probably be much greater in the future when executives exercise their options rather than when their companies grant these options.

Restricted Stock Plans and Restricted Stock Units

Under **restricted stock plans**, a company may grant executives stock options at market value or discounted value, or they may provide stock. Under restricted stock plans, executives do not have any ownership control over the disposition of the stock for a predetermined period, often many years. This predetermined period is known as the vesting period, much like vesting rights associated with employer-sponsored retirement plans (Chapter 4). Alternatively, companies may provide executives with restricted stock units. **Restricted stock units** are shares of company stock that are awarded to executives at the end of the restriction period.

Similar to restricted stock plans and restricted stock units in terms of the vesting period, a company may choose to add to the vesting period a performance criterion for determining whether to award stock options or stock units. This type of equity agreement is referred to as a **performance plan**. A company's board of directors determines the performance criteria. For example, a company's earnings per stock share is often used. The Coca-Cola Company recently modified its executive-level and top-management equity agreements to follow performance plan standards. These leaders will receive fewer stock shares, but additional performance share units. One of the main reasons for this change was shareholders' dissatisfaction with the company's weak performance in the U.S. market.

Stock Appreciation Rights

Stock appreciation rights provide income to executives at the end of a designated period, much like restricted stock options. However, executives never have to exercise their stock rights to receive income. The company simply awards payment to executives based on the difference in stock price between the time the company granted the stock rights at fair market value to the end of the designated period, and the executives are permitted to keep the stock. Executives pay taxes on any income from gains in stock value when they exercise stock rights, presumably after retirement, when tax rates are lower.[5] Employers receive a tax deduction in the same amount. Neither the employee nor the employer pays taxes when stock appreciation rights are granted.

Phantom Stock Plans

A **phantom stock** plan is a compensation arrangement whereby boards of directors promise to pay a bonus in the form of the equivalent of either the value of company shares or the increase in that value over a period of time. Phantom stock plans are similar to restricted stock plans because executives must meet specific conditions before they can convert these phantom shares into real shares of company stock. There are generally two conditions. First, executives must remain employed for a specified period, usually several years. Second, executives must retire from the company. Upon meeting these conditions, executives receive income equal to the increase in the value of company stock from the date the company granted the phantom stock to the conversion date. Phantom stock plans provide executives with tax advantages. Executives pay taxes on the capital gains after they convert their phantom shares to real shares of company stock during retirement.

Employee Stock Purchase Plans

A company may choose to offer a formal employee stock purchase plan that allows participating employees to purchase stock after a designated period of time. In anticipation of making a stock purchase, employees set aside money through payroll deduction for this specific purpose during the offering period, which is the point in time when they may purchase the employer's stock based on the money set aside in their accounts. The span of time over which employees are permitted to contribute to their accounts is referred to as the **offering period**. Companies have the option of setting up employee stock purchase plans as qualified or nonqualified. To qualify for favorable tax treatment, companies' plans must meet several criteria. For example, all full-time employees with two or more years of service must be allowed to participate.

SEPARATION AGREEMENTS

Separation agreements specify compensation and benefits an executive will receive after the company's board of directors terminates the executive. These agreements are negotiated during the hiring process, approved by the board of directors, and subsequently documented by written contract. Golden parachutes and platinum parachutes are the most well-known types of executive separation agreements.

Golden Parachutes

Most executives' employment agreements contain a golden parachute clause. **Golden parachutes** provide pay and benefits to executives after a termination that results from a change in ownership or corporate takeover, that is, the merger or combining of two separate companies. Approximately 80 percent of Standard & Poor's 500 companies offer golden parachute packages to CEOs who are replaced due to corporate takeover.[6] For example, Compuware, which developed software for use on mainframe computers, was taken over by a private equity firm Thoma Bravo, LLC. in 2014. The top six executives of the company held golden parachute agreements equaling approximately $23 million in cash, stock, and other benefits.[7] Among these top executives, former CEO Bob Paul's golden parachute was valued at approximately $6.6 million. Boards of directors often approve golden parachute clauses for three reasons. First, golden parachutes limit executives' risks in the event of these unforeseen events. Second, golden parachutes promote recruitment and retention of talented executives. Third, in the event that a takeover bid would benefit the company, it is possible that a CEO would work against it in order to save his or her job. Companies benefit from golden parachute payments because they can treat these payments as business expenses. This means that companies can reduce their tax liability by increasing the parachute amount. The total value of golden parachutes came to exceed executives' annual income levels by far. Public outcry led to government-imposed intervention that limited tax benefits to companies.

Platinum Parachutes

In an ideal world, CEOs will perform on an exemplary basis, making decisions to drive up company profits. As you know, we do not live in a perfect world; sometimes, CEOs do not perform their jobs well and companies lose out on profit opportunities. After a period of unsatisfactory performance as determined by shareholders and other company executives, CEOs may often be terminated even before the expiration of their employment contracts. Many companies reach agreements with CEOs to terminate employment, awarding a platinum parachute as an incentive. **Platinum parachutes** are lucrative awards that compensate departing executives with severance pay, continuation of company benefits, and even stock options. Companies typically use platinum parachutes to avoid long legal battles or critical reports in the press, essentially by paying off a CEO to give up his or her post. For example, Louis Chenevert resigned from United Technologies amid growing criticism from investors that he had become disengaged from the business. He left the company with a platinum parachute worth $195 million including approximately $136.3 million in stock options and about $31 million in pension benefits.[8] Apart from this example, it is important to reiterate that golden parachutes became common when hostile corporate takeovers were occurring in large numbers during the 1980s and 1990s. As such activity slowed down, many companies continued to offer golden parachutes, but extended the use for a CEO's termination for other reasons, such as poor performance. For this purpose, it is not uncommon to see the terms golden parachute and platinum parachute used interchangeably.

REPORTING AND DISCLOSURE REQUIREMENTS

Disclosure of executive compensation components and engagement of shareholder opinion set executive compensation and benefits practices apart from compensating other employee groups. Two laws, in particular, are responsible for these requirements: The Securities Exchange Act of 1934 and the Wall Street Reform and Consumer Protection Act of 2010 (Dodd-Frank Act).

Securities Exchange Act of 1934

Companies that sell and exchange securities (e.g., company stocks and bonds) on public stock exchanges are required to file a wide variety of information with the **Securities and Exchange Commission (SEC),** including executive compensation and benefits practices. One of the main goals is to help prospective investors understand the financial matters of importance to themselves. The SEC is a nonpartisan, quasi-judicial federal government agency with responsibility for administering federal securities laws. The **Securities Exchange Act of 1934** applies to the disclosure of important company financial information as well as information about executive compensation practices. For executive compensation and benefits, companies are required to complete a **Definitive Proxy Statement** under Section 14A of the Securities Exchange Act, typically referred to as a DEF 14A. It reveals detailed information about the compensation and benefits of the CEO and **Named Executive Officers (NEOs),** who generally are the four most highly compensated officers after the CEO. Within the DEF 14A, companies must disclose multiple types of information, which are listed in Exhibit 11.1.

The information should be presented in narrative and tabular form. The narrative is referred to as the **Compensation Discussion and Analysis (CD&A),** where it must present an unambiguous explanation of all executive compensation and benefits information contained in the tables. Disclosing detailed information

EXHIBIT 11.1
Securities and Exchange Commission Disclosure Requirements for Executive Compensation

- Stock option and stock appreciation right tables.
- Long-term incentive plan table.
- Pension plan table.
- Performance graph comparing the company's stock price performance against a market index and a peer group.
- Report from the compensation committee of the board of directors explaining compensation levels and policies.
- Description of the directors' compensation, disclosing all amounts paid or payable.
- Disclosure of certain employment contracts and golden parachutes.

about executive compensation and benefits should increase the accountability of company boards of directors for executive compensation policies and decisions. Failure to comply with SEC reporting rules can lead to hefty monetary penalties.

There are several tables contained within the DEF 14A, but the most important here is the Summary Compensation Table, which discloses compensation information for the CEO and the NEOs over a three-year period. As you can see in Exhibit 11.2, the Summary Compensation Table for the Boeing Company covers the compensation paid to the named executive officers during the past completed fiscal year and the two preceding fiscal years. The table contains two main subheadings: annual compensation and long-term compensation. Annual compensation includes salary (i.e., base pay), bonus, and other annual compensation. Long-term compensation includes restricted stock awards, stock appreciation rights, and long-term incentive payouts. The last column, "All Other Compensation ($)," is a catchall column to record other forms of compensation. Information in this column must be described in a footnote. It should be noted that the CD&A contains additional tables further elaborating on components of executive benefits.

In 2008, the SEC unveiled additional rules for disclosing executive compensation. These rules require that companies reveal how much executives are paid, making such previously hard-to-find information as pension and estimated separation totals transparent. Although the new rules represent a substantial improvement in pay disclosure, the SEC made a revision that resulted in a less-meaningful disclosure of stock options.

In 2009, the SEC chairperson announced further changes in the disclosure of executive compensation in a company's Summary Compensation Table. The change pertains to the reported value for stock options and stock awards. The SEC disclosure rules show components of compensation previously hidden as well as provide clarity into elements of compensation already disclosed. The most significant changes follow:

Total The Summary Compensation Table of a company's proxy will now have a column that adds up and displays the total compensation an executive received for the previous year. In the SEC pay database this year, this is labeled SEC Total.

Change in Pension Value and Nonqualified Deferred Compensation This column in the Summary Compensation Table shows the increase in actuarial value to the executive officer of all defined benefit pension plans and earnings on nonqualified deferred compensation plans.

All Other This column captures compensation that does not fit in any other column of the Summary Compensation Table, including perquisites and other personal items (e.g., aircraft usage, car service, and club memberships). Each item of compensation included in All Other that exceeds $10,000 will now be separately identified and quantified in a footnote.

Pension Benefits The new rules require companies to disclose the present value of accumulated pension benefits, showing the total lump sum amount of money an executive would receive in retirement.

EXHIBIT 11.2 2015 Summary Compensation Table, The Boeing Company

The following table sets forth information regarding compensation for each of our 2015 named executive officers.

Name and Principal Position	Year	Salary ($)[1]	Stock Awards ($)[2]	Option Awards ($)[3]	Non-Equity Incentive Plan Compensation ($)[4]	Change in Pension Value ($)	All Other Compensation ($)	Total ($)
Dennis A. Muilenburg, *Chairman, President and Chief Executive Officer*	2015	$1,354,269	$5,105,064	—	$4,568,549	$1,848,002	$349,449	$13,226,333
	2014	1,135,389	2,474,990	—	4,117,900	3,917,410	152,712	11,798,401
	2013	941,004	1,156,567	1,156,559	3,494,900	717,653	254,929	7,721,612
Gregory D. Smith, *Chief Financial Officer, Executive Vice President, Corporate Development and Strategy*	2015	841,154	1,500,009	—	2,248,649	122,333	107,670	4,819,815
	2014	809,231	6,495,646	—	2,663,600	498,085	112,989	10,579,551
	2013	685,700	616,608	616,597	1,553,042	28,930	95,135	3,596,012
W. James McNerney, Jr., *Former Chairman and Chief Executive Officer*	2015	1,779,962	6,272,444	—	11,338,320	0	586,220	19,916,946
	2014	2,004,231	6,272,517	—	14,475,000	5,350,097	760,075	28,861,920
	2013	1,930,000	3,763,534	3,763,503	12,920,972	0	885,553	23,263,562
Raymond L. Conner, *Vice Chairman, President and Chief Executive Officer, Commercial Airplanes*	2015	1,016,154	2,071,912	—	2,843,850	2,995,344	160,326	9,085,586
	2014	1,002,500	8,497,786	—	2,072,500	4,576,995	271,533	16,421,314
	2013	828,846	843,743	843,743	2,052,960	985,652	107,224	5,662,168
J. Michael Luttig, *Executive Vice President and General Counsel*	2015	870,577	1,700,094	—	2,787,846	913,922	212,991	6,490,430
	2014	877,480	1,548,377	—	3,359,100	1,463,310	199,677	7,448,444
	2013	822,373	850,048	850,083	3,486,856	32,679	125,226	6,167,265
Diana L. Sands, *Senior Vice President, Office of Internal Governance and Administration*	2015	470,577	3,599,069	—	751,748	242,239	74,286	5,137,919

(1) Amounts reflect base salary paid in the year, before any deferrals at the executive's election and including salary increases effective during the year, if any.

(2) Amounts reflect the aggregate grant date fair value of PBRSUs and RSUs granted in the year computed in accordance with FASB ASC Topic 718. These amounts are not paid to or realized by the executive. The grant date fair value of each PBRSU and RSU award in 2015 is set forth in the 2015 Grants of Plan-Based Awards table on page 40. A description of PBRSUs and RSUs appears on page 41.

(3) Amounts reflect the aggregate grant date fair value of stock options granted in the year computed in accordance with FASB ASC Topic 718. These amounts are not paid to or realized by the executive. Assumptions used in the calculation of these values are included in Note 15 to our audited financial statements included in our 2015 Annual Report on Form 10-K. We have not granted stock options since 2013.

(4) Amounts reflect (a) annual incentive compensation, which is based on Company, business unit, and individual performance pursuant to the annual incentive plan, and (b) any payout of performance awards for the three-year performance period that ended in the relevant year pursuant to the long-term incentive program, in each case including amounts deferred under our deferred compensation plan.

305

Severance Benefits Companies must disclose any termination or change-in-control agreements with executives. They must disclose the specific circumstances that will trigger payment and the estimated total payments and benefits provided for each circumstance.

Wall Street Reform and Consumer Protection Act of 2010 (Dodd-Frank Act)

President Barack Obama signed the **Wall Street Reform and Consumer Protection Act of 2010** to further enhance the transparency of executive compensation practices. Also commonly referred to as the **Dodd-Frank Act,** the act requires the companies that trade stock on public exchanges comply with numerous major provisions, three of which encompass employee-benefits practices. The first provision requires **say on pay.** Say on pay gives company shareholders the right to vote yes or no on executive compensation proposals that are contained in proxy statements, including current and deferred components and golden parachute agreements. The frequency is determined by shareholder vote. Although the say on pay provision guarantees shareholders the right to vote on executive compensation proposals, the vote is nonbinding. That is, the outcome of shareholders' voting does not overrule any compensation decision made by the company's board of directors. The nonbinding vote advises the company's board of directors of possible concerns about the structure of executive compensation packages, including excessive perks and the lack of clarity between compensation and business results.

The second provision details independence requirements for compensation committee members and their advisors, such as compensation consultants and legal counsel. Members of compensation committees typically receive compensation and some employee benefits for their services, and this practice is considered to be acceptable. However, possible violations of the Dodd-Frank independence requirement may arise when at least one committee member also receives compensation as a company employee. For example, a compensation committee member who also serves as the company's executive vice president may be considered violating the independence requirement. On the other hand, a compensation committee member who does not receive compensation from the company as an employee or external consultant would not violate the independence requirement.

The third provision requires that companies disclose the circumstances under which an executive would benefit from a golden parachute arrangement. Specifically, disclosure is required of all agreements and understandings that the acquiring and target companies have with the executive officers of both companies.

Concluding Comments

The structure and regulations pertaining to executive employee benefits are extremely complex. Fully understanding them requires expertise that is often found in leading executive compensation and benefits consulting firms, public accounting firms, and specialized law firms. Some of the leading and most well-respected consulting firms include the following:

- Frederic W. Cook & Company (www.fwcook.com)
- The Hay Associates (www.haygroup.com)
- Pearl Meyer & Partners (www.pearlmeyer.com)
- Towers Watson (www.towerswatson.com)
- William M. Mercer (www.mercer.com)

Useful updates about executive compensation and benefits can be found on these firms' Web sites.

Summary

We discussed NQDC arrangements, which are significant elements of executive compensation packages. The primary goals are to restore retirement income disallowed by qualification rule, and to award benefits at substantially higher levels than restoration plans achieve. The security of retirement benefits depends on whether a plan is funded (rather than unfunded) and on the particular funding mechanism. This chapter concludes with a review of the key regulatory and disclosure requirements for companies that publicly trade stock.

Key Terms

Key employee, *290*
Highly compensated employee, *291*
nonqualified deferred compensation plans (NQDC), *293*
nondiscrimination rules, *293*
funded plans, *293*
unfunded plans, *293*
normal retirement age, *294*
mandatory retirement age, *294*
bona fide executive, *294*
high policymaking position, *294*
excess benefit plans, *295*
supplemental executive retirement plans (SERPs), *295*
top hat plan, *296*
funding mechanisms, *296*

constructive receipt, *297*
split-dollar life insurance, *298*
rabbi trust, *298*
secular trust, *299*
employee-owned annuities, *299*
company stock, *299*
company stock shares, *299*
stock option, *299*
stock grant, *299*
exercise of stock option, *299*
disposition, *299*
fair market value, *299*
incentive stock options, *300*
capital gains, *300*
capital loss, *300* nonstatutory stock options, *300*
restricted stock plans, *300*
restricted stock units, *300*

performance plan, *300*
stock appreciation rights, *301*
phantom stock, *301*
offering period, *301*
golden parachutes, *302*
platinum parachutes, *302*
Securities and Exchange Commission (SEC), *303*
Securities Exchange Act of 1934, *303*
Definitive Proxy Statement, *303*
Named Executive Officers (NEOs), *303*
Compensation Discussion and Analysis (CD&A), *303*
Wall Street Reform and Consumer Protection Act of 2010, *306*
Dodd–Frank Act, *306*

Discussion Questions

1. What are the main objectives of nonqualified plans?
2. Why are unfunded plans the riskiest from an executive's perspective? How can companies justify the use of unfunded plans?
3. Discuss the funding mechanisms for NQDC plans.
4. Describe the reporting and disclosure requirements for executive compensation and benefits.
5. Having studied employee-benefit practices in this book, do you believe that treatment of executives is fair compared to that of employees of lesser ranks? Explain your answer.

Cases

1. Understanding Your Employee Benefits: Executive Compensation in a Corporation

After 15 years working at a small, family-run business, you have received an offer for a new opportunity in a large corporation. During a series of interviews with executives in the company, you learn about a variety of avenues to move up the corporate ladder. You believe that the position as a department manager provides you an opportunity to join a company where you could spend the rest of your career. As an executive position with the company could be in your future, you think that you should learn more about the compensation that executives at this company receive. Further, you want to make sure that you will be joining an organization that behaves ethically and pays all employees fairly.

You have a concern about what you have heard in the media about excessive executive compensation in large companies such as the one you are thinking about joining. You have read stories about public protests of large corporations and have also heard about executive scandals in which organizational leaders have inflated expenses to companies and spent money on excessive parties and furnishings for private residences. You are curious about whether such protests or scandals have involved your potential future employer.

You start to research this issue and are relieved to learn that there have not been any executive scandals at this organization. There is an article, however, about a previous CEO receiving a platinum parachute. You aren't sure what this means, but you understand that the company lost quite a bit of money while that person was the CEO, and it seems as if he still received a fairly generous separation package from the company. The article also states that most top executives at this organization have a golden parachute clause in their contracts, and you aren't sure what the difference is between platinum and golden parachutes.

The company is publicly held, and you learn that its executives do participate in an incentive stock option plan. Executives are granted a certain number of stock options each year that they are able to exercise after five years. As a result, there is an incentive for executives to work to increase the overall value of the company stock. This part of executive compensation seems to make sense. You hope that someday you also will be rewarded by the company's success.

In the company's annual report, you are able to see the total compensation of many of the company's top executives, and overall, it seems that the executive pay and benefits at the company are not generally considered to be excessive. It also seems that executive compensation is attractive and in line with something that you should aspire to receive. Based on your research so far, this opportunity might just be the right move for your career.

1. What is the purpose of the platinum parachute? Why would the company provide this benefit? How does it compare to the golden parachute?
2. Why does the company offer an incentive stock option plan?
3. What other protections are in place for the shareholders and employees relative to executive compensation in organizations?

2. Managing Employee Benefits: Compensating Executives at Safeguard Insurance

The executives at Safeguard Insurance are focused on continuing efforts that have brought the company significant growth in the past 15 years. Director of Human Resources Beth Frazier is considering how to provide more incentives to executives to continue this focus. Two years ago, the company went public and began selling shares of stock on the stock market. While executives were granted some stock in the company's initial public offering, Beth now wants to examine the best way to use the company's stock value in the executive compensation plan. She knows that company ownership can help incentivize executives to increase the value of the company stock, and thus the ongoing success of the company.

Safeguard Insurance is led by an executive team that includes the chief executive officer, the chief operating officer, and functional area leaders, including chief legal counsel, the director of finance, the director of operations, the director of marketing and sales, and Beth's position. There are also leaders within the different lines of business, including the director of personal lines insurance and the director of commercial lines insurance. Beth is working with the company's board of directors to examine the compensation structure of this team of leaders. In addition to a retirement plan and other basic benefits such as time off, the company offers a competitive base salary plus a bonus plan that is tied to company revenue. Beth believes that a more direct tie to the company's stock value may add just the right incentive for executives.

Since the company's stock went public, its value has been a key indicator of the overall success of the company. As the company executives are closely monitoring the company stock value, Beth believes that tying executive compensation to the stock value will provide a clear incentive for executives. If executives remain focused on increasing the overall value of the stock, they should make decisions that are in the best interest of the company. Further, both executives and the company will benefit if the value of the stock continues to increase.

Initially, Beth thought granting the executives annual incentive stock options would create the right incentive for the team. By doing so, the company would grant the executives the option to purchase stock at a later date at the price on the date of the grant. The executives would then have an incentive to grow the stock value over time. However, a member of the board of directors suggested considering offering a phantom stock plan instead. A phantom stock plan exists when executives are compensated with hypothetical company shares rather than actual shares of company stock. Upon meeting certain conditions, executives receive income that is equal to the increase in the value of the company stock from the date that the phantom stock was granted until the conversion date.

Beth needs to conduct more research on both types of plans in order to formulate a recommendation for an incentive plan for executives. She must first decide if an incentive plan tied to the value of company stock is a good alternative for the company. It seems that this is a logical move to make, but Beth also needs to determine the best way to structure the plan. She thinks that the phantom stock plan may offer some advantages, but as she starts her research, she knows she needs to consider all of the options.

1. How does a stock option plan provide an incentive for executives?
2. Which plan would be better for Safeguard Insurance, the incentive stock option plan or the phantom stock plan?

Endnotes

1. 29 U.S.C. §623(c)(1).
2. ERISA §§201(2), 301(a)(3), 401(a)(1).
3. *Ibid.*
4. Treas. Reg. §1.451-2(a).
5. I.R.C. §61, 83, 162, 451; Treas. Reg. §1.83.
6. P. Joshi, "Golden Parachutes Are Still Very Much in Style." *New York Times*, June 29, 2013. Accessed March 31, 2016, www.nytimes.com.
7. J. C. Reindl, "Compuware Execs Could Get Millions in Golden Parachutes." *Detroit Free Press*, November 7, 2014. Accessed April 4, 2016, www.freep.com.
8. T. Mann, "A $195 Million Exit for United Technologies CEO." *The Wall Street Journal*, February 5, 2015. Accessed February 10, 2016, www.wsj.com.

Chapter **Twelve**

Global Employee Benefits at a Glance*

Chapter Outline

Quantifying Elements of Employee Benefits Outside the United States

North America
Canada
Mexico

South America
Brazil
Argentina

Europe
France
Germany
United Kingdom

Asia
The People's Republic of China
Japan
India

Africa
South Africa

Australia

Summary

Key Terms

Discussion Questions

Cases
1. *Understanding Your Employee Benefits: Working Abroad*
2. *Managing Employee Benefits: Expanding Internationally at Suds Microbrewery*

Endnotes

Learning Objectives

In this chapter, you will gain an understanding of:

1. The differences among benefits in the United States and around the world.

2. Paid time-off benefits in various continents and countries.

3. Protection benefits such as retirement, health care, and social security in various continents and countries.

4. Legal and regulatory influences on employee-benefits practices.

5. Other practices that distinguish various countries' benefits programs.

*This chapter was prepared by Professor Niti Pandey of the Department of Business Administration, Eastern Connecticut State University, and updated for this edition by Joseph Martocchio.

In his bestselling book *The World Is Flat,* Thomas L. Friedman talks about how the current state of technology-driven globalization has resulted in a high level of interconnections among the economies of various parts of the world. This means that U.S. employers will be increasingly required to do business with entities in many other countries as erstwhile underdeveloped parts of the world experience tremendous economic, trade, and standard-of-living growth. Additionally, the move from traditional manufacturing to knowledge- and service-based employment also means that jobs, as well as markets, are more likely to be geographically dispersed. As the need increases for employers to interact globally, human resource management (HR) professionals will have increased opportunities to develop employment practices for U.S. employees in foreign assignments, as well as deal with indigenous employees in the parent company's foreign offices. While most employers may choose to offer attractive benefits above and beyond the minimum required by the host nations so as to attract the desired talent, it is important to first know the basic legal employment context and the minimum statutory employment standards of the country where the employer proposes to do business—just as has been discussed throughout this book for U.S. employment. This chapter provides a glimpse of the wide variety of employment practices around the world. For each country, benefits issues, including paid time off, protection programs (e.g., retirement, health care), and stand-out benefits in particular regions are reviewed. Each review starts off with a brief treatment of governmental structure, norms, and historical events to help shed light on its version of employee benefits.

QUANTIFYING ELEMENTS OF EMPLOYEE BENEFITS OUTSIDE THE UNITED STATES

When referencing employee benefits in all countries, it is important to note some of the important concepts and measures. First, the **gross domestic product (GDP)** describes the size of a country's economy. Size is expressed as the market value of all final goods and services produced within the country over a specified period. The GDP is typically calculated by the country's national statistical agency. Second,

EXHIBIT 12.1
Gross
Domestic
Product (GDP),
Per Capita
GDP, Health
Expenditures,
and Labor
Force Size

Country	Gross Domestic Product (GDP) ($ trillions)	Per Capita GDP ($)	Per Capita Health Expenditures ($)	Labor Force Size (millions)
United States of America	17.97	56,300	9,627	156.40
Canada	1.62	45,900	5,003	19.30
Mexico	2.22	18,500	1,147	52.81
Brazil	1.80	15,800	1,532	109.20
Argentina	0.57	22,400	1,635	17.47
France	2.42	41,900	4,902	29.84
Germany	3.84	44,400	5,017	45.04
The United Kingdom	2.86	41,000	3,731	32.94
The People's Republic of China	19.51	14,300	800	804.00
Japan	4.65	38,200	7,446	64.32
India	8.02	5,800	232	502.10
South Africa	0.72	13,400	1,192	20.86
Australia	1.24	65,400	6,147	12.50

Notes: The GDP, per capita GDP, and per capita health expenditures are expressed in U.S. dollars adjusted for the PPP exchange rate and are based on 2015 estimates.

Source: Central Intelligence Agency. *The World Factbook 2016.* Accessed April 8, 2016, https://www.cia.gov/library/publications/the-world-factbook/index.html.

GDP per capita generally indicates the standard of living within a country: The larger the per capita GDP, presumably the better the standard of living. Exhibit 12.1 lists GDP per capita for the United States and the countries reviewed in this chapter. These figures represent each nation's GDP at **purchasing power parity (PPP)** exchange rates. That is, these figures indicate the worth of all goods and services produced in the country valued at prices prevailing in the United States. This is the measure most economists prefer when looking at per capita welfare and when comparing living conditions or use of resources across countries. Third, the **per capita expenditure on health care**, defined as the sum of Public Health Expenditure and Private Expenditure on Health, is another important measure. This measure helps employee-benefits professionals understand the standard of health care, addressing an important element of discretionary and legally required benefits.

NORTH AMERICA

This section offers a brief glimpse at employment relationships and employee benefits in Mexico and Canada. Both countries, along with the United States, are part of a trade bloc known as **NAFTA—the North American Free Trade Agreement**. As an aside, every HR professional should recognize the role of **trade blocs**. A trade bloc is a group of countries that agree to reduce trade barriers between themselves, often by lowering tariffs and sometimes restricting non-participating countries from engaging in trade relationships. As a result, many trade blocs promote regional trade and create economic growth for participating countries. Also, some trade bloc agreements include worker provisions, which is why all HR professionals should understand them. NAFTA is the second-largest free trade area—in terms of exports—behind the European Union. Trade between the United States and its NAFTA partners has soared since the agreement entered into force. Under NAFTA, trade restrictions were removed from industries such as motor vehicles and automotive parts, computers, textiles, and agriculture. In addition, the treaty also delineated the removal of investment restrictions among the three countries.

The labor side of NAFTA is the **North American Agreement on Labor Cooperation (NAALC),** which was created to promote cooperation between trade unions and social organizations to champion improved labor conditions. Overall, NAFTA is reported as having been good for Mexico, which has experienced a fall in poverty rates and a rise in real income as a result of the trade agreement.[1] This section presents a brief overview of employment relationships in Canada and Mexico and information about some of the employee benefits required by law.

Canada

Canada is a constitutional monarchy that is also a parliamentary democracy and a federation consisting of 10 provinces and 3 territories.[2] While Canada has enjoyed a trade surplus and balanced budgets for many years, recent concern and debate have grown over the increasing cost of the publicly funded health-care system.

The basic rule of Canadian law holds that labor and employment law fall within the exclusive jurisdiction of the provinces.[3] Thus, both individual and collective employment relationships are controlled at the provincial level, and federal legislation cannot override provincial laws, even when an industry or employer primarily conducts business overseas (except in cases in which the industries are expressly assigned to federal jurisdiction). The origins of the common law governing individual employment contracts are the **English Statute of Labourers** of 1562, which established working hours and wages. This statute was eventually repealed in the early 19th century but became part of the English common law and later, part of the common law governing all the provinces except Quebec. Quebec, instead, operates under the Civil Code of Quebec (instituted in 1866), whose modernized version became effective January 1, 1994.

Paid Time-Off Benefits

Canadian employment law holds that employees are entitled to several paid holidays, the number of which varies by province. Typically, the number of paid holidays ranges between 6 and 10 days per year. For example, the number is 6 on Prince Edward Island and 10 in the Northwest Territories. Employees are also entitled to two weeks' paid vacation time, along with a sum of money as vacation pay (increasing to three weeks after six years of employment).[4] Weekly vacation pay is equal to 2 percent of the employee's pay for the preceding year. Slight variations are evident from province to province. Maternity and paternity leave provisions are coordinated under the Federal Employment Insurance Act. Employees are permitted to take job-protected, paid maternity leave up to 17 weeks and paid parental leave up to 35 weeks.[5] More recently, the Canadian government introduced compassionate care leave, which provides up to 26 weeks of paid leave for an employee to care for a seriously ill family member. For the purposes of this type of leave, family members include a spouse, a common law partner, children, and parents.[6] There are no laws that require granting time off for military service.

Protection Benefits

Pensions and Retirement Benefits   Canada has two state pension plans, one for Quebec residents only and one for all other Canadians. Both are funded by matching contributions from employers and employees and are fully portable upon employment changes, much like 401(k) plans in the United States.[7] Employees contribute 4.95 percent of gross earnings (5.325 percent in Quebec), while self-employed individuals contribute 9.9 percent of declared earnings (10.65 percent in Quebec). Employers contribute the same amount as employees.[8] In addition to these public plans, many employers provide supplementary pension plans that are regulated by provincial or federal legislation, which establishes minimum funding standards; specifies the types of investments the plans may make; and deals with matters such as portability, benefit vesting, and locking in contributions. Employers frequently have different plans for executive and managerial employees.

Health and Disability Benefits   Medical and basic hospital care in Canada are paid for by provincial medical insurance plans with compulsory coverage for all residents and by funding revenue derived from both general federal taxes and provincial taxes. While public health plans normally do not provide employed persons with prescription drugs except while they are hospitalized, additional benefits are covered by private supplementary insurance, which is offered by the employer, including dental and vision care. The government provides short- and long-term disability plans.[9] Employers also provide long- and short-term disability benefits for sickness or injury as part of a benefits package.

Mexico

Mexico is a federal republic,[10] and Mexican labor law is based on the Mexican Federal Labor Law.[11] Mexico's free market economy is comprised of agriculture and a mix of new and old industries, which have become increasingly dominated by the private sector. The **Labor and Social Security article** of the constitution is still in effect.[12] Employment relationships in Mexico fall under the Federal Labor Law, which clearly defines the terms *worker* and *employer*.[13] Some of the employee benefits ensured under federal jurisdiction in Mexico are discussed below.

Paid Time-Off Benefits

Mexican employment laws stipulate certain paid time-off benefits for all employees.[14] Workers are entitled to paid time off during public holidays, and those who are required to work during a mandatory holiday are entitled to double pay. Female employees are entitled to maternity leave—six weeks of leave prior to giving birth, and six weeks of leave after birth—with full salary.[15] Maternity leave can also be extended with half pay for as long as necessary and does not affect seniority rights. Employees are entitled to 6 vacation days after being employed for one year, and they receive 2 more days for each subsequent year, up to a maximum of 12 days. Starting in the fifth year, an employee is entitled to 14 days of vacation, and for each additional period of five years, 2 more vacation days are added. Employers must pay workers a vacation premium equivalent to 25 percent of salary earned during scheduled vacation days.

Protection Benefits

Social Security Social security programs are administered by the Mexican Social Security Institute, which protects employees in matters of occupational accidents and illnesses, maternity, sicknesses, incapacitation, old age, retirement and survivor pensions, day care for children of insured workers, and social services.[16] Employees contribute 1.125 percent of gross earnings for pensions and 0.625 percent for disability and survivors' insurance. Self-employed individuals contribute 6.275 percent of declared earnings for pensions and 2.375 percent for disability and survivors' insurance. Employers contribute a substantially larger amount—5.15 percent of payroll for pensions and 1.75 percent for disability and survivors' insurance.[17]

The benefits are set forth as follows.[18] Workers with at least 52 weeks' worth of payments into the system who withdraw from employment are entitled to continue making voluntary payments. Should they return to salaried employment, they may return to the system and maintain all benefits, which may be in cash or in kind. Cash benefits take the form of payments in the early stages of illness or incapacitation, depending on the medical condition and its effects on work and pensions. In-kind benefits take the form of medical attention, including surgery, medicines, hospitalization services, and so forth.

Pensions and Retirement Benefits All workers must join the mandatory individual account system, which is slowly replacing the former social insurance system.[19] At retirement, employees covered by the social insurance system before 1997 can choose to receive benefits from either the social insurance system or the mandatory individual account system.

Health Benefits Medical services are normally provided directly to patients (including old age pensioners covered by the 1997 law) through the health facilities of the Mexican Social Security Institute.[20] Benefits include general and specialist care, surgery, maternity care, hospitalization or care in a convalescent home, medicines, laboratory services, dental care, and appliances. These benefits are payable for 52 weeks and may be extended in some cases to 78 weeks.[21] In addition, the wife of an insured man also receives postnatal benefits, and medical services are provided for dependent children up to age 16 (age 25 if they are students; no limit if disabled).[22]

Other Benefits Mexico has a national system of worker housing, paid for by employer contributions in the form of payroll taxes fixed at 5 percent; this helps workers obtain sufficient credit for the acquisition of housing. Workers who are not employed after age 50 are entitled to receive the full balance of contributions made in their names to the housing fund.[23]

SOUTH AMERICA

According to the International Monetary Fund's World Economic Outlook Database, Brazil, Argentina, Colombia, and Chile are the largest economies in South America.[24] Venezuela and Peru are experiencing economic development as well. On the other hand, Argentina and Chile have the best **human development index (HDI),** which is a comparative measure of life expectancy, literacy, and standard of living measured by the United Nations.[25] Venezuela has large oil reserves, which have turned the nation into an important player in world trade. The biggest trade bloc in South America used to be Mercosur, also called the Southern Common Market, which was comprised of Argentina, Brazil, Paraguay, Uruguay, and Venezuela as its main members, and Bolivia, Chile, Colombia, Ecuador, and Peru as associate states. The second-biggest trade bloc was the Andean Community of Nations, made up of Bolivia, Colombia, Ecuador, Peru, Venezuela, and Chile.

These two trade blocs merged in a declaration signed on December 8, 2004, at the Third South American Summit and formed one large trade bloc known as the South American Community of Nations, which has modeled itself on the European Union.[26] This section takes a brief look at the two largest economies in this potentially formidable global economic bloc: Brazil and Argentina.

Brazil

Brazil is a federal republic. The country has a well-developed mining, manufacturing, agricultural, and services sector, and it is increasingly taking on a larger share of global trade and work.[27] The **Consolidation of Labor Laws** (*Consolidacao das Leis do Trabalho*) accords many employee benefits the status of fundamental constitutional rights, and, in general, employment relationships in Brazil are highly regulated by statute.[28] For example, Brazilian law states that employer-sponsored benefits cannot be eliminated. Employment contracts are based on the country's legal principle of continuity. This principle applies to all employment contracts, both written and oral. However, in practice, employers discharge employees arbitrarily because there is a substantial supply of readily available workers who are willing to accept lower pay.[29] There simply is not enough incentive provided for employers to engage in good-faith labor relations, and job security is often lacking for most employees.[30]

Paid Time-Off Benefits

Brazilian labor law stipulates annual 30-day paid vacation plus a bonus equivalent to one-third of an employee's monthly salary. Maternity leave is 120 days and paid for by social security. In addition, paternity leave of five consecutive days is allowed as of a child's date of birth.[31]

Protection Benefits

Social Security   The social security system that went into effect in 1991 details various benefits for workers in Brazil.[32] Comprehensive social security benefits are provided by law to all workers for retirement for illness, old age, or length of service; death benefit pensions; assistance during imprisonment; savings funds; social services; professional rehabilitation assistance; work accident payments; maternity leave payments; family salary support; accident insurance; and sick leave benefits.

Pensions   Social insurance is provided to employed persons in industry, commerce, and agriculture; domestic servants; some categories of casual workers; elected civil servants; and the self-employed.[33]

There is also voluntary coverage for students, women who work in the home, the unemployed, and other categories, and also a special system for public-sector employees and military personnel. Monthly benefits are equal to 70 percent of the average earnings plus 1 percent of the average earnings for each year of contributions, up to a maximum of 100 percent. Employees contribute between 8 percent and 11 percent of gross earnings, while self-employed individuals contribute 20 percent of declared earnings. These contributions also finance sickness and maternity benefits and family allowances.

Employers are required to contribute 20 percent of payrolls. There are no maximum monthly earnings for contribution purposes. Small-enterprise employers may contribute from 2.75 percent to 7.83 percent of monthly declared earnings, depending on annual earnings declared in the last year.

Health Benefits   In Brazil, medical services are provided directly to patients in rural and urban areas through the Unified Health System. These services include such benefits as general, specialist, maternity, and dental care; hospitalization; medicines (some cost-sharing is required); and necessary transportation.[34]

Argentina

Argentina is a democratic republic that benefits from strong educational resources and rich natural resources.[35] The country had suffered economic decline and depression in the 1990s—a huge fall from being one of the world's wealthiest countries 100 years ago. With various successive governments trying to revive the economy with International Monetary Fund (IMF) aid and measures to cut the fiscal deficit, in 2002, the Argentinean president finally devalued the peso compared to the dollar and also froze utility tariffs, curtailed creditors' rights, and imposed high taxes on exports, which helped the economy rebound strongly.

Paid Time-Off Benefits

Employees are entitled to 14 days of paid vacation each year when seniority does not exceed 5 years, 21 days when seniority is between 5 and 10 years, 28 days for between 10 and 20 years of seniority, and 35 days for more than 20 years of seniority. Employees are also entitled to between three and six months of sick leave, based on seniority. Female employees are entitled to maternity leave for 45 days before birth and 45 days after birth, and these employees are entitled to cash benefits paid out by the social security funds. All employees are entitled to short leaves of absence for familial events or for examinations. There are 12 paid holidays, and employees who work on these days must be paid overtime at 100 percent of the regular hourly rate.[36]

Protection Benefits

Pensions A mandatory retirement and pension system exists in Argentina, and all employees must be covered by the social security system. Both employees and employers are required to contribute a percentage of the employee's gross wages—11 percent of covered earnings. These contributions also finance disability and survivor benefits and administrative fees (limited to 1 percent of covered earnings), for those who opt into the individual account system.[37] Voluntary contributions are the same. Employers contribute 10.17 percent or 12.71 percent of their payrolls, according to the type of enterprise. Additional contributions are made on behalf of workers in hazardous or unhealthy occupations.

Health Benefits Employee health insurance is mandated by statute, and the cost of health insurance is financed by a 6 percent employer contribution of the gross payroll. Employers must also obtain and pay the premium for collective life insurance for employees.[38] Benefits include medical, hospital, dental, and palliative care; rehabilitation; prostheses; and transportation. Benefits are defined by the schedule in law issued by the Ministry of Health and Environment. Pharmaceutical products for chronic diseases are either free or require a 30 percent copayment; 60 percent for other diseases. Pharmaceutical products are free during pregnancy, childbirth, and for postnatal care; for children until age 1; and in cases of hospitalization.[39]

EUROPE

The **European Union (EU)** is a unique international organization that aims to become an economic superpower while retaining quintessential European practices, such as high levels of employment, social welfare protection, and strong trade unions.[40] While the EU has its own legal powers and performs executive, legislative, and judicial functions just like any other governing body, it has limited authority in the area of labor and employment laws. The EU does not attempt to harmonize the employment laws of member states; under the laws of all member states, employers must provide each employee with a written document about the terms of the employment contract. The concept of "employment at will" does not exist in the EU as in the United States. (The "Employment at will" doctrine indicates that either an employee or employer may terminate employment for any reason, unless otherwise specified in a labor agreement or contract.) The EU makes use of directives and community legislation to ensure that some minimum standards are adopted by member states. All member states either have specific legislation or unfair dismissal or general civil code provisions that apply to termination of employment contracts. They all provide employees with a substantive basis for challenging employment dismissal and procedural mechanisms for adjudicating claims.[41]

The EU Web site reports that community labor law was designed with the aim of ensuring that the creation of the single market did not result in a lowering of labor standards or distortions in competition. However, it has been increasingly called upon to play a key role in making it easier for the EU to adapt to evolving forms of work organization. On the basis of Article 137 of the Treaty of Maastricht, the European Community must support and complement the activities of the member states in the area of social policy. In particular, Article 137 defines minimum requirements in the areas of working and employment conditions, and information provided to workers and the consultation of workers. Improvement of living and working conditions in member states is governed by national legislation, but also to a large extent on agreements concluded by the social partners at all levels (country, sector, and company). This section briefly presents some of the basic employee benefits practices in the EU member states of France, Germany, and the United Kingdom.

France

France is a democratic republic and is currently transitioning from the traditional model (in which government ownership and intervention were strongly featured) to greater reliance on free market mechanisms.[42] The government has given up stakes in such large companies as Air France, Renault, and Thales, while still maintaining a strong presence in public transport and defense. The population, however, has resisted reforms targeted at labor market flexibility.

With 35-hour-long workweeks and five weeks of paid vacation, French workers typically get better benefits than their U.S. counterparts.[43] Employment laws are incorporated in the **French Labor Code** *(Code du Travail)* and reflect the social-democratic ideology that has guided the employment relationship. Employees must be informed in writing about essential aspects of employment, including working hours and amount of paid leave. Such features as mandatory profit sharing and greater employee participation in management, as well as "just cause dismissal" (an acceptable reason must be given for employment termination such as insubordination), make French employment relationships different from those in the United States.

Paid Time-Off Benefits

French law grants every employee the right to a minimum of 25 days of paid vacation after one year of employment. Also, employees receive pay for 11 statutory holidays. Of these 11, the only mandatory public holiday in France is Labor Day (May 1), and employees who work on this day must be paid double time. Paid vacation cannot exceed 25 working days; a period of vacation is decided by the employer after consultation with employee representatives or based on mutual agreement; paid leave cannot be replaced by a cash payment. All women are entitled to maternity leave for an uninterrupted period of at least 14 weeks before and/or after delivery (with at least two weeks before and/or after delivery). They are entitled to receive payment or an allowance during the period of leave at a rate at least equivalent to sick pay. Coincidentally, this regulation applies to all European Union member states.[44] Following a mother's return to work, the employer will grant the employee an interview to help place her in an equivalent activity. At the time the revision of this book was being prepared, the European Union was formulating new rules and standards to establish a more comprehensive parental leave policy.

Protection Benefits

Retirement   Effective August 21, 2003, the French government mandated that employees must work longer before they may receive full government pensions. The increase from 40 to 41 years took effect in 2012. Retirees will also be prohibited from receiving their pensions while working on a part-time basis, because the pension amount is set at a generous level—85 percent of annual earnings prior to retirement. In 2016, rules were put into effect that will reduce pension benefits by 10 percent effective in 2019. And, in 2017, the minimum retirement age rose to 62. All of these actions became necessary because of a rapidly increasing government deficit.[45]

Social Security   Social security benefits granted to employees contain three components: health insurance, unemployment insurance, and retirement insurance. A base system of social insurance applies equally to all employees, with rules on reimbursement rates for medical expenses, rules on calculation of unemployment allowance, and the right to a retirement allowance. Each is the same for all employees. Also, private employers can provide company benefits such as additional medical coverage and additional retirement benefits. Furthermore, French law provides for mandatory profit sharing for employers with more than 50 employees. Employers and employees may also enter into a variety of voluntary profit-sharing programs.

Health Insurance   Employers pay for employee health insurance. Medical benefits include general and specialist care, hospitalization, laboratory services, medicines, optical and dental care, maternity care, appliances, and transportation.[46] The insured normally pays for services and is reimbursed by the local sickness fund. A €1 flat-rate contribution is paid for each medical service up to an annual ceiling (pregnant women and women on maternity leave, hospitalized persons, and persons with low income are exempt). After the deduction of the flat-rate contribution, the sickness insurance reimburses fully or in part the cost incurred by the insured depending on the type of service: 100 percent of the medical service cost for certain severe illnesses, for work injury beneficiaries who are assessed as 66.6 percent or more disabled, and for pregnant women from the sixth month of pregnancy up to the 12th day after childbirth, regardless of whether the costs are related to the pregnancy or not; 70 percent for medical services; 60 percent for paramedic services; 35 percent or 65 percent for pharmaceuticals; 60 percent or 70 percent for laboratory services; 65 percent for optical and appliance fees up to an annual ceiling; and 80 percent for hospitalization after a nominal copayment.

Other Benefits As an exception, French law provides more-flexible rules for management-level employees. Executive managers (*cadres dirigeants*) and top executives are not subject to French regulation. Integrated managers (*cadres integers*) such as office managers and forepersons are subject to regulations similar to those for regular employees, and autonomous managers (*cadres autonomes*) and managers whose work schedules cannot be determined in advance can enter into individual agreements with employers.[47]

Germany

Germany is a federal republic with the fourth-largest economy in the world.[48] The integration of the former East German economy is a strain on the overall economy of unified Germany, and unemployment rates have been very high. Germany has recently been pushing labor market reforms, such as increasing the retirement age and increased female workforce participation. And, there have been increasing concerns about the aging workforce and high unemployment.

Paid Time-Off Benefits

Employees cannot be required to work on official holidays, ranging from 9 annual holidays in northern Germany to 13 in southern Germany. The statutory minimum vacation is 24 working days (or four weeks, because Saturdays are counted). Younger workers have a right to a vacation of 25 to 30 working days; disabled workers receive an additional 5 days. A minimum of six months of employment is necessary to be eligible for vacation.[49] Under the terms of the **Maternity Leave Law,** time away from work must be counted as time worked for determining vacation entitlement. Employees may take 5 days annually or 10 days every two years (under individual state-level statutes) as paid holidays for continuing education. An employee retains his job if he is drafted into the military or called for military exercises, which creates a suspended employment relationship. Employees receive regular pay during an illness for a period of up to six weeks.

Expectant mothers can take six weeks, leave before giving birth and an additional eight weeks after giving birth, and at least an average salary or wages calculated on the basis of the last 13 weeks before commencement of leave. An employee can request up to three years of child-rearing leave, and employers must guarantee return to the same job. Payments for child-rearing leave are made by the national health authority.

Both parents are eligible for paid family leave. The government bestows the right to receive the parental allowance for a period of up to 24 months, or up to 28 months if both parents share caregiver responsibility. Employers are not required to pay salaries while on leave, but the government provides a parental allowance of about 67 percent of pay for 14 months. Alternatively, employees receive the same amount but paid over the 24-month period.

Protection Benefits

Pensions   Germany has a statutory pension system similar to the U.S. Social Security system. In addition, an employer offers a pension plan and a tax-favored investment plan. Pension benefits originate from three sources: statutory pension insurance, company pension plans, and private life insurance.[50] The retirement age under the statutory pension plan has been increasing gradually until it reaches 66 in 2023 and 67 in 2029.

Health Insurance   German laws stipulate guidelines for the minimal health welfare of workers.[51] For blue-collar workers (and some white-collar workers), mandatory state health insurance premiums are borne 50 percent by the insured and 50 percent by the employer. Employees whose income exceeds a certain amount can opt out of the state plan and purchase private health insurance. In such cases, employees may request that the employer's health insurance contribution be included in their salary.

United Kingdom

The United Kingdom (U.K.) is a constitutional monarchy and it is the second-largest economy in Europe following Germany.[52] Employment relationships are governed by a variety of common law and statutory provisions.[53] The most significant reforms, instituted by the Labour government, resulted in the **Employment Relations Act of 1999.** Employers are generally free to negotiate terms of employment, with a few statutory restrictions.

Paid Time-Off Benefits

Workers are entitled to 28 days of annual paid leave, including statutory and public holidays, and 28 weeks of statutory sick pay in any three-year period. The employer reserves the right to require the employee to undergo a medical examination to verify an illness.[54] Employers cannot permit women to work in the two weeks immediately following birth. Employees can receive a leave of 26 weeks, which may not begin prior to 11 weeks before birth. Contractual benefits other than remuneration, such as health insurance, are preserved during maternity leave. The employee also has a right to statutory maternity pay. Employees with one year of service are entitled to take 13 weeks of unpaid leave related to child care. Fathers can receive paid paternity leave within eight weeks of the child's birth. An employee is entitled to take a reasonable amount of time off during working hours to take care of *dependents,* a term that includes a spouse, children, parents, and relatives living under the same roof. Parents of young children have the right to flexible work arrangements in relation to hours/times/place of work, though requests can be refused if such arrangements were to cause disruptions to the employer. Employees must have at least 26 weeks of qualifying service to be eligible for these benefits, as well as a sufficient relationship with the child and responsibility for child care.

Protection Benefits

Pensions   All employees with the requisite National Insurance Contributions are entitled to a basic state pension. However, this is a small amount, and employees must supplement it in at least one of four ways:

- State Second Pension—Pays a certain proportion of lifetime average earnings over a quite limited band.
- Company pension—Occupational plans such as defined contribution and defined benefit plans are available from individual employers.
- Personal pension—Established arrangements between employees and insurance companies; an employer need not be directly involved, although it may choose to contribute.
- Stakeholder pension—May be operated by insurers and other providers in much the same way as personal pensions, or established by employers and administered by trustees as occupational pension plans, and are defined contribution arrangements with strict statutory limits.[55]

The retirement age will rise gradually from age 65 to age 68 from 2020 to 2046.

Health Benefits   Medical services are provided by public hospitals and by doctors and dentists under contract with, and paid directly by, the **National Health Service.** Benefits include general practitioner care, specialist services, hospitalization, maternity care, dental care, medicines, appliances, home nursing, and family planning. Patients pay £7.40 (7.40 British pounds) for each prescription and 80 percent of the cost of any dental work, up to a maximum of £204. Those receiving means-tested benefits and their adult dependents, children younger than age 16 (age 19 if a student), pregnant women, and nursing mothers are exempt from dental and prescription charges.

ASIA

As of 2016, China has had the largest economy in Asia, followed by India and Japan. Asia has several trade blocs, such as the **Asia-Pacific Economic Cooperation,** the **Asia-Europe Economic Meeting,** the **Association of Southeast Asian Nations,** and the **South Asian Association for Regional Cooperation,** to name a few. After seven years of negotiations, the final terms of the **Trans-Pacific Partnership (TPP)** were set in 2016, but it had not been put into effect at the time of this book's revision. The TPP is a trade agreement among 12 Pacific Rim countries. However, given the wide variation and diversity in the world's largest and most populous continent, there is no unifying economic body (like the EU or NAFTA) that represents all the countries of Asia. This section examines a representative sample of the relatively more-developed and developing economies in Asia: China, Japan, and India. A bloc of countries that is not examined here, but that nonetheless deserves mention since considerable jobs are being outsourced there, are those in southeast Asia: Thailand, Vietnam, Singapore, Malaysia, Philippines, Cambodia, and Laos. These economies are experiencing a current influx of foreign investment, though they are not even close to the countries discussed below in terms of annual growth rates.

The People's Republic of China

The People's Republic of China (PRC) is a communist state characterized by a fast-growing economy, which, over the past couple of decades, has been shifting from a centrally planned system to a more market-oriented one. One of the key challenges has been sustaining adequate job growth for tens of millions of workers laid off from state-owned enterprises and finding work for migrants.

The PRC Labor Law was established in 1995, resulting in a break from the traditional "iron rice bowl" system of employment, with a shift from state-owned enterprises to private ones, a move that has given rise to new employment relationship issues.[56] Under the older welfare system, the workforce was considered the property of the state, and many benefits, such as housing, medical, and retirement systems, were payable directly by state-owned enterprises to the employees. With the introduction of the PRC Labor Law, employment relationships are now defined by individual contracts.[57]

Paid Time-Off Benefits

The length of an employer-approved medical treatment period generally depends on the employee's age and length of service and can range from 3 to 24 months. During this period, the salary paid to the employee may not be less than 80 percent of the local minimum wage. Employees who have worked for one or more years are entitled to paid annual leave, but no binding laws exist about this; national policy guidelines recommend 7 to 14 days. Employees who have worked for more than one year are entitled to "home leave" if they do not live in the same place as their spouse or parents. Employees earn normal wages during this period, and employers are obligated to pay all travel expenses for employees visiting their spouses and for unmarried employees visiting their parents. Women are entitled to no less than 90 days of paid maternity leave, starting 15 days prior to birth.[58]

Protection Benefits

Pensions   A new law decoupled employment relationships from the social insurance system and set up a unified basic pension system.[59] The system now has social insurance and mandatory individual accounts. (Provincial and city/county social insurance agencies and employers adapt central government guidelines to local conditions.) Coverage includes employees in urban enterprises, urban institutions managed as enterprises, and the urban self-employed. In some provinces, coverage for the urban self-employed is voluntary. (Urban enterprises comprise all state-owned enterprises, regardless of their location.) Old age provisions in rural areas is based mainly on family support, as well as community and state financial support. Pilot systems in the form of individual accounts, supported at the town and village level, and subject to preferential support by the state, operate in some rural areas. Employees of government and Communist Party organizations, as well as those in cultural, educational, and scientific institutions (except for institutions financed off-budget), are covered under a government-funded, employer-administered system. Enterprise-based pension systems cover some employees (including the self-employed) in cities.

An employee contribution to mandatory individual accounts is 8 percent of gross insured earnings. (The contribution rate is higher in some provinces.) The minimum earnings for employee contribution and benefit purposes are equal to 60 percent of the local average wage for the previous year. The maximum earnings for employee contribution and benefit purposes vary, but may be as much as 300 percent of the local average wage of the previous year. There are no employer contributions to mandatory individual accounts. Central and local government subsidies are provided to city/council retirement pension pools as needed.

Health Insurance   China has a unified medical insurance system, with all employers and workers participating in the system. Employers contribute 6 percent of the payroll, while employees contribute 2 percent of their salary. Health insurance is based on a **Basic Medical Insurance Fund** consisting of a **Pooled Fund** and **Personal Accounts.** Employees' contributions go directly into their Personal Accounts, and 30 percent of employer contributions are paid into these accounts. Covered workers receive medical benefits at a chosen accredited hospital or clinic on a fee-for-service basis. The individual account is used to finance medical benefits only, up to a maximum equal to 10 percent of the local average annual wage. The social insurance fund reimburses the cost of the medical benefit from 10 percent up to 600 percent of the local average annual wage, according to the schedule. Medical treatment in high-grade hospitals results in lower-percentage reimbursements, and vice versa. Reimbursement for payments beyond 600 percent of the local average annual wage must be covered by private insurance or public supplementary systems. Contract workers receive the same benefits as permanent workers.[60]

Japan

Japan is a constitutional monarchy. The Japanese economy is characterized by government-industry cooperation, a strong work ethic, and mastery of high technology. A unique characteristic of the Japanese economy used to be *keiretsu*, or the close-knit relations among manufacturers, suppliers, and distributors, representing a guarantee of lifetime employment for a substantial portion of the urban labor force—a system that has now been eroded considerably.

Employment relationships[61] are based on the traditional notion of freedom of contract, and some basic employment provisions are contained in the Civil Code of 1896. However, the outdated Civil Code has been replaced, and there are currently numerous laws enacted post World War II that deal with labor standards, unions, minimum wages, child care, and family leave—just to name a few—as well as employee-benefits laws. Employee-benefits laws include various insurance schemes, participation in which is mandatory, with premiums borne either solely by the employer or by a combination of the employer and employee.

Paid Time-Off Benefits

Workers are entitled to 10 days of leave after six months. After 1.5 years of continuous employment, workers earn an additional day for each year of continuous service up to a maximum of 20 days. At the time of revision, a proposal was being considered to mandate that workers take vacation time. The strong work culture has led the majority of workers taking far fewer days off than they earned. Currently, there are no legal provisions granting employees paid time off to celebrate holidays. Maternity leave is granted if requested within six weeks of giving birth. Postbirth leave of eight weeks is mandatory, although an employee may return to work after six weeks with the approval of a physician. Employer-specific contracts determine the rate of pay during maternity leave; if the employer does not pay anything, then employment insurance pays for 42 days before birth and 56 days after birth at the rate of 60 percent of standard wages. Employees must be granted child care leave upon request for the duration of one year if the child is less than one year old. Family care leave for three months is allowed to care for family members. Employers are not required to pay wages; however, employment insurance provides up to 40 percent of regular wages. There is no military leave policy. Employers must give time off for civic duties such as voting in political elections.[62]

Protection Benefits

Pensions   Japan has a social insurance system involving a flat-rate benefit for all residents under the national pension program and earnings-related benefits under the employees' pension insurance program or other employment-related program; residents aged 20 to 59; voluntary coverage for residents aged 60 to 64 (aged 65 to 69 in special cases); and for citizens residing abroad (aged 20 to 64). The national pension program is one in which the contribution is included in the insured person's contribution to the employees' pension insurance or other employment-related program. A proportionate amount is transferred to the national pension program. All other insured persons contribute 16,900 Japanese yen monthly beginning in 2017. Low-income spouses of workers insured under the employment-related program may apply for exemption from payment. Employees' pension insurance includes 9.150 percent of basic monthly earnings and salary bonuses before tax for most employees. If the employee is contracted out, the contribution ranges between 5.47 and 5.77 percent of monthly earnings, including salary bonuses before tax. The minimum monthly earnings for contribution and benefit purposes are 98,000 yen. The maximum monthly earnings for contribution and benefit purposes are 620,000 yen. The minimum and maximum earnings levels are adjusted on an *ad hoc* basis in line with any increases in the national average wage. The government covers 50 percent of the cost of benefits, plus 100 percent of administrative costs.[63]

Health Benefits   Japan's National Health Insurance program covers medical care and treatment, which is usually provided by clinics, hospitals, and pharmacists under contract with, and paid by, the insurance carrier (some carriers provide services directly through their own clinics and hospitals).[64] Benefits include medical treatment, surgery, hospitalization, nursing care, dental care, maternity care (but only for difficult childbirths), and medicines.

There is no limit to duration. The cost-sharing amount depends on the person's age: under age 3, 20 percent of the cost; ages 3 to 69, 30 percent of the cost; ages 70 or older, 10 to 20 percent based on income. Japan's national program is available to all individuals unless they are covered by an employer-sponsored health plan. These health insurance benefits are similar to those provided under the country's national health insurance program.

India

India is a democratic federal republic with a diverse economy ranging from traditional farming to high-technology industries.[65] The Indian economy is plagued with income disparity and developmental challenges similar to China's. More than half of India's output is created with less than one-quarter of its labor force, and services are the major source of economic growth. Strong economic growth combined with easy consumer credit and a real estate boom are fueling inflation concerns, and the huge and growing population poses fundamental social, economic, and environmental problems. Basic constitutional legislation governs employment relationships for all employees, ensuring equality of opportunity to public employment and prohibition of child labor.

The **Directive Principle of State Policy** has statutes that affect various aspects of employment relationships, such as working conditions and participation in management.[66] Some of the key employee benefits provided by employers in India are provident funds, gratuities (bonuses), pension (either defined benefit or defined contribution), housing, cars, loans, life insurance protection for dependents, health/disability benefits, medical benefits for employees and their families, and leave encashment.[67] The Employees' Provident Fund Organization is one of the world's largest social security programs. Gratuities apply to most employees in India, and these are funded through employer contributions averaging approximately 4.5 percent of the payroll.

Wide variations exist between the public and private sectors, with the **Ministry of Labour** and labor laws governing employment relationships in the public sector and more employer discretion allowed in the private sector. Additionally, all blue-collar employees and factory workers are governed under existing labor laws.

Paid Time-Off Benefits

Workers employed in privately owned factories, mines, and plantations are entitled to one day off for every 20 days worked during the previous year. Typically, this accrual method provides 12 days off with pay each year. These rules do not apply to workers employed in government-owned factories or railroads. Paid leave policies are usually determined by states and industries where local governments set the number of minimum required days off and companies choose whether to offer additional paid time-off benefits. Local governments also determine the number of paid holidays, varying between 15 and 20 days.

Leave is usually calculated for each year based on the number of days worked in the previous year, and if a worker does not take all the accumulated leave, a maximum of 30 days is allowed to roll over to the succeeding calendar year. There is no statutory provision for paternity leave, but maternity leave is allowed in the form of paid time off and a possible medical bonus. All employees get paid time off for various public and national holidays.

Protection Benefits

Pensions   The first and current laws regarding pensions were passed in 1952 (employees' provident funds), with amendments in 1972 (payment of gratuities), 1976 (employees' deposit-linked insurance), and 1995 (employees' pension scheme and the national social assistance program). Pension benefits include provident funds with survivor (deposit-linked) insurance and pension funds, gratuity schemes for industrial workers, and a social assistance system. In 2004, a voluntary old age, disability, and survivors' benefits scheme was enacted. This program is part of the Unorganized Sector Social Security scheme for employees and self-employed persons aged 36 to 50 with monthly earnings of 6,500 rupees or less but without mandatory coverage, and it was introduced as a pilot program in 50 districts. Contributions are income-related and flat-rate. Coverage includes employees (such as casual, part-time, and daily wage workers and those employed through contractors) with monthly earnings of 6,500 Indian rupees or less working in establishments with a minimum of 20 employees in one of the 182 covered industries (the establishment remains covered even if the number of employees falls below 20).[68]

Employees covered by equivalent occupational private plans may contract out. Voluntary coverage exists for employees of covered establishments with monthly earnings of more than 6,500 rupees, with the agreement of the employer and for establishments with fewer than 20 employees if the employer and a majority of the employees agree to contribute. Provident fund contributions include 12 percent of basic wages (10 percent of basic wages in five specified categories of industry) in covered establishments with fewer than 20 employees, and some other specific cases.

Health Benefits   State governments arrange for the provision of medical care on behalf of the **Employees' State Insurance Corporation.**[69] Services are provided in different states through social insurance dispensaries and hospitals, state government services, or private doctors under contract. Benefits include outpatient treatment, specialist consultations, hospitalization, surgery and obstetric care, imaging and laboratory services, transportation, and the free supply of drugs, dressings, artificial limbs, aids, and appliances. The duration of benefits ranges between three months and one year, according to the insured's contribution record.

AFRICA

According to the United Nations' Human Development Report, the bottom 25 ranked nations in the world were all in Africa.[70] This is due, in large part, to corrupt governments, despotism, and constant conflict, making the entire continent of Africa—the second-largest and second-most populous—the world's poorest place. Economic conditions in Africa have stagnated and moved backward in many cases, plagued by low per capita income, lack of foreign trade and investment, poverty, low life expectancy, violence and instability, and a debilitating spread of HIV/AIDS. Some areas of economic success are South Africa and Botswana, in the southern part of the continent. Some comparable success is also being made by Ghana, Kenya, Cameroon, and most notably Nigeria, which has large proven oil reserves as well as the highest population in Africa. It is expected to boom economically. In this section, a brief review is provided of the most developed African economy, South Africa.

South Africa

South Africa is a republic and one of the few relatively more-developed economies in Africa. The country is a middle-income, emerging market with an abundant supply of natural resources as well as well-developed financial, legal, communications, energy, and transport sectors, and it has a modern infrastructure supporting an efficient distribution of goods to major urban centers throughout the region. However, there is a noteworthy social disparity, which has held over from the apartheid era with continued poverty and lack of economic empowerment among the disadvantaged groups.

Labor rights in South Africa stem from its constitution and its newest legislation, the **Labour Relations Act of 1995,** under which there is no distinction between union and nonunion employees. All employment relationships are dealt with under this law. For example, *unfair labor practice* as a term applies to individual employment contracts, as opposed to collective contracts found in the United States.[71]

Paid Time-Off Benefits

All employees are entitled to 21 consecutive days of annual leave each year (or, one paid day off for every 17 days of work), and there are 12 paid public holidays. Sick leave is calculated over a 36-month period with the same employer, and an employee is entitled to paid sick leave that is equal to the number of days an employee would normally work during a six-week period, subject to a 30-day maximum. A female employee is entitled to four months of unpaid maternity leave, and she may not work for six weeks after the birth of a child. Employees are also entitled to family responsibility leave if they have been employed for longer than four months and work at least four days per week. Leave entitlement is three days of paid child care leave per year or for the death of a family member. This leave does not carry over from one leave cycle to another.[72]

Protection Benefits

Pensions State pensions are available to all persons of relevant age, but the payout is very modest. Bargaining councils have pension or provident schemes to which employers and employees make equal contributions. The social assistance system provides coverage for citizens with limited means, and the government bears the total cost. Government contributions also finance medical benefits.[73]

Health Insurance Many private medical plans exist in South Africa, and employers that do have health insurance plans require equal contribution from employees. Retirees are entitled to subsidized medical care at provincial health-care facilities with such benefits as hospitalization and medication.[74]

AUSTRALIA

Australia is a federal parliamentary democracy. Its economy is fueled by high export prices for raw materials and agricultural products. In recent years, the country has emphasized growing ties with China and has utilized conservative fiscal policies to sustain its high economic standards. As far as employment regulations are concerned, variations exist among each of the states, as well as the Commonwealth, and the vast majority of large employers are now covered by the 2005 Work Choices Act. Employment contracts are affected by awards or industrial agreements that detail working conditions and various employee benefits (paid time off, training, and so on), and approximately 50 percent of all Australian workers are employed under awards made by the **Australian Industrial Relations Commission.**

Paid Time-Off Benefits

Full-time employees are entitled to 10 days of paid personal time off per year. Employees are also entitled to annual leave of 20 days at the end of every year of service, with unused leave accumulating from year to year. Long-service leave accrues after a period of continuous service. A minimum entitlement to unpaid parental leave exists for permanent employees, up to 52 weeks (on an unpaid basis, shared between the working parents). Paid maternity and paternity leave maximums are 18 weeks.[75]

Protection Benefits

Pensions Employers are required to make annual contributions to help support the government pension.[76] Mandatory pension requires employee contributions that are tax deductible up to a maximum of A$5,000 (5.000 Australian dollars) plus 75 percent of contributions in excess of this amount, or the age-based contribution (younger than age 35, A$15,260; ages 35 to 49, A$42,385; ages 50 or older, A$105,113), whichever is lower.[77] There is no upper limit for voluntary contributions. Employer contributions are 9.5 percent of basic wages, and this rate is rising gradually until it reaches 12 percent by 2025. Employer contributions are tax deductible. Government matches voluntary contributions made by the insured from A$20 up to A$500 for annual incomes up to $34,488. The co-contribution gradually decreases to zero as income rises.

Health Benefits Workers' medical benefits include free care by staff doctors in public hospitals. The patient pays 15 percent of the scheduled fee for outpatient ambulatory care or A$50.10, whichever is less (indexed annually for price changes). Private benefit organizations pay for private hospital stays, or public hospitals charge for those who choose treatment by their own physician in public hospitals. A fee of up to A$36.90 per prescription applies to most medicines.

Summary

This chapter reviews benefits offerings mandated by the governments of several countries around the world. The review reveals that extensive variation exists in minimum standards. A striking difference between the United States and other countries is the less-generous family leave benefits in the United States and the relatively fewer paid days off. Governments in other countries mandate paid time off, reflecting the importance of family and religion. Most countries offer social security pensions, but, in many cases, these benefits are not lucrative. The countries we reviewed offer comprehensive health-care programs, and, as is the case in the United States, mounting costs are straining these systems. In many countries, employees are required to make larger contributions to help offset higher costs.

Key Terms

gross domestic product (GDP), 312

GDP per capita, 313

purchasing power parity (PPP), 313

per capita expenditure on health care, 313

North American Free Trade Agreement (NAFTA), 314

trade blocs, 314

North American Agreement on Labor Cooperation (NAALC), 315

English Statute of Labourers, 315

Labor and Social Security article (Mexico's constitution), 317

human development index (HDI), 318

Consolidation of Labor Laws (Brazil), 319

European Union (EU), 321

French Labor Code (Code du Travail), 322

Maternity Leave Law (Germany), 324

Employment Relations Act of 1999 (United Kingdom), 325

National Health Service (United Kingdom), 326

Asia-Pacific Economic Cooperation, 327

Asia-Europe Economic Meeting, 327

Association of Southeast Asian Nations, 327

South Asian Association for Regional Cooperation, 327

Trans-Pacific Partnership (TPP), 324

Basic Medical Insurance Fund (People's Republic of China), 329

Pooled Fund (People's Republic of China), 329

Personal Accounts (People's Republic of China), 329

Unemployment Insurance Fund (South Korea), 333

Directive Principle of State Policy (India), 334

Ministry of Labour (India), 334

Employees' State Insurance Corporation (India), 335

Labour Relations Act of 1995 (South Africa), 337

Australian Industrial Relations Commission, 338

Discussion Questions

1. Discuss the main differences between health-care offerings in the United States and one other country's practices discussed in this chapter. How do these differences affect companies' ability to compete with other companies worldwide?

2. Discuss the main differences between retirement systems in the United States (taking into account legally required and discretionary programs) and one other country discussed in this chapter. Does it appear that the cost of retirement programs are creating burdens for competitive advantage?

Cases

1. Understanding Your Employee Benefits: Working Abroad

The time you dedicated to studying and preparing for an opportunity in international business is finally paying off. You have been interviewing for jobs abroad and have just received two job offers for similar positions at multinational companies, both located in South America. While you have traveled abroad extensively, either one of these jobs would help you fulfill your dream of working and living in another country. Now, you just need to decide which offer to accept. As you begin considering the options, you need to make sure you fully understand each opportunity.

One offer is for a company in Rio de Janeiro, Brazil, and the other is for a company in Buenos Aires, Argentina. Both cities have many opportunities for an exciting living and working experience. South America seems like an ideal location to start your international career, and your studies of Spanish and Portuguese should prepare you to be successful. As a global marketing expert, you are confident that your skill set will be valued at either company and that both opportunities will provide you with solid experience that will help you advance and grow in your career. Both companies are successful and growing, and you genuinely enjoyed everyone you met in the interview process at each company. Your currency conversion calculation suggests that the salary offers are similar, as is the cost of living in these two countries. All in all, this is going to be a difficult decision.

One thing you are not clear about is the type of employee benefits you should expect in each country. Each company will soon send you a complete offer letter outlining the pay and benefits, but you decide to do some research to see what you can expect. Although you are generally healthy, you are concerned about the health benefits. You think it is particularly important to understand the health-care system and costs, as you will be away from your own doctors and preferred health-care providers. You also want to make sure you understand typical retirement benefits provided to workers in both of these countries, as you are at a point in your career in which you should be concerned with your savings for retirement. Finally, you plan to travel while you are living in South America, so you want to know what kind of time-off benefits you should expect. As you wait for the details of each of the offers, you decide to start doing some research on your own.

1. How do the benefits offered in Brazil compare to those offered in Argentina?
2. How do benefits offered in these countries compare to those typically offered in the United States?

2. Managing Employee Benefits: Expanding Internationally at Suds Microbrewery

Director of Human Resources Ellie Gomez at Suds Microbrewery has helped successfully open 20 new brewery locations across the United States in the past 10 years. Suds Microbrewery is a successful chain that started with one location in the Midwest and quickly grew. The company brews several variations of its award-winning beers at each location and ships them to restaurants and retail outlets within a short radius of each brewery. Thus, company growth requires opening new breweries. Suds Microbrewery had had success in the 20 major markets that it has entered thus far in the United States, and the company is now ready to expand internationally. The company's market research has identified Canada and the United Kingdom as the company's first international locations. While Ellie is now an expert in opening a new location, she knows that hiring employees in different countries will create a lot of new challenges.

The company has secured locations in Toronto and London, and Ellie is in the process of determining the staffing plan for each new brewery. While a staff from another brewery will help open the new locations and train the new employees, Suds Microbrewery plans to hire local employees to staff each brewery. Ellie has a lot of research to do to understand local labor markets and how to recruit the right staff, but she knows the total compensation package that the company offers will be important. She has started to explore local pay rates but needs to also outline the employee benefits package to offer at each location. This is a new challenge for Ellie, as all the company's U.S. locations have the same benefits package.

The U.S. locations offer standard benefits to all full-time employees. The U.S. benefits offerings include a company-paid health insurance option, in which employees can enroll after one month of employment. To support the retirement savings of workers, the company offers a 401(k) retirement plan with a match of employee contributions of up to 5 percent of an employee's annual pay. The employees also receive six paid vacation days plus seven paid holidays each year.

Ellie knows that it is important to establish a benefits package that is not only comparable to the U.S. benefits offerings, but also competitive with the benefits offerings of competitors in the local markets where the new breweries will open. Several of the employees at the new locations, managers in particular, will be communicating with employees at U.S. locations, and thus they will have an opportunity to compare benefits. Ellie is aware, however, that employee-benefits practices are generally different in these countries from those in the United States. In particular, health insurance, retirement benefits, and time-off requirements may be regulated by law. Before Ellie can begin to make recommendations, she must first conduct research to understand what is required in each country and how the requirements compare to Suds Microbrewery's current offerings.

1. What are some challenges that Ellie is going to face in creating the new benefits packages for the international locations?
2. What are some general recommendations for Ellie as she plans these benefit offerings?

Endnotes

1. M. A. Sergie, "NAFTA's Economic Impact," Council on Foreign Relations, February 14, 2014. Accessed March 31, 2016, www.cfr.org/trade/naftas-economic-imact/p15790.
2. Accessed April 5, 2016, https://www.cia.gov/library/publications/the-world-factbook/geos/ca.html.
3. P. L. Benaroche. In P. M. Berkowitz, A. E. Reitz, and T. Muller-Bonnani (eds.), *International Labor and Employment Law*, 2nd ed., Vol. II, 2008, 53.
4. Accessed March 31, 2016, www.publicholidays.ca/.
5. Accessed April 15, 2016, www.esdc.gc.ca/en/reports/ei/maternity_parental.page.
6. Accessed, April 21, 2016, www.esdc.gc.ca/en/reports/ei/compassionate_care.page.
7. Accessed April 21, 2016, www.socialsecurity.gov/policy/docs/progdesc/ssptw/2014-2015/americas/canada.html.
8. Accessed April 23, 2016, https://www.ssa.gov/policy/docs/progdesc/ssptw/2014–2015/americas/canada.pdf.
9. Accessed April 21, 2016, https://www.canada.ca/en/services/benefits/disability.html.
10. Accessed April 19, 2016, https://www.cia.gov/library/publications/the-world-factbook/geos/mx.html.
11. V. Escoto-Zubiran. In P. M. Berkowitz, A. E. Reitz, and T. Muller-Bonnani (eds.), *International Labor and Employment Law*, 2nd ed., Vol. II, 2008, 157.

12. National Employment Law Council. *Basics of Mexico Labor Law.* Accessed October 28, 2016, http://www.nationalemploymentlawcouncil.org/nonmember/agenda_PDFs/2013/Basics_of_Mexican_Labor_Law.pdf

13. *Ibid.*

14. V. Escoto-Zubiran, 158–160.

15. N. de Buen Lozano and C. de Buen Unna. In W. L. Keller and T. J. Darby (eds.), *International Labor and Employment Laws,* 2nd ed., Vol. I, 2003, 22–60.

16. Accessed April 22, 2016, https://www.ssa.gov/policy/docs/progdesc/ssptw/2014-2015/americas/mexico.pdf.

17. *Ibid.*

18. N. de Buen Lozano and C. de Buen Unna, 22–68.

19. Accessed April 22, 2016, https://www.ssa.gov/policy/docs/progdesc/ssptw/2014-2015/americas/mexico.pdf.

20. *Ibid.*

21. *Ibid.*

22. *Ibid.*

23. *Ibid.*

24. Accessed April 15, 2016, www.imf.org/external/pubs/ft/weo/2014/02/pdf/c2.pdf.

25. Accessed April 15, 2016, http://hdr.undp.org/en/statistics/.

26. Accessed April 15, 2016, http://www.cfr.org/trade/mercosur-south-americas-fractious-trade-bloc/p12762.

27. Accessed April 15, 2016, https://www.cia.gov/library/publications/the-world-factbook/geos/br.html.

28. P. R. F. Pires and L. C. M. Gomes. In W. L. Keller and T. J. Darby (eds.), *International Labor and Employment Laws,* 2nd ed., Vol. I, 2003, 30–32, 30–19.

29. *Ibid.* 30–33.

30. *Ibid.* 30–33.

31. I. C. Franco and C. Pizzotti. In P. M. Berkowitz, A. E. Reitz, and T. Muller-Bonnani (eds.), *International Labor and Employment Law,* 2nd ed., Vol. II, 2008, 39.

32. Accessed March 31, 2016, www.socialsecurity.gov/policy/docs/progdesc/ssptw/2014-2015/americas/brazil.html.

33. *Ibid.*

34. *Ibid.*

35. Accessed March 28, 2016, https://www.cia.gov/library/publications/the-world-factbook/geos/ar.html.

36. A. Bronstein, "National Labour Law Profile: Republic of Argentina." International Labor Organization. Accessed April 22, 2016, www.ilo.org/ifpdial/information-resources/national-labour-law-profiles/WCMS_158890/lang--en/index.htm.

37. Accessed April 22, 2016, https://www.ssa.gov/policy/docs/progdesc/ssptw/2014-2015/americas/argentina.pdf.

38. J. D. Orlansky. 2008. In W. L. Keller and T. J. Darby (eds.), *International Labor and Employment Laws,* 3rd ed., Vol. IIB, 2008, 76-57.

39. Accessed April 22, 2016, http://www.ssa.gov/policy/docs/progdesc/ssptw/2014-2015/americas/argentina.html.

40. J. Kenner. In W. L. Keller and T. J. Darby (eds.), *International Labor and Employment Laws*, 2nd ed., Vol. I, 2003, 1-1–1-2.

41. *Ibid.* 1-68.

42. Accessed April 3, 2016, https://www.cia.gov/library/publications/the-world-factbook /geos/fr.html.

43. Accessed April 7, 2016, https://www.cfe-eutax.org/taxation/labor-law/france.

44. European Commimssion, "Professional, Private, and Family Life." Accessed April 21, 2016, http://ec.europa.eu/justice/gender-equality/rights/work-life-balance/index_en .htm.

45. U.S. Social Security Administration, "International Update, 2016," March 2016.

46. Accessed April 22, 2016, www.socialsecurity.gov/policy/docs/progdesc/ssptw/ 2010-2011/europe/france.html.

47. S. E. Tallent, B. Grinspan, and F. Sauvage. In W. L. Keller and T. J. Darby (eds.), *International Labor and Employment Laws*, 2nd ed., Vol. I, 2003, 3-65.

48. Accessed March 31, 2016, https://www.cia.gov/library/publications/the-world-factbook /fields/2195.html.

49. R. Lutringer and M. S. Dichter. In W. L. Keller and T. J. Darby (eds.), *International Labor and Employment Laws*, 2nd ed., Vol. I, 2003, 4-86–4-91.

50. *Ibid.*

51. *Ibid.* 4-103.

52. Accessed April 21, 2016, https://www.cia.gov/library/publications/the-world-factbook /geos/uk.html.

53. K. Jack. In W. L. Keller and T. J. Darby (eds.), *International Labor and Employment Laws*, 2nd ed., Vol. I, 2003, 7-1–7-9.

54. *Ibid.* 7-104–7-121.

55. *Ibid.* 7-151–7-153.

56. Accessed April 5, 2016, https://www.cia.gov/library/publications/the-world-factbook /geos/ch.html.

57. A. W. Lauffs *et al.* In W. L. Keller and T. J. Darby (eds.), *International Labor and Employment Laws*, 2nd ed, Vol. I, 2003, 31-5.

58. *Ibid.*

59. *Ibid.* 31-38–31-39.

60. Accessed April 22, 2016, www.socialsecurity.gov/policy/docs/progdesc/ssptw/ 2014-2015/asia/china.html.

61. Accessed April 22, 2016, www.cia.gov/library/publications/the-world-factbook/geos/ ja.html.

62. J. S. Siegel, M. Ogawa, and G. J. Bengoshi. In W. L. Keller and T. J. Darby (eds.), *International Labor and Employment Laws*, 2nd ed, Vol. I, 2003, 32-3–32-4.

63. Accessed April 17, 2016, https://www.ssa.gov/policy/docs/progdesc/ssptw/2014-2015 /asia/japan.pdf.

64. Accessed April 17, 2016, https://www.ssa.gov/policy/docs/progdesc/ssptw/2014-2015 /asia/japan.pdf.

65. Accessed April 24, 2016, https://www.cia.gov/library/publications/the-world-factbook /geos/in.html

66. *Ibid*

67. R. Singhania. In W. L. Keller and T. J. Darby (eds.), *International Labor and Employment Laws*, 3rd ed, Vol. IIB, 2008, 57-11–57-13.

68. R. Singhania, *International Labor and Employment Laws*, 2008, 57-64–57-65.

69. Accessed April 20, 2012, www.socialsecurity.gov/policy/docs/progdesc/ssptw/2010-2011/asia/india.html.

70. United Nations, "Human Development Report." Accessed April 3, 2016, http://hdr.undp.org/en/composite/HDI.

71. Accessed August 15, 2012, https://www.cia.gov/library/publications/the-world-factbook/geos/sf.html.

72. S. Stelzneer. In P. M. Berkowitz, A. E. Reitz, and T. Muller-Bonnani (eds.), *International Labor and Employment Law*, 2nd ed, Vol. II, 2008, **221**.

73. *Ibid.* 224–225.

74. E. J. Lubbe and H. J. Datz. In W. L. Keller and T. J. Darby (eds.), *International Labor and Employment Laws*, 2nd ed, Vol. I, 2003, 33-94–33-95.

75. J. Cooper *et al.* In W. L. Keller and T. J. Darby (eds.), *International Labor and Employment Laws*, 3rd ed, Vol. IIB, 2008, 70-1–70-6.

76. *Ibid.* 70-71–70-73.

77. *Ibid.* 70-87.

Glossary

133⅓ percent rule   Guards against backloading in retirement plans. The annual accrual rate cannot exceed 133⅓ percent of the rate of accrual for any prior year.

401(k) plans   Qualified retirement plans named after the section of the Internal Revenue Code that created them. These plans permit employees to defer part of their compensation to the trust of a qualified defined contribution plan. Only private-sector or tax-exempt employers are eligible to sponsor 401(k) plans.

457 plans   Nonqualified retirement plans for government employees; named after the section of the Internal Revenue Code that created them.

A

accidental death and dismemberment insurance (AD&D)   Covers death or dismemberment as a result of an accident. Dismemberment refers to the loss of two limbs or the complete loss of sight (i.e., blindness). Compared to life insurance, AD&D generally does not pay survivor benefits in the case of death by illness.

accommodation and enhancement benefits   Promote opportunities for employees and their families, such as educational scholarships and transportation services.

accrual rules   Specify the rate at which participants accumulate (or earn) retirement benefits.

accrued benefits   The benefit amount that a participant has earned under the plan's terms at a specified time or account balances for key employees.

accumulated benefit obligation   The present value of benefits based on a designated date. Actuaries determine a defined benefit plan's accumulated benefit obligation by making assumptions about the return on investment of assets and characteristics of the participants and their beneficiaries, including expected length of service and life expectancies.

adverse selection   The tendency of an insurance pool to disproportionately attract "bad risks" and discourage the participation of "good risks."

after-tax contributions   Do not enable employees to exclude contributions from annual income before calculating federal and state income tax obligations.

Age Discrimination in Employment Act of 1967 (ADEA)   A federal equal-employment opportunity law that protects older workers age 40 and over from illegal discrimination in the workplace.

age-weighted profit-sharing plan   A type of hybrid retirement plan; fundamentally a defined contribution plan because benefit amounts fluctuate according to how well the investments of plan assets perform. Consideration of age in these plans is similar to defined benefit plans because employers contribute disproportionately more to the accounts of older employees based on a projected hypothetical benefit at normal retirement age.

Americans with Disabilities Act (ADA)   Prohibits discriminatory employment practices against qualified individuals with disabilities.

Americans with Disabilities Act Amendments Act of 2008   Made important changes to the definition of the term *disability*. These changes make it easier for an individual seeking protection under the ADA to establish that he or she has a disability within the meaning of the ADA.

annual addition   The annual maximum allowable contribution to a participant's account in a defined contribution plan, including employer contributions allocated to the participant's account, employee contributions, and forfeitures allocated to the participant's account.

annuities   A series of payments for the life of the participant and beneficiary. Annuity contracts are usually purchased from insurance companies, which make payments according to the contract.

automatic cost-of-living adjustments (COLAs)   Annual increases to Social Security benefits that approximate rises in the cost of goods and services, such as items regularly purchased (e.g., food, medical care).

average benefit test   A test for coverage requirements that determines whether qualified plans benefit a "nondiscriminatory classification" of employees and possess an "average benefit percentage" for non highly compensated employees that is at a minimum 70 percent of the average benefit percentage for highly compensated employees covered by the plan.

averaged index monthly earnings (AIME) Refer to a factor in determining a person's Social Security benefits, specifically, age 62, disability, or death, adjusted for changes in the person's earnings over the course of his or her employment and changes in average wages in the economy over the same period.

B

backing-in approach A reactive process for making possible changes to benefits. Companies evaluate the benefits program only when unexpected problems arise.

backloading Occurs whenever benefits accrue at a substantially higher rate during the years close to an employee's eligibility to earn retirement benefits. The Internal Revenue Service discourages backloading; employers must follow one of three rules to ensure regular accumulation of retirement benefits: three percent rule, 133⅓ percent rule, or fractional rule.

back care programs Educational programs designed to help workers reduce back injuries through training, exercise programs, ergonomic evaluations of the work environment, and relaxation techniques.

banking hours A feature of flextime schedules that enables employees to vary the number of work hours daily as long as they maintain the regular number of work hours on a weekly basis.

base pay The monetary compensation employees earn on a regular basis for performing their jobs. Hourly pay and salary are the main forms.

base period The minimum period of time an individual must be employed before becoming eligible to receive unemployment insurance under the Social Security Act of 1935.

benefits strategy The use of benefits practices that support total compensation strategies, human resource strategies, and competitive strategies.

bereavement leave Provides paid time off for employees, usually following the death of a relative. A bereavement policy specifies the relatives whose death qualifies employees for leave. Also known as *funeral leave.*

bona fide executive In the context of the mandatory retirement age for employer-sponsored retirement plans, this person primarily manages the overall company and directs the work of two or more people.

business necessity A legally acceptable defense against charges of alleged discriminatory employment practices in Title VII of the Civil Rights Act of 1964 and the Civil Rights Act of 1991 claims. Under the business necessity defense, an employer proves that the suspect practice prevented irreparable financial damage to the company.

C

Cadillac tax Based on a provision of the Patient Protection and Affordable Care Act of 2010, a tax that is (scheduled to be) collected from employers that offer high-cost employer-sponsored health plans.

cafeteria plans Enable employees within a company to choose from among a designated set of benefits and different levels of these benefits. These plans meet the IRC Section 125 criteria and represent one type of *flexible benefit plans.*

capital gains The difference between the company stock price at the time of purchase and the lower stock price at the time an executive receives stock options.

capital loss Refers to the difference between the company stock price at the time of purchase and the lower stock price at the time an executive receives the stock options when the stock price at disposition is lower.

carryover provisions Permit employees to take unused vacation time at a later time.

carve-out plans A contract entered into between an insurance company and another company to provide special services such as prescription drugs or cancer treatment to its members or beneficiaries. Sometimes, carve-out plans are purchased to cover dental care, vision care, or mental and substance abuse services.

case management A means by which companies ensure that patients receive essential medical attention on a cost-effective basis.

cash balance plan A type of hybrid retirement plan that defines benefits for each employee by reference to the amount of the employee's hypothetical account balance.

cash-out provisions Pay employees an amount equal to the unused vacation days based on regular daily earnings.

Centers for Medicare & Medicaid Services One of two federal agencies with primary responsibility for the programs established by the Social Security Act of 1935 and its subsequent amendments. See also *Social Security Administration*.

child care Programs that focus on supervising preschool-age dependent children whose parents work outside the home.

Civil Rights Act of 1991 A federal law that shifted the burden of proof of disparate impact from employees to employers, overturning several 1989 Supreme Court rulings. Previously, employees were responsible for indicating which employment practices created disparate impact in employment discrimination suits, and for demonstrating how the employment practice created disparate impact (intentional discrimination).

Clean Air Act Amendments of 1990 Require employers in smoggy metropolitan areas such as Los Angeles to comply with state and local commuter-trip-reduction laws.

cliff vesting Enables employees to earn 100 percent vesting rights after no more than three years of service.

coinsurance A feature of health plans that refers to the percentage of covered expenses or a fixed dollar amount paid by the insured.

company stock Total equity or worth of a company.

company stock shares Equity segments of equal value. Equity interest increases with the number of stock shares.

compensable factors Job attributes that compensation professionals use to determine the value of jobs, and whether jobs are equal for the purposes of the Equal Pay Act of 1963. These factors pertain to skill, effort, responsibility, and working conditions.

compensation discussion & analysis (CD&A) A section contained within the definitive proxy statement (DEF 14A), must present an unambiguous explanation of all executive compensation information contained in the tables.

competitive strategy The planned use of company resources—technology, capital, and human resources—to promote and sustain competitive advantage.

comprehensive major medical plans Replace traditional fee-for-service plans by extending coverage to a broader array of services (similar to supplemental plans).

compressed workweek schedules Enable employees to perform their work in fewer days than a regular five-day workweek.

concurrent reviews Conducted by health insurance companies to determine whether additional hospitalization is medically necessary. The main goal of such reviews is cost control.

Consolidated Omnibus Budget Reconciliation Act of 1985 (COBRA) An amendment to ERISA that provides employees and beneficiaries the right to elect continuation coverage under group health plans if they would lose coverage due to a qualifying event.

consortium EAPs Establish contracts with sets of numerous smaller employers. Smaller companies combine limited resources to establish a contract with a third-party provider.

constructive confrontation Entails discussing incidents of poor performance with a troubled employee, citing the necessity of improving job performance within a designated period. In many instances, employees recognize that personal problems are responsible for poor performance and voluntarily seek help through an EAP.

constructive receipt A legal concept that guides the timing of an executive's obligation to pay income taxes. Under this doctrine, the plan is subject to taxation if the assets are available to the employee without substantial restrictions, limitations, or risk of forfeiture.

consumer-driven health care The objective of helping companies maintain control over costs while also enabling employees to make greater choices about their health care. CDHPs combine a pretax payment account with a high-deductible health plan.

Consumer Price Index (CPI) Indexes monthly price changes of goods and services that people buy for day-to-day living.

continuation coverage Refers to extended healthcare plan participation mandated by COBRA up to 36 months following a qualifying event.

contributory financing (contributory plans) The company and its employees share the costs of discretionary benefits.

copayment Nominal payments an individual makes as a condition of receiving services

core hours The time when employees must be present in the workplace; a feature of flextime schedules.

core plus option plans Extend a pre-established set of benefits such as medical insurance and retirement plans as a program core.

corporate-owned life insurance A particular supplemental executive retirement plan based on the use of whole life insurance.

cost-of-living adjustments (COLAs) Periodic base pay increases that are based on changes in prices as indexed by the consumer price index (CPI). COLAs enable workers to maintain their purchasing power and standards of living by adjusting base pay for inflation.

coverage requirements Limit an employer's freedom to exclude employees from qualified plans. Tests to determine whether coverage requirements are met include the ratio percentage test and the average benefit test.

current profit-sharing plans Award cash to employees, typically on a quarterly or annual basis.

D

day care Programs involving the supervision and care of children or the elderly.

death benefits Awarded in two forms under workers' compensation: burial allowances and survivor benefits. Burial allowances reflect a fixed amount, varying by state.

death claim Workers' compensation claim for deaths that occur in the course of employment or that are caused by compensable injuries or occupational diseases.

deductible The amount an individual pays for services before health benefits become active.

DEF 14A See also *definitive proxy statement.*

deferred compensation An agreement between an employee and a company to render payments to an employee at a future date. Deferred compensation is a hallmark of executive compensation packages.

deferred profit-sharing plans Place cash awards in trust accounts for employees. These trusts are

set aside as a source of retirement income on behalf of employees.

defined benefit plans A retirement plan that awards a monthly or annual sum equal to a percentage of a participant's preretirement pay multiplied by the number of years he or she has worked for the employer. Defined benefit plans are also referred to as pension plans.

defined contribution plans Employees make contributions to their accounts based on a chosen percentage of annual pay. At their discretion, the company makes matching contributions, which are determined by a formula.

definitive proxy statement Companies must file this statement under Section 14a of the Securities Exchange Act. This statement is typically referred to as a DEF 14A, revealing detailed information about the compensation of the chief executive officer (CEO) and named executive officers (NEOs), who are the four most highly compensated executives after the CEO. Within the DEF 14A, companies must disclose multiple types of information about compensation. This information should be presented in narrative and tabular form. The narrative is referred to as the Compensation Discussion & Analysis (CD&A) and it must present an unambiguous explanation of all executive compensation information contained in the tables. See also *Compensation Discussion & Analysis (CD&A).*

deliberate and knowing torts Torts that entail an employer's deliberate and knowing intent to harm at least one employee.

dental fee-for-service plans Fashioned after general fee-for-service insurance programs, these plans provide protection against dental health care expenses in the form of cash benefits paid to the insured or directly to the dental care provider.

dental HMOs Prepaid dental services.

dental care plan Covers routine preventative procedures and necessary procedures to promote the health of teeth and gums.

dental maintenance organizations Deliver dental services through the comprehensive health-care plans of many health maintenance organizations (HMOs) and preferred provider organizations (PPOs).

dental service corporations Nonprofit corporations of dentists owned and administered by state dental associations.

disposition The sale of stock by the stockholder.

distribution Payment of vested benefits to participants or beneficiaries.

distributive justice Perceived fairness about how rewards are distributed.

Dodd-Frank Act. See *Wall Street Reform and Consumer Protection Act of 2010.*

Drug-Free Workplace Act of 1988 A federal law mandating that companies holding federal contracts worth at least $100,000 or grants in any amount promote a drug-free workplace.

dual capacity A legal doctrine that applies to the relationship between employers and employees. Specifically, a company may fulfill a role for employees that is completely different from its role as employer.

duration of work test Determines eligibility for disability benefits under Social Security based on whether an individual has worked sufficiently long enough (and contributed to Social Security).

E

economic exchange As with wages and salary, an agreement whereby the nature of the exchange has been specified at the time of employment. Economic exchanges can also be renegotiated at any time during employment, as with yearly pay raises. Explicit company policies and procedures help to ensure that each party (i.e., the employer and the employee) fulfills the obligations in the exchange relationship. In other words, in exchange for continued employments and wages, employees are obligated to work for the employer.

Economic Growth and Tax Relief Reconciliation Act of 2001 Created tax benefits to individuals and companies in various ways, such as increasing the amount that companies and employees can contribute to qualified retirement plans on a pretax basis.

economies of scale The idea that it is more efficient or less costly to provide the same benefit to larger groups of individuals than to smaller groups of individuals.

educational assistance benefits Payments for tuition, fees and similar expenses, books, supplies, and equipment. The payments may be for either undergraduate- or graduate-level courses and do not have to be for work-related classes.

educational assistance program Allows employees to exclude as much as $5,250 of annual gross income for educational assistance.

elder care Programs that provide physical, emotional, or financial assistance for aging parents, spouses, or other relatives who are not fully self-sufficient because they are too frail or disabled.

election period Relating to the Consolidated Omnibus Budget Reconciliation Act, refers to the period that begins on or before the occurrence of the qualifying event, and it extends for at least 60 days.

elimination period Minimum amount of time an employee must wait after becoming disabled before disability insurance payments begin. Elimination periods follow the completion of the pre-eligibility period.

Emergency Unemployment Insurance (EUC) Program established in June 2008 by the Supplemental Appropriations Act of 2008; provides 13 additional weeks of federally funded unemployment insurance benefits to the unemployed who have exhausted all state unemployment insurance benefits for which they were eligible.

employee assistance programs (EAPs) Help employees cope with personal problems that may impair their personal lives or job performance. Examples of these problems are alcohol or drug abuse, domestic violence, the emotional impact of AIDS and other diseases, clinical depression, and eating disorders. EAPs also assist employers in helping troubled employees identify and solve problems that may be interfering with their job or personal lives.

employee benefits Compensation other than hourly wage or salary. Examples include paid vacation, health-care coverage, and tuition reimbursement.

Employee Benefits Security Administration Agency of the U.S. Department of Labor that possesses responsibility for enforcing Title I of ERISA. This agency conducts investigations through its 10 regional offices and 5 district offices located in major cities throughout the country.

employee-financed benefits Employers do not contribute to the financing of discretionary benefits because employees bear the entire cost.

employee-owned annuities Offer executives the greatest degree of financial security because they own the annuities. An executive sets up an annuity arrangement with a third-party vendor such as a mutual fund company; then, the company pays the cost for the annuity. An executive's vested retirement benefit usually determines the amount of the annuity.

employee (individual) mandates Something that an individual must do because it is required by law.

Employee Retirement Income Security Act of 1974 (ERISA) Regulates the establishment and implementation of discretionary benefits practices. These include medical, life, and disability programs as well as pension programs.

employee stock option plans (ESOPs) Provide shares of company stock to employees. It can be thought of as stock bonus plans that use borrowed funds to purchase stock.

employer mandate Under the Patient Protection and Affordable Care Act of 2010, a requirement that companies with at least 50 employees offer affordable health insurance to its full-time employees. For the purposes of this law, full-time employees work on average at least 30 hours per week or 130 hours per month.

Employment and Training Administration U.S. Department of Labor agency that oversees unemployment insurance programs.

equal-employment opportunity (EEO) Related to federal laws prohibiting discrimination against various protected classes of individuals regarding all employment practices, including employee benefits.

Equal Employment Opportunity Commission (EEOC) Federal government agency that oversees the enforcement of EEO laws.

Equal Pay Act of 1963 A federal EEO law requiring that companies pay women equally when performing work equal to that of men as defined by compensable factors. This act does specify permissible exceptions, allowing companies to pay women less than men for jobs of equal worth, based on seniority, merit, quantity of work, or other factors besides sex.

equal payments Reflect a belief that all employees should share equally in the company's gain to promote cooperation among employees.

essential benefits A requirement of the Patient Protection and Affordable Care Act of 2010, include items and services within 10 categories, for example, ambulatory patient services, emergency services, and hospitalization.

establishment funds Primitive forms of disability insurance created and funded by employers that provided minimal cash payments to workers who became occupationally ill or injured.

excepted benefits Benefits not subject to requirements of the Patient Protection and Affordable Care Act of 2010 that apply to group health plans.

excess approach A method approved by the Internal Revenue Service for integrating qualified defined contribution plans with Social Security benefits. This approach stipulates a compensation amount, which is known as the integration level. Companies contribute to the pension plan or offer benefits at a lower rate for compensation below the integration level than above the integration level.

excess benefit plans Executive retirement plans that extend the provisions of existing qualified plans. The objective is to increase retirement benefits by the amount lost due to contribution and annual addition limits set by the Internal Revenue Service.

exclusion provisions In insurance plans, a list of the particular conditions that are ineligible for coverage. For example, most disability insurance plans do not provide coverage for disabilities that result from self-inflicted injuries.

exclusive provider organization (EPO) A variation of preferred provider organizations (PPOs). EPOs do not offer reimbursement for services provided outside the established network of health-care providers. See *preferred provider organization.*

executive compensation consultants Recommend alternative pay packages to compensation committees.

executive perquisites Cover a broad range of benefits from free lunches to the use of corporate jets. These benefits help recognize the attained status of executives.

exempt jobs Not subject to the overtime pay provisions of the Fair Labor Standards Act (FLSA).

exercise of stock option An employee's purchase of stock using stock options.

experience rating A system that establishes higher contributions (to fund insurance programs) for employers with higher incidences of claims (i.e., more people using the insurance).

experience rating system Establishes higher contributions to fund unemployment insurance programs for employers with higher incidences of unemployment.

extrinsic compensation Includes both monetary and nonmonetary rewards.

F

Fair Labor Standards Act of 1938 (FLSA) Contains provisions for minimum wages, overtime pay, and child labor restrictions.

fair market value The average value between the highest and lowest reported sales price of a stock on the New York Stock Exchange on any given date.

Family and Medical Leave Act of 1993 (FMLA) Provides protection in cases of family or medical emergencies. FMLA permits eligible employees to take up to a total of 12 workweeks of unpaid leave during any 12-month period for family or medical emergencies.

family assistance programs Help employees provide care to young children and dependent elderly relatives.

family coverage Offers health insurance benefits to the covered employee and qualified dependents.

FAS 106 Created by the Financial Accounting Standards Board; a rule that changed the method of how companies recognize the costs of nonpension retirement benefits, including health insurance, on financial balance sheets. This rule effectively reduces a company's net profit amounts listed on the balance sheet.

FAS 132 requires that companies disclose substantial information about the economic value and costs of retiree health-care programs.

Federal Employees' Compensation Act Created a workers' compensation program for federal civilian employees.

Federal Insurance Contributions Act (FICA) Mandatory taxes employees and employers pay to finance the Social Security Old-Age, Survivor, and Disability Insurance Program (OASDI).

Federal Unemployment Tax Act (FUTA) Mandatory tax employers pay to fund state unemployment insurance programs.

fee-for-service plans Provide protection against health-care expenses in the form of cash benefits paid to the insured or directly to the health-care provider after receiving health-care services. These plans pay benefits on a reimbursement basis.

fiduciaries Individuals who manage employee-benefits plans and retirement plan funds.

fiduciary responsibilities The duties of managers of employee-benefits programs and pension plan funds. Established by ERISA to ensure prudent choices in managing and administering pension or welfare plans that are in the best interest of participating employees. Fiduciaries can be insurance companies, employee-benefits professionals, or others who are deemed qualified to make prudent decisions.

Financial Accounting Standards Board (FASB) Nonprofit company responsible for improving standards of financial accounting and reporting in companies.

flat benefit formula In retirement plans, it designates either a flat dollar amount per employee (flat amount formula) or dollar amount based on an employee's compensation (flat percentage formula). Annual benefits are usually expressed as a percentage of final average wage or salary.

flexible benefit plans See *cafeteria plans*.

flexible scheduling Allows employees the leeway to take time off during work hours to care for dependent relatives or react to emergencies.

flexible spending accounts Permit employees to pay for certain health-benefits expenses or to pay the premium or cost for at least one of these benefits.

flexible work arrangements Create the flexibility for employees to balance work and nonwork demands or interests.

flextime schedules Allow employees to modify work schedules within specified limits set by the employer. Employees adjust when they will start work and when they will leave.

floating holidays   Allow employees to take paid time off to observe any holiday not included on the employer's list of recognized paid holidays.

forfeitures   Amounts from the accounts of employees who terminated their employment prior to earning vesting rights.

Form 5500   Guides employers in reporting detailed financial and actuarial data about pension and welfare plans to the U.S. Department of the Treasury.

formularies   Lists of drugs proven to be clinically appropriate and cost effective. The basis for setting formularies varies for each insurance plan.

fractional rule   Guards against backloading in retirement plans. This rule applies to participants who terminate their employment prior to reaching normal retirement age. It also stipulates that benefit accrual upon termination be proportional to normal retirement benefits.

full retirement age   Age at which individuals become eligible to receive full old-age (retirement benefits) Social Security benefits. This age began rising slowly from age 65 in 2000 and will reach age 67 for individuals born in 1960 or later.

full-integration approach   Reduces an individual's company-sponsored disability benefits by the amount of public disability benefits.

full-service EAPs   Include service providers such as alcohol treatment programs. Employers offer full-service EAPs through in-house services, third-party providers, or participation in a consortium EAP.

fully insured plans   Based on a contractual relationship with one or more insurance companies to provide health-related services for employees and their qualified dependents. Under fully insured arrangements, insurance companies assume the risk for paying medical claims, and insurers take responsibility for administering the plan.

funded plans   Allocate money or property (i.e., company stock or securities) to trust funds or insurance company contracts established in an executive's name without risk of forfeiture.

funding mechanisms   Provide for executive retirement plans, the financial resources for funded or unfunded plans. Funding mechanisms vary according to the level of security, from least amount of security to the greatest amount: general asset approach, corporate-owned life insurance, split-dollar life insurance, rabbi trusts, secular trusts, and employee-owned annuities.

funeral leave   See *bereavement leave*.

G

Genetic Information Nondiscrimination Act of 2008 (GINA)   Protects job applicants, current and former employees, labor union members, and apprentices and trainees from discrimination based on their genetic information by making unlawful the misuse of genetic information to discriminate in health insurance and employment.

Giles v. General Electric Co.   A case in which the U.S. Court of Appeals for the Fifth District upheld a lower court's decision to award a former General Electric machinist $590,000 for damages, front pay, and attorney fees. Giles injured his back while performing his job.

golden handcuffs   The idea that defined benefit pension plans provide strong financial incentive for employees to build seniority because pension income is much more generous for these individuals (compared to those who leave the company after a few years).

golden parachute   Refers to a clause in most executive employment agreements that provides pay and benefits to executives following their termination resulting from a merger.

grandfathered plans   Individual and group health plans already in existence prior to March 23, 2010, which is the enactment date of the Patient Protection and Affordable Care Act of 2010.

Great Depression   A period during the 1930s in which scores of businesses failed and masses of employees became chronically unemployed.

gross domestic product (GDP)   Describes the size of a country's economy. Size is expressed as the market value of all final goods and services produced within the country over a specified period. The GDP is typically calculated by the country's national statistical agency.

GDP per capita   Generally indicates the standard of living within a country: The larger the per capita GDP, presumably the better the standard of living.

group coverage Extends health insurance coverage to a group of employees and their qualified dependents.

group model HMOs Primarily use contracts with established practices of physicians that cover multiple specialties. Each group model HMO contracts exclusively with one practice of physicians at a time. These HMOs do not employ physicians directly. Instead, they compensate physicians according to a pre-established schedule of fees for each service, or on a capitation basis by setting monthly amounts per patient.

H

Health Care Financing Administration The previous name for the current Centers for Medicare & Medicaid Services.

health-care plans Cover the costs of services that promote sound physical and mental health, including physical examinations, diagnostic testing, surgery, hospitalization, psychotherapy, dental treatments, and corrective prescription lenses for vision deficiencies.

Health Insurance Portability and Accountability Act of 1996 (HIPAA) An amendment to ERISA, this act imposes requirements on group health and health insurance issuers relating to portability, increased access by limiting preexisting limitation rules, renewability, and health-care privacy.

Health Maintenance Organization Act of 1973 (HMO Act) Promoted company use of health maintenance organizations by providing HMOs with financial incentives subject to becoming federally qualified.

health maintenance organizations (HMOs) Sometimes described as providing prepaid medical services because fixed periodic enrollment fees cover HMO members for all medically necessary services only if the services are delivered or approved by the HMO.

health protection programs A host of practices geared toward promoting sound health. Health protection programs subsume health insurance and a variety of programs designed to promote physical and mental health.

health reimbursement arrangements Reimburse employees for health-care expenses.

health risk appraisals Wellness programs that inform employees of potential health risks based on a physical examination and responses to questions about certain habits (e.g., diet and family members' health histories).

health savings accounts (HSAs) For employees who are enrolled in an HDHP to help pay for medical expenses. It is important to note that HSAs are not available for any other type of health-care plan.

high-deductible health insurance plans Require substantial deductibles compared to managed care plans and traditional fee-for-service plans.

highly compensated employees Defined in the Internal Revenue Code as a 5 percent owner at any time during the year or the preceding year, *or* for the preceding year: the employee had compensation from the employer in excess of $120,000 in 2017, *and* if the employer so chooses, the employee was in the top-paid group of employees where top-paid employees are the top 20 percent of most highly compensated employees.

high policy-making position In the context of the mandatory retirement age for employer-sponsored retirement plans, refers to those who play a significant role in the development of company policy but do not have direct line control (e.g., over business functions such as accounting, finance, human resources).

hospitalization benefits The items that a health plan will provide coverage for, related to stays in the hospital such as the cost of the room and necessary medical supplies.

hospital insurance tax Mandatory tax that employers and employees pay to help fund the Medicare Part A program. A taxable wage base does not apply. Also known as *Medicare tax.*

HR strategies (human resource strategies) Specify the use of multiple human resource (HR) practices that are consistent with a company's competitive strategy.

hybrid plans Combine features of defined benefit and defined contribution plans. Four common hybrid retirement plans include cash balance plans, target benefit plans, money purchase plans, and age-weighted profit-sharing plans.

I

illegal bargaining subjects Proposals for contract revisions that are either illegal under the National Labor Relations Act or violate federal or state law.

impairment approach Bases workers' compensation benefit amounts on the physical or mental loss associated with an injury to a bodily function. This approach does not account for loss of future earnings because it ignores the physical and mental capacities necessary to perform the essential functions of one's job.

incentive pay Defined as compensation, other than base wages or salaries, that fluctuates according to employees' attainment of some standard such as a pre-established formula, individual or group goals, or company earnings. Also known as *variable pay.*

incentive stock options Entitle executives to purchase their companies' stock in the future at a predetermined price. The predetermined price usually equals the stock price at the time an executive is granted the stock option. In effect, executives are purchasing the stocks at a discounted price. Executives generally exercise their option to purchase the stock after the price has increased dramatically.

indemnity plan Traditional health insurance plans in which the insurance company reimburses the patient or health-care provider a designated amount.

individual coverage Health insurance purchased outside the employment setting for herself and qualified dependents.

individual mandate Under the Patient Protection and Affordable Care Act of 2010, a requirement that individuals who can afford to purchase health insurance must do so either by participating in an employer-sponsored plan or purchasing health insurance coverage independently.

individual practice associations Partnerships of independent physicians, health professionals, and group practices. IPAs charge lower fees to designated populations of employees (e.g., Company A's workforce) than fees charged to others. Physicians who participate in this type of HMO practice from their own facilities and continue to see HMO enrollees and patients who are not HMO enrollees.

informational justice Fairness of the accounts given for certain procedures.

in-house EAPs Rely on employees of the company to provide EAP services.

injury claims Workers' compensation claims for disabilities that have resulted from accidents such as falls, injuries from equipment use, or physical strains from heavy lifting.

inpatient benefits Covered expenses associated with hospital stays.

insurance policy Contractual relationship between an insurance company and beneficiary that specifies the obligations of both parties. For example, a health insurance company specifies that it will cover the cost of physical examinations, and a life insurance company agrees to pay a spouse an amount equal to double of his deceased wife's annual salary.

insured A person covered by an insurance policy.

integrated paid time-off policy Enables employees to schedule time off without justifying the reasons.

Internal Revenue Code (IRC) The set of federal government regulations pertaining to taxation in the United States, for example: sales tax, company (employer) income tax, individual (employee) income tax, property tax.

International Employee Assistance Professionals Association (EAPA) A professional organization dedicated to promoting standards for EAPs.

interpersonal justice Perceived fairness of the interpersonal treatment people receive from others

J

job-lock phenomenon Occurs whenever an employed individual experiences a medical problem, and this individual is "locked" into his or her current job because most health insurance plans contain preexisting condition clauses.

jury duty Leave and witness duty policies protect employee rights to serve on a jury or as a witness in courts of law. Participation may be paid or unpaid, depending upon various factors. Jury duty is guided by federal and state law; witness duty policy is guided by state law in only about one-third of all states.

Jury Systems Improvement Act of 1978 A federal law recognizing that participation on a jury in federal court is a protected individual's right.

K

key employees Defined in the Internal Revenue Code as any employee who during the current year is an officer having an annual pay greater than $175,000 in 2017, a 5 percent owner of a business, or a 1 percent owner of the a business whose annual pay is more than $150,000.

L

leveraged ESOPs Stock option plans that borrow money from a financial institution to purchase company stock. Over time, the company makes principal and interest payments to the ESOP to repay the loan.

liability management For the purposes of executive retirement plans, liability management speaks to adequate preparation to honor financial obligations to executives as set forth in nonqualified plans.

life insurance Protects the families of employees by paying a specified amount upon the employee's death. Most policies pay some multiple of the employee's salary.

lifetime limits refers to the maximum amount a plan would cover.

Longshore and Harborworkers' Compensation Act Created a workers' compensation program for maritime workers.

long-term disability Refers to illnesses or accidents that prevent an employee from performing his or her own occupation over a designated period, oftentimes up to two years.

long-term disability insurance Provides benefits for extended periods of time anywhere between six months and life.

loss of wage earning capacity approach Factors in two important issues that are likely to affect an injured worker's ability to compete for employment: human capital (e.g., work experience, age, and education) and the type of permanent impairment.

lump sum distributions Single payments of benefits. In defined contribution plans, lump sum distributions equal the vested amount (sum of all employee and vested employer contributions, and interest on this sum).

M

mail order prescription drug program Dispenses expensive medications used to treat chronic health conditions such as HIV infection or neurological disorders such as Parkinson's disease.

managed care plans Emphasize cost control by limiting an employee's choice of doctors and hospitals. They also provide protection against health-care expenses in the form of prepayment to health-care providers.

mandatory bargaining subjects Employers and unions must bargain over these subjects if either constituent makes proposals about them. These subjects include disability pay, health care, paid time off, and retirement.

mandatory retirement age Illegal under the Aged Discrimination in Employment Act (ADEA) with the exception of limited circumstances.

matching contributions Money the employer deposits into an employee's defined contribution account contingent on the employee making contributions first.

maximum excess allowance Amount by which the excess benefit percentage exceeds the base benefit percentage for permitted disparity rules involving Social Security OASDI payments and employer-sponsored defined benefit payments.

maximum offset allowance Limits the amount by which benefits may be reduced. The maximum offset allowance may be the lesser of 50 percent of the benefit the employee would have earned without the plan's offset reduction (i.e., gross benefit percentage), or 0.75 percent of the participant's final average compensation multiplied by the participant's years of service (up to a maximum of 35 years).

Medicaid A jointly funded, federal–state health insurance program for low-income people and a variety of people in need, including children, the elderly, the blind, or disabled people who are

eligible to receive federally assisted income maintenance payments.

Medicare Programs that serve nearly all U.S. citizens
aged at least 65 or disabled Social Security beneficiaries by providing insurance coverage for hospitalization, convalescent care, and major doctor bills.

Medicare Advantage Variety of health insurance
coverage options for individuals eligible for Medicare protection who choose not to participate in
Parts A and B.

Medicare Advantage or Medicare Part C One of
four Medicare programs; offers beneficiaries additional choices in health-care providers.

Medicare Part A One of four Medicare programs;
provides compulsory hospitalization insurance.

Medicare Part B One of four Medicare programs;
provides voluntary supplementary medical insurance.

**Medicare Prescription Drug, Improvement and
Modernization Act of 2003** Led to changes in the
Medicare program by adding prescription drug
coverage and recognizing health savings accounts
(HSAs).

Medicare Select plans Medigap policies that offer
lower premiums in exchange for limiting the
choice of health-care providers.

Medicare tax See *hospital insurance tax.*

Medigap Insurance that supplements Part A and
Part B coverage, available to Medicare recipients
in most states from private insurance companies
for an extra fee. Most Medigap plans help cover
the costs of coinsurance, copayments, and
deductibles.

mental health and substance abuse plans Cover
the costs for treating mental health ailments such
as clinical depression and the abuse of alcohol or
chemical substance abuse.

Mental Health Parity and Equity Act A federal
law that established parity requirements for mental health plans being offered in conjunction with
a group health plan that contains medical and surgical benefits. This act requires that any group
health plan that includes mental health and substance use disorder benefits along with standard
medical and surgical coverage must treat them
equally in terms of out-of-pocket costs, benefit
limits, and practices such as prior authorization
and utilization review.

mergers and acquisitions The combination of
once-separate business entities or companies into a
single business.

merit pay programs Reward employees with permanent increases to base pay according to differences in job performance.

military leave Enables employees who are members of the National Guard to report for military
duty when ordered just as civilians do in the
event of a mandatory military draft. Employers
choose whether to pay employees while on military leave.

minimum funding standards Ensure that employers contribute the minimum amount of money necessary to provide employees and beneficiaries
promised benefits.

mix-and-match plans Permit employees to purchase any benefit (and benefit level).

modular plans Offer numerous fixed benefit
packages to meet the lifecycle needs and priorities
of different employee groups. Examples include
single employees with no dependents, single
parents, married workers with dependents, and
employees nearing retirement.

money purchase plan A type of hybrid retirement
plan that is a defined contribution plan because
the benefit is based on the account balance (i.e.,
the employer contributions plus returns on investment of the employer contributions) at retirement.
However, these plans possess the funding requirements of defined benefit plans because employers
must make annual contributions according to the
designated formula for the plan.

morbidity tables Express annual probabilities of
the occurrence of health problems. In general,
insurance companies set insurance rates higher as
the probability of death or the occurrence of health
problems increases.

mortality tables Indicate yearly probabilities
of death based on factors such as age and sex established by the Society of Actuaries. Insurance companies rely on these tables in the underwriting process.

multiemployer plans Pension or welfare plans for
workers in industries in which it is common to
move from employer to employer when work
becomes available, such as in the skilled trades (for
example, carpentry). The Labor Management

Relations Act of 1947, also known as the Taft-Hartley Act, spurred the growth of multiemployer plans in the private sector. These plans are also referred to as *Taft-Hartley plans*.

multiple-payer system Refers to a system in which more than one party is responsible for covering the cost of health care, including the government, employers, labor unions, employees, or individuals not currently employed (e.g., retirees, the unemployed, and employees whose employers do not pay for health-care coverage).

multiple tiers Specified copayment amounts an individual will pay for a specific prescription.

N

named executive officers (NEOs) The four most highly compensated after the CEO, and detailed information about their compensation must be disclosed in the definitive proxy statement DEF 14A.

National Association of Insurance Commissioners (NAIC) A nonprofit organization that addresses issues concerning the supervision of insurance within each state. Specifically, the NAIC has three main objectives: maintaining and improving state regulation, ensuring the reliability of insurance companies in matters of financial condition, and promoting fair, just, and equitable treatment of policyholders and claimants.

National Labor Relations Act of 1935 (NLRA) Established the right of employees to bargain collectively with employers on such issues as wages, work hours, and working conditions.

National Labor Relations Board (NLRB) Oversees the enforcement of the NLRA.

network model HMOs Contract with two or more independent physicians' practices. These HMOs usually compensate physicians according to a capped fee schedule.

Newborns' and Mothers' Health Protection Act of 1996 Sets minimum standards for the length of hospital stays for mothers and newborn children, and prohibits employers and all insurers (independent and self-funded indemnity plans as well as managed care plans) from using financial incentives to shorten hospital stays.

noncontributory financing (noncontributory plans) The company pays the total cost of designated discretionary benefits.

nondiscrimination rules These rules prohibit employers from discriminating in favor of highly compensated employees in contributions or benefits, availability of benefits, rights, or plan features. Also, employers may not amend pension plans to favor highly compensated employees.

nonexempt jobs Subject to the FLSA overtime pay provision.

non-grandfathered plans New health plans (or preexisting plans that have been substantially modified after March 23, 2010, that is, the enactment date of the Patient Protection and Affordable Care Act of 2010.

nonleveraged ESOPs A company contributes stock or cash to buy stock. The stock is then allocated to the accounts of participants. Nonleveraged plans are stock bonus plans.

nonproduction time A variety of possible uses of time related to, but not actually performing, an employee's main job duties or to periods of nonwork time during a work shift. Nonproduction time related to the performance of job duties includes cleanup, preparation, and travel between job locations. Nonwork time during a work shift includes rest periods or breaks and periods to eat a meal.

nonqualified deferred compensation (NQDC) plans Specify the payment of compensation in the future.

nonscheduled injuries As classified in workers' compensation programs, these are general injuries of the body that make working difficult or impossible. Examples of nonscheduled injuries include back or head damage.

nonstatutory stock options Deferred compensation that does not qualify for favorable tax treatment. Executives pay income taxes on the difference between the discounted price and the stock's fair market value at the time of the stock grant, not at the time of disposition, and they do so at their ordinary income tax rate. They do not pay taxes in the future when they choose to exercise their nonstatutory stock options.

normal retirement age Lowest age specified in a pension plan. Upon attaining this age, an employee gains the right to retire without the consent of the employer, and to receive benefits based on length of service at the full rate specified in the pension plan.

O

occupational disease claims Workers' compensation claims for disabilities caused by ailments associated with particular industrial trades or processes.

offering period Refers to the span in time over which employees, including executives, may purchase the employer's stock based on the money set aside in their accounts established through payroll deduction.

offset approach A method approved by the Internal Revenue Service for integrating qualified pension plans with Social Security benefits. This approach subtracts a particular fraction of the qualified pension plan benefit from the total benefit without integration.

offset provisions Reduce company-sponsored retirement, disability, or life insurance by subtracting a particular percentage of these benefits from workers' compensation or Social Security disability plans.

Old-Age, Survivor, and Disability Insurance (OASDI) Programs that provide retirement income, income to the survivors of deceased workers, and income to disabled workers and their family members under the Social Security Act of 1935.

Older Workers Benefit Protection Act (OWBPA) The 1990 amendment to the Age Discrimination in Employment Act of 1967.

on-call time Requires employees to spend time on or close to the employer's premises so that they cannot use the time effectively for their own purposes. Virtually every employer can demand that nonexempt employees be available on an as-needed basis. In general, on-call time is paid leave.

organizational citizenship behavior Employees' discretionary behavior, not explicitly or directly recognized by the formal reward system of the employer, but in aggregate promoting organizational effectiveness.

out-of-pocket maximum Refers to the maximum amount a policyholder must pay per calendar year or plan year.

outpatient benefits Covered expenses for treatments in hospitals not requiring overnight stays.

outplacement assistance Programs that provide technical and emotional support to employees who are being laid off or terminated. Companies assist through a variety of career and personal programs designed to develop employee job-hunting skills and self-confidence.

outsourcing A contractual agreement by which an employer transfers responsibility to a third-party provider. In the case of benefits, third-party providers are independent companies with expertise in benefits design and administration.

P

paid time off Policies that compensate employees when they are not performing their primary work duties. Companies offer most paid time off as a matter of custom, particularly paid holidays, vacations, and sick leave.

partial disabilities Provide supplemental benefits in long-term disability plans to cover a portion of income loss associated with part-time employment.

partial disabilities inclusion Refers to a provision of many company-sponsored long-term disability plans. Specifically, this provision offers supplemental benefits to cover a portion of income loss associated with part-time employment.

Patient Protection and Affordable Care Act of 2010 (PPACA) Enacted on March 23, 2010, a comprehensive law that mandates health insurance coverage and sets minimum standards for insurance.

Pension Protection Act of 2006 (PPA) Designed to strengthen employee rights as retirement plan participants. Is an amendment to ERISA.

pension equity plans Hybrid retirement plans that are similar to cash balance plans, except that these plans credit employees' accounts with points based on years of service.

pension plans Provide income to individuals and beneficiaries throughout their retirement.

per capita expenditure on health care Defined as the sum of Public Health Expenditure and Private Expenditure on Health, is an important measure that helps employee-benefits professionals understand the standard of health care, addressing an important element of discretionary and legally required benefits.

percentage discounts Fees that are discounted from the amounts health-care providers would usually charge.

performance plan Refers to a type of equity agreement whereby a company's board of directors establishes performance criteria that an executive must meet before receiving a reward of stocks or stock options.

permanent partial disabilities Limit the kind of work an individual performs on an enduring basis.

permanent total disabilities Prevent individuals from ever performing any work.

permissive bargaining subjects Subjects on which neither the employer nor union is obligated to bargain. These subjects include administration of funds, retiree health benefits, and workers' compensation (within the limits of various state laws).

permitted disparity rules Allow companies to explicitly take into account Social Security OASDI benefits when determining pension benefits. Subject to established limits, qualified plans may reduce benefits based on the benefits owed under the Social Security program. Companies rely on either the excess approach or offset approach to integration. Also known as *Social Security integration.*

person-focused pay General rewards to employees for acquiring job-related competencies, knowledge, or skills rather than for demonstrating successful job performances.

phantom stock A compensation arrangement whereby boards of directors compensate executives with hypothetical company stock rather than actual shares of company stock. Phantom stock plans are similar to restricted stock plans because executives must meet specific conditions before they can convert these phantom shares into real shares of company stock.

plan termination rules Specifications set forth by the Pension Benefit & Guaranty Corporation regarding the discontinuation of an employer's defined benefit pension plan.

platinum parachutes Lucrative awards that compensate departing executives with severance pay, continuation of company benefits, and even stock options. Companies typically use platinum parachutes to avoid long legal battles or critical reports in the press, essentially by paying off a CEO to give up his or her post.

point-of-service plans (POSs) Combine features of fee-for-service systems and health maintenance organizations. POS plans are almost identical to PPOs except, like HMOs, POS plans require the selection of a primary care physician.

preadmission certification Certification by a medical professional of a health insurance company may be necessary before a doctor can authorize hospitalization of a policyholder. Failure to ascertain preadmission certification may lead to denial of hospitalization benefits.

precertification reviews Evaluate the appropriateness of proposed medical treatment as a condition for authorizing payment. Also known as *prospective reviews.*

pre-eligibility period Spans from the initial date of hire to eligibility for coverage in a disability insurance program.

preexisting condition A mental or physical disability for which medical advice, diagnosis, care, or treatment was received during a designated period preceding the beginning of disability or health insurance coverage.

preferred provider organization (PPO) A type of managed care plan that refers to a select group of health-care providers who agree to furnish health-care services to a given population (for example, Company B's employees) at a higher level of reimbursement than under fee-for-service plans.

Pregnancy Discrimination Act of 1978 (PDA) Amendment to Title VII of the Civil Rights Act of 1964. The PDA prohibits discrimination against pregnant women in all employment practices.

premium Amount of money an individual or company pays to maintain insurance coverage.

premium-only plans Enable employees to pay their share of the cost to receive health insurance, dental insurance, and other company-sponsored health insurance.

prepaid group practice Provide medical care for a set amount.

prepaid plan   Pays health-care providers a fixed amount according to the number of individuals covered by the plan.

prescription card program   Operates like an HMO by providing prepaid benefits with nominal copayments for prescription drugs.

prescription drug plans   Cover a portion of the costs of legal drugs that state or federal laws require be dispensed by licensed pharmacists.

pretax contributions   Enable employees, with tax regulation approval, to exclude contributions to benefits from annual income before calculating federal and sometimes state income tax obligations.

primary care physicians   Designated by HMOs to determine whether patients require the care of a medical specialist. This functions to control costs by reducing the number of medically unnecessary visits to expensive specialists.

primary insurance amount (PIA)   Equals the monthly benefit amount paid to a retired worker at full retirement age or to a disabled worker.

probationary period   Initial term of employment (the length of which is set by the employer) during which companies attempt to ensure that they have made sound hiring decisions. Often, employees are not entitled to participate in discretionary benefits programs during their probationary periods.

procedural justice   The perceived fairness of processes.

prospective reviews   Also known as precertification reviews; help control health insurance expenditures by evaluating the appropriateness of proposed medical treatment as a condition for authorizing payment. Specifically, prospective reviews aim to verify a patient's coverage, determine whether the health plan covers the treatment, judge whether the proposed treatment is medically appropriate, and specify whether a second surgical opinion is necessary.

protection programs   Provide family benefits, promote health, and guard against income loss caused by catastrophic factors like unemployment, disability, or serious illnesses.

provider payment systems   Payment arrangements between health-care providers and managed care insurers.

psychological contracts   Implicitly establish terms of employment. This is in contrast to more explicit economic exchange agreements such as wage or salary levels.

purchasing power parity (PPP)   Exchange rates that indicate the worth of all goods and services produced in the country valued at prices prevailing in the United States. This is the measure most economists prefer when looking at per capita welfare and when comparing living conditions or use of resources across countries.

Q

qualified beneficiary   For the purposes of the Consolidated Omnibus Budget Reconciliation Act, any individual who is a beneficiary under the group health plan such as the spouse of the covered employee or dependent child of the covered employee. Qualified beneficiaries include the covered employee when the qualifying event is termination of employment (other than by reason of misconduct) or a reduction in work hours.

qualified benefits   Any employer-sponsored benefit for which an employee may exclude the cost from federal income tax calculation. For example, an employee's monetary contribution to an employer-sponsored medical insurance plan is excluded from the calculation of annual federal taxes.

qualified domestic relations orders (QDROs)   In qualified plans, QDROs permit a retirement plan to divide a participant's benefits in the event of divorce. Dividing a participant's benefits without a QDRO is a violation of ERISA and the IRC.

qualified individual with a disability   Person who possesses the necessary skills, experience, education, and other job-related requirements and, regardless of reasonable accommodation, can perform the essential functions of the job; related to the ADA.

qualified joint and survivor annuity (QJSA)   In qualified plans, a QJSA is an annuity for the life of the participant with a survivor annuity for the participant's spouse.

qualified plans   Welfare and pension plans that meet various requirements set forth by the Employee

Retirement Income Security Act of 1974; these plans entitle employees and employers to favorable tax treatment by deducting the contributions from taxable income. Qualified plans do not disproportionately favor highly compensated employees.

qualified preretirement survivor annuity (QPSA) In qualified plans, a QPSA provides payments for the life of the participant's surviving spouse if the participant dies before he or she has begun to receive retirement benefits.

qualified scholarship programs Established by Section 117 of the Internal Revenue Code, these programs grant tax benefits to employees for their own or their children's education below graduate-level work. The tax benefit equals the amount of qualified tuition reduction plus related expenses (e.g., fees, books, supplies).

qualified tuition reductions Reduction in tuition granted by the employer's program of qualified scholarship programs.

qualifying events Pertain to an employee's right to elect continuation coverage under the Consolidated Omnibus Budget Reconciliation Act. Qualifying events include the death of the covered employee, termination or reduction in hours of employment (other than by reason of misconduct), divorce or legal separation, dependent child ceasing to meet the health plan's definition of a dependent child, and eligibility for Medicare benefits under the Social Security Act.

R

rabbi trusts Irrevocable grantor trusts named after an Internal Revenue Service ruling that created them. Grantors of a rabbi trust, in this case, employers, maintain ownership of the trust. Companies establish rabbi trusts to provide executives and key employees or beneficiaries with deferred compensation upon retirement or termination without cause.

ratemaking service organizations Recommend rates that states charge companies to provide workers' compensation insurance.

rating manuals In workers' compensation programs, these manuals specify insurance rates based on classifications of businesses.

ratio percentage test A test for coverage requirements that determines whether qualified plans cover a percentage of non highly compensated employees that is at least 70 percent of the percentage of highly compensated employees covered by the plan.

recent work test Determines the eligibility for disability benefits under Social Security based on the age at which an individual becomes disabled.

referral EAPs List of names and contact information for a variety of professional help services, ranging from crisis hot lines to alcohol and substance abuse treatment programs.

rehabilitative services Cover physical and vocational rehabilitation in workers' compensation. Rehabilitative services are available in all states.

relational psychological contracts Employees' expectations from the employer that might be either economic or noneconomic, but are also emotional, subjective, and intrinsic in nature.

restoration An objective of executive retirement plans that addresses the gap between the maximum retirement benefits allowed by the Internal Revenue Service for qualified plans and the more substantial retirement income benefits absent IRS regulations.

restricted stock A type of long-term executive compensation. Specifically, restricted stock means that executives do not have any ownership control over the disposition of the stock for a predetermined period, often 5 to 10 years.

restricted stock plans A company may grant executives with stock options at market value or discounted value, or they may provide stock instead. Under restricted stock plans, executives do not have any ownership control over the disposition of the stock for a predetermined period, often many years. This predetermined period is known as the vesting period, much like vesting rights associated with employer-sponsored retirement plans.

restricted stock units Shares of company stock that are awarded to executives at the end of the restriction period.

retirement plans Provide income to individuals and beneficiaries throughout their retirement.

retrospective reviews Following medical treatment but prior to disbursement of benefits, help control health insurance expenditures by determining whether the health insurance program covers the patient, the medical condition, and the medical treatment. These reviews also judge whether claims are nonfraudulent by confirming that medical treatments were actually given and appropriate for the medical condition.

risk-of-loss rules Alternatively, *uniform coverage requirement;* rules that require that employers make the full amount of benefits and coverage elected under a flexible spending account (FSA) plan available to employees from the first day the plan becomes effective regardless of how much money an employee has actually contributed.

Roth individual retirement account (Roth IRA) A tax-free, nondeductible IRA introduced by the Taxpayer Relief Act of 1997. Withdrawals are nontaxable, including the account's earnings if distributions meet certain criteria. See also *traditional individual retirement account.*

S

sabbatical leave Paid time off for professional development activities such as certification, conducting research, and curriculum development.

safe harbors Compliance guidelines in a law or regulation.

salary reduction agreements Permit an employer to defer a specified amount of pay, often expressed as a percentage of pay, into the employee's defined contribution retirement account each pay period.

Sarbanes-Oxley Act of 2002 Mandated a number of reforms to enhance corporate responsibility, enhance financial disclosures, and combat corporate and accounting fraud in response to corporate accounting scandals in Enron, Tyco, and other large U.S. corporations.

savings incentive match plans for employees (SIMPLEs) May be the basis for individual retirement accounts or Section 401(k) plans in small companies.

say on pay This provision of the Dodd-Frank Act gives company shareholders the right to vote yes or no on executive compensation proposals that are contained in proxy statements, including current and deferred components and golden parachute agreements. The frequency is determined by shareholder vote. Although the say on pay provision guarantees shareholders the right to vote on executive compensation proposals, the vote is nonbinding.

scheduled injuries The loss of a member of the body, including an arm, leg, finger, hand, or eye, as classified in workers' compensation programs.

scholarship programs Cover some or all of the tuition and related expenses for employees or family members pursuing undergraduate degrees in two- or four-year colleges.

second-injury funds Cover a portion or all of the costs of a current workers' compensation claim associated with preexisting conditions from a work-related injury during prior employment elsewhere.

second surgical opinions A feature of many health insurance plans, reduces unnecessary surgical procedures and costs by encouraging an individual to seek an independent opinion from another doctor.

secular trusts Similar to rabbi trusts with one exception: Secular trusts are not subject to a company's creditors in the event of bankruptcy or insolvency.

Securities and Exchange Commission (SEC) A nonpartisan, quasi-judicial federal government agency with responsibility for administering federal securities laws.

Securities Exchange Act of 1934 Applies to the disclosure of executive compensation in companies that trade stock on public stock exchanges.

Self-Employment Contributions Act (SECA) Mandatory tax that self-employed individuals contribute to the OASDI and Medicare programs, but at a higher tax rate than required for non-self-employed individuals.

self-funded plans Refer to health plans that pay benefits directly from an employer's assets.

seniority pay systems Employees rewarded with permanent additions to base pay periodically according to employees' length of service performing their jobs.

short-term disability For the purposes of private disability insurance plans, an inability to perform the duties of one's regular job for a limited period (e.g., six months).

short-term disability insurance   Provides income benefits for limited periods of time, usually less than one year.

sick leave   Benefits that compensate employees for a specified number of days absent due to occasional minor illness or injury.

single coverage   Extends health insurance benefits only to the covered employee.

single-payer system   Refers to a health-care system in which the government regulates the health care and uses taxpayer dollars to fund health care such as in Canada and some other economically developed countries. Single-payer systems are often referred to as universal health-care systems because the government ensures that all its citizens have access to quality health care regardless of ability to pay.

six-year graduated schedule   Allows workers to become 20 percent vested after two years and to vest at a rate of 20 percent each year thereafter until they are 100 percent vested after six years of service.

smoking cessation   A type of wellness program designed to help employees quit smoking tobacco products.

social exchange   The most basic concept explaining social behavior. All social behavior can be seen as an exchange of activity (work effort), tangible (visible performance) or intangible (motivation and commitment), and more or less rewarding or costly (pay and benefits), between at least two persons (employee and employer).

social good   Refers to a booming economy, low levels of unemployment, progressive wages and benefits, and safe and healthful working conditions.

Social Security Act of 1935   Established four main types of legally required benefits: unemployment insurance, retirement income, benefits for dependents, and medical insurance (Medicare).

Social Security Administration (SSA)   One of two federal agencies with primary responsibility for the programs established by the Social Security Act of 1935 and its subsequent amendments. See also *Centers for Medicare & Medicaid Services.*

Social Security credits   Used by the Social Security Administration to determine whether eligible individuals qualify for benefits. Employees accumulate credits based on their payment of Social Security taxes withheld from earnings.

Social Security integration   See *permitted disparity rules.*

Social Security numbers   The nine-digit numbers used to keep track of employee wages and benefits under the original OASDI and unemployment insurance programs.

split-dollar life insurance   Policies that provide separate life benefits and death benefits. The employer and executive share the premium payment. An agreement between the employer and executive determines the relative share of the premium and the policy's owner.

staff model HMOs   Medical facilities owned by the HMO that employ medical and support staff on the premises. These practices compensate physicians on a salary basis. Staff physicians treat only HMO members.

state compulsory disability laws   See *workers' compensation.*

stock appreciation rights   A type of executive deferred compensation that provides income to executives at the end of a designated period, much like restricted stock options. However, executives never have to exercise their stock rights to receive income. The company simply awards payment to executives based on the difference in stock price from the time the company granted the stock rights at fair market value to the end of the designated period, permitting the executives to keep the stock.

stock grant   A company's offering of stock to employees.

stock options   Describe employees' right to purchase company stock.

strategic benefit plans   Detail different scenarios that may reasonably affect the company, and these plans emphasize long-term changes in how a company's benefit plans operate.

strategic planning   Entails a series of judgments, under uncertainty, that companies direct toward achieving specific goals. Companies base strategy formulation on environmental scanning activities. The main focus of environmental scanning is discerning threats and opportunities.

stress management A type of wellness program that helps employees cope with many factors inside and outside the work environment that contribute to stress.

suitable work For purposes of unemployment insurance benefits, suitable work refers to jobs that require skills, knowledge, and ability similar to a person's customary work. Unemployed workers must demonstrate that they are actively seeking suitable work to maintain unemployment insurance benefits.

summary compensation table Discloses compensation information for CEOs and the four most highly paid executives over a three-year period employed by any company whose stock is traded on public stock exchanges. The information in this table is presented in tabular and graphic forms to make information more accessible to the public. Required by the Securities Exchange Act of 1934.

summary of material modification Describes important (i.e., material) changes to the benefits plan. Material information applies to changes in the benefits program, including plan administrators, claims procedures, eligibility rules, and vesting provisions of retirement plans. Required by the Employee Retirement Income Security Act.

summary plan descriptions Specify essential information about employer-sponsored benefits as required by the Employee Retirement Income Security Act. Essential information includes the names and addresses of the employees responsible for developing and administering the benefits plan, disclosure of employee rights under ERISA, eligibility criteria for participating in the benefits program, and conditions under which an employee becomes disqualified for benefits or is suspended, claims procedures for receiving payments and for appealing denial of claims, and whether a retirement plan is insured by the Pension Benefit Guarantee Corporation.

supplemental executive retirement plans (SERPs) Provide executives with supplemental retirement benefits, usually increasing an executive's total retirement benefits to a substantially greater sum than restoration plans.

supplemental retirement benefits Increase an executive's total retirement benefits to a sum that is substantially greater than benefits provided by restoration plans.

T

Taft-Hartley plans See *multiemployer plans*.

target benefit plan A type of hybrid retirement plan that calculates benefits in a fashion similar to defined benefit plans based on formulas that use income and years of service. However, these target benefit plans are fundamentally defined contribution plans, because the benefit amount at retirement may be more or less than the targeted benefit amount based on the investment performance of the plan assets.

taxable wage base Limits the amount of annual wages or payroll cost per employee subject to taxation to fund OASDI programs.

tax-deferred annuity (TDA) Established by Section 403(b) of the Internal Revenue Code, the TDA is a type of qualified retirement plan for employees of nonprofit organizations such as churches, private and public schools and colleges, hospitals, and charitable organizations.

Taxpayer Relief Act of 1997 Introduced a tax-free nondeductible individual retirement account (IRA), referred to as the Roth IRA.

telecommuting Alternative work arrangement in which employees perform work at home or some other location besides the office.

temporary partial disabilities Individuals may perform limited amounts of work until making a full recovery.

temporary total disabilities Prevent individuals from performing meaningful work for a limited period. Individuals with temporary total disabilities eventually make full recoveries.

term life insurance The most common type of life insurance offered by companies; provides protection to an employee's beneficiaries only during a limited period based on a specified number of years or maximum age. After that, insurance automatically expires.

three percent rule Guards against backloading in retirement plans. A participant's accrued benefit cannot be less than 3 percent of the normal retirement benefit, assuming the participant began participation at the earliest possible age under the plan and she or he remained employed without interruption until age 65 or the plan's designated normal retirement age.

Title VII of the Civil Rights Act of 1964 A federal equal employment opportunity (EEO) law that makes it an unlawful employment practice for an employer to discriminate against any individual with respect to his compensation, terms, conditions, or privileges of employment, because of such individual's race, color, religion, sex, or national origin.

top-down approach A proactive process for benefits planning. Companies regularly review the entire benefits program or particular parts of the program.

top hat plan Unfunded deferred compensation plan for a select group of managers or highly compensated employees.

top-heavy provisions Apply to minimum benefits accrual and vesting rights. Plans are said to be top-heavy if the accrued benefits or account balances for key employees exceed 60 percent of the accrued benefits or account balances for all employees.

total compensation strategies The use of compensation and benefits practices that support both human resource strategies and competitive strategies.

trade blocs Groups of countries that agree to reduce trade barriers between themselves, often by lowering tariffs and sometimes restricting nonparticipating countries from engaging in trade relationships.

traditional individual retirement account (IRA) Provides for a tax-free deduction when a contribution is made, and the IRA is subject to income tax in its entirety when distributed. See also *Roth IRA.*

transactional psychological contracts Employees' expectations from the employer are more economic and extrinsic in nature.

transportation services Companies may sponsor public transportation subsidies, vanpools, or employer-sponsored vans or buses that transport employees between their homes and the workplace. These services promote attendance and help retain employees for whom transportation between home and work is either challenging (because of heavy traffic or unreliable transportation) or too expensive.

trust Obligation to protect the interests of designated trustees who are the individuals or organizations that have responsibility to manage employee-benefit plans.

tuition reimbursement programs Fully or partially reimburse an employee for expenses incurred for education or training.

U

underwriting Decision process that insurance companies rely upon to decide whether to offer insurance.

Unemployment Compensation Act of 2008 Expanded the Emergency Unemployment Compensation Program benefits to 20 weeks nationwide (from 13 weeks) and provided for 13 more weeks of emergency unemployment compensation (for a total of 33 weeks) to individuals who reside in states with high unemployment rates.

unfunded plans Do not guarantee retirement benefits because companies may choose to use any money set aside for an executive's retirement for other purposes and a company's creditors.

Uniformed Services Employment and Reemployment Rights Act of 1994 A federal law that gives individuals the right to employment by the company in which they worked prior to military service (i.e., reemployment rights). Individuals reemployed after military service are entitled to the seniority and other rights and benefits they would have had by remaining continuously employed.

unit benefit formulas Recognize length of service in retirement plans. Typically, employers decide to contribute a specified dollar amount per years worked by an employee. Alternatively, they may choose to contribute a specified percentage amount per years of service.

universal health care Refers to systems in which the government ensures that all its citizens have access to quality health care regardless of ability to pay.

universal life insurance Provides protection to employees' beneficiaries based on the insurance feature of term life insurance and a more flexible savings or cash accumulation plan than is found in whole life insurance plans.

use-it-or-lose-it provision Does not permit employees to have unused vacation time awarded in one year available in subsequent years.

usual, customary, and reasonable charges   Defined as not more than a physician's usual charge, within the customary range of fees charged in the locality, and reasonable, based on the medical circumstances.

utilization reviews   Evaluate the frequency of employee's usage and cost of health insurance based on a review of insurance claims and the quality of specific health-care services. Also, employers offering health benefits and insurers depend on utilization reviews to ensure that medical treatments received by participants were medically appropriate.

V

vesting   An employee's nonforfeitable rights to retirement plan benefits. There are two aspects of vesting: Employees acquire vesting rights on either a cliff vesting schedule or on a gradual vesting schedule.

violations of an affirmative duty   Such violations take place when an employer fails to reveal the exposure of one or more workers to harmful substances, or the employer does not disclose a medical condition typically caused by exposure.

vision care plan   Covers eye examinations, prescription lenses, frames, and fitting of prescription glasses.

volunteerism   Refers to giving of one's time to support a meaningful charitable cause. More and more companies are providing employees with paid time off to contribute to causes of their choice.

W

wage-loss approach   Bases workers' compensation benefits on the actual loss of earnings that results directly from nonscheduled injuries. Application of this approach requires monitoring of an individual's income following an injury. The objective is to replace a part of or all of the earnings loss due to the injury.

wage test   Criterion specified in the Federal Unemployment Tax Act (FUTA) to determine whether employers must participate in state unemployment insurance programs.

waiting period   Specifies the minimum number of months or years an employee must remain employed before becoming eligible for one or more benefits. Waiting periods often correspond to the length of probationary periods. For Social Security unemployment insurance benefits, the waiting period is usually one week following submission of a claim.

Wall Street Reform and Consumer Protection Act of 2010   Enhances the transparency of executive compensation practices. Also commonly referred to as the *Dodd-Frank* Act, the act requires the companies that trade stock on public exchanges to comply with the act's provisions.

wearaway   Some (usually older) employees do not accrue benefits for a period of time following conversion of a defined benefit plan to a cash balance plan, while other (usually younger) employees do not experience an interruption in accruing benefits.

weekly benefit amounts (WBAs)   The amount an individual receives from unemployment insurance programs, usually ranging between 50 and 67 percent of previous earnings.

weight control and nutrition programs   Wellness programs that educate employees about proper nutrition and weight loss to promote sound health.

welfare plan   Generally refers to nonpension benefits for the purposes of ERISA.

welfare practices   Historical term for employee benefits: "anything for the comfort and improvement, intellectual or social, of the employees, over and above wages paid, which is not a necessity of the industry nor required by law."

wellness programs   Promote and maintain the physical and psychological health of employees.

whole life insurance   Pays an amount to the designated beneficiaries of the deceased employee. Unlike term life insurance, whole life plans do not terminate until payment to beneficiaries.

witness duty   See *jury duty*.

Women's Health and Cancer Rights Act of 1998   Requires group health plans to provide medical and surgical benefits for mastectomies.

Worker Adjustment and Retraining Notification (WARN) Act   Requires that management give at least a 60-day advance notice of a plant closing or mass layoff. An employer's failure to comply with the requirement of the WARN Act entitles employees to recover pay and benefits for the period for which notice was not given, typically up to a maximum of 60 days.

workers' compensation benefits Include unlimited medical care, disability income, rehabilitation services, and death benefits.

workers' compensation Established state-run insurance programs that are designed to cover medical, rehabilitation, and disability income expenses resulting from employees' work-related accidents. Also known as *state compulsory disability laws.*

working condition fringe benefit Any property or services provided to an employee of the employer to the extent that, if the employee paid for such property or services, such payment would be allowable as a deduction under Section 162 (trade or business expenses) or 167 (depreciation of the property used in the trade or business) of the Internal Revenue Code.

Y

yearly limits Refer to the maximum amount a plan would cover each year.

Employee Benefits Index